The Colours of the Empire

European Anthropology in Translation
Published in Association with the Society for the Anthropology of
Europe (AAA)
General Editor: **Sharon R. Roseman,** Memorial University of
Newfoundland

This new series introduces English-language versions of significant works
on the Anthropology of Europe that were originally published in other
languages. These include books produced recently by a new generation
of scholars as well as older works that have not previously appeared in
English.

The Colours of the Empire

Racialized Representations during Portuguese Colonialism

Patrícia Ferraz de Matos

Translated by
Mark Ayton

berghahn
NEW YORK · OXFORD
www.berghahnbooks.com

Published by
Berghahn Books
www.berghahnbooks.com

English-language edition
©2013 Berghahn Books

Portuguese-language edition
© 2006 Imprensa de Ciências Sociais
As Côres do Império. Representações Raciais no Império Colonial Português
by Patrícia Ferraz de Matos

Library of Congress Cataloging in Publication Data

Matos, Patrícia Ferraz de.
[Cores do império. English.]
The colours of the empire : racialized representations during Portuguese
colonialism / Patricia Ferraz de Matos ; translated by ; Mark Ayton.
p. cm. — (European anthropology in translation ; v. 4)
Translation of: As cores do império.
Includes bibliographical references and index.
ISBN 978-0-85745-762-2 (hardback : alk. paper) -- ISBN 978-0-85745-763-9
(ebook)
1. Portugal—Colonies--History. 2. Racism—Portuguese-speaking countries.
3. Indigenous peoples—Portuguese-speaking countries. I. Title. II. Title: Colors
of the empire.
JV4227.M37413 2012
325'.3469—dc23

2012012562

British Library Cataloguing-in-Publication Data

A catalogue record for this book is available from the British Library

Funded by Direcção-Geral do Livro e das Bibliotecas / Portugal

Printed in the United States on acid-free paper

ISBN 978-0-85745-762-2 (hardback)
ISBN 978-0-85745-763-9 (ebook)

To look for the Other in these images, drawings and moving pictures is to find a paradigmatic Western discourse and to understand the gaze We bring to bear on Elsewhere

PASCAL BLANCHARD, *L'Autre et Nous,*
«Scènes et Types»

Contents

Tables and Illustrations

Tables

Illustrations

Acknowledgements

The text which follows was written under the guidance of Professor José Manuel Sobral during my sojourn at the University of Lisbon's Instituto de Ciências Sociais. It is primarily the fruit of my work, discussions and exchanges of ideas with Professor José Manuel Sobral. I am eternally indebted to Professor Sobral for the way he encouraged me to carry on my research, the untiring availability he showed, his readiness to read and critique my work chapter by chapter, and the constant interest he showed in it. I would also like to thank him for encouraging me to bring out this English edition. Professor Sobral knows this book better than anyone except myself.

The University of Lisbon's Instituto de Ciências Sociais is not just a working laboratory but also a meeting place for social scientists from all countries. The dynamics of the institute, and the assistance it gave me, were major factors in the final outcome of my work.

My interest in racial issues was first awakened when I was invited by Professor Susana de Matos Viegas to work as an assistant (1997–2000) on a project designated *Power and Differentiation on the Coast of Bahia: Cultural Identities, Ethnicity and Race in Multi-ethnic Contexts,* under the direction of Professor Miguel Vale de Almeida. The opportunity to participate in this project, and a field visit to Brazil in 1998, consolidated this interest and served as the stimulus for later research, the results of which are published here. I thank Professor Viegas for her invitation and for her confidence in my work.

I would also like to thank everyone in the various locations where I carried out my research: the Instituto de Zoologia e Antropologia of the Faculty of Science of the University of Porto, the Biblioteca Nacional of Lisbon, the Anthropology Department of the Faculty of Science and Technology of the University of Coimbra (with special thanks to Lina), Cinemateca Portuguesa's Arquivo Nacional das Imagens em Movimento (especially Dr Sara Moreira and Luís Gameiro), the Instituto de Ciências Sociais of the University of Lisbon (and especially Dr Goretti Mattias, for her encouragement and for allowing me to consult uncatalogued materials from the Arquivo de História Social, and the librarians of the ICS) and Casa-Museu Bissaya Barreto in Coimbra (especially Dr Isabel Horta e Vale, curator of the Casa-Museu and director of Portugal dos Pequenitos).

I am also thankful for the grant I was awarded by the Instituto de Ciências Sociais, and for the scholarship awarded by the Fundação para a Ciência e a Tecnologia as part of its human resources training service. Both were indispensable to the completion of this book. I also extend my gratitude to all the people I interviewed, especially the alumni of the former Escola Superior Colonial, and all those who provided me with valuable information during my research.

My thanks go to my original publishers, Imprensa de Ciências Sociais, for making the original publication possible in 2006. To Berghahn Books and all those who represent it, and especially Sharon R. Roseman, editor of Berghahn's European Anthropology in Translation series, I express my gratitude for making this English translation possible.

Still more thanks to professors Miguel Vale de Almeida, António Medeiros and João de Pina-Cabral for encouraging me with my work on this English edition, and for the suggestions they gave me. I am also grateful to Ana Pinto Mendes for the valuable help she gave me when approaching the publishers of this English edition, and for her unceasing friendship. This book was translated by Mark Ayton, with whom I worked on the preparation of its final version, and whom I thank for his professionalism and diligence. This edition would not have been possible without the translation subsidy granted by the Direcção Geral do Livro e das Bibliotecas in Portugal.

Thanks also to: my parents, Isilda Toscano and Sílvio Ferraz, and my aunt and uncle, Irene Toscano and Alfredo Cerveira, for all their support, both moral and financial; my dear friend Manuela Garcia, for reviewing the original versions of parts of the text and for helping out on the family front when I was busy; and Susana de Matos Viegas, Gonçalo Duro dos Santos and Nuno Porto for their critical input.

Finally and no less importantly, my son Afonso was born as I was working on this book, and he has grown as this book took form. His liveliness and energy always encouraged me in the more difficult days. To him, and to his father António who was always by our side, this book is dedicated.

Acronyms and Abbreviations

AGC – Agência Geral das Colónias / *Central Agency for the Colonies*

AGU – Agência Geral do Ultramar / *Central Overseas Agency*

AHC – Arquivo Histórico Colonial / *Colonial Archive*

AHU – Arquivo Histórico Ultramarino / *Overseas Archive*

ANIM – Arquivo Nacional das Imagens em Movimento / *National Moving Pictures Archive*

BGC – Boletim Geral das Colónias / Central Colonial Bulletin

BN – Biblioteca Nacional / *National Library*

CEEP – Centro de Estudos de Etnologia Peninsular / *Peninsular Ethnology Studies Centre*

CEEU – Centro de Estudos de Etnologia do Ultramar / *Centre for Overseas Ethnological Studies*

CML – Câmara Municipal de Lisboa / *Municipal Council of Lisbon*

CNCDP – Comissão Nacional para as Comemorações dos Descobrimentos Portugueses / *National Commission for the Commemoration of the Portuguese Discoveries*

ESC – Escola Superior Colonial / *Higher Colonial College*

FBB – Fundação Bissaya-Barreto / *Bissaya-Barreto Foundation*

IICT – Instituto de Investigação Científica e Tropical / *Institute for Scientific and Tropical Research*

IP – Indústria Portuguesa / Portuguese Industry

ISCSP – Instituto Superior de Ciências Sociais e Políticas / *Higher Institute for Social Sciences and Politics*

ISCSPU – Instituto Superior de Ciências Sociais e Política Ultramarina / *Higher Institute for Overseas Social Sciences and Politics*

ISEU – Instituto Superior de Estudos Ultramarinos / *Higher Institute of Overseas Studies*

IST – Instituto Superior Técnico / *Higher Technical Institute*

JIU – Junta de Investigações do Ultramar / *Overseas Research Board*

MCCA – Missão Cinegráfica às Colónias de África / *Cinematic Mission to the African Colonies*

MEMEUP – Missão de Estudos das Minorias Étnicas do Ultramar Português / *Mission for the Study of Ethnic Minorities in Overseas Portugal*

PP – Portugal dos Pequenitos / 'Little People's Portugal'

SGL – Sociedade de Geografia de Lisboa / *Geographic Society of Lisbon*

SNI – Secretariado Nacional de Informação, Cultura Popular e Turismo / *National Bureau for Information, Popular Culture and Tourism*

SPAC – Sociedade Portuguesa de Actualidades Cinematográficas / *Portuguese Newsreel Society*

SPAE – Sociedade Portuguesa de Antropologia e Etnologia / *Portuguese Society of Anthropology and Ethnology*

SPN – Secretariado de Propaganda Nacional / *National Propaganda Office*

UTL – Universidade Técnica de Lisboa / *Technical University of Lisbon*

Introduction

My motivation for examining the 'race' issue in the context of the Portuguese Colonial Empire dates from 1998, when I first came into contact with this subject in my new job as a research assistant. I later had the opportunity to expand upon and indulge my interest in the subject with the inclusion of a module on representations inherent to racial discrimination – unquestionably a source of distress for much of humanity – in the fourth master's degree course of the Instituto de Ciências Sociais of the University of Lisbon, which was dedicated to the issue of global suffering. Although racism and racist interpretations of reality have fallen into disrepute since the end of the Second World War, this does not mean they have disappeared. 'Phenomena' such as the greater or lesser aptitude of certain groups for certain tasks continue to be debated. Science may have discredited the concept of 'race', but the preconceptions associated with it can still emerge where we least expect them to.

Scientific output on the subject of racism is still a very recent phenomenon in Portugal. Examples include the recent series of publications organized by Jorge Vala,[1] which denounce the 'subtle racism' of the Portuguese. On the national level, however, research into racial representations remains scarce – especially with regard to the representations produced in the so-called Portuguese Colonial Empire. My intention with this book is to fill this gap via an analysis of racial representations in the early decades of the Estado Novo (which lasted from 1933 to 1974), a question which overlaps with that of racism. The classic rationale of racism is based on the unequal treatment of those seen as different and thus held to be inferior, and we shall frequently come across manifestations of this rationale in this book. Racial discrimination[2] exists when

---

1. *Expressões dos racismos em Portugal,* by Jorge Vala, Rodrigo Brito and Diniz Lopes (Instituto de Ciências Sociais da Universidade de Lisboa, Lisbon 1999).

2. Cashmore (1996: 306) sees *racial* discrimination as different from other kinds. Groups subject to discrimination are denied opportunities not on the basis of their individual merits and abilities, but on their belonging to a certain group, which is erroneously conceived in racial terms.

individuals of a certain physical appearance are associated with certain traits of personality or conduct held to be positive or negative. According to Giddens, a racist is someone who believes there are biological reasons for classifying people with certain physical characteristics as inferior or superior (1989: 246). Thus, racism is the inferiorization or exclusion of a group on the basis of reasons presented as 'natural' (Wieviorka 1996: 345).

I'd also like to use this introduction to point out that my use of the word 'Colours' in the title of this book alludes to the fact that colour has always been a primary (since apparently objective) criterion of classification. However, colour later became a synonym or near-synonym of 'race', i.e. a more abstract notion for which attempts were made to establish scientific credibility. This book seeks to determine how the different populations under Portuguese rule were represented in the specific context of the Colonial Empire; and to do so it examines the relationship between these representations and the meanings attached to the notion of 'race'.[3] I shall discuss the racial representations which informed the policy of the Estado Novo – within the international context of the time – and the production of academic literature on 'race' in Portugal. I shall also examine the relationship between the racial formulations disseminated in Portugal in the period under review and the racial theories produced from the eighteenth century onwards in Europe and beyond. My examination centres on 'representations', as these are cultural markers, 'worldviews' which shape the action of individuals. This book draws primarily on work in the fields of anthropology and history, the two disciplines most involved in the production of representations of the 'Natives' of the former Portuguese colonies. Most of my sources are to be found in Portuguese libraries and archives. I also carried out interviews to fill in any gaps in the literature, and to complement the information obtained from historical records.

With regard to the terminology and expressions used in this book, I have tried where possible to avoid employing terms which are politically and historically specific. In some cases I wrap them in inverted commas; in others I have tried to find a more neutral substitute. But on occasion it is almost impossible to find an acceptable workaround, and sometimes when we invent new expressions to replace those which are 'politically incorrect' we run the risk of detaching ourselves from the milieu we propose to examine. Some of these terms[4] have been the ob-

---

3. On the debate on the idea of race in Portugal, see Amorim et al. (1997).

4. The earliest criticism of the use of certain of these terms dates from the mid-1950s with authors such as Balandier (1955). It was later applied to the debate on colonialism

ject of much theoretical debate on the colonial question, and sometimes no consensus as to their validity exists within the scientific community. Therefore, when I refer to 'colonized populations' or 'native populations' I am designating the Indigenous populations or 'Natives' subject to Portuguese rule (meaning, of course, *colonial* rule, with its connotations of an unequal power relationship between 'colonizers' and 'colonized') in the period under review. As for the expression 'colonial populations', this embraces all the inhabitants of the former Portuguese overseas territories, including, for example, settlers, traders and those working in the colonial administration, who were neither 'Natives' nor 'Indigenous'.

This book is divided into three chapters. In the first chapter I outline the meanings which over time have attached to the idea of 'race'. This term emerged in a specific historical context, and its origins are to be found in the sixteenth and seventeenth centuries. The great sea voyages of this period were important, as they were decisive episodes for the production of representations. New conceptions, attitudes and arguments arose with regard to 'difference', as observed and articulated, during this period. Their 'pedigree' influenced, and was a determining factor in, the construction of the meaning given to 'race' and the importance it was to have for the racist doctrines of the eighteenth and nineteenth centuries. Most researchers locate the emergence of racism[5] in the eighteenth century, a time when the groundwork was being laid for the emergence of 'modern' science and when debates on the origins of humanity proliferated. Philosophers, writers, historians, travellers and specialists from the nascent 'modern' sciences, including anthropology, all made their contribution to the emerging idea of 'race'.

As we shall see, the classical revivalism of the Enlightenment fuelled discrimination against those who did not match the classical ideal of beauty – an ideal that was to become the standard against which human beings were measured. Driven by their curiosity, the scientists of the Enlightenment observed, measured and compared skulls, searched for explanations for differences in skin pigmentation, and ranked individuals on 'racial scales', with Europeans at the top of the scale. It is important to bear these historical aspects in mind, for through them we can trace a history of the relationship between biological and cultural approaches to the physical and behavioural diversity of humankind.

---

as a cultural process by, for example, Dirks (1992) and to the tensions generated by 'empires' in Stoler and Cooper (1997).

5. The term itself was coined between the two World Wars. For the present purposes 'racism' shall be taken to designate manifestations of discrimination informed by a belief in the existence, and inequality, of 'races'.

In Chapter II, I examine the 'discourse, images, and knowledge' connected with the former Portuguese colonies and their inhabitants in the early decades of the Estado Novo. I begin with an account of the constitution of Portuguese colonialism and the development of 'colonial knowledge' from the late nineteenth century onwards, with the emphasis on studies in the field of anthropology, a discipline then still in its infancy. I shall examine how the idea of a 'Portuguese Colonial Empire' was institutionalized, and how the populations which belonged to this empire were conceptualized, classified and ranked. In Portugal, the early twentieth century – and the 1930s and '40s especially – was a period in which a great deal of theory and propaganda was produced on the subject of the colonies. It was also a time of major congresses such as the First National Congress on Colonial Anthropology (1934) and the Congresses of the Portuguese World (1940). I shall therefore be examining a wide range of phenomena and the ways they reached different strata of the population, viewed not only in terms of social class but also age group. In other words, I shall try to determine which messages were directed primarily at the uneducated masses and which at a more elite target group, which were directed at adults and which at children and youths, in an attempt to identify differences and similarities from one message to another. It is from this perspective that I shall examine how the populations under Portuguese colonial rule were represented in school and college readers, and in documentaries and films which explored the 'overseas' theme. We shall see how these materials acted as vehicles for the transmission of the prescribed ideals, and we shall investigate how 'Native populations' were depicted and what treatment they received. During my research for this book I often encountered recurrent ideas with regard to these populations, and I have attempted to arrange these ideas within a framework which classifies written discourse by its origins – the political and academic worlds, the mass media, and missionaries.

Chapter II also examines the role of the institutions that were the leading producers of 'anthropological knowledge' of the inhabitants of the Portuguese overseas territories, the degree to which 'scientific' representations influenced the political representations of these inhabitants, and the possible impact of the former representations on colonial policy. I shall then discuss some of the clichés most frequently invoked in connection with Portugal's colonial expansion. Preeminent among these are the claims that the Portuguese were not racist, that during the colonial period especially they did not put up racial barriers against other cultures, that there was a certain originality about the Portuguese.

And yet for centuries emphasis was placed on the concept of 'cleanliness' or 'purity of blood' (Boxer 1969: 212), while in the 1930s and '40s some scientists warned of the catastrophic effects of miscegenation. Not until the postwar period was the racial question reformulated in an attempt to place the 'colonized populations' on an equal footing with the Portuguese of the metropolis. However, some preconceptions would persist.

Chapter III is dedicated to an analysis of the major exhibitions in which Portugal participated, or its government organized, in the period from 1924 to 1940. The presence of the colonies in these exhibitions was an opportunity to glorify the image of the 'Colonial Empire'. I shall examine how the exhibitions were constructed, what their objectives were, and the place of the 'Natives' in them, in terms of how they were represented and treated. These exhibitions were designed to give visitors the sensation that they were actually travelling through the colonies and meeting their populations, so Indigenous inhabitants were brought from the overseas territories to participate in them. These living representations were not only 'on show' but also worked in the construction of the events, for example, by building their traditional dwellings.

In Portugal, the two biggest events of this kind were the First Portuguese Colonial Exhibition, held in Porto in 1934, and the Exhibition of the Portuguese World, held in Lisbon in 1940. Central Portugal also got in on the exhibition act with Portugal dos Pequenitos. Built in Coimbra, Portugal dos Pequenitos (PP)[6] did not put any actual Natives on display, but instead featured sculptures, drawings and photographs. Interestingly, Portugal dos Pequenitos ended up as a permanent exhibition and can still be visited today. Taking these exhibitions as a whole, I propose to investigate the status they accorded the Indigenous inhabitants of the territories under Portuguese rule, and how their representations of the latter were related, or not, to the 'race' factor.

In my view, the issues addressed in this book remain relevant in these postcolonial times. Although the concept of 'race' has been discredited by science, much prejudice persists. Of course, some of the observations made in this book relate to their context and not to the present day; although discrimination continues to exist, today's circumstances are very different. Nevertheless, the concepts of 'race' and ethnic discrimination continue to appear in political, social and economic dis-

---

6. For reasons of brevity, the names of many of the organizations and institutions cited in the text are replaced by abbreviations. A list of these abbreviations and what they stand for is given at the beginning of this book.

course on issues such as political reform, immigration policy, crime and punishment, and affirmative action.[7] It is my hope that by shedding light upon a relatively recent past we can improve our perceptions of current problems.

---

7. The term 'affirmative action' refers to programmes designed to implement racial equality in the workplace and other spheres of society, as extensively introduced in the United States.

Chapter I

Origins of a Prejudice
The Roots of Racial Discrimination

The discovery of human variety: early formulations

According to some authors,[1] racial exclusion cannot be seen as an operative concept in the structure of ancient Greek society. Since no racial conception of the individual seems to have existed in this period, no term existed to designate it (Goldberg 2002). The same holds for medieval society, although in a more complex sense. The word 'race' occasionally appears in translations of classical and medieval texts as a rendering of 'species', and what it designates is typically 'populations' or humankind in general. Ancient Greek society *did* practise discrimination and exclusion, but neither seems to have been based on racial factors. In Herodotus (fifth century BC), for example, we can observe a discourse which excludes 'barbarians' from Greek society on ideological grounds – but an interest in 'scientifically'[2] describing those excluded, determining to what extent they were or were not 'barbarians', is equally evident. Ancient authors also mentioned 'anthropophagites' or 'man-eaters', later known as 'cannibals'.[3] And in the Hippocratic Corpus (fourth century BC) we find an attempt to explain the physical and mental differences between the inhabitants of Europe and Asia in terms of environmental influence. So while the Greek texts do contain instances of ethnocentric

---

1. The authors cited in this chapter are those who most frequently appear in the literature published in Portugal in the early twentieth century or who had the greatest influence on an international level.

2. The case of the Pygmies, for example, as reported in Herodotus (Jahoda, 1999: 1).

3. 'Cannibalism' is also one of the 'key symbols' by which we recognize 'savagery' (Jahoda 1999).

and xenophobic discrimination and claims of cultural superiority, these differences do not seem to have been based on biological factors.

Just as Antiquity referred to them in cultural terms, 'modern' discourse has located racial differences in 'nature'. But if racial prejudice did not exist in Antiquity, how do we explain the emergence of the idea of White superiority during the Enlightenment? There are, after all, European texts (written by Greeks) which discuss the parity of Europeans and Blacks in terms of beauty, culture and intellectual capacity. Why then did the Renaissance exclude statues of Black people from its supposed revival of classical aesthetic ideals? It would seem that in ancient Greece and Rome statues of Black Africans, with the bodily proportions and physical characteristics proper to them, were marginal to cultural life. The presence of Blacks was tolerated, sometimes even venerated, but not in association with ideals of beauty.

In medieval European thought, individuals were conceived as subject to theological categories. Classification and discrimination operated from a different perspective. Discourse on the 'other' was principally informed by the distinction between Christians and non-Christians. However, the artistic depictions found in medieval literature include strange and exotic beings which are a mixture of human and animal elements. Many of these show the influence of the mythological figures of Antiquity, but others are based on accounts of human beings who were different, were from remote places or had physical defects (Jahoda 1999). In these representations it is common for the devil to be depicted as a Black person or dressed in black. On the level of language, Western discourse is full of dichotomies in which white represents purity and virginity and black represents impurity, evil and, therefore, inferiority. One work containing representations similar to those described above and influential in the medieval period was the *Natural History* of Pliny the Elder (AD 23?–79?), with its accounts of strange, exotic and frightening humanoid creatures of all shapes and sizes. Pliny's catalogue drew largely on Greek sources. In the Middle Ages, individuals who were exotic or in any way different were designated 'monsters', and the birth of a baby with physical defects was seen as a portent of celestial and terrestrial calamity. Generally speaking, these beings elicited disgust, and their only chance of salvation lay in baptism, whereby they could become rational creatures endowed with souls. This definition of humanity in relation to its rationality predates the modern emphasis on rational capacity, which was seen as differing across different racial groups (Goldberg 2002: 285). And yet, the Middle Ages still lacked a specific category for designating 'race' or racial differentiation. By the late Middle Ages, however, there was increased contact between peoples of diverse geographic origins and with physical and cultural differences. The classical ideas of Pliny and Strabo (60 BC–AD 25?)[4] considering the equatorial regions to be unfit for human habitation were proven wrong. Western Africa was conquered and exploited, its populations enslaved by the Spanish and Portuguese, in a process which had its parallels across the ocean in the New World. Although an explorer such as Christopher Columbus might have expected to encounter the monstrous beings described in Antiquity, this was not what he found. As Pliny's categories grew increasingly ill-defined, the monster of the popular imagination was supplanted by the 'savage' – a human being similar to a monkey, naked, hirsute but lacking facial hair, carrying a club or even a tree trunk. This caricature bears comparison with later depictions of the 'caveman'. The 'savage' as thus depicted represented violence, indiscipline, wantonness, absence of civilization, sin, irrationality and immorality (Jahoda 1999). At the same time, the concept of 'race' began to emerge as part of the European social consciousness. From the fifteenth century onwards, non-European Christians were gradually excluded from the domain of Christendom. In papal documents of this period we find Europe described as a collective 'we'; the term 'race' was to emerge shortly afterward. *Race* as we use it in English is believed to derive from a French word which originally designated the royal families which ruled France in the Middle Ages (Augstein 1996).

By the sixteenth century, the cultural centre of gravity had shifted from Jerusalem to Europe. Under the influence of mercantile capitalism and advances in technology, race began to be defined in relation to 'others' – Africans, Native Americans, Asians – who were held to be inferior. Over the course of four centuries of conquest and colonial exploitation, the West imposed its dominion over non-European societies. By the sixteenth and seventeenth centuries we begin to see value judgements in the accounts of travellers and European *conquistadores*. Cortés described Aztec societies as most agreeable, and said that their qualities revealed what was best in America. For Cortés, the New World seemed to lie somewhere between two Old Worlds: one was White, Christian Europe, and the other was Africa, which was neither Christian nor White. For the Dominican friar Bartolomé de las Casas,[5] the 'Indians' of the New World were docile and fit to receive the holy Catholic faith; but

---

4. At a time when Africa was still confused with Asia, Strabo attempted to describe a number of population groups, although he had no firsthand experience of them, on the basis of the accounts brought home by travellers. See *The Geography of Strabo*, 1932, in Jahoda (1999).

5. Bartolomé de las Casas was born in Seville in 1470. He studied in Salamanca and first travelled to the Americas as a counsellor in 1502. Here he was deeply struck by the

their 'physical weakness' and 'scant inclination for heavy work' placed them in opposition to the 'physical vigour of the Africans' – reflections which made Bartolomé de las Casas hit on the idea of 'exporting the Blacks to America' to relieve the Indians (Mazzoleni 1992: 60). In the famous letter of Pêro Vaz de Caminha to Manuel I of Portugal on the 'finding' of Brazil, written in Porto Seguro de Vera Cruz on 1 May 1500, we can clearly detect the curiosity and sense of enchantment elicited by the 'Natives',[6] who are described in minute detail. Pêro Vaz de Caminha emphasizes their nudity, which seems to have been the source of some discomfiture:

> The men of the land are young and well built ... In complexion they are *pardo*,[7] with a reddish tinge, with fine, well made faces and good noses. They go around naked with no covering, and think nothing either of covering or showing their modesties. And this they do with as much innocence as they show their faces ... Also there were plenty of comely young women, with long black hair over their shoulders, and their modesties so high, so tight and so hairless.

The poet Luís Vaz de Camões (1524?–1580) worked in the service of the Portuguese empire from 1553, the year of his arrival in Goa, until 1570, when he returned to Lisbon. Camões's descriptions of the peoples he meets on his travels reveal fascination, revulsion and estrangement. In his references to Africans in his epic poem *The Lusiads*, Camões uses expressions such as 'peoples denied the colour of day by the son of Clymene', 'strange people', 'Black people', 'strange black-skinned being', 'naked and the colour of darkest night' (Canto V). They inhabited an Africa that was 'ignorant and full to brimming with ugliness'; the Africans were, in essence, a 'lawless', 'wild', 'Black and naked' people (Canto X).

In the languages of early sixteenth-century Europe, the word 'race' designated 'lineage', i.e. a group of people descending from a common ancestor believed to have endowed them with identical characteristics. This remained the predominant acceptance of 'race' until around 1800 (Banton [1987] 1998). In the 'lineage' conception of 'race', physical ap-

---

ill-treatment of the Indian slaves, and crossed the Atlantic on several occasions to solicit the Spanish king on their behalf.

6. Until then, the only ethnic groups known to the Portuguese were Arabs, Africans, Jews and Asians. Africans began arriving in Portugal in the fifteenth century as slaves, disembarking in the Algarve, the Sado and later Lisbon. They later began to be sent to Brazil. The price of an African slave varied depending on sex, age and health. Africans also appeared in the theatre and dances, or were employed as court jesters. In the eighteenth century they are known to have taken part in bullfights (Tinhorão 1988).

7. Light brown.

pearance was not the fundamental index of difference. In the eighteenth century, 'race' appeared in translations as one of the many renderings of the Latin *gens* ('clan') and *genus* ('kind'); other synonyms were 'stock', 'tribe', 'family' and 'nation'. From now on, social differentiation acquired a more specifically racial dimension.

Human variety was also addressed in political and philosophical treatises. In his *First Treatise on Government* (1689), John Locke[8] (1632–1704) argued against slavery. For this influential British empiricist, all human beings were free, with equal rational capacities. However, some commentators on Locke's work argue that he contradicted his own principle not only in his comments on slavery in the *Second Treatise,* but also in his conduct as a colonial administrator and secretary to the Lords Proprietor of South Carolina. Generally speaking, empiricism encouraged the tabulation of perceptible human differences, from which it then deduced 'natural' differences. Rationalism, meanwhile, posited innate, and especially mental, differences[9] in its explanation of behavioural differences. As Goldberg (2002: 289) wrote, this 'contrast between Lockean empiricism and Leibnizean[10] rationalism on the nature of racialized subjectivity and the implications for the domain of the moral stand as prototype of the contrast between two great philosophical representatives of the Enlightenment, Hume and Kant'.

The emergence of 'modern' racism

For some authors, 'modernity' can be associated with 'a time period and with an initial geographical location' (Giddens [1990] 1998: 1). For others, it is a period of 'movement, of flux, of change and of unpredictability' (Lash and Friedman 1992: 1). The rhetoric and discourse

---

8. Locke's key work, *An Essay Concerning Human Understanding* (1690), proposed a systematic analysis of the origin, essence and certainty of human knowledge. According to Marvin Harris, the period elapsing between the publication of this work and the French Revolution marks the limits of the Enlightenment, during which anthropological theory began to develop ([1968] 1981: 1).

9. According to this theory, a form of rationalism which we find in Descartes and his follower Leibniz, certain categories of knowledge are innate to us, deriving not from experience but from the structures inherent to reason. Leibniz argued in favour of innate ideas, and of our innate ability to formulate certain concepts independently of experience (Hessen [1926] 1980).

10. In his posthumously published *Nouveaux essais sur l'entendement humain* (1765), Leibniz rebutted the epistemological point of view supported by Locke. George Berkeley's *A Treatise Concerning the Principles of Human Knowledge* (1710) and David Hume's *A Treatise of Human Nature* (1739–40) and *An Enquiry Concerning Human Understanding* (1748) further developed Locke's views (Hessen [1926] 1980).

of modernity are generally characterized in terms of rupture, ongoing quest and innovation. Its logic appears to be rooted in three major phenomena and their respective constructs: production, organization and power (Balandier 1988: 10–20, 148–49). Owing to a whole series of favourable factors, ranging from climate to politics, the rise of the West had begun with the Neolithic Revolution. This development continued through the period of the maritime discoveries and the Renaissance. Transformations in the mechanisms and technologies of power began to emerge in the seventeenth and eighteenth centuries (Foucault [1975–76] 1992). In the nineteenth century came the 'subjection of Nature's forces to man: machinery, the application of chemistry in industry and agriculture, steam navigation, railways, electric telegraphs, clearing of whole continents for cultivation, canalization of rivers' (Marx and Engels 1848: 12). One century later, we can add to that list automobiles, electronics, nuclear energy, cybernetics and the increasing presence of information technology in everyday life, air travel, genetics, biotechnology and major breakthroughs in medicine. However, what makes these changes distinctively 'modern' is not their invention per se, but rather a process of investigation, discovery and innovation allied with the determination to transform theory into practice and use knowledge to change the world (Berman 1992: 35). But modernity can also be described in terms of a rupture in the passage of time. This rupture comes about as a consequence of the reification of the opposition between an obsolete past and a heroic, triumphant present. For the 'moderns', to speak of progress and the accumulation of knowledge was to speak of a past which investigated without systematically arranging, and of a present and future which investigate, classify, and systemize, which devise methods and look for solutions to problems. 'Modern' science therefore construed nature as something which had to be appropriated (Escobar 1994: 213) and (re)ordered if progress was to be made. According to Latour ([1991] 1997), however, if the success of modernity depends on its ability to produce ontologies which ensure nature does not interfere with culture, and vice versa, such a task of purification lies well beyond the scope of modernity, for there are many situations in which 'hybrids' persist; which is to say, they have not been subjected to purification and therefore cannot be represented in 'modern' terms. Similarly, the difficulty of representing these hybrids, of giving them a place in a system which establishes a clear separation of nature from culture, made them figures of suspicion. And so the difficulty of representing *Mestiços* – individuals who cannot be assigned a given 'type' – led some scientists to consider them as a threat. For those who sought to isolate the primary essences of the world, the hybrid should not exist. Yet 'modern' anthropological practice found it difficult to separate Black from White, Western from non-Western, and failed to prevent the propagation of the *Mestiço* person, the embodiment of the hybridism which supposedly threatened to bring humanity to degeneracy.

The invention of the norms and ideals of beauty

The Enlightenment was a dual revolution: in aesthetic and intellectual conventions on the one hand, and against Christianity and its old superstitions on the other. Racial categorization at this time was to be found not only in political and philosophical debate but also in art. The structure and language of the 'modern' discourse typically employed in describing what we see as 'beautiful', 'important', 'reasonable' and 'valuable' were influenced by the idea of White superiority (Mosse 1992). One idea never brought into the epistemological field of this discourse was the idea of the equality of Black people in terms of beauty, culture and intellectual capacity. This was an act of discursive exclusion whereby the idea is effectively silenced. It is more than a reflection of the fact that at this time Blacks were not associated with power; it also reveals that through the late seventeenth century and for most of the eighteenth century – i.e. the period we designate the Enlightenment – 'modern' discourse was structured in a way which promoted the idea of 'white supremacy' (West 2002). Attitudes such as differentiating, comparing, hierarchizing and excluding were adopted with reference to a 'norm'. But the 'power of the norm' only operates 'within a system of formal equality, since within a homogeneity that is the rule, the norm introduces, as a useful imperative and as a result of measurement, all the shading of individual differences' (Foucault 1977: 184). In other words, only within a relatively uniform complex can we encounter a 'norm' which serves as the benchmark from which we can compile an inventory of the differences existing within this complex. Applying this formula to human groups, it is only because they are similar to one another that we can make comparisons and identify differences between them. The 'norm' against which human differences were thrown into relief was the European body; and the discrepancies between White and non-White bodies supposedly evidenced 'racial' differences.

Knowledge in the Enlightenment was a means of wielding power, and power itself was also constructed by knowledge. 'Modern' discourse therefore incorporates concepts, metaphors and norms which shape the understanding of those who evaluate and formulate value judgements. The norms incorporated in 'modern' discourse shaped these formulations, while the language used denoted what was valued, in opposition to what was not valued and was therefore omitted. The Scientific Revo-

lution,[11] whose principal origins lie in the pre-Enlightenment intellectual watersheds of the seventeenth century, was important because it
heralded a new age in which the authority of science was paramount.
More than that, it made two fundamental concepts central to its world-
view: 'observation' and 'evidence'. Descartes played a key role in this
process, in associating the scientific urge to explain the world with the
philosophical urge to portray and represent it. When 'modern' science
emerged, it was already primed with this urge to represent, re-represent
and expound everything that exists. As Mosse (1992) noted, science
and aesthetics exerted a mutual influence on one another. Science, influenced by 'modern' philosophical discourse, promoted and stimulated
the observation, comparison and ordering of the physical characteristics
of bodies, and in each of these activities the cultural and aesthetic norms
of the classical world were the benchmark. Behind these norms, then,
was an ideal against which observations could be ordered and compared
– an ideal informed by the aesthetic values of beauty and the proportions
of the human form, and of classical cultural models of equilibrium, self-
control and harmony. When combined with the need to justify practices
of domination, 'modern' discourse helped unleash 'modern' racism.

One of the new sciences to emerge in the latter half of the eighteenth century was anthropology: the study of humanity and its place
in nature, and based in its early days on the observation, measurement
and comparison of different groups of men and animals. But these
observations, measurements and comparisons were grounded in value
judgements themselves based on the aesthetic criteria of Antiquity. This
explains, in part, the Enlightenment's enthusiasm for reviving the 'clas-
sics' and reinstating the authority of classical authors. For the new science of anthropology, therefore, the nearer an individual approximated
to the ideal proportions and profiles of Antiquity, the greater the value
assigned to him. And these 'norms' were also embraced by many writers, artists and academics of the Enlightenment. In his *History of Ancient
Art,* for instance, J. J. Winckelmann described ancient Greece as a world
of beautiful bodies. Taking the Greek world as his inspiration, Winckelmann devised a set of rules for art and aesthetics designed to determine
the relative proportions of eyes and eyebrows, shoulder blades, hands
and feet, and – especially – noses. These rules could serve as a guide
for measuring individuals or whole 'cultures'.[12] For classical aesthetics,

---

11. Leading names in this revolution included Copernicus and Kepler in astronomy,
Galileo and Newton in physics, Descartes and Leibniz in mathematics, and Francis Bacon in philosophy.

12. Mosse (1992) has analyzed the aesthetic strain in 'race' theorists such as Buffon,
Camper and Lavater, and the influence of the art historian J. J. Winckelmann on their
work.

beauty was a property which the individual possessed, in much the same way as goods are possessed in classical economic theory. On this view, individuals not possessing certain 'natural' qualities were poor; and just as with laissez-faire economics, this was the responsibility of the individual and no one else. Beauty was gauged in terms of characteristics such as fair skin, straight hair, balanced bodily proportions and so on. Thus, just as Locke suggested that economic poverty inevitably drives individuals to work in factories and mines for scant recompense, 'racial poverty' (an expression used by Goldberg [2002]) would justify the inferiorization and subjugation of people who did not conform to the 'norm'.

Theories on the origin of humanity: monogenism and polygenism

As we have seen above, the eighteenth century devoted considerable attention to human variety and the issues this variety raised. One of the dominant models in attempts to explain phenotypical variation in human beings was the Chain of Being, a theory founded on the supposed immutability of the species, which were ranged in a hierarchy rising from the humblest of living beings all the way up to God. It was this theory of creation around which the debate on the origins of human life revolved – a debate which opposed monogenist and polygenist interpretations of human origins and continued from the eighteenth into the nineteenth century. The debate between monogenists and polygenists placed the egalitarian model of the Enlightenment in opposition to racial doctrines. According to the monogenist view, which predominated until the mid-nineteenth century, all humanity had common origins but had been divided by language since the Tower of Babel. It had then undergone physical and cultural degeneration in the following millennia, as it spread into ever more inhospitable regions. This was the doctrine supported by organized religion, which maintained that all human beings descended from Adam and Eve – and that all differences, therefore, were merely superficial (Banton [1987] 1998). The proponents of monogenism vehemently believed in Scripture and saw the progress of humanity as a journey from perfection – the Garden of Eden – to imperfection and ultimate degeneration.[13] They also maintained that differences were caused by the climate, milieu and living conditions of each population group. For the monogenists, ever since the expulsion from Eden the 'races' had been undergoing a process of degeneration which caused changes on various levels, with 'Whites' having been the least affected by this process of degeneration and 'Blacks' the most (Gould 1983: 36). In addition, the Bible – itself the source of the monogenist

---

13. Note that evolutionary theory plays no part in this debate, as this was an idea that appeared later.

principle – seemed to indicate that Africans were inferior. In the story of the Curse of Ham (Genesis 9:20–27), Noah[14] puts a curse on his son Ham after the latter 'saw him' drunk and naked and reported the incident to his two brothers, Shem and Japheth. When Noah 'awoke from his wine' he pronounced a curse on Ham's son Canaan, making him a servant of his uncles, Ham's brothers Shem and Japheth: 'a servant of servants shall he be unto his brethren'. One interpretation of this story held that Africans who became slaves were the descendants of Ham. And yet it was largely the social, economic and political conditions in which colonialism, slavery, the exploration of Africa and the conquest of the New World occurred which were decisive in the discrimination and subjugation of the Africans (Smedley 1993).

Polygenism emerged in the mid-nineteenth century as a counterblast to the monogenist doctrine embraced by the church, and as a consequence of advances in the natural sciences. According to the polygenist view, 'creation' occurred in several different places, and this explained why human beings were different. The polygenists rejected the influence of the environment on physical appearance. On this view, the emphasis therefore shifted to the examination of the relations between biological data and human behaviour. Disciplines such as phrenology and anthropometrics, which sought to evaluate human capacities on the basis of the size and proportions of the brain, emerged as offshoots of polygenism.

The influence of Enlightenment thought

The thinkers of the eighteenth century played a major role in the formulation of discriminatory ideas. In the one camp were the humanist inheritors of the French Revolution of 1789, whose ideal was the equality of humankind; in the other were thinkers who emphasized not similarities but differences. Humanist literature and philosophy, and Rousseau's celebration of the unity of humanity, were influential on the one side; as were the ideas of Buffon, with his insistence on essential differences between men, on the other. And it was to the great thinkers of the eighteenth century that the theorists of 'race' of the following century so often appealed. In the Enlightenment alone, figures such as Rousseau, Montesquieu and Voltaire in France, Hume and Jefferson in the English-speaking world, and Kant in the German orbit committed racist views to paper, in writings which ultimately conferred authority on the naturalists, anthropologists, physiognomists and phrenologists who sought to to give 'scientific' legitimacy to such views. In the humanist view, all men had a singular and inherent ability to improve

---

14. According to the story in the Bible, it is from Shem, Ham and Japhet, all sons of Noah and fellow survivors of the Flood, that all the peoples of the earth descend.

themselves – an idea which was quite different from the view later expounded by the evolutionists of the nineteenth century. The idea that all men are born equal but incomplete is associated with Rousseau's idea of the 'good savage', the 'other' who in Rousseau's view was remote from and morally superior to Western man (Schwarcz 1995: 44–45). Rousseau also devised the notion of the 'primitive man' to designate human beings with desirable, i.e. uncorrupted, characteristics. Yet these notions must be seen as part of Enlightenment discourse on the exotic, not as an overestimation of the 'other'. So how did some Enlightenment philosophers manage to embrace ideas of equality without being inconsistent on the question of racial inferiority? The only way of sidestepping this problem was to deny Blacks their rational faculties and human condition. The categories 'pre-civilized' and 'primitive' designate beings with neither 'reason' nor 'autonomy'; and so they 'cannot be party to the general will and civil society' (Goldberg 2002: 294, 303). Despite the emergence of movements committed to the abolition of slavery based on the 'race' factor and appealing to none other than the universalist doctrines of the Enlightenment, in reality the equality model was applied only to the European, and more generally Western, subject. 'Race' became a natural, intemporal factor, and so discrimination was seen as unavoidable, something to be tolerated. For the polygenist Voltaire, for example, a hierarchy among the different 'races' could be established based on the analysis of their powers of reasoning and their capacities of affirmation and resistance: the 'Black race' was 'a species of men as different to ours as the race of Spaniards is to greyhounds' ([1756] 1963: 305). And in his *Peuple d'Amérique,* Voltaire argued that 'Negroes' (and 'Indians') were different people from Europeans.

Then there was David Hume (1711–76), whose essay *Of National Characters* identified moral and physical determinants of various nations. Physical determinants were climate and environment, i.e. the elements which the monogenists of the eighteenth century believed were responsible for human variations; moral determinants were customs, government, economic conditions and the external influences which affected the minds and habits of a population. According to Hume, the Jews were 'fraudulent', the Arabs 'uncouth and disagreeable', the Greeks 'deceitful, stupid and cowardly' – in contrast with the 'ingenuity, industry and activity' of their ancestors and the 'integrity, gravity and bravery' of their Turkish neighbours (Goldberg 2002: 292). For Hume, the English were superior to all others,[15] in large part because they 'benefited from

---

15. Bacon and Berkeley had earlier assigned inferiority to the inhabitants of the far North and of the tropics, by contrast with those living in the temperate zones (Goldberg 2002: 292).

their governmental mixture of monarchy, aristocracy and bourgeois democracy' (Goldberg 2002: 292). As for 'non-whites', and 'negroes' especially, these were 'naturally inferior' (Wade 1997: 9; Goldberg 2002: 293). Hume's argument was an empirical one: 'only whites had produced anything notable and ingenious in the arts and sciences, and even the most lowly of white peoples ... had something to commend them.' But the 'negroes', 'even those living in Europe, had no accomplishments they could cite' (Goldberg 2002: 293). Like Locke before him, Hume thought there must be 'natural' differences between the descendants of these groups, a difference which justified their relative superiority and inferiority. Jefferson came to similar conclusions in *Notes on the State of Virginia,* where he maintained that the intellectual capacity of the 'black' was inferior to that of the 'white'. Hume's contemporary Immanuel Kant (1724–1804) was driven by the same curiosity when he adduced national characteristics in justification of racial differences. For Kant ([1764] 1953), the Germans were the exemplar of superiority to all others. He saw in them a 'synthesis of the English intuition for the sublime and the French feeling for the beautiful' (Goldberg 2002: 293). Kant ranked the peoples of the Orient (also designated the 'Mongolian race') variously. The Arabs were 'hospitable, generous and truthful', but were 'troubled by an "inflamed imagination" that tends to distort'; the Japanese were 'resolute but stubborn'; and the Indians and Chinese were 'dominated in their taste by the grotesque and monstrous' (Goldberg 2002: 293). On the lowest level of civilization, among the 'savages' bereft of 'moral understanding', came the Blacks, whom Kant described as 'stupid'. Slightly less savage were the Native Americans, described by Kant as 'honourable' and 'honest'. Basing his analysis partly on the arguments of Hume, Kant drew a distinction between the Native Americans, who were capable of being civilized, and the Africans, who were not.

The Enlightenment's most widely cited reason for human variety was climate – an idea first found in the Hippocratic Corpus. In *De l'esprit des lois* (1748), Montesquieu drew parallels between climatic variations and levels of civilization. The farther south we travelled, according to Montesquieu, the more defects and fewer virtues we encountered in men. Building on Montesquieu's foundations, Adam Smith, Adam Ferguson and William Robertson considered levels of civilization to be related to means of subsistence. This idea that milieu explained physical differences prevailed right to the end of the eighteenth century. Some of the views of the most radical 'environmentalists' of the period also demonstrate how the restrictive power of 'modern' discourse delimited the theoretical alternatives and options with regard to the idea of 'White supremacy'. Samuel Stanhope Smith, for example, opposed the idea of hierarchies of 'race' and argued in favour of intermarriage in the United States; humanity, for Stanhope Smith, was a single species and human diversity was due to natural, environmental causes. Swayed by the ideals of classical aesthetics, however, he also affirmed in his *Essays* (1787) that physical variations were degenerations relative to an ideal state as embodied by the civilized White.

For the Scottish philosopher Henry Home, Lord Kames (1696–1782), humankind derived from not one but several sources.[16] Kames combined polygenism with climatic factors, but did not view the latter as decisive in the development of civilization. Indeed, the polygenists generally insisted on the inefficacy of the environment for altering human constitutions, arguing that the 'races', since they were adapted to one milieu, could not adjust to another. They contended, therefore, that the different 'races' in fact constituted different species[17] and that, as in the animal world, one species could not breed with another. One of the major figures in this debate was Georges Louis Leclerc, Comte de Buffon (1707–88), author of the 44-volume *Histoire naturelle* published between 1749 and 1804. For Foucault (1966), Buffon's work constituted the beginnings of a 'general science of man'. This work centred on the evolution of physical characteristics such as skin colour and stature. Like the eighteenth-century naturalist Linnaeus (1707–78), Buffon saw the 'races' as random variations; but 'white' was the 'real and natural colour of man', with the 'Blacks' and other 'races' examples of variations on the original. According to Buffon, the darkest 'Blacks' were to be found in the hottest regions of the planet. In addition, a 'savage' transported to Europe would gradually become not only 'civilized', but also White. Although an opponent of slavery, Buffon affirmed that 'Blacks' were lacking in intellect. His definition of species was based 'not on the criterion of resemblance but ... that of lineage' (Augstein 1996: xvi): all animals that could procreate among themselves belonged to the same species, and, since all the human 'races' were capable of reproducing among each other, they therefore all belonged to the same species. The example of horses showed that 'it was necessary to cross breeds in order

---

16. Not an entirely new idea: in 1520 Paracelsus had argued that 'Blacks' and 'primitives' had separate origins from Europeans. In 1591, Giordano Bruno made a similar claim, this time with regard to the Jews and Ethiopians. His fellow Italian Lucilio Vanini maintained that the Ethiopians were descended from monkeys and had formerly gone around on all fours. These arguments in favour of the separate origins of humanity went against the position of the church, and Bruno and Vanini were among many heretics condemned to burn at the stake (West 2002).

17. The number varied from author to author – for some there were two, for others, dozens (Stocking 1988: 6).

to maintain the quality of the parent generation' (Augstein 1996: xvi). For the German physician Franz Joseph Gall (1758–1828), the intellectual faculties were 'impressed' upon each individual while still in the fetal state, and could therefore be read in the shape of the head. Taking this physiological premise as their starting point, Gall and his collaborator Johann Caspar Spurzheim (1776–1832) set about establishing phrenology[18] as a science. To do so, they visited 'learned institutions …in order to convince their scientific peers that the conformation of the skull was indicative of individual character and abilities' – or defects – of its owner (Augstein 1996: xix–xx; Baroja [1987] 1995: 205).

Another product of eighteenth-century thought was the discipline of physiognomical character studies. One major name in this field was Johann Caspar Lavater (1740–1801). For Lavater, painting was the 'mother' of the new discipline of physiognomy, and Greek statues embodied the ideals of beauty. Unlike the naturalists, Lavater did not advance a set of 'ideal' measurements. Instead, he argued that certain combinations of elements were apt to cause awestruck admiration, and that our first visual impression of a person was always the most accurate. A Protestant pastor from Zürich and a profoundly religious man, Lavater maintained that the facial appearances of living creatures indicated their internal, moral configuration and denoted the influence of the divine on man (Augstein 1996; Baroja 1995). For Kant, our appraisal of physical appearances was always subjective. In his observations on the Greek ideal of beauty, Kant revealed a knowledge of the comparative studies of Camper and Blumenbach,[19] the precursors of modern 'physical anthropology', or anthropometrics as it is now better known. For Kant, physiognomic studies designated the identification of the internal characteristics of man by the examination of external, involuntary features (Kant 1935: 195–96). The two most civilized peoples on earth in terms of their innate characters, according to Kant, were the English and the French.[20]

Finally, a word about the contribution of philology to the debate. In the 1780s, William Jones (1746–94), a judge in Calcutta, discovered a

---

18. Phrenology or cranioscopy attracted criticism from the anatomist Cuvier, and from theologians. It was taken up with much enthusiasm in Britain and the United States, however. And it gained a new lease of life with the systemization of racist ideology in the nineteenth century, thanks not only to Spurzheim but to other theorists such as Anders Retzius and Carl Gustav Carus.

19. Kant knew these natural historians personally. Camper's conclusions were based on the examination of only eight skulls; Blumenbach's, on 245. The latter's work was a precursor of 'ethnic craniology'.

20. Kant's classification did not include the Germans – as a German himself, Kant perhaps wished to avoid charges of vanity.

genealogical link between ancient Sanskrit and the modern European languages. Jones believed that a comparative study of these languages could yield valuable data on the origins of humanity. For Jones and other authors, languages were 'living' organisms whose history shadowed the history of mankind. This connection legitimized philology as a science, placing it on a level with other historical sciences like geology and comparative anatomy (Augstein 1996).

Natural history, classifications and the emergence of 'race' as a category

To understand how the concept of 'race' operates, it is important first to examine the contexts in which the concept functions as an element in a system of classification. Until the end of the eighteenth century, natural history was essentially a static discipline. Investigation centred not on the history or evolution of phenomena, but instead on their classification and relations. The criteria of classification were based not so much on anatomical and physiological knowledge as on external observation. This method took its cue from the Chain of Being model mentioned above, which viewed creation as a continuous, interlinking series, arranged hierarchically, from the celestial creatures down to the human, animal, vegetable and mineral worlds. The principal objective of natural history was to observe, compare, measure and order animal and human bodies on the basis of the visible (particularly physical) characteristics whereby living beings could be identified and differentiated in classifications, taxonomies, tables, indexes and inventories. Or as Foucault put it, 'natural history is no more than the naming of the visible' (1966: 178). However, as the sheer variety of taxonomies shows, one thing that this approach failed to deliver was consensus. In the pre-Darwinian context, the species were considered as unchanging, and the members of each species as holders of an essence which distinguished them from all other species. In connection with this view there emerged notions such as 'racial purity',[21] according to which miscegenation would be disastrous, as it would contaminate that same 'essence' which – since it was presumed to exist – ought to be preserved. Of all the taxonomies devised, the one proposed by Linnaeus gained the widest acceptance.[22] Like other contemporary biologists, Linnaeus believed that the species

---

21. The concept of 'purity of blood' enjoyed much currency in the sixteenth century as justification of discrimination against the Jews and people of Jewish descent. But it died out over time, and should not be viewed as a precedent of what occurred in Europe in the twentieth century (Mosse 1992).

22. However, as early as 1684 the French doctor François Bernier had used 'race' as a differentiating category in the classification of individuals of different skin colours – in Bernier's case, Europeans, Africans, Orientals and Lapps.

were indivisible units created by God at the beginning of the world, and that variations within species were due to imperfections in the reproduction of the original 'type'. In his *Systema Naturae,* published in 1735, Linnaeus classified all living organisms by genus and species, laying the foundations for later taxonomies. Linnaeus organized the various species – each an immutable prototype – by number and kind (variations found within a single species, e.g. 'race'). All members of a given species were capable of generating fertile offspring by reproducing with fellow members of their species. For Linnaeus, there were four human 'races' – *Homo europaeus, Homo asiaticus, Homo afer* and *Homo americanus.* He also presented considerations on the subdivisions within the *Homo* genus, and classed humans with monkeys.

Some authors argue that Linnaeus merely organized living organisms into one great chain, but without arranging them in hierarchical order. Yet the classification criteria he applied to humans were not restricted to the physical sphere – they also included evaluatory aspects we would now call sociocultural, psychological and temperamental. For example, he drew a distinction between the civilized *Homo sapiens* – European – and *Homo afer* – African. And while Linnaeus devoted special attention to the African woman, he had nothing to say of her European, American or Asian counterparts. In Linnaeus's taxonomy the 'Yellow' man was described as vainglorious, greedy, stern and melancholic, the 'Black' man as slothful, lazy and negligent, the American as stubborn and timid and the 'White' as lively and inventive.[23] But advances in anatomical studies were to prove Linnaeus wrong in many aspects. It wasn't just his thesis that humanity was one animal species among many that was contentious.[24] The evidence of human variety posed a number of questions: If all the groups of humanity descended from Noah and his offspring, why did people look so different? Why did some groups seem to be more advanced than others? This brings us to another major figure in this period. Georges Cuvier (1769–1832) was a French anatomist who introduced into the specialist literature of the early nineteenth century the term 'race' and the idea of the inheritance of physical characteristics among the various human groups (Stocking 1968). Cuvier showed that comparative anatomy could be useful for the study of the past, and suggested that there were differences between the physiological types of

---

23. The distinctions Linnaeus draws between the European (sanguine), American (choleric), Asian (melancholic) and African (phlegmatic) are styled on the Galenic theory of humours (Stocking 1988).

24. Aristotle included man in the animal kingdom, but distinguished him from other animals by virtue of his physical and cultural characteristics.

'savages' and Europeans. Perhaps because he was a devout Protestant, Cuvier did not follow through on this idea (Augstein 1996).

'Modern' discourse thus played an important role in the development of classificatory schemes which used 'race' as a category of natural history.[25] Since 'race' was held to be 'natural', it could be used as a tool for making social, moral and cultural distinctions between individuals. The origins of the racial theories of the nineteenth century must therefore be understood in the context of the eighteenth-century vision of humanity. As Augstein (1996) noted, no single philosophy, movement or author can be considered the sole precursor of these theories. Instead, we have to look to a confluence of different phenomena: the formation of a liberal, secular and antimonarchical politics; the emergence of what would come to be known as the nation-state; the increase in biological and zoological research; phrenological and physiognomical research; political imperatives and the need to scientifically justify slavery; and philology and the study of language as a mirror of national character.

Racialism: the racial theories of the nineteenth century

In the nineteenth century, one trend of thought upheld the place of Blacks as members of humanity, while another (the evolutionist view) maintained that the Blacks were somewhere between the animal and human state. The nineteenth century has been called the 'age of scientific racism', and it was in this century that the emphasis on the differences between human individuals gained the ascendancy, with links and correlations being established between genetic data, intellectual capacity and moral behaviour.[26] According to some naturalists, the basis for these correlations could be physical features such as the skull, chin or nose. As variation was a phenomenon of no importance for the early taxonomists, organisms were classified into 'types', or predetermined categories, in accordance with their correspondence with the 'type' by which the species

---

25. Ashley Montagu was one of the authors who argued that the genealogy of racism in the 'modern' West is inseparable from the emergence of 'race' as a category of classification in natural history (Montagu 1974).

26. The correlation – or the attempt to establish a correlation – between body and behaviour, between bone structure and other physical features such as the appearance of the hair or colour of the skin, is examined in *Bones, Bodies, Behavior* (Stocking 1988). On the attempts to correlate morphological characteristics with behavioural patterns in the North American and French traditions in the nineteenth century, see Stocking (1968), Stepan (1982) and Gould (1983); on similar attempts in Brazil, see Correia (1982) and Schwarcz (1995).

had been defined. In the mid-nineteenth century, this practice extended
to subspecies and to geographic 'race'. Mayr (1963) designated this particular manifestation of essentialism as 'typological thinking'. The naturalists of the nineteenth century sought to order, organize and classify
existing facts and new discoveries as they emerged. The concept of 'type'
was borrowed from botany and zoology, and based on the assumption
that each 'race' was a permanent type with certain innate characteristics
which passed from one generation to the next.[27] The racial 'types' were
ordered hierarchically, just as racial 'lineages' had been previously; but
the reasons for establishing the hierarchy were now given as innate, biological differences, as Lamarck (1744–1829) proposed in 1802 (Mayr
1982: 108). And if 'natural' differences were 'biological' (Wade 1997:
10), then individuals conforming to, for example, the Native American
'type' might be encountered anywhere in the world, on any continent
– it was enough for them to have phenotypical characteristics in common with the Indigenous people of the Americas. Once the racial types
had been established, they could be used as a template by which the be-
haviours and cognitive capacities of the different groups could be read.
Together with other determinants such as climate and geography, the
taxonomy of bodies could, it was believed, explain social and cultural
differences. One idea to emerge from this methodology in the nineteenth
century was that northern Europeans were 'superior races' who enjoyed
the 'ideal climate'. Thus, the darker races and tropical climates would
never be capable of producing civilizations as evolved as those of northern Europe (Skidmore [1974] 1989: 44). And yet these 'tropical climates'
belonged to the very same places Europe had been appropriating for itself
since the fifteenth century – Africa and Latin America.

The earliest studies in craniology were conducted by Johann Friedrich Blumenbach (1752–1840), a professor of medicine at the University of Göttingen. Blumenbach's findings led him to question the views
on hybridism held by Buffon, whose work had inspired Blumenbach's
own research. But since, like Buffon, he was a monogenist, Blumenbach looked for other ways of proving the unity of the species (Augstein
1996). For Blumenbach, physical variations were due to circumstances
of climate. Like Linnaeus and Buffon before him, he maintained that
'races' were merely variations. Blumenbach's work was also influenced
by the aesthetic and cultural ideals of ancient Greece. Following the
monogenist model, he saw 'original' man – the 'Caucasian' – as having

27. The polygenists preferred the concept of 'type' to 'species' or even 'race', as it allowed them to counter the monogenist argument that variations within a given group
were sometimes greater than the variations observed between one group and another.

degenerated in two different directions, in both cases driven by climatic influences: to the American and thence to the Mongol, and to the Malayan and thence to the Ethiopian. He also maintained that the more moderate the climate, the prettier the face. As they lived in latitudes far removed from a temperate climate, therefore, Blacks were necessarily less handsome (Mosse 1992; Stocking 1988). Blumenbach's division of humanity into five varieties – Caucasian, Mongolian, Ethiopian, American and Malayan – dates from 1781 (Augstein 1996). It was based on such criteria as skull size and the shape of the chin and nose, and it was to prove highly influential in the following century.

The Dutch anatomist Pieter Camper (1722–89) devised a system of cranial measurement based on 'facial angle', i.e. the degree of facial prognatism. For Camper, the 'ideal' facial angle was 100 degrees, as found in the statues of the ancient Greeks. This standard squared with Winckelmann's classical ideal of beauty, on which Camper's belief that the Greek proportions exemplified beauty and embodied perfection was based. Using this technique, Camper claimed that the facial angle of Europeans was approximately 97 degrees, while that of Blacks was between 60 and 70 degrees, i.e. closer to the measurements recorded for apes and dogs. Some anthropologists later appropriated Camper's 'facial angle' technique as a scientific method, although Camper himself claimed his main objective in devising it had been to stimulate an interest in classical Antiquity among young artists. Like other theorists of 'race', Camper actually had a background in the visual arts (Mosse 1992).

Another metric, the cephalic index, was devised by the Swiss anthropologist Anders Retzius (1796–1860) in the mid-nineteenth century. An expression of the ratio of head width to length, the cephalic index classified human heads into three categories – dolichocephalic, mesocephalic, and brachycephalic – in quantitative studies on variations in brain size and shape. With this index, each element, isolated from its original context, could be classified and assigned its level on a scale of evolution.

Meanwhile, the rivalry between monogenists and polygenists continued, with the appearance of learned societies such as the Société d'Anthropologie de Paris, founded in 1859 by the anatomist, craniologist and polygenist Paul Broca (1824–80). A disciple of William Frederic Edwards (1777–1842) early in his career, Broca took the skull as his primary object of study, on the basis of which he sought to establish a correlation between physical and mental inferiority. This method, Broca believed, would enable the reconstitution of 'types' or 'pure races' – hybridization was to be condemned, as it could cause sterility (Schwarcz 1995: 54). Broca maintained that 'in general, the brain is larger in men than in women, in eminent men than in men of mediocre talent, and in

the superior races than in the inferior' (Gould 1986: 168). A polygenist like Gall and Topinard, Broca insisted on the 'immutability of races'
– going so far as to link the infertility of the mule with sterility in the
Mulatto (Broca 1864). Both Broca (1861) and Haeckel some time later
(1900) classified the 'races' on a scale ranging from the most to the least
evolved, with the White European or 'Caucasian' at the top of the scale
(Coon[28] 1962). Another polygenist and a follower of L. Agassiz, Samuel
George Morton (1799–1851) drew physical and moral comparisons between the populations of the United States and Egypt on the basis of
their skull measurements. The findings of this research were published in
Crania Americana (1839) and *Crania Aegyptya* (1844). Morton believed
his method would enable comparisons between the human 'races', and
between these and the animal kingdom.

As craniology became increasingly refined over the course of the nineteenth century with the development of craniometry, attempts were now
made to confirm earlier theories on racial variation. Armand de Quatrefages (1810–92), a professor of anthropology at the Muséum National
d'Histoire Naturelle in Paris, refined a number of cranial and facial metrics in his belief in the accuracy of anthropometric data. Similarly, for
Topinard the 'measurement method' stood in opposition to the 'senti-
ment method' (Dias 1996: 31–33).

The earliest comprehensive expositions of racial theory were advanced
by the anatomist Robert Knox (1793–1863) in Britain and by Joseph
Arthur, Comte de Gobineau (1816–82), in France. In 1850, Knox published *Races of Men,* in which he asserted that 'race is everything'. In addition to refloating 'race' as a biological concept, Knox argued (against
the views of the nineteenth-century naturalists) that the 'races' should
not mix, for a 'Mixed race' was doomed to perish. Knox also rejected the
idea that 'race' was influenced by the environment. Like Gobineau, he
drew on the theories of the German author Gustav Klemm, who made
a distinction between 'active races' and 'passive races'.

Polygenism thus came to reject the idea of equality in variety, and
denied Rousseau's 'noble savage' any hope of improvement. The polygenists explained human variety in terms of racial theory, and in so doing provided a justification for inequality. Once legitimized in this way,
inequality led to discrimination and various forms of social domination.
Generally speaking, racial inferiority meant the inferiority of Blacks,
outsiders and criminals. Classifications were used as the foundations of
theories which, at bottom, legitimized imbalances of power. In other
words, racial theories were racist not only because they upheld the exis-

---

28. Carleton S. Coon (1904–81) was a US physical anthropologist whose racial theory
was based on his research on hominoid fossils.

tence of different 'races', but also because they ordered them according to a hierarchy. Based on the idea that, like animals, humans were divided into 'races', each with its own biological equipment, these theories were advanced as the explanation for differences in social development. The 'Whites', as conquerors and bringers of civilization, must be biologically superior. They were followed by the 'Yellows', then by the Native Americans, and then, in last place, by the African Blacks. The latter were considered to be incapable of initiative or any creative act, and therefore closer to the animal state. The anthropological method which legitimized these theories appealed to facts and numbers, which were to be allowed to speak for themselves without the intervention of the scientist and his subjectivity. The supposed objectivity of its methodology was designed to invest 'physical anthropology' with scientific legitimacy. But this way of conceiving science in terms of quantifiable data – and the use of instruments to obtain the data – was not exclusive to anthropology; it was common to all disciplines with aspirations to scientific status. And by the second half of the nineteenth century, 'race' (regardless of whether it was interpreted in monogenist or polygenist terms) was already being used as an ideological weapon in social and political debate.

Racial theories also made their presence felt outside the scientific sphere. The 'physiognomy of the peoples' was a recurrent theme in nineteenth-century art publications. One example, published in German and French in 1835 (see Baroja 1995: 223), was a picture album with accompanying text. Its author, Godefroy Schadow, was an artist with intellectual pretensions. His book contained drawings by travellers and artists of the racial physiognomic features of the peoples they had encountered. Schadow's work included reproductions of the skulls of different peoples, portraits of individuals in full face and profile, physiognomies of individuals supposedly representative of the 'Yellow' and Mongolian 'races', Oceania and 'Black Africa', Native Americans, Hindus, Jews, Spanish, French, Italians (these taken from classical portraits) and Germans, along with profiles of the faces of Spaniards and Russians, etc. On a more scientific level, Darwin (1809–82) attempted during his journeys to analyze the facial expressions of various peoples from supposedly different 'races'. Darwin arrived at the conclusion that facial expressions are the same in all people, regardless of racial variations (Baroja 1995: 223–30). Attempts at interpreting physiognomy continued, however. As late as the twentieth century the Portuguese anthropologist Mendes Correia could still claim that

> [t]here are, in truth, simian features in the physiognomy of some degenerates and some inferior populations. But simian features are [also] found in mentally and morally superior individuals. The correspondence

between the physical and the moral exists. Some faces cannot fool us (M. Correia 1932: 1).

Race in theory and slavery in practice

Interestingly, racial theory reached its height just when slavery[29] and the slave trade were being abolished. As John Rex noted, in colonial societies the slave occupied the lowliest social position, and in extreme cases was considered not a man but property, a mere tool ([1986] 1988: 81). Those who defended slavery considered Africans to belong to the lowest echelons of the great Chain of Being, alongside the orangutang, for example. They saw darkness of skin as a degenerative variation of what had been the original colour of man's skin – white. Therefore, they argued, Blacks should serve White people, who were superior in beauty and intelligence. Some racial theorists opposed slavery; but as abolitionism began to gain momentum in Europe, theories began to emerge according to which Blacks, like the Native Americans and Asians, were innately and permanently inferior to Whites.

The division between the proslavery and abolitionist lobbies of the nineteenth century was not always as clear-cut as we might imagine. For the former, forced labour was the destiny of an inferior species – the Africans. Yet some abolitionists called for an end to slavery not because they felt pity for the Blacks, but because they desired the extinction of the 'less capable' (Spencer, 1820–93) – an evolutionist idea – and considered that slavery merely ensured the survival of 'Blacks'. It was on these grounds that the anthropologist Lewis Henry Morgan (1818–1881) came to support abolitionism after 1850. An end to slavery would bring an end to the Black 'race'. The doctor James Cowles Prichard (1786–1848) was another author who put his knowledge in natural history at the service of his abolitionist stance. In his *Researches into the Physical History of Man* (1813), Prichard 'attempted to prove that the story of Genesis was correct and that all human tribes had, indeed, descended from one original couple' (Augstein 1996: xxiii).

In the first decade of the nineteenth century, some Portuguese abolitionists[30] called for European immigration to Brazil as an alternative to

---

29. Slavery had its beginnings in the civilizations of the Fertile Crescent. The practice later spread to Egypt, Syrio-Palestine and the eastern Mediterranean, Greece and the Roman empire. There were probably slaves in Portugal before it even existed as a nation. On slavery in Portugal, see Carreira (1979), UNESCO (1979), Tinhorão (1988), Rodrigues (1999) and Marques (1999).

30. Valentim Alexandre (1993) locates the emergence of abolitionism in Portugal between 1817 and 1820. For João Marques (1999), the abolitionist cause emerged a little earlier, in 1815.

African slave trafficking.[31] At issue was the fact that the 'colour' of the Blacks was considered an obstacle to their assimilation. There was, then, a link between abolitionism and hostility towards Black people. While some among the proslavery contingent saw trafficking in Black people as having a civilizing and integrative function, there were abolitionists who favoured immigration by the 'White man' on the grounds that it would even out the Brazilian racial spectrum: miscegenation between Brazilians and European immigrants would lead to the dilution of 'Negroid' characteristics in just a few generations. Of similar persuasion in this respect were the lieutenant António de Oliva, who proposed offering incentives for 'White' men to marry 'Black' or 'Indigenous' women, and the doctor Soares Franco,[32] who suggested barring unmarried men from working or receiving pay (Marques 1999: 130–35).

Slavery can be explained in economic terms, but not exhaustively so; on an entirely economic paradigm, people would be exploited indiscriminately, not on the basis of a belief in the racial inferiority of some and their 'propensity' for forced labour. Some authors have argued that slavery and racism were driven by utilitarian imperatives:[33] both one and the other were acceptable by virtue of the benefits they brought. This is the attitude found among colonial administrators such as James Mill and his son John Stuart Mill. For James Mill, an employee of the East India Company from 1819, the Indians, like the Chinese, were deceitful, two-faced, treacherous, cowardly, bereft of feeling and dirty. Mill recommended that the Indian government be subjected to the benevolent guidance of the British parliament. His son, John Stuart Mill, was also of the view that India should be governed by a colonial administration, but unlike his father he believed the colony was capable of governing itself once it had acquired civilized societal norms. Both Mills viewed the 'Natives' as children who required the guidance and supervision of rational, capable administrators. These 'Natives' 'ought not to be brutalized … nor enslaved but directed – administratively, legislatively, pedagogically and socially' (Goldberg 2002: 296). It was in the name

---

31. The end of the slave trade did not mean the end of slavery. Trafficking was not made illegal until 1831. The effective end of legal slave trafficking came in 1851; but slavery was not actually abolished in Portugal until 1888, when it was also banned in Cuba and Puerto Rico. In the United States, abolition came in 1865 (Wolf 1982; Skidmore [1974] 1989).

32. Appeals such as those made by Oliva and Franco seem to have been rare, and radical, cases in Portugal after 1815, however.

33. The theory of utility insists on treating every individual equally and impartially, and rejects paternalist interpretations. In other words, every individual is responsible for his or her own happiness and success.

of 'the Natives' own happiness, their future good defined in utilitarian terms, that they should have been willing to accept this state of affairs' (Goldberg 2002: 297). This added up to a justification of racialized colonialism, and consolidated it as an institution.

Racialism under attack

In the middle of the nineteenth century, when debate still raged between two opposing views – race as lineage (associated with an ethnological approach, upholding the idea of change and the importance of environmental circumstances) and race as type (associated with an anthropological approach, upholding the view that racial differences had arisen in the remote past, and supporting the idea of 'continuity' based on heredity) – along came Charles Darwin (1809–82), who undermined both theories with a new synthesis which explained both 'change' and 'continuity' (Banton [1987] 1998: 81). Drawing on Malthusian population theory, Darwin posited a process of 'natural selection' among the species. The publication of *The Origin of Species* (1859) rendered the debate between monogenists and polygenists irrelevant; both camps embraced the new evolutionist model. Contrary to popular belief, it was not Darwin who coined the phrase 'survival of the fittest' but Herbert Spencer (Poliakov [1971] 1974: 282). The following paragraphs will nevertheless concentrate on Darwin, who was after all the prime spokesman of evolutionary theory.

Darwinian biology showed that man was the descendant of a number of other animals, to which he did not stand in a superior position. What made Darwinian biology so radically different from earlier theories was that while Darwin sought to identify the differences between all the animals, and thereby determine man's place in the world, the anthropologists and naturalists who were his contemporaries looked for the differences between humans, appealing to the animal world for justification of certain differences they viewed as 'inferior' and therefore not part of the human world. This was to construct the inferiority of the 'other' (Gould 1983). The central thesis of *The Origin of Species* was that natural selection acted to preserve favourable differences and variations, while eliminating harmful ones (Darwin [1859] 1968: 84). It therefore made no sense to talk of permanent racial 'types', since all life, including humanity, adapted over time. Notwithstanding its biological focus, *The Origin of Species* reached a diverse reading public. Various interpretations of it have been applied to other areas of knowledge, including psychology, linguistics, sociology, politics and anthropology. Monogenists such as Quatrefages and Agassiz used the evolutionist model to hierarchize the different 'races' and peoples according to their 'mental and moral' qualities. The polygenists, meanwhile, accepted the common ancestor thesis but argued that the 'human species' had gone their own separate ways a long time ago, and now developed along different lines. The polygenists also expressed concern at the question of the mixing of the 'races'. Broca argued that the mixed-blood person, like the mule, was infertile; but Gobineau and Le Bon instead lamented his or her formidable propensity for reproduction, as a throwback to the more negative characteristics of their forebears.

As the nineteenth century ended and the twentieth began, there emerged a pseudo-scientific discourse on the subject of the 'primitive man' – who in a certain sense was the successor to the idea of the 'noble savage'. This discourse is to be found in the texts which were to form the foundations of a new branch of knowledge – ethnology. In their research into the rhythms of sociocultural growth, anthropologists such as Morgan, Tylor and Frazer (the 'social evolutionists') examined cultural development from a comparative perspective. According to social evolutionism, the superior 'races' were those who had shown themselves most successful in their ability to dominate others (Stocking 1968, 1988). Two strands of determinism emerged in parallel with this theory: geographic determinism and 'social Darwinism' (Cashmore [1984] 1996: 348–50), also known as 'race theory'. Advocates of geographic determinism, such as Henry Thomas Buckle (1821–1862) and Friedrich Ratzel (1844–1904), saw the cultural development of a nation as being totally subject to the influence of environment. Social Darwinism, meanwhile, promoted the 'pure type' – unsullied by miscegenation – and condemned mixed-blood reproduction as a phenomenon linked to social and 'racial' degeneracy (Schwarcz 1995: 58).

One movement that emerged concomitantly with evolutionism was eugenics, a political creed whose aim was to improve the physical and moral qualities of future generations. As 'a kind of advanced practical form of social Darwinism' (Schwarcz 1995), eugenics proposed intervention in population dynamics with the aim of subjugating or even eliminating the 'inferior races'. The term 'eugenics' (from the Greek *eu* – well, *genos* – birth) was coined in 1883[34] by Francis Galton (1822–1911), a half-cousin of Darwin. In his *Hereditary Genius* (1869), Galton

---

34. Eugenics was a new term in 1883, but the idea it embodied was far from new. Elimination of the incapacitated was an idea current among the ancient Greeks, as the British eugenicists themselves acknowledged – perhaps to mitigate the impact of the shocking notion that since not all individuals are equally endowed, some should not be allowed to reproduce (see Stepan 1991).

applied statistical and genealogical methods in an attempt to prove that human ability was influenced by heredity, not education, and called for interracial marriages to be prohibited. And he again drew on Darwinism in his *Inquiries into Human Faculty* (1883), in which he formulated his eugenicist theory of 'racial perfection'. In Galton's view, however, the Darwinian process of natural selection was no longer operative under 'civilized' conditions, and therefore active intervention in human development was necessary. In 1907 Galton was appointed the inaugural president of the Eugenics Education Society, the world's first eugenics association. He was succeeded by Leonard Darwin, Charles's son. Eugenics attracted the attention of many scientists and specialists, but this interest has to be seen as the culmination of the process of intellectual and social change which occurred in the nineteenth century, a process whereby human life was increasingly seen in terms of the natural laws of biology (Stepan 1991: 21). New questions began to arise with regard to miscegenation, too: now the risk was that it would trigger uncontrollable combinations. Some theorists argued that miscegenation would favour the 'inferior races' to the detriment of the 'superior', for whom degeneracy awaited. To prevent miscegenation, its opponents called for the segregation of certain groups, the isolation of 'inferiors' and even their extermination. Ultimately, eugenics revealed the incompatibility of cultural evolutionism and social Darwinism. 'Degeneration'[35] came gradually to depose 'evolution' as the watchword. For the social evolutionists, mankind was a hierarchy of unequal parts; for the social Darwinists, it was divided into diverse species.

Polygenists such as Gustave Le Bon, E. Renan and Gobineau drew their own conclusions from the social Darwinist view. For Gustave Le Bon (1841–1931), one of the most influential and widely quoted authors in Portuguese racial doctrine, inequalities of 'race', gender and social grouping were innate ([1894] 1910: 6). Le Bon saw 'race' as a fixed quantity that predetermined the evolution of the peoples:

> Each people possesses a mental constitution that is as fixed as its anatomical characters are ... Institutions exert an extremely weak influence on the evolution of civilizations, in most cases being effects, and only very rarely causes ... Man is always ... and above all else the representative of his race ([1894] 1910: 9–10, 18).

---

35. Vice, crime, immigration, female labour and the urban milieu were other commonly cited causes of degeneration. The belief that many of the afflictions associated with the poor – tuberculosis, syphilis, alcoholism and mental illness – were hereditary also fuelled fears of social decadence.

Le Bon did not just associate 'type' with 'race'; he also associated 'race' with 'species'. What he proposed was to identify the characteristics that endured over a prolonged course of time, the factors that constituted 'race' and that 'ended up acquiring great fixity' in determining 'the type of each people' – identifiable via a set of characteristics which remained unchanged over time. Basing his evaluation on behavioural, cultural and psychological criteria, Le Bon divided humanity into four groups: 'the primitive races, the inferior, the mediocre and the superior' ([1894] 1910: 23, 31–32). He also drew distinctions between the relative aptitudes of the sexes. Referring to an earlier study,[36] Le Bon wrote:

> Races in which cranial volume exhibits the greatest individual variations are the highest in civilization ... Among the members of a tribe of savages, all of them dedicated to the same occupations, the difference is ... minimal; between the peasant who only has three hundred words ... and the wise man who has a hundred thousand with the corresponding ideas, the difference is ... enormous [1894] 1910: 48–49).

A Frenchman, Le Bon did not omit to mention that the skulls of Parisian males were among the 'largest skulls known'. In excluding not only females but also males living in other French cities – not to mention the nonurbanites – Le Bon revealed his approach to be ethnocentric and classist.

For E. Renan (1823–92) there were three 'races' – White, Black and Yellow – each with its own specific origin and development. The 'Blacks', 'Yellows' and 'Mixed-breeds' were inferior not because they were uncivilized, but because they were uncivilizable ([1872] 1961). On the subject of the European nations, Renan denied German superiority by arguing that no pure 'races' existed, and that the more 'noble' countries such as England, France and Italy were those in which blood was more mixed – with Germany being no exception. But to apply the concept of 'race' in this way to any given European group was to make it a totally malleable category, of interest only to students of the history of humankind, with no political application ([1882] 1992: 46–48).

This brings us to Gobineau, the author of *Essai sur l'inégalité des races humaines* (1853), for whom the value of a 'race' was to be judged by its ability to create an original civilization. A novelist, philosopher, historian and would-be anthropologist, Gobineau maintained that the origins of all the Indo-European civilizations, with the exception of Assyria, could ultimately be traced to the Aryan 'race', the ethnic group whose languages formed the root of the Indo-European family of languages

---

36. Le Bon (1879).

and whose blood supposedly ran in the veins of all conquering peoples. For Gobineau, the purest representatives of the Aryan 'race' in his day were the Germanic peoples. Gobineau did not, however, view the Jews as an inferior 'race' (Ruffié 1983: 167–71). The Aryan 'type',[37] argued Gobineau, was the result of a process of racial refinement conducive to civilization and progress (Schwarcz 1995: 61–64). Sharing the ideas of the social Darwinists, he introduced the idea of 'racial degeneration' as a result of the crossbreeding of different human 'species'.

New developments emerged with the dawn of the twentieth century. Craniology and methods such as the cephalic index came in for criticism. Anthropology was now drawing on data from the fields of biology and morphology, including stature and length of limbs, eye colour and hair texture. The idea of 'race' and racial 'type' itself began to be questioned, especially in light of the findings of the Austrian botanist and monk Gregor Johann Mendel (1822–84) and his discovery that 'specific traits ... were controlled by specific elements (that is, genes) which were passed from one generation to another as independent components' (Wade 1997: 13); this discovery 'meant that the idea of type, whereby an unchanging bundle of traits was passed down the generations, was untenable' (Wade 1997: 13). Mendel's work was to contribute to the triumph of Darwinism. Another author, W. E. B. du Bois, questioned the idea that 'race' was 'natural' in *The Conservation of Races* (1897) (McGary 2002: 433-36). But the most important contribution in this period came from Franz Boas (1858–1942) and his critiques of Darwinian anthropology and evolutionism in anthropology.[38] Although he started by accepting many of the methods, premises and conclusions

---

37. 'Aryan' was a term first used in nineteenth-century linguistics in reference to the Indo-Iranian language group. The term derives from *arya*, which is classical Sanskrit for 'nobleman' or 'leader'. Perhaps Hitler would not have been so fond of the term if he had considered that the Indians differed far more from the blond, Nordic type than the Jews he hated and condemned to extermination.

38. 'Physical anthropology' developed along different lines in different countries, according to the anthropological traditions of each. It had considerable projection in France and Germany, and in Europe in general, where it was known simply as 'anthropology' – often in opposition to 'ethnology', which was culturally oriented. In the case of Anglo-American anthropology, where the ethnological tradition was more deeply rooted and the evolutionary tradition stronger, 'physical anthropology' – sometimes designated 'somatology' – became one of the four branches of a new 'general anthropology' which also embraced ethnology, linguistics and prehistoric archaeology. With his grounding in ethnology and 'physical anthropology', Boas soon acclimatized himself to the more encompassing American discipline and became one of the few social scientists to make a significant contribution to each of the four branches of anthropology. Other anthropologists rejected evolutionary racialism too, but it was Boas who actually laid out the groundwork for modern anthropological theory on the problem of 'race' vs. 'culture'.

of classical/physical anthropology, Boas leaned towards the monogenist view, and his epistemological and scientific orientation led him to adopt a critical posture with regard to this kind of anthropology. Boas showed that the variations in the dimensions of the same head over the course of a lifetime, or between two consecutive generations, were greater than those found between different 'races'.[39] Along with his disciples, like Ashley Montagu, he questioned theories of innate racial differences and heredity, while he also criticized the disciples of Morgan and the advocates of evolutionary theory in general. Boas turned his critical ammunition on evolutionist classifications, emphasizing instead the importance of environmental, regional and geographic factors in the study of human variety. Physical, cultural and linguistic characteristics were all subject to the influence of external processes, and therefore different results would be obtained depending on the template used for the classification – 'race', language or culture. Furthermore, argued Boas, the elements of a 'culture' can spread from one group to another, making reconstruction of a linear evolutionary sequence of cultural development a difficult or even impossible task (Boas [1940] 1982).

The anthropological tradition of Boas and the North American social determinists and culturalists has its foundations in the critiques of racialism and eugenics in the period between the two World Wars. These critiques rejected the concept of 'race' in favour of 'cultural determinism'. For Boas, human variety was to be explained by the geographic and 'cultural' isolation of the 'races'. Lamarck had already argued that evolution occurred not by way of selection but adaptation. As opposed to the Darwinists, and insofar as Lamarckism favoured the influence of environmental circumstances, all Lamarckians had a certain affinity with the supporters of geographic determinism. Boas's initial sources were the ethnographic data he had gathered in the Pacific Northwest and the arguments that Rudolf Virchow advanced against the Darwinists. Boas and his followers rejected evolutionist schemata and the classifications of the natural sciences applied to man. In their view, American anthropology had gone astray with Morgan (Stocking 1968; Kuper 1988). In the 1920s and '30s, a new generation of Boasians developed a theory of cultural determinism designed on the one hand to fill the vacuum left by earlier, discredited theories and on the other to counter the growing influence of eugenics, biological reductionism and behaviourism, which contended that the environment, not genetics, was the key determinant.

---

39. In *Changes in Bodily Form of Descendants of Immigrants* (1911), Boas showed that the shape of the human head is subject to modification by environmental influence in a relatively short span of time.

With the rise of fascism in Europe and the new impetus it gave to racist theories, at a time when the evolutionary racism of the nineteenth century was so powerful an influence in Nazi Germany that it became state policy, the Boasians now levelled new critiques at an old enemy.

In parallel with social determinism, anthropology promoted the notion of cultural relativism, i.e. the idea that no culture is superior to another but is merely *different,* and must therefore be understood according to its own context. On this view, biological, sociobiological and genetic factors did not determine the social and cultural destiny of human beings. What was specifically human about humans was the cultural nature of their social life, i.e. the attribution of sense and meaning to human actions.

The race debate has endured right through the twentieth century and into the twenty-first. Many authors now point to the inconsistencies in understanding 'race' as a 'natural' concept. Some contend that 'race' is a concept devoid of meaning (Appiah 1992); others that it has significance only when viewed as a social construct (Mills 1997; Outlaw 1996). The idea of 'race' may be suggested by what we might call somatic visibility, i.e. the elements which make up skin colour, texture and colour of hair, facial lineaments, shape of head, and stature; and yet certain formulations derive not from what we see but from the preconceived ideas of the observer, and this is to forget that what we see is also part of a process of construction of social meaning that has been underway throughout the centuries. Discrimination is based not on demonstrable biological facts, but rather on the 'biologization' of social facts. The belief in a biologically underwritten essence led to social exclusion, which has perpetuated the emphasis on phenotypical differences and in turn led to the creation of a 'culture' within which we can meaningfully speak of a 'racial' group. As we can still observe today, somatic differences can be replaced by so-called cultural – or even imaginary – characteristics. This is what happened when phenotypical characteristics were invented to set the Jews apart in European anti-Semitism. When the cultural and physical characteristics of individuals are considered together – when the characteristics we would designate as cultural are seen as natural – we are 'naturalizing' those differences (Wade 1997: 7). The notion of 'race' as applied to humanity may therefore have purposes of a social and political nature that we cannot exclude from our analysis. And in European terms, the colonial situation played a decisive role in the invention of a racial ideology which must be examined with caution.

Chapter II

Discourse, Images, Knowledge

The Place of the Colonies and Their Populations in the Portuguese Colonial Empire

The formation of Portuguese colonialism and 'colonial knowledge'

The following quotation is from Gonçalves Pereira, a professor at the Universidade Técnica of Lisbon (UTL) and an advocate of colonialization and eugenics:

> Everyone knows the extent of the plan of Albuquerque, who did not hesitate in conferring the highest functions on the Natives of India and led his soldiers to breed with the Native women, at the same time respecting the age-old civilization he had encountered ... This was also the orientation that dominated our colonization of Brazil, which was transformed from a region ... populated by decadent races into a prosperous nation which Portugal would not deny, when the time came, its own independence. But it is above all in the colonization of Africa that we can find ample testimony of the eminently moral and humanitarian character of colonization ... The Portuguese transformed nomadic races into sedentary ones, warlike and anarchic populations into peaceful, hardworking peoples. They saved thousands of human beings [and] showed themselves always superior to differences of race, caste or religion. [Their] superiority ... in the moral sphere is recognized by all colonialists and we can therefore say that we have little to learn ... from the modern colonizing movement (Pereira 1935: 13–14).

Pereira, writing in 1935, was invoking the plan of Afonso de Albuquerque, the sixteenth-century governor of Goa, as a strategy to be followed in the Portuguese colonies. Further reference was made to Albuquerque's plan in a text published as part of the 1934 colonial exhibition in Porto; here the emphasis fell on Albuquerque's endeavours to give new blood to the population of India and encourage 'Portuguese men to marry local women'. This would 'Christianize the women, children and, perhaps too, the families of Oriental women married to Portuguese men' – women who would show themselves to be 'rich and covered in distinction'; thus ensuring the transmission of 'the language, customs, institutions, religion of Portugal – everything which is dear to the Portuguese – to this far eastern population, turning it Portuguese'. This was 'the force which Albuquerque wished to set against the Oriental forces. The purpose of the new race would be to counterbalance, or more accurately prevail over, the force represented by the pure Natives' (*Portugal através do tempo e da história* 1934).

In this chapter[1] I propose to examine the status of the 'colonized populations', the images of these populations in metropolitan Portugal and the racial representations conveyed by these images, and the studies carried out on these populations, in an effort to understand them better and to determine whether miscegenation between Portuguese and 'Natives' of the colonies was viewed as favourably as it was by Albuquerque in the early sixteenth century. For Albuquerque's policy, although it was often referred to by the colonizers of the twentieth century, was not the policy which was implemented in Portugal's African territories, and some twentieth-century Portuguese academics, such as Mendes Correia and Eusébio Tamagnini, actually argued against interracial reproduction.

With the breakup of the Luso-Brazilian empire (a process which lasted from 1808 until 1825, the year of the treaty in which Portugal recognized the independence of the kingdom of Brazil), Portugal found it necessary to reinforce its presence in Africa (Alexandre 1993). The Sá da Bandeira plan, set down in a report of 1836, called for the abolition of the trans-Atlantic slave trade, but the reasons for this appeal were at bottom economic: to divert the capital mobilized by the slave trade into productive activities and to use African labour in Africa instead of exporting it (Santa-Rita 1955). In other words, there already existed a

---

1. Much of the empirical sources used in this chapter come from a bibliographical database I have compiled and which now contains over one thousand entries – *Discursos e Saberes sobre Raça: Bibliografia Portuguesa (1870–1970)*. This database was created as part of the research project *Poder e Diferenciação na Costa da Bahia. Raça e Etnicidade em Contextos Multiétnicos*, funded by the Fundação para a Ciência e a Tecnologia, Lisbon, and coordinated by Miguel Vale de Almeida.

plan for the reconstruction of the colonial economy in Africa, based on the abolition of trafficking in slaves in favour of the local exploitation of labour. This context was propitious to the increase in studies of the colonized territories and efforts to manage the subjugated populations. Until then, Portuguese colonizers had essentially dealt only with the coastal populations, not with the inhabitants of the interior. Where such dealings did exist, they were mainly trade-based. This remained the case until the end of the nineteenth century, when the Berlin Conference (15 November 1884 to 26 February 1885) defined the overseas possessions of Portugal. From this point on we can speak of a form of colonialism that rationalized natural and human resources and that was responsible for the political, economic and social management of these possessions. This was only possible after the African wars of pacification of the late nineteenth century, which in some places extended well into the twentieth century (Pélissier 1986).[2] Now that the African continent had been divided up, the next step was to discover it – and this meant geography, fauna and flora, geology and hydrography, health and hygiene in the tropics, agriculture and livestock farming, trade and colonial ethnology. Scientific expeditions were organized with the mission of gathering data on populations considered to be endangered, and the desire to catalogue humanity in all its diversity began to take form.

Although an 'evocative designation', the phrase 'Portuguese Colonial Empire' does not appear in any Portuguese legislation of the nineteenth century; its official revival was to come under the minister João Belo (*Álbum-Catálogo Oficial,* 1934: 72). With the legislation of November 1933,[3] Portugal divided its 'empire', 'for administrative purposes', into eight 'colonies' which were 'an integral part of the Nation': Cape Verde, Guinea, São Tomé e Príncipe, Angola, Mozambique, the State of India (Goa, Damão and Diu), Macao and Timor. Under the new colonial project, national identity, scientific research and political goals were closely interwoven. Thus we find much discourse which was simultaneously political and scientific in import, defining the Portuguese nation as a 'colonial nation'. Much of the attention of authors who examined the questions of 'race' and 'national identity' was therefore directed at the colonies. With regard to the production of 'colonial knowledge', science came to an accommodation with politics. Fuelling this new area of study were institutions, schools, and museums with vast collections of

---

2. The Guinea revolt took place on 17 April 1931, when a revolutionary junta undertook military action.

3. The *Carta Orgânica* published in the *Diário do Governo* was enacted by *Decreto-Lei* no. 23 228 of 15 November 1933, later amended by *Lei* no. 1948 of 13 February 1937, passed by the minister for the colonies, Vieira Machado.

books, works and artefacts that funded and sponsored publications, exhibitions, congresses and similar events designed to disseminate colonial
knowledge. Then again, many authors of the late nineteenth century
– the novelist Eça de Queirós is one example among many – never wrote
about the colonies, for they did not see them as relevant. In the view of
the historian Oliveira Martins,[4] a great deal of money was being wasted
on the colonies ([1880] 1888: 237).

Notwithstanding these unfavourable views, the fact remains that in
the mid-nineteenth century legislation was passed which acknowledged
the importance of anthropological knowledge of the colonies. However,
since there was no tradition of such research, it seems that little interest
was shown in it by the scientific community of the time. Then in 1874
came another two pieces of legislation designed to 'reiterate the instructions sent to the colonial authorities to ensure the continuation of these
anthropological studies' (Henriques 1997: 61). These instructions were
designed to promote research in the field of 'physical anthropology', a
discipline then emerging in Portugal, the rest of Europe, and the United
States. Travellers, traders, missionaries and others were instructed to collect body parts (bones, skin, hair), take physical measurements or complete questionnaires sent from metropolitan Portugal. They took their
inspiration from the 'instructions' that Guérando and Cuvier issued to
travellers in the early nineteenth century (Centlivres 1982). Their objective was to classify the people encountered and establish racial and cultural typologies. They also prescribed measurements of physical strength
and resistance and sketches of heads, frontally and in profile. Several
European institutions were already working on colonial research at this
time, either in Europe or its colonies,[5] but none were to be found in
Portugal.

By the end of the nineteenth century, however, Portugal began to
wake up to the need to invest more in the training of its colonial administrators, and to make them aware of the importance of learning
about the local populations. The research carried out by Portuguese
scientists helped justify the exercise of power and sovereignty over the
subject populations, while also affirming the civilizing power of colonial rule. Yet the findings of such research were mainly empirical, and
either lacked theoretical backing or rested on outmoded theory. At this
time, 'race' was a key instrument of classification. And yet as a polysemic

---

4. Oliveira Martins was the first Portuguese author to embrace the idea that 'races'
viewed as inferior should be subjugated by those seen as superior, and in the long term
were doomed to disappear. His ideas were primarily influential on the generation that
took part in the African wars of occupation.

5. E.g. Britain, France, the Netherlands and Italy (A. Costa 1940).

term, 'race' offered fertile ground for all kinds of taxonomies to flourish. Sometimes it was used not in a strictly racial sense at all, but rather as a means of distinguishing or elevating one group relative to others, or to differentiate the inhabitants of a certain territory. For example, some authors referred to the Portuguese as a good example of the 'spirit of the race' or as expressing the 'virtues of the race'. What interests us here, however, is the discrimination of colonial peoples based on the belief in the existence of 'races' as innate entities among which a hierarchy could be established. Many authors did not properly believe in the existence of 'races', but still believed there were sufficient differences to merit the establishment of a hierarchy.

The creation of the Sociedade de Geografia de Lisboa (SGL) gave new impetus to colonial studies. It was part of an initiative designed to encourage geographic exploration[6] and to illustrate the value of the colonies – which other colonial powers eyed with envy. The SGL was founded in 1875 by the writer and publicist Luciano Cordeiro, with the assistance of Andrade Corvo.[7] Its membership was a diffuse elite of professors of higher education, the liberal professions, intellectuals, traders, industrialists and army officers. The SGL gave its backing to a number of initiatives designed to increase studies on Portugal's overseas territories and their populations.[8] In its attempts to stimulate such research, in 1880 the SGL proposed that the government create a course in colonial studies, to be administered in an 'Instituto Oriental e Ultramarino Português'. This marked the beginning of 'scientific colonialism' in action. The course was to include materials on the history of colonization and colonial geography, colonial administration and common law, and the languages and ethnographic studies of the colonial territories (Guimarães 1984). Then, in 1894, Lisbon's Instituto 19 de Setembro introduced a colonial course with ten component modules, although only one module, Colonial Hygiene, was ever actually administered – and that for only a short time (J. Paulo 1992: 11). Other institutions which later offered colonial studies were the Escola de Medicina Tropical and the Escola Colonial, although the content of these disciplines, under legisla-

---

6. Although Silva Porto had made an expedition from Angola to Mozambique as early as 1853.

7. On the SGL and its activities between 1875 and 1895, see Guimarães (1984).

8. The SGL was something of a latecomer if we take into account the fact that geographic societies had already been created in Paris, London, Berlin and St Petersburg in the first half of the nineteenth century. Both the Berlin Conference (1884–85) and the British Ultimatum (1890) alerted the SGL to the need to defend Portugal's territories in Africa. The SGL organized a number of exploratory expeditions to, and studies on, Africa.

tion introduced in 1902, was also available in the geography and history disciplines of the Curso Superior de Letras. The first of these schools was created in 1902, with the support of the SGL. It was renamed the Instituto de Medicina Tropical in 1935. The second was created in 1906 with the mission of training the civil administration personnel of the overseas territories and the then Ministry for the Navy and Overseas. The Escola Naval and the Escola de Guerra also offered modules on colonial subjects as part of their legal and historical courses.

Anthropological studies of the populations of Portugal's overseas territories did not properly exist until the twentieth century. Perhaps the only exception was Fonseca Cardoso (1865–1912),[9] who for many historians was a pioneer of 'colonial anthropology' with his studies in Angola, Timor and India. Although other texts revealed a degree of acquaintance with the colonial populations, their principal objective was not to relate aspects of local ethnography; instead, they belonged to other scientific contexts, like the work of the geographic missions. They did, however, address certain aspects of the populations – exoticism, a tribal chief or other particulars. Many of these texts are by military men or missionaries. Invariably, however, and although they do reveal the importance attached to knowledge of the colonial populations, they were written by people whose ideas were imbued with Western concepts and criteria of evaluation, and were therefore ethnocentric. Furthermore, and despite the fact that Portugal was a colonial power, the anthropology of this time did not exclusively concentrate on the 'colonized populations'. Contrary to what the Italian researcher Donato Gallo (1988) asserts, perhaps it is more accurate to say that anthropology as an emerging science was not properly at the service of colonialism, but rather flourished in its midst. In addition, Portuguese anthropology did not limit its research to the populations under Portuguese rule but also examined other groups, such as the mentally and physically ill, sufferers of various ailments, prostitutes, delinquents and criminals, as happened, or had happened earlier, in the European and American schools of anthropology. The colonial populations did claim the bulk of the attention; but if there had been no colonies, anthropology would have turned its attentions elsewhere. And if anthropology was ever in the service of colonialism, this happened not at the outset but later, when the regime took on board certain scientific theories in an attempt to justify the colonization of territories inhabited by populations considered to be bereft of civilization. One generalization we can safely make about this anthropology is

---

9. On the career of Fonseca Cardoso, see Roque (2001).

its emphasis on the physical metrics[10] which fuelled the racial theories of the nineteenth century.

The Portuguese could not exactly be described as producers of groundbreaking scientific theories, or at least did not recognize their own theories as such; instead, they incorporated ideas from abroad, and some people were more alert to these ideas than others. There was some degree of international exchange, however. In 1880, Lisbon's Academia das Ciências hosted the 9th International Congress of Anthropology and Prehistoric Archaeology. This same year marked the emergence of the earliest anthropological research in Portugal – research which essentially belonged to the 'physical' domain. We can also mention the Sociedade Carlos Ribeiro, founded in 1888, and the *Revista de Ciências Naturais e Sociais* (1889–98), a publication founded the following year and the predecessor of another scientific review, *Portugália* (1899–1908). The creation of the Sociedade Carlos Ribeiro marked the emergence of the city of Porto as a centre of anthropological studies. Some of the most respected researchers of the day pubished their work in the four volumes of the *Revista de Ciências Naturais e Sociais;* they included Teófilo Braga (1843–1924), Santos Rocha (1853–1910), Basílio Teles (1856–1923), Adolfo Coelho (1847–1919), Martins Sarmento (1833–99), Ricardo Severo (1869–1940), Rocha Peixoto (1866–1909), Leite de Vasconcelos (1858–1941), Júlio de Matos (1856–1922) and Fonseca Cardoso (1865–1912) (Pereira and Pita 1993: 660). These studies aspired to a degree of rigour comparable to that of the mathematical and physical sciences. They were characterized by their descriptive, comparative and classificatory tenor, and were similar to the evolutionist models being advanced in geology and biology by Lyell and Darwin, respectively.[11]

The Sociedade Portuguesa de Antropologia e Etnologia (SPAE) was founded in Porto in 1918 by Mendes Correia (1888–1960). Despite its 'predilection for physical anthropology and archaeology', the SPAE was also created 'to stimulate a certain amount of ethnographic research' (Leal 2000: 35). In 1921, on an initiative by Portuguese anthropolo-

---

10. 'Physical anthropology' was also afoot in Brazil with the work of Agassiz and Nina Rodrigues, a disciple of Broca, although more emphasis was placed on cultural anthropology in the Brazilian case (Schwarcz 1995). Nevertheless, as Broca's work illustrates, cultural aspects were still seen in the light of 'physical anthropology' – data collected from physical measurements was applied as a metric of social and cultural development.

11. On the influence of Darwin on the Portuguese authors of the the generation of 1870, see A. Pereira (1997). According to Pereira, Darwin is rarely depicted in this literature as the man who ushered in 'the hells of the twentieth century, of race struggle, eugenics and crime'.

gists, the Portuguese branch of the International Anthropology Institute was founded in Coimbra. This institute also had a delegation in India, staffed by researchers from the medical school of Goa.

In parallel to the investment being made on the institutional level, various congresses were held on colonial questions in the early twentieth century. Three congresses in particular are worth mentioning. The first was the inaugural National Colonial Congress of 2 December 1901. The second National Colonial Congress, promoted by the SGL, came in 1924. According to José Gonçalo Santa-Rita, although scientific research was not directly addressed at the 1901 congress, things had changed by 1924, when there was much debate on recent research on the colonies – albeit mainly in the fields of geography and botany. Meanwhile, in July and August 1923 the first West African Congress of Tropical Medicine, organized by Norton de Matos, was held in Luanda. The objective of this congress was not only to contribute to successful colonization and solve sanitary and public health problems, but also to identify the problems faced by colonizers and Natives. This, in the opinion of Rui Pereira, was 'the most important scientific event to have occurred in the Portuguese colonies' (1986: 204). In the specific field of anthropology, two important congresses were held outside Portugal: the First Universal Races Congress, held in London in July 1911, and the International Congress of Ethnology and Ethnography, held in Neuchâtel in 1914, which gave preference to ethnological studies over 'physical anthropology'. At this second congress Bezemer delivered a paper on the 'importance of ethnography in colonial policy', in which he argued that a knowledge of ethnography among the colonial administrators was necessary to avoid bloody conflict (Lima 1934: 107). Anthropological data on the Natives was not the most pressing necessity at this initial stage. For many colonizers, driven by their desire for a utilitarian form of colonialism, it was more important that the Natives submitted to the colonial authorities, and that neither agreements nor the use of force should be necessary. Nevertheless, interest in the anthropology of Indigenous peoples was growing by this time, and it was clearly driven by the need for the colonizers to know their subjects better. In 1912, Portugal opened the Ethnographic Museum of Angola and Kongo. Such efforts did not always produce significant results, however. In many texts the principal – or near-omnipresent – theme was how to make the colonies economically viable on the basis of their natural resources – and these resources included the Natives. Anthropological motives per se came later.

In the period under review in this book, we encounter a number of people who define themselves as opponents of the regime yet also support the existence of the colonies. And the republican regime was every bit as colonialist as the monarchy it had replaced. The expression that defined Portugal as 'a single, indivisible whole' belonged to Afonso Costa (1871–1937), a leading political figure of the First Republic who was an opponent of the Estado Novo in its first decade of existence – Costa was even driven into exile because of his views. Another major figure of the First Republic was Norton de Matos, who favoured a more philanthropic policy towards the Natives of the colonies. His governance[12] promoted and funded ethnographic studies in Angola. However, by the 1930s and '40s projects such as these had all but fizzled out. Although an innovator in terms of certain ideas and their implementation, Norton de Matos was still very much a man of his time. He viewed the African from a European, prejudice-laden perspective; while he favoured a colonization that recognized, respected and showed an interest in the 'usages and customs' of the Natives, he still identified real (i.e. Western) civilization with that of the colonizer, whose job it was to bring this civilization to 'backward countries' (Matos 1944: vol. 1, 51). Before Norton de Matos, there already appeared to exist in Angola a certain 'awareness of Indigenous usages and customs' – awareness which was enshrined in certain pieces of legislation (R. Pereira 1986). Only with Norton de Matos, however, were more decisive measures taken to carry out scientific research. In 1913, the Indigenous Affairs, Reconnaissance and Scientific Exploration – later renamed the Secretariat for Indigenous Affairs – was created with the mission of conducting a survey of 'Indigenous usages and customs'. One man who played a major role in this process was Ferreira Dinis, author of the exhaustive ethnographic survey *Populações Indígenas de Angola* (1918). This survey was based on 'ethnographic' questionnaires completed by employees of the colonial administration, and later became part of the module in Colonial Anthropology, directed by António de Almeida, which was attached to the Escola Superior Colonial's (ESC) chair in Colonial Ethnology and Ethnography.

Interest in colonial ethnography seems to have faded in the 1920s, to be replaced by other concerns. A new orientation now guided colonial policy, and when he returned to Luanda to take up his office as high commissioner on 16 April 1921, Norton de Matos was saddened by what he found. With regard to the 'education and instruction' of the Na-

---

12. Norton de Matos was appointed colonial and war minister in 1915, after having served as governor of Angola from 17 June 1912 to 8 March 1915. He was later appointed high commissioner for Angola, an office he held from 16 April 1921 to 18 September 1923. Before becoming a republican and joining the Democratic Party, he had been a monarchist deputy and later became an opponent of the Estado Novo. He was also a grand master in the Masons.

tives, Norton de Matos felt that 'the *Indígena*[13] would only be reborn to a new life … when his language was Portuguese and his level of instruction increased commensurately with that of our children' (1944: vol. 3, 301). Norton de Matos divided the indigenous Angolan population into three groups: 'the great mass of Blacks, almost completely benighted by primitive civilization'; 'a small number of Blacks and *Mestiços,* with a rudimentary education which served only to remove them from their own civilization without inserting them in ours and to form men without character'; and 'an increasingly large group of Blacks and *Mestiços,* worthy of our full consideration and attaining, thanks almost exclusively to their own efforts and their overcoming of unfounded oppositions, to our level of civilization' (1944: vol. 3, 302). This classification formed the backdrop against which 'the necessary measures' should be taken 'to ensure that no more pseudo-educated, pseudo-civilized Blacks were produced like those of the second group'. In Norton de Matos's view, it would be better 'to leave the Blacks of Angola forever illiterate rather than create that degenerate hybrid that goes by the name of *Ambaquista,* and whose principal characteristics are disdain for manual labour and insubordination to the Western morality and civilization, which they would declare, in their mangled Portuguese, to be theirs' (1944: vol. 3, 302). The best way of preventing the growth of these demographic elements was to connect instruction in literacy with the learning of trades and crafts. Instead of 'wrenching the *Indígenas* from their way of life', from their 'usages and customs', they should be encouraged to 'evolve … towards a more perfect level of civilization', for 'education geared exclusively towards literacy and proselytism, in isolation and as the only objectives to be attained', would always produce 'the worst results'. As for the religious missions, these constituted 'elements of significant value for the education and instruction of the *Indígenas*' (1944: vol. 3, 303–4, 318). For Norton de Matos there was no such thing as 'colonial policy' but rather a 'policy of the Nation'. Hence his 'work towards development' in the colonial territories, his quest for the 'improvement in

---

13. Under article 2 of colonial ministerial decree 16473 of 6 February 1929, which defined the political, civil and criminal status of Natives, '*Indígenas*' (i.e. Natives) were 'individuals of the Black race, or descended from it, or who by their ornament and custom, are indistinguishable from the common type of that race'; '*não Indígenas*' (non-Natives) were 'those of any race who did not meet those conditions'. The guidelines for colonial policy were established by the Colonial Act *(Acto Colonial)* of 1930, which laid down differences in rights and duties between those born in the mother country and those born in the colonies, and between the Assimilated and the *Indígenas.* The 1954 *Indígena* statute of the Portuguese provinces of Guinea, Angola and Mozambique incorporated an integration policy, but continued to impose segregation. The *Indígena* statute was finally abolished in 1961.

the living conditions, material and spiritual, of all Portuguese, White and Coloured', his support for the colonization of Portugal's African territories 'by way of White Portuguese families',[14] and his calls for the 'transformation of the lives ... of the *Indígenas*' (1944: vol. 1, 19, 21, 28). When he announced his candidacy for President of the Republic in 1948, Norton de Matos appealed to the Portuguese at home and overseas on behalf of the unity of nation, economy and action. He called for intensive settlement of the overseas territories and the promotion of agriculture, which he saw as the basis of 'the whole civilization of the Indigenous populations of the overseas provinces'. On the subject of the rights of the citizen, he upheld the 'equality of all before the fundamental law, without discrimination by race, sex, language, religion or public opinion'.[15] In other words, although he spoke of the existence of different 'races', he argued that these should have equal rights – which was hardly surprising in the post–Second World War context.

The Colonial Act and the 'creation' of the *Indígena*

In the military dictatorship instituted by the coup of 28 May 1926, António Oliveira Salazar was minister of finance until 1932, when he was appointed head of government. He had previously served as colonial minister in 1930. Salazar's policy was based on reducing public expenditure to a minimum, and it was the colonies which suffered most from these cuts, which were in marked contrast to the investment made in Angola under the governorship of Norton de Matos. The two men shared one point in common, however: the idea of the 'nationalization' of the colonies. The myth of the colonizing mission of Portugal also fuelled the development of colonial ideology, as did the 'creation' of the *Indígena*. The guiding principles of colonial policy were set down in the 47 articles of the Colonial Act of 1930. João Belo, minister for the colonies from 1926 to 1928, attempted to maintain and legitimize

---

14. While Norton de Matos sought to encourage 'White' families to relocate to Africa (more specifically, Angola), Armindo Monteiro, minister for the colonies from 1931 until his appointment to the ministry of foreign affairs in 1935, tried to restrict Portuguese emigration to the colonies – those wishing to depart could only leave with a 'letter of summons', for it was important to avoid projecting the idea that the colonies were havens for 'fugitives' or the unemployed. The 'Whites' were not to project a 'bad' image to the Natives, but rather one in which they were seen as superior.

15. Anonymous, 1948, *General Norton de Matos, Candidato à Presidência da República apresentou a sua candidatura no Supremo Tribunal de Justiça, em 9 de Julho de 1948, nos termos do Art. 27 da Lei Eleitoral em vigor*, Bequest of Pinto Quartim, Arquivo de História Social do Instituto de Ciências Sociais da Universidade de Lisboa, no. 46, doc. 212.

Portugal's overseas possessions by institutionalizing the ideal of 'empire' in a project overseen by Salazar and Quirino de Jesus (a member of the Seara Nova group). It was this project that later gave rise to the Colonial Act. In its first section ('On General Guarantees') we read: 'It is of the organic essence of the Portuguese Nation to discharge the historic function of possessing and colonizing overseas domains and civilizing the Indigenous populations contained therein' (article 2). Article 3 states: 'The overseas domains of Portugal are designated as colonies and constitute the Portuguese Colonial Empire.' The Colonial Act also reduced the powers and autonomy of the colonial governments, which now fell under the control of the ministry for the colonies and the central (i.e. Lisbon) administration. The intention was to exercise greater power over the colonies so they could be better exploited. In essence, the Colonial Act had a political intent, and it heralded a new phase of colonial administration that was imperialist, nationalist and centralizing. It also established differences between the rights and duties of those who had been born in metropolitan Portugal and those of the Assimilated and Indigenous populations. These differences were established on the basis of criteria such as manner of dress, educational qualifications and social conduct, and distinctions could also be drawn between *Assimilado* and *Indígena* if the differences between them were significant. This made it possible for certain *Assimilados* to become 'real' Portuguese. The Colonial Act also instituted a policy of *tutela* (supervision) in regard to the populations of São Tomé e Príncipe, Guinea, Angola, Mozambique and Timor. Natives of Cape Verde, the State of India and Macao were given special status.

Although united under a common nationality, the many societies that populated the Portuguese 'empire' were subjected to distinctions based on the 'races' to which they supposedly belonged. They were denied autonomy, as this would have led to a forced assimilation. Furthermore, the inferior status of these populations would justify the investments made by Portugal in its efforts to protect, civilize and evangelize them. Thus, the Colonial Act gave official sanction to difference and hierarchy. A shared nationality – Portuguese – was no guarantee of equality.[16] In other words, the 'empire' was a political entity founded on the existence of hierarchically arranged identities, all subsumed under their common belonging to the same 'nation'.

---

16. France also passed a Colonial Act which denied its colonial subjects equality, driven by the development of a discourse founded on a 'racial hierarchy' and concealed behind an ideology which trumpeted the 'union of the races'. This discourse exalted the 'union of peoples' within the empire, but political realities showed that the underlying purpose was to bring into evidence their differences of origins (Blanchard and Blanchoin 1995: 227).

The Colonial Act was debated from 13 to 16 May 1930 at the third National Colonial Congress. It was then referred to the Colonial Council. The proposals it contained divided opinions. One man who spoke out against what he called the 'inappropriate and pretentious' expression 'Portuguese Colonial Empire' was the governor of the Bank of Angola, Cunha Leal, who preferred the 'traditional designation of overseas provinces' as the only one which conveyed 'the historic conception of the indivisibility and integrity of the national territory' (quoted in R. Silva 1990: 105–6). Norton de Matos and Bernardino Machado (the inaugural director of the course in anthropology at the University of Coimbra in 1930, and a former president who was deposed by the military coup of 1926) disagreed with many of the premises of the Act. Despite these misgivings, the Colonial Act was passed on 8 July 1930[17] and entered the Constitution in 1933. It was not abolished until 1951. The principles it enshrined were enacted under other legislation, such as the Labour Code of the *Indígenas* of the Portuguese Colonies in Africa (1928), the Organic Diploma on Relations Between *Indígenas* and Non-Indígenas under Private Law (1929), the Organic Charter of the Portuguese Colonial Empire[18] and the Overseas Administrative Reforms (both 1933). The Organic Charter, for example, established 'the right of the *Indígena* to live and work' and awarded official legal status to 'the overseas religious missions' (*O Século* 1940b: 54–55). For Silva Cunha, these and other basic laws constituted 'the Portuguese system of Indigenous policy'. But this 'policy' promoted the subjection of Natives to special restrictions, such as the 'prohibition from leaving their district (a crime punishable by law) and the obligation to enrol in the census records,[19] so that they cannot avoid the strictest supervision' (Cameroto 1936: 102). Writing on the Colonial Act, Santa-Rita (1936) argued:

> If ... it is the job of the State to defend the Indigenous population against exploitation by the Whites and prevent it from being considered as goods or draft animals as it was in the days of slavery, the fact remains ... that the Black man cannot be accorded the right to idleness which is denied the White man (Santa-Rita 1936: 232).

One stratagem whereby the Natives were forced to work was the mandatory 'Indigenous tax'.[20] Since the White man was not allowed to be

---

17. *Decreto* no. 18 570.

18. The Organic Charter was the consequence of changes to the legal foundations of the Colonial Act, and comprised 248 articles in its 8 sections (Cameroto 1936).

19. At these census enrolments, it was common for the administrative staff to give names to the Natives, many of them abusive or humorous.

20. One former district manager revealed in an interview that '[t]here was a census every year because there was this Indigenous tax and everyone who was legally adult came

idle, Blacks too should be obliged to carry out the tasks assigned them, even it meant using a degree of violence. Some, though not many, critics spoke out against forced labour in Africa, and called for the formation of more egalitarian societies. Freire de Andrade (1925) and Norton de Matos were among these critics, although their objections were voiced before the advent of the Estado Novo (and in Norton de Matos's case, during it, too).

Legislation on the status of the *Indígena* remained in effect until 1961, when it was abolished under Adriano Moreira. It was outlined in three specific statutes: the Political, Civil and Criminal Statute of the Indigenous Populations of Angola and Mozambique, passed in 1926 when João Belo was minister for the colonies; the Political, Civil and Criminal Statute of the Indigenous Population (1929, under the minister Bacelar Bebiano); and the Statute of the Indigenous Populations of Guinea, Angola and Mozambique (1954, with Sarmento Rodrigues the overseas minister). The initial *Indígena* statute (1926) applied only to Angola and Mozambique, 'the two large colonies where the problem [had] greater amplitude' and required 'more attention'.[21] In 1927, the legislation was enforced in Guinea and the territories leased to the Mozambique and Nyassa Companies; in 1946 it was extended to São Tomé e Príncipe and Timor. The *Indígenas* in question were defined as 'individuals of the Black race or descendants thereof who, by their enlightenment and customs, cannot be distinguished from the bulk of that race'.[22] No other elements of identification were taken into account. Furthermore, it was the colonial governments who were responsible for determining who was and who was not 'Indigenous', although administrative employees were not always capable of making the distinction. As a former district manager active in the 1930s told me in interview:

> Fine, I gave the king of Kongo a slap in the face and shoved him off his chair, because they told me I wasn't to allow a Black to remain sitting when I arrived … And so the administrator said: 'Hey listen, so you slapped the king of Kongo then?' And I answered: 'Don't ask me who the king of Kongo is; all I saw was a Black sitting there and he didn't stand up.' And he says to me: 'Ah, but that's not allowed, you can't do that'. 'Oh no?' I said. 'I'm not going to apologize to him. He's taken it in good part; he says the White man didn't know he was a king' (28 and 29 March 2003).

---

to pay it … Cadá [an agricultural estate in Angola] needed 900 Blacks; the Blacks went around doing nothing, they had to pay their tax … and so the State supplied them with the money in return for working there. Where's the forced labour in that? I don't see it.'

21. *Decreto–Lei* no. 12 553 of 23 October 1926.
22. *Decreto–Lei* no. 13 698 of 30 May 1927.

Individuals classed as *Indígenas* could, however, be reclassified as *Assimilados* and gain the right to Portuguese citizenship. Following amendments introduced in 1929, the *Indígena* legislation remained unchanged until 1954, when it was again revised.[23] For Angola, Legislative Decree no. 237 of 26 May 1931 defined the

> necessary conditions for an *Indígena* to be 'Assimilated' as a European: 1 to have fully relinquished the usages and customs of the Black race; 2 to be able to speak, read and write the Portuguese language; 3 to adopt monogamy; and 4 to exercise a profession, craft or office compatible with European civilization, or to have income obtained by licit means which is sufficient to procure food, sustenance, housing, and clothing for him and his family (Osório and Rodrigues 1940: 552–53).

This was obviously seeing African societies in light of Western values. The regime itself acknowledged that 'the general equation of the overseas *Indígena* with the European' was merely theoretical: it was an idea which had already been current during the liberal monarchy, which established a basic distinction between 'citizen' and *Indígena*. On the face of it, the Indigenous statute of 1926, the Labour Code and the Colonial Act seemed to respect the 'usages and customs' of the Natives, their freedom to enter into employment contracts, their protection from forced labour, and their right to remuneration and to medical assistance. It was argued that the Natives were defended and protected by their 'Indigenous' status. The question of the Indigenous statute was not addressed in the constitutional review (the sixth) of 1945. In the same year, however, the revised Organic Charter tells us that 'in the State of India and the colonies of Macao and Cape Verde the respective populations are neither classed nor treated as *Indígenas*' – they had the status, therefore, of 'citizens'. The later constitutional review of 1951 led to the repeal of the Colonial Act and its removal from the Constitution of 1933, an attempt to lessen the qualitative charge of the *Indígena* statute. In 1953, the reformulation of the Organic Charter as the Organic Law on Overseas Portugal withdrew 'Indigenous' status from the natives of Timor and São Tomé e Príncipe. These changes were not extended to the populations of Angola, Guinea and Mozambique, who remained subject to the classification imposed on them in 1929.

At bottom, the idea behind the Indigenous statute, and the difficulties encountered in amending it, were indicative of a camouflaged

---

23. One of the features of this statute most fiercely criticized by the anticolonialist movement was the racial discrimination it enshrined. The review of the legislation eliminated the duality of personal status at the level of political rights: now all colonial subjects were entitled to obtain identity cards as Portuguese citizens.

racism which manifested itself in paternalism and evangelization, and whose ultimate objective was to keep the overseas possessions and their populations in the sphere of colonial rule. In the Portuguese overseas territories as a whole, the various subject populations were accorded varying degrees of importance. The lowest levels of the hierarchy were occupied by Angolans, Guineans and Mozambicans; then came the inhabitants of Timor and São Tomé e Príncipe; then, higher still, were the inhabitants of the State of India, Macao and Cape Verde.

As for the Labour Code,[24] this was passed on 6 December 1928 as a result of international pressure (from the League of Nations especially) which had been growing since 1926. Until the new legislation was passed in 1928, forced labour was common practice in the Portuguese colonies. The colonial authorities were actively involved in recruiting Indigenous labour both for public and private ends, and they continued to do so after the new legislation was introduced; the changes never left the paper they were written on.[25] And yet this review of the Labour Code came in for considerable criticism, especially from settlers who believed that they would be unable to satisfy their labour needs without the intervention of the authorities. Some settlers even saw the Portuguese as blameless, arguing that other colonial powers treated their Natives with cruelty because they felt hatred and racial prejudice – sentiments which they, the Portuguese, did not harbour, as they were tolerant by nature. It was commonly asserted in the 1930s and '40s that slavery did not exist in Portugal but was still to be found in certain foreign colonies and protectorates. However, the plantations of São Tomé e Príncipe, one of the world's biggest producers of cocoa, were worked by 'servant' labour recruited in Angola and Mozambique. These workers could only become 'freedmen' if they possessed a 'letter of enfranchisement'. Most of them ended up signing away their rights in 'contracts' which made them dependent on the plantation owners; in other words, they were slaves, although their condition was long concealed by the Portuguese political and legal system. In most cases, the real beneficiaries of this labour were not the Natives but the factories, companies, agricultural estates and their owners – those who depended on such labour to run their businesses. Furthermore, representing the Natives as 'uncivilized' meant they could be considered as suitable for labour.

---

24. I consulted the following text of this legislation: República Portuguesa, 1936, *Código do Trabalho dos Indígenas nas Colónias Portuguesas de África, Aprovado por Decreto no. 16 199 de 6 de Dezembro de 1928...*

25. On this subject see various texts by Silva Cunha in the 1950s. On 'Indigenous labour' and colonial legislation, see S. Cunha ([1949] 1955). Silva Cunha lectured at the Faculty of Law in Lisbon, where he specialized in problems related to 'Indigenous labour'. He was overseas minister from 1965 to 1973 and a professor at the ESC.

Some African labour was exported outside the empire, on a seasonal basis or otherwise. Mozambican labour was exported to South Africa and Rhodesia, for example. These exported labourers were not fully aware of their rights and they could be exploited even more in the foreign colonies than in the Portuguese ones. Armindo Monteiro himself admitted at the Imperial Conference of 1933 that 'a mistake' had been made when

> in their eagerness to reap dividends and to get public projects finished quickly, the nations sacrificed the Black's freedom of labour, severing him from his family environment, removing him from the institutions that ... gave him refuge, giving him as companions men of other tribes [and] other creeds, other traditions, sowing anarchy in his social life (*Álbum-Catálogo Oficial*, 1934: 87).

Monteiro acknowledged that this was a 'bad method' because 'the essential datum of colonization' should be of a 'human order' and 'spiritual nature'. Other acts he justified by arguing that with 'scant military resources we rule over Indigenous populations in their millions, because we stand for the protection that they desire and respect, for it respects them in their deepest aspirations and beliefs.' After all this talk about respecting the way of life of the Natives, Monteiro then goes on to contradict himself: 'What we have to do is change the lives of the Indigenous population, bringing them closer to ours, making them evolve, first within the bounds of their own disciplinary structures, then as part of the institutions which we efficiently impose upon them' (*Álbum-Catálogo Oficial*, 1934: 87).

Acting in parallel with the political regime, and reinforcing it, was the church. The image cultivated by the church was that of an institution which supported the civilizing mission of the Portuguese and their duty to educate, protect and evangelize the Natives, so that they could become 'Assimilated' and shake themselves free of their state of savagery (in some cases) and barbarism (in others). Vocational training was organized in the colonies in keeping with the perceived habits and aptitudes of the Natives. Although they were often viewed as idle, overgrown children, the Natives could be assimilated into civilization via the endeavours of the Portuguese colonizers and missions (Lobato 1952). As the legislation of 22 November 1913 appeared to omit to mention the missionary vocation of Portugal, João Belo drafted the Missionary Statute. Article 66 of this statute[26] entrusted the education of the *Indígenas* to 'missionary personnel and their auxiliaries'. According to the missionary Joaquim Mendes, the missions were 'the only entity' with

---

26. *Decreto* no. 31 207 of 5 April 1941.

the 'right to instruct the Blacks', although the State was responsible for 'covering expenditure on education' (Mendes 1955: 434). We can now understand the intentions behind this legislation and the reasons for the hierarchies established. And yet with all these changes to the legislation, and despite all the efforts made in political and religious circles, illiteracy rates among the native populations was still at nearly 100 per cent at the beginning of the 1950s. According to official censuses, in 1950 the 'Assimilated' or 'civilized' sections of the African population accounted for less than 0.02 per cent (Anonymous 1953: 65).

Colonial propaganda: 'marketing the empire'

A number of institutions specializing in colonial issues were created under the Estado Novo, while others which had already existed were reinforced. However, in comparison with other 'empires' – the French, Belgian, British and Dutch – Portugal was less well endowed with such institutions. It had no colonial or ethnographic museum, for example.[27] The Agência Geral das Colónias (AGC) was created in 1924, and existed for over fifty years, although its name was changed in 1951 to the Agência Geral do Ultramar (AGU). It was to be one of the most important producers of events and disseminators of information on the colonies.[28] Other official bodies like the Secretariado de Propaganda Nacional (SPN)[29] had the job of disseminating expressions such as 'Indigenous' and 'colonies'. These notions thereby acquired a new dynamic. Imperial propaganda was also spread in exhibitions, the press, literature, posters, picture postcards, the education system, cinema, the arts (architecture, music, drawings, paintings) and theatre. The state broadcaster, Emissora

---

27. Not until 1965 did the country have a national ethnological museum, for example.

28. The AGC/AGU published the periodicals *Boletim Geral das Colónias (BGC)* and *O Mundo Português* as well as a number of collections, such as *Pelo Império* (1935–61), the *Biblioteca Colonial Portuguesa, Temas Lusíadas, Clássicos da Expansão Portuguesa no Mundo, Colecção de relatórios e documentos coloniais* and the *Anuário do Império Colonial Português*. Its materials – books, newsletters, films and pictorial matter – were lent to schools, scientific societies and associations. Other contemporary periodicals carried articles on the colonies: examples were *Vida Colonial, Portugal Colonial e Marítimo* (vol. 1 covered the period 1897–98), *Boletim da Sociedade de Geografia de Lisboa, Portugal em África, Portugal d'Aquém e d'Além Mar, Cadernos Coloniais, Notícias do Império* and *Informação Colonial.*

29. On the activities of the SPN (1933–44), later the Secretariado Nacional de Informação, Cultura Popular e Turismo (SNI) (1944–74), in Portugal, and of the Departamento de Imprensa e Propaganda (1939–45) in Brazil, see Paulo (1994).

Nacional, created in 1935 with Henrique Galvão (1895–1970) at its head, was also a vehicle of this propaganda. The cultural propaganda, centenary celebrations and other cultural events sponsored by the SPN (created in 1933) were collectively designated a *política do espírito*[30] by its director António Ferro (1895–1956). In 1944 the SPN was succeeded by the Secretariado Nacional de Informação, Cultura Popular e Turismo (SNI), with Ferro appointed its director-general the same year. The SPN-SNI promoted events, sponsored a law protecting the cinema and organized awards. Emissora Nacional (with its board that vetted prospective broadcasts for their airworthiness), although nominally an autonomous body, ultimately reported to the SPN-SNI. The SNI also published periodicals directed at the Portuguese and foreign public.[31] These publications, like all media, were subject to censorship. After the approval of the new Constitution on 11 April 1933, a new law[32] sanctioned the inspection of periodicals,[33] posters, fliers and leaflets whose subject matter touched (or was considered to touch) on 'matters of a political or social nature' (Pires 2000: 14). Other periodicals whose stock-in-trade was not specifically the colonies, such as *O Século*, dedicated special issues to them. Periodicals on missionary work included *Missões de Angola e Congo, Revista de Cultura Missionária*[34] and *O Pretinho. Boletim para a mocidade a favor das Missões Africanas publicado pelo Sodalício de S. Pedro Cláver,* which was published in several languages. This last publication – *O Pretinho* means 'The Little Black Boy' – adopted a characteristically lamenting tone in relation to the Africans, and especially African children, who were seen as the victims of negligent parents who forbade them to go to school and catechism, beating them and forcing them to observe irrational rites.

Other initiatives were organized with the aim of projecting the grandeur of the 'empire', such as cruise voyages[35] and 'colony weeks'. The SGL organized one such colony week from 30 April to 8 May 1935.

---

30. The expression is by Paul Valéry and was encouraged by Ferro. On the work of Ferro, see Ó (1999).

31. Examples included *Panorama* (a magazine specializing in art and tourism), *Atlântico* (a Luso-Brazilian cultural review), *Portugal* (a monthly newsletter published in five languages), *Informações* (a weekly newsletter) and *Notícias de Portugal* (sent by airmail to Portuguese consulates and communities around the world).

32. *Decreto-Lei* no. 22 469.

33. These publications did not normally include a forum for debate between authors and readers, or between the authors themselves. Ideas were projected as self-evident truths, and little room was available to dispute them.

34. Vol. 2, in 1895, and vol. 16, in 1959.

35. In 1935 the *Cruzeiro da Juventude* made a journey to the colonies, while the *Cruzeiro dos Estudantes dos Liceus Coloniais* made a visit to metropolitan Portugal. In the

As an article in *Vida Colonial* reported, this event did not count on 'the cooperation of the Natives of Overseas Portugal', of whom there were 'many spirits of rare mental acuity' living in metropolitan Portugal, 'nor did the speeches given make clear allusion to the Indigenous populations, the grave problem of their colonization, to clear and focused thinking' that would guide the development of the colonies. According to this same article it was necessary to develop a 'colonial consciousness' and awaken an interest in colonization, which was 'above all a civilizing work, an educational and moral work, a spiritual work' (Anonymous 1935a: 4). The development of this 'consciousness' was supported by the researchers of the ESC and by institutions with links to the colonies, who were frequently called upon to participate in conferences and exhibitions, colony weeks and programmes broadcast by Emissora Nacional, and to contribute texts for school readers. The endeavour to train colonial administrators and educate metropolitan Portugal on the colonies and their inhabitants was therefore a joint effort involving institutions, intellectuals and the state itself. A similar effort was evident in the congresses, which in general sought to showcase technological and material advances, i.e. all the elements which contributed to development and brought Portugal closer to other major imperial powers. Among the most significant of these congresses were the third National Colonial Congress of May 1930, organized by the SGL, and the International Congress of Prehistoric Anthropology, held in Coimbra and Porto. A number of Portuguese specialists participated in this congress, in which human 'types' and exotic customs were discussed. In the same year, the fifteenth International Congress of Anthropology and Prehistoric Archaeology[36] was held in France,[37] with the Portuguese contribution essentially focusing on 'physical anthropology'. Portugal also participated in the International Colonial History Congress, held in parallel with the Colonial Exposition of Paris (1931), at which the importance of colonial studies was proclaimed. Numerous events took place during Armindo Monteiro's tenure as minister for the colonies (1931–35): the first Conference of Colonial Governors (1933), the National Imperial

---

following years the *Cruzeiro dos Velhos Colonos* visited metropolitan Portugal, and in 1941 another cruise was organized to bring young colonials to Portugal.

36. Session IV of the International Anthropology Institute. Portugal: 21–30 September 1930. Portugal session – third section. Among the Portuguese contributions were papers by M. Correia (1931), Correia and Athayde (1930), Lima and Mascarenhas (1930), Correia and Athayde (1931), Pina (1931) and C. Ferreira (1932).

37. France also hosted the Congrès de la société indigène in 1931 and the Congrès des peuples coloniaux in 1937, where issues such as colonial populations and interracial reproduction were on the agenda.

Conference (1933), and several which were held in 1934 – the first Portuguese Colonial Exhibition, the Colonial Agriculture Congress, the first National Colonial Anthropology Congress, the first National Congress on Colonialization, the Congress on Colonial Education in the Metropolis,[38] the first National Unity Congress, the first Congress on Commercial Exchange with the Colonies, and the first Military and Colonial Congress.

Of those mentioned, I will examine in detail the Colonial Anthropology Congress of 22–26 September,[39] held in Porto with the SPAE as its sponsor and organizer, and assisted by the directorate of the Colonial Exhibition, which was held in the same city from 15 June to 30 September. Although a congress on anthropology had been held as part of the International Colonial Exhibition of Paris in 1931, it did not focus exclusively on colonial populations as the Colonial Anthropology Congress in Porto did. As the 1934 Porto congress showed, Portugal was now turning a scientific eye on its colonial populations. A number of papers were presented on the subject of 'colonial anthropology', and it was hoped that the congress would encourage the production of more. Its organizers sought to bring together scholars who addressed 'the varied and complex problems of the colonial populations', since 'knowledge of these populations in their multiple biological, ethnic and social aspects' formed the 'basis of any rational plan for the organization and improvement of the colonies'. The publicity in advance of the congress[40] stated that 'numerous ethnographic artefacts' would be on display at the exhibition, as would 'specimens of various Indigenous races'. With the arrival of these Natives in Porto, the city's Anthropology Institute had real 'human material' at its disposal for several months. The Natives were

---

38. This congress was organized by the ESC and took place on 26–28 September. Participants included teachers working in colonial research and education, including Mendes Correia, Sampaio e Mello and Lisboa de Lima (*Congresso do Ensino Colonial na Metrópole. Organização, Programa e Regulamento das Sessões* 1934).

39. Initially scheduled to be held from 7–11 October, this conference was brought forward because the colonial exhibition with which it was designed to coincide was to close at the end of September.

40. The congress was divided into three sections. Papers presented in section 1 (the largest) were on the subject of 'Physical Anthropology; Ethnic Biology; Cross-breeding; Blood Groups'. A total of twenty-five papers were presented in section 1. The presiding committee was composed of J. Pires de Lima, Germano Correia, João G. Barros e Cunha and Lt. Colonel Leite de Magalhãis. Section 2 covered 'Ethnology; Folklore; Linguistics; Psychology; Sociology; Religions' (vol. 2), with the presiding committee comprising E. Tamagnini, J. Oliveira Lima, Amândio Tavares, and Canon António Miranda Magalhãis. Section 3, 'Prehistory and Archaeology; Human Geography; Migrations; Demographics; Criminology and Acclimation', operated jointly with the second section, except on the last day, when it convened separately with Penha Garcia as chairman.

considered to represent the human population of the places from which they hailed, and their examination served as the basis for generalizations in regard to larger groups.

Some of the papers presented at the congress were compiled on the basis of observations of the Natives – 79 Guineans, 40 Angolans, 139 Mozambicans, 4 Bushmen and an assortment from Timor, Macao and India (Anonymous 1935b). The need to know more about the populations of the colonies led Vítor Fontes, chairman of the Anthropology Committee of the SGL, to underline the need for medical and administrative personnel to follow the instructions of anthropologists in the colonies to collect materials for analysis: 'bones, hairs and casts of the hands, ears and feet' (1934: 189). In a similar strain, Mendes Correia noted that the staff of the Anthropology Institute was dedicating its attention to the anthropological study of the *Indígena,* and had identified their 'descriptive and anthropometric traits, blood groups, basal metabolic rate, and a few physiological and psychological traits'. Mendes Correia reported that contrary to what had occurred in France, where even the 'illustrious French anthropologist Prof. Vallois' lamented the fact that the 'directors of the 1931 Colonial Exhibition of Paris have not permitted the use of the *Indígenas* there assembled', the Portuguese exhibition had assembled 'anthropological documentation superior to that of many important foreign scientific missions' (1934e: 15, 19). Aires Kopke, too, called for more research into the 'different human races' of the 'Metropolis and Colonies' (*Trabalhos do I Congresso* 20–21).

At the inauguration of this congress, Mendes Correia stressed the 'formidable contribution of our discoverers to the progress of Anthropology, revealing to Europe the existence of populations and races which were hitherto unknown and which, in some cases, have now disappeared or have been transformed under the influence of other ethnic or cultural elements'. Correia evoked the 'amazement' and 'enthusiasm' awakened in the readers of 'our rutters', 'chroniclers' and 'old authors' on 'unknown … populations'. And he noted that at a time when scientific anthropology had not even been born, they combined 'somatological descriptions of the most evident characters' with 'precious first-hand accounts of the customs, social organizations etc. of these peoples'. In this connection he cites Pêro Vaz de Caminha, Duarte Pacheco, Duarte Barbosa, Tomé Lopes, Damião de Góis, João de Barros and António Galvão, among others. Giving as an example the *Notícia do Brasil, Descrição verdadeira da costa daquele Estado,* a manuscript dating from 1589 and published in 1825 by the Academia Real das Ciências, Correia describes the manuscript as a 'precious mine of information on the geography, natural history and ethnology of Brazil' (despite its account of 'mermen', one fable among many). Correia went on to discuss the pioneers of the nineteenth century, in whose work the roots of 'colonial anthropology' were to be found, singling out the work of Fonseca Cardoso, 'the anthropologist of the pleiad of *Portugália* in Angola, India and Timor'. The component disciplines of 'colonial anthropology' listed by Professor Correia were 'physical anthropology on skeletons and living subjects', 'ethnography' and 'linguistics'. He also noted that while Portugal had produced research comparable to what was being done in other countries, other work 'lacked real scientific preparation and orientation', and he drew attention to the lack of 'broad and systematic research that only expeditions expressly sent to the colonies with the suitable personnel and the necessary material resources' could conduct (M. Correia, 1934d: 21–26).

At the centre of the preoccupations of those participating in this congress was the issue of 'race'. In a paper entitled 'The Marathas in Portuguese India', Germano da Silva Correia (Nova Goa) presented the results of the analysis of the blood of four hundred Goan Marathas and of the anthropometric and haemoethnological studies carried out at the laboratory of the school of medicine and surgery in Goa. On their 'general morphological appearance', this researcher described his specimens as 'men of *pardo* colour, medium stature, well proportioned, resilient, uncommunicative, agile and with a rather inexpressive gaze' (G. Correia, 1934a: 271). As for their skin colour, 'numbers XIV, XVII, XVIII and XXII on the Von Luschan scale predominated, indicating a bronzed colour in nearly all its tonalities' (G. Correia, 1934a: 272) (Figure 1). The analysis also included indexes based on head and body measurements. Germano Correia confused 'race' with 'caste', which replaced the former as the key indicator of differentiation in India.

Other papers presented at the congress examined

Figure 1. 'Adult Maratha – native of Goa, frontally and in profile' (G. Correia 1934a: 81).

the issues of interracial reproduction[41] or 'race' and cultural aspects, addressing these latter two issues together.[42] A number of contributions addressed cultural aspects or the need for ethnological studies. With a single exception,[43] all of these papers were presented in the second section of the congress. Another paper presented in the second section was Mendes Correia's 'Comparative Psychosocial Value of the Colonial Races', which revealed the findings of a survey[44] sponsored by the Anthropology Institute (director: Mendes Correia), distributed either directly or through the AGC, the SGL and the Portuguese missions, evaluating the same qualities examined by Porteus and Babcock in their formulation of the 'Racial Efficiency Index'.[45] Mendes Correia also cited the work of Roquette Pinto, a Brazilian researcher who had attempted to identify qualities specific to the different 'races' existing in Brazil. But racial bias and the personal coefficient interfered with Correia's survey method, and therefore scientific objectivity was seriously compromised. Yet Correia followed a similar method in his appraisal of the psychosocial qualities of the populations of the colonies, of which Porteus and Babcock and Roquette Pinto made no mention but which Correia considered interesting. The survey was in two parts: one was directed at the 'pure races' and the other at *Mestiços*. However, Correia's paper only mentioned the former group – 'the metropolitan Portuguese or a Black African population of a given region'. Creoles, Mulattoes and *Macaistas* (inhabitants of Macao) were ignored (M. Correia 1934c). The target groups were the 'Blacks' of Guinea, São Tomé e Príncipe, Angola and Kongo, the 'Blacks of Mozambique', Indians, Chinese Macanese and Timorese. The survey analyzed parameters such as impulsiveness, morality (which Mendes Correia acknowledged as difficult to evaluate, based as

41. 'The Problems of Miscegenation', by E. Tamagnini (Coimbra) (inaugural conference minutes, vol. 1); *'Mestiços* in the Portuguese Colonies', by Mendes Correia (Porto); 'The Euro-Africans of Angola', by Germano Correia. The last of these texts examined themes such as 'interhuman panmixia', the crossbreeding of human groups, the implementation of favourable eugenic conditions in the work of colonization and 'civilization', morphology, and anthropometrics. Sources cited included Roquette Pinto, Baptista Lacerda, Paul Broca, and Georges Papillault (G. Correia, 1934b).

42. This was the case of 'The Races and Monuments of Hindustan' (inaugural conference minutes, vol. 1) by Germano Correia.

43. 'Black Art' by Aarão de Lacerda (Porto) (conference minutes, vol. 1).

44. Twenty-seven individuals completed the questionnaire: eleven missionaries, six army officers, five doctors, two civil servants and three respondents from other occupations. No farmers, industrialists or traders completed the questionnaire.

45. The qualities evaluated were: 1. Group planning capacity; 2. Resistance to suggestion – Self-determination; 3. Inhibition to impulse – Prudence; 4. Resolution – Determination; 5. Self-control; 6. Stability of interest; 7. Conciliatory attitude; 8. Dependability.

it was on different foundations which did not bear comparison), openness to persuasion, self-control, resolve/decisiveness, foresight, tenacity, general intelligence and openness to education. As Correia observed, it was not possible to draw any major conclusions from the findings, and significant variations were to be detected in the findings on aptitudes. He did, however, indicate that, although lacking in initiative, the Bantu were suitable for work, a 'quality' which was also found in the Guineans and Timorese.

In 1936, Vieira Machado was appointed as the new minister for the colonies. Congresses and exhibitions held during his period of office (1936–44) were the Conferences on Higher Colonial Culture (1936), the first Economic Conference on the Colonial Empire[46] (June 1936), the second Conference of Colonial Governors, the Historic Exhibition of the Occupation, the first Congress of Portuguese Expansion in the World (all 1937), and the Congresses of the Portuguese World and the Exhibition of the Portuguese World, both in 1940. Among the most interesting of these for our purposes were the Conferences on Higher Colonial Culture,[47] an initiative of Vieira Machado, promoted by the ministry of the colonies and held in March and April 1936 in the offices of the SGL. Participants included major colonial figures and members of the regime's political apparatus: administrators, managers and representatives of Portuguese 'colonial knowledge'. A total of sixteen papers were presented (*BGC* 1936, no. 129: 72), ranging in subject matter from the history of Portugal to the current situation and the destiny of the 'empire'. According to Vieira Machado, Portuguese expansion had been made possible due to an alliance between 'wise men' and 'men of action' (*BGC* 1936, no. 129: 13). Each element connected with and mutually fortified the other.

In some of the papers presented at this conference we can detect a touch of Luso-tropicalist discourse. The agenda, however, was not to acknowledge the equality of two different spheres (colonizers and colonized), but rather to argue that the two could coexist in harmony. Other contributors proclaimed Portuguese colonialism as Christian. Agostinho Campos, a senior professor of history at the Faculty of Letters in Coimbra, informed the conference that settlers were expected to bring faith to the colonies, and that it was its 'tolerance' and 'understanding of other peoples' that allowed Portugal to 'spread Western civilization overseas'.

---

46. See *Primeira Conferência Económica do Império Colonial Português – Parecer, Projectos de Decretos e Votos*, vol. 2, Lisbon, 1934. This conference was the idea of Armindo Monteiro, who appointed the then undersecretary of state for the colonies, Vieira Machado, to coordinate the preparatory work for the first conference.

47. On these conferences, see also Thomaz ([1996] 1998).

Not only this, but the *simpatia* of the Portuguese colonizer attracted and assimilated the *Indígena*. Thus,

> the colonizing race ... 'digests' the colonized, to the point that neither problems of irreducible racial encystment, nor the revolt of the civilized against the civilizer, which are easy to predict or to fear in other forms of Western colonization, are possible (*BGC* 1936: no. 129, pp. 38, 46).

For Campos, the missionary was characterized by his ability to detect in the Natives individuals capable of being elevated to higher stages of development, but only in the sense that they were 'assimilated' and 'digested' by the colonizer. For the minister for the colonies, meanwhile, the elevation of the *Indígena* to the status of 'Portuguese' was a 'miracle', although the teaching of Portuguese in the colonies had contributed towards this miracle by enabling communication among their inhabitants: a situation contrary to the segregation practised by other imperial powers, who kept their native languages to themselves so that Whites and Blacks would remain separated. By being educated, evangelized and 'digested', the Natives could become 'Portuguese'.

1940 was the year of the Congresses of the Portuguese World, organized as part of the 'Centenary Celebrations' held in Coimbra, Porto and Lisbon. The official opening ceremony took place in the National Assembly in Lisbon on 1 July and the celebrations ran until 13 July. Present at the opening ceremony were the cardinal-patriarch of Lisbon, Manuel Cerejeira, government dignitaries including Salazar, and leading academic and cultural figures. The proceedings of the congresses[48] were published in eighteen long volumes. Ten independent congresses were held in all, with a total of 231 Portuguese and 121 foreign participants. In all, 515 papers were presented. The sheer quantity of papers did not always translate into a significant qualitative contribution to their field, however. But there were exceptions, and differences of opinion, too – all the more so in that the congresses brought together figures from various scientific areas, of different political persuasions, and from different countries.

Generally speaking, overseas issues were at the fore, not just in terms of the number of papers on this subject (more than forty, and most of them long) presented at the Colonial Congress of 11–15 November,

---

48. The conferences were: Pre- and Protohistory of Portugal, Medieval History, History of the Discoveries and Colonization, History of the Dual Monarchy and the Restoration, Modern and Contemporary Portuguese History, the Congress of Luso-Brazilian History, History of Science in Portugal, the Colonial Congress and the National Population Science Congress.

but also in papers presented at the other congresses and whose subject matter touched on, or directly addressed, important overseas issues such as the history of Portuguese colonialism or investment in agriculture, the economy, technology, medicine and social welfare in the colonies. Despite the variety of participants, they did appear to be in unison with regard to the existence and the permanence of the colonies, and the need to carry out more research on them. Examples of this can be found in the titles of papers on the colonies and their populations: the need to intensify colonial research (Costa 1940); the colonial populations in the domain of 'physical anthropology' (A. Correia 1940a; A. Ferreira 1940; A. Correia 1940b; Lima and Paulo 1940; Serra 1940); and contact between the 'races' (M. Correia 1940b: 113–33; Santa-Rita 1940b; A. de Azevedo 1940; M. Correia 1940c; Lima 1940). Other papers addressed themes in the domain of ethnology (Pina 1940; Estermann 1940; A. Almeida 1940b; Nogueira 1940) or called for more such research; some were based on secondary sources. Another issue discussed at the Colonial Congress was 'Indigenous labour', with a number of papers presented on this subject (Freire 1940; Cabral 1940; Fontoura 1940). One of the studies carried out on the Natives on show at the exhibition was by Azambuja Martins (1940), with the title 'Research on the Mentality of the Indigenous Mozambican Soldier'. This study examined the 'mental characteristics of the Landin soldier and the tendency for the latter to constitute the typical Mozambican soldier' (Martins, 1940: 443). Many of the tests designed to evaluate the capabilities of this 'typical soldier' were carried out by officers and military. On the Landin company present at the Porto exhibition of 1934 we read:

> Discipline was always easy to maintain, and the docility of temperament of the Landin was evident, as was the joy they showed at the festivities they attended … In six months, only three Landin soldiers were punished with detention or confinement. Curiously … the Indigenous musical group from Angola initially disrupted discipline … with some of the most undisciplined elements being severely punished; their subsequent behaviour was good (*Soldado Africano de Moçambique*, 1936, Lisbon, AGC, p. 117, quoted in Martins, 1940: 456).

This company had visited Vigo on 10 August 1934 to take part in the Luso-Galician festivities. Three years previously, a 'detachment of Landins, formed by ten soldiers and two corporals, under the command of a European sergeant', had been sent to the Colonial Exhibition of Paris as the guard of the Portuguese pavilion, where it made an 'excellent impression' (Martins, 1940: 457). This was an illustration of the important role played by the armed forces in 'civilizing the Natives'.

An examination of the papers reveals which authors were read, quoted or served as inspiration. For example, in 'The Mentality of the African Black and the Past Portuguese Evangelization', a paper presented by J. Alves Correia (1940), one of the authors cited was Lévy-Bruhl.[49] This paper also quotes Raimundo Nina Rodrigues[50] (1862–1906) and Artur Ramos[51] on the subject of the religious syncretism resulting from the combination of Catholicism, Amerindian animist beliefs and fetishism, and quotes Gilberto Freyre on the Franciscan missions in Brazil. This proves, to some extent, that there existed a circulation of ideas between Portugal, the rest of Europe and the Americas. Most of the authors cited were not contemporary, but from the late nineteenth and early twentieth centuries. Brazil features strongly in the proceedings, not only in the Luso-Brazilian History Congress but also in contributions by speakers in other congresses. For Mendes Correia, Brazil was an admirable nation (1940d: 254) which was undergoing a process of 'whitening'[52] – a phenomenon welcomed by some authors, including Mendes Correia himself:

> My illustrious friend Oliveira Viana has observed in Brazilian life of recent decades a curious phenomenon which he designates the Aryanization of Brazil. This takes the form of a constant increase in Europoid elements and the regression of *pardo* and Negroid ethnic factors ... The coloured elements do not seem to me to belong to the socially, politically and economically dominant majority of the population. On the contrary, their presence in the senior posts, the dominant classes, the middle

49. In *Les fonctions mentales,* Lévy-Bruhl attacks attempts to explain the mentality of 'primitives' in terms of processes and habits which belong to the 'civilized' mentality, arguing that some elements are so deeply ingrained in the representation of the 'savage' that they leave no room for the cognitive faculties of the subject group – faculties which are common in representations of the 'civilized' individual.

50. A Brazilian anthropologist, Rodrigues was a disciple of Broca and had his own followers in Oscar Freire, among others. In his lifetime he published one book, *O problema da raça negra na América Portuguesa.* His research, conducted over a fifteen-year period (1890–1905), was published in various volumes. The first volume, *Os africanos no Brasil* (5th ed. 1977; 1st ed. 1933?), was later published separately.

51. A Brazilian anthropologist whose *O Negro Brasileiro* (1934) examined the syncretism resulting from the confluence of Catholic doctrine, Amerindian animist beliefs and Yoruba fetishism. Ramos concurred with Nina Rodrigues that the beliefs of the Amerindian population revealed a pregenital state of development corresponding to the birth-fantasy phase in children (J. Correia 1940: 493–506).

52. Elsewhere, Mendes Correia observes: 'On Avenida Beira Mar in Rio, on a Sunday afternoon or on my way back to my hotel, when I saw ... many couples walking together, I encountered only White men with White women, *Mulatos* with *Mulatas,* Black men with Black women, in an electivity of attraction of individuals of the same race. At the basis of the love which inspired those idyllic states there seems to be an anthropological affinity' (1935: 13).

and upper schools, on the beaches and in the fashionable resorts, is not very high (M. Correia, 1940d: 254).

In addition to Oliveira Viana,[53] Mendes Correia also cites Sílvio Romero,[54] Roquette Pinto,[55] Lôbo de Oliveira, Óscar Brown,[56] Pedro Calmon, Euclides da Cunha and Alfredo Ellis Júnior. A general review of the congresses suggests that where colonial issues were concerned, and despite the fact that some papers were less well researched than others, all contributed to an event whose aim was the better to dominate and guide the Natives. Knowing his muscular strength as measured with a dynamometer made it possible to diagnose which tasks the Native was most suited to. Anthropobiological studies were the most prevalent; sociocultural studies were less well represented. In its attempts to assert itself as a science, anthropology had taken as its earliest subject matter the 'physical' human traits; and various papers made reference to authors like Broca and Topinard. All this classifying and compiling of inventories inevitably reified the Natives, making them passive subjects of measurements and examinations whose objectives were to determine their resilience and capacity for work; studies which addressed the social and cultural realities of the Natives' lives served only, on occasion, to provide the setting for studies in 'physical anthropology'. And it is mainly in the works of missionaries that we find more attention given to sociocultural matters. This tendency would remain the norm until the work of Jorge Dias (1907–73), who focused on the social and cultural aspects of the Native populations in the project 'Studies of Ethnic Minorities in the Portuguese Overseas Territories' (MEMEUP), which he directed in the early 1950s. Although some papers presented at the congress were rather rudimentary, it seems the underlying objective was to give an impression of many papers reporting studies on the colonies and their populations, and preferably that the conclusions of each be echoed in other authors, for if everyone came to the same conclusions it would be easier to impose these views as 'knowledge' – views which, if not always totally scientific, could still be touted as such while they

---

53. A historian and contemporary of Roquette Pinto, Lôbo de Oliveira and Óscar Brown.

54. A historian who saw Brazil as the product of three races: the European White, the African Black and the Aboriginal Indian.

55. A historian who classified humanity into 'leucoderms, faioderms and melanoderms'.

56. An anthropologist and biotypologist and the author of *O normótipo brasileiro*. For Mendes Correia, this book offered a simplified classification of humanity into not one but at least three 'normotypes', 'respectively corresponding to the leucoderms, faioderms and melanoderms of Roquette Pinto's classification' (1940d: 255).

served their real purpose, that of legitimizing colonialization. A battery of empirical data, test, tables, graphs, photos and diagrams was presented in support of this aim.

After 1940, the next congresses to discuss colonial issues were the second National Unity Congress of 1944,[57] the Commercial Congress on the Fifth Centenary of the Discovery of Guinea in 1946, and the International Congress on the History of the Discoveries, held in 1960 as part of the commemorations of the fifth centenary of the death of Henry the Navigator. Looking over the proposals, minutes and papers of all these congresses since 1901, we can see that certain topics were always debated as problems which required a solution. This was the case of Indigenous labour, welfare for Natives and settlers, colonial education, the religious missions and the absorption of Indigenous institutions in the administrative apparatus.

It was one of the desiderata of the Estado Novo that metropolitan and colonial Portugal be a single political, legal, moral and economic continuum. On this view, Portugal was one big nation made up of territories scattered all over the world (E. Vasconcelos 1929: 7). In 1932 the minister for the colonies, Armindo Monteiro, made a visit to Portugal's overseas possessions.[58] In an interview given to the *Diário de Notícias* on the eve of his departure, Monteiro revealed that the administration of the 'empire' was to be raised 'to a perfect unity of interests and sentiments'.[59] Monteiro also claimed that Portugal had a good record of colonization in the past. Brazil was an example to be followed in the modern colonies, especially in Africa. For a later colonial minister, Vieira Machado, what happened in Brazil during the colonial period was nothing short of a 'miracle'.[60] In similar spirit, at a speech delivered at the first Colonial Anthropology Congress, Mendes Correia had described Brazil as the 'most brilliant accomplishment of the colonizing spirit of the Portuguese' (1934d: 24). And Brazil occupied a major place in the Congresses of the Portuguese World and the Exhibition of the Portuguese World, in which it was an official participant, with a pavilion opened by its then

---

57. The section dedicated to colonial policy included a number of appeals for the revision of the Colonial Act.

58. Monteiro had visited Angola and Mozambique earlier, in 1929. In the years following Monteiro's second overseas trip general Carmona, Portuguese President from 1926 to 1961, travelled to Guinea and Angola (1938), and to Mozambique (1939). As minister for the colonies, Marcelo Caetano made a visit to the overseas territories in 1945.

59. I found this interview not in the *Diário de Notícias* but *Indústria Portuguesa*, no. 51, p. 30.

60. The term used by the colonial minister Vieira Machado at the Conferences on Higher Colonial Culture in 1936.

president, Getúlio Vargas. The good example of Brazil therefore offered a justification for continued Portuguese colonialization, even if in other territories.

French colonization was also widely cited as examplary. In an article published in *Vida Colonial,* Viana de Almeida argued that the colonial policy of France was an example to follow, as it made an effort to incorporate 'Indigenous elements' in the life of the nation. The French, he argued, were a great nation which was not afraid of 'treating the Blacks as equals and brothers'. Other authors were critical of French colonial policy, arguing that 'relations between the French Blacks and their European compatriots would introduce corruption into the purity of Gallic blood'. Some dismissed these accusations as the views of countries who were the enemies of France. Opinions were not so divided on the subject of German colonialism. In 1935 the issue of whether Germany should be permitted to have colonies again was raised. In *Vida Colonial* there appeared an article based on a text by François Tessan published in *Tribune des nations* on the colonial claims then being made by Germany. The examples given in this article were intended to show that for Germany, colonies were only of use as 'exploitation camps' while the 'lot of the Indigenous populations' merited 'not the slightest consideration'. In other words, 'the social function of colonization' – the 'unavoidable duty of all colonizing nations' – was 'unknown to the Germans'. It was therefore concluded that utilitarianism was 'the dominant principle in German colonization' and various episodes were evoked in illustration of the way the 'Indigenous populations', considered by many to be condemned to extinction, had been treated by the Germans. The utilitarian conception of colonization which was attributed to the Germans, and the idea of Black inferiority which persisted among the Germans, for whom Black people were valuable only as labour, concurred to produce the conclusion that Germany did not have the capacity to manage 'Indigenous populations', which were considered as 'backward in terms of civilization' (ZZ, 1935: 12, 15) by the author of the article, despite the good intentions he seems to show elsewhere in his text.

Broadly speaking, this book proposes to analyze the colonial messages (including texts, images and their legends) which codified relations of domination and power. Therefore, we will also examine images, and how they showed, exaggerated or obfuscated alterity, and to what extent. These images are found in many spheres of life: education, entertainment, science, politics (i.e. propaganda), trade and tourism. In my analysis of these images, I shall attempt to articulate them with colonial discourse – which is essentially political – and academic discourse on 'race' (i.e. anthropology) and culture (i.e. ethnology or pseudo-ethnology). Little research has been conducted on images representing the 'other' in Portugal.[61] But it was these images, and the discourse which accompanied them, which conveyed ideas and constructed stereotypes on what the autochthonous inhabitants of the colonies were like. Therefore they should not be interpreted only in terms of their documentary value (which they certainly have), content (the people they depict, and their description) or supposed veracity. They also constitute processes of signification which, in the final analysis, enable the invention[62] and propagation of identities (Edwards 1990).

These images are frequently found in photographs, posters, drawings, paintings, books, postcards and films. And their dissemination seems to have helped convince many Portuguese of their civilizing and evangelizing mission. In identical fashion, academics used images to demonstrate the quality of their 'scientific' findings: from the analysis of these images it was concluded that certain individuals had a more robust profile, while others were more delicate, some more crafty, others more given to laziness, and others still bereft of a moral faculty. Photography, for instance, was seen as an instrument which revealed the real and the natural. As the saying goes, "to see is to know": and photography materialized reality. But every image was carefully selected for its ability to illustrate what the scientist proposed to demonstrate. Broca (1879) was the first anthropologist to propose the use of photography, with the bust photographed frontally and in profile, and with the arms outstretched. What we immediately notice in photographs of this kind – a practice later taken up by Portuguese anthropologists – is the absence of expression on the faces of the subjects. And from a sample of one single individual considered as a representative specimen, all the individuals belonging to his or her group were considered to have been studied too, while analysis of the photographic evidence would yield elements supposedly enabling the typification of each individual, with each assigned his place in a previously defined classificatory grid. And there is another factor: capturing the *other* in an image, photograph or indeed classification may tell us more about the capturer than the captured. On many occasions the photographs did not even require titles,[63] for the mere exhibition of the difference was illuminating enough. But photography

61. On representations of the other, see *L'Autre et Nous. Scènes et Types,* a UNESCO-sponsored publication with contributions by biologists, anthropologists, historians, philologists, doctors and political scientists (Blanchard et al. 1995).

62. On this subject, see Edwards (1990), who examines the role of photography in anthropological methods in the late nineteenth century. Edwards discusses two projects from this period, one from England and the other from Germany.

63. Even where they have a caption, the exact provenance of certain images and the subjects they depict cannot always be determined.

is not just a method of recording or fixing an image; it also evokes the past, and imprisons its subject in the past. What's more, it is in the act of revealing the individual that discrimination is consummated. The individual is not there of his own volition, has no control over the montage of the photographic process and, in all likelihood, does not even identify with the end product; he is merely a means to the ends of the person capturing his image. In the next section we shall examine the colonial messages – in both text and image format – conveyed in the school readers and films of the period under review.

Colonial representations in primary and secondary school readers

Portugal's colonial consciousness was also cultivated in its schools, and the analysis of this consciousness can be most revealing. As Marc Ferro wrote:

> The image we have of other peoples, and of ourselves, is bound up with the history we were told when we were small. It marks us for the rest of our lives (Marc Ferro, *Comment on raconte l'histoire aux enfants à travers le monde entier*).

One way of cultivating the colonial consciousness was in activities such as school parties and 'colony weeks'. The SGL promoted a school exchange scheme[64] intended to foster friendships between students of the metropolis and colonies and the children of Portuguese residents in Brazil. On 31 March 1934, the SGL sent a letter[65] to the head teacher of every school in the country, indicating that the correspondents could 'exchange postcards ..., postage stamps, drawings, photographs and generally speaking everything that served to illustrate their country and living conditions'. Another letter,[66] dated 11 December 1935 and sent to the minister for the colonies, stated that the objective of such propaganda was to awaken in metropolitan inhabitants the desire to

> visit the Overseas Lands that they know from the descriptions in the letters and where they know friendly arms are waiting for them. Similar

---

64. This came after a parliamentary vote of 12 March 1932, in which the president of the SGL, Penha Garcia, proposed implementing the plan of Albano Mira, director of the SGL's school exchange service.

65. Available from: AHU. School Exchange Programme. Room 6, order no. 538, bundle 5.

66. Available from: AHU. School Exchange Programme. Room 6, order no. 538, bundle 5.

longings ... will stir the colonials: ... A student at a school in Guinea tells his friend in Alcobaça: '... I liked your picture very much and I'd like to send you mine too, but ... you won't like it because I'm Black, but ... look now ... I, MY FATHER, MY MOTHER AND MY BROTHERS AND SISTERS ARE AS PORTUGUESE AS YOU ARE.'

This is clearly an expression of the sense of inferiority a boy feels because he is 'Black'. But it also echoed the prevailing ideology, according to which Africans were as Portuguese as the inhabitants of the metropolis. And yet although they could call themselves Portuguese, they felt different and feared not being accepted. And in most cases they were not indeed treated as if they were Portuguese. Nevertheless, the exchange programme was praised in various quarters. An article published in the *Nouvelle dépêche* on 24 March 1936 with the title 'Gosses blancs et gosses noirs' lauded the initiative, and even wondered why France did not launch a similar scheme whereby 'Whites and Blacks' could be 'in contact'. Whatever the value of these school-level initiatives, in my view the colonial ideas they transmitted probably had little influence on most Portuguese, and the same can be said of primary and secondary school textbooks. A contributing factor here was that secondary school teachers received no instruction in colonial matters during their training, unless they specifically chose to do so as an option. Among 'some of the topics for the students of secondary and technical schools' addressed in the colony week of 1940, most of which were on historical subjects, was one entitled 'The Indigenous Races of our Colonies: Their Usages and Customs' (SGL archives, Semana das Colónias, 1940; quoted in J. Paulo, 1992: LXXXVII). What exactly was discussed under this title, and how it was discussed, we do not know. Not until the 1950s and '60s did a greater concern with the overseas territories begin to emerge. And even then, history as it was taught revealed little of the colonial territories and their natives. The general idea conveyed was simply that of a single, multiracial state.

Most of our attention here will go to the *livros de leitura* or readers, as these were household objects of mass social diffusion in which we can readily identify the ideas transmitted to children.[67] Although colonial representations were not the primary motive of these readers, it's nev-

----

67. There was no official encouragement for the education of the masses in the 1930s and '40s. The regime promoted an education system which taught the populace to read, but did not encourage it to develop any critical faculties. And in many instances the masses had no great aspirations to receiving schooling anyway. In 1926, only one-third of Portuguese children attended primary school, a situation which remained unchanged until the 1960s (see Mónica 1977, 1979).

ertheless interesting to examine how these representations were transmitted, and with what means. The readers I have selected are from the
third and fourth years of primary school and the first years of secondary
school, and include technical, vocational and commercial instruction.
It is in these years that we find the greatest numbers of students, for in
this period the populace[68] generally attended primary school only, and
in many cases did not even complete it. Another reason for choosing
readers from the third year of primary school upwards is that it was
in the third year that the teaching of history and geography was introduced. My analysis will also include the 'Guide for the Instruction and
Education of the Soldier' (Santos and Guimarães 1939),[69] as well as a
book published by the Portuguese Catholic Mission in Angola and used
in the schooling of Angolan Natives (Molar 1947). In these two books,
something which we immediately notice is the size of the typeface: it
is exceptionally large in the soldier's book, and larger still in the book
for the Angolan Natives. Thus, less information could be carried on the
same number of pages.

The content of the books and readers I examine in this section followed an officially approved programme which included obligatory texts
and authors, regardless of the edition; and it also echoed the ideology of
the regime, its way of revealing the world and Portuguese society. The
normative ideas they contained also served to reproduce social values.
Some of their central themes related to the heroes of Portuguese history. As in the Exhibition of the Portuguese World and Portugal dos
Pequenitos, these heroes were mainly from the Middle Ages and the
Renaissance; no attention was given to the period ranging from the Restoration of 1640 to the Estado Novo. Instead we encounter emblematic figures – the kings and conquerors of old Portugal, the heroes of
the wars of pacification in Africa, the missionary, the soldier and the
teacher. All are extolled for their efforts and the devotion they showed
the *pátria*. Texts on the existence of *other* populations are mainly limited
to accounts of distant places in geography manuals; actual references to
geographic and/or historic questions are generally rare or even nonexistent. Accounts of the history of Portugal in the readers do, however, in-

---

68. The expression *povo* (people, masses) is a 'mythic and ambiguous designation', but
this was the 'intended' meaning, i.e. the 'collective of citizens who may have extensive
experience of life but no formal learning, and need to read simple and direct texts' (Torgal
1996: 503).

69. This book was written by a colonel, João A. Correia dos Santos, and a major,
João Carlos Guimarães. It was originally intended for adults in metropolitan Portugal.
The level of instruction is, however, the level of children's classes, so the texts have been
adapted.

clude episodes describing the encounters of the Portuguese with Nordic
peoples, Romans and Arabs, the intention being to show that large-scale
miscegenation had first occurred on Portuguese soil a long time ago,
and that the Portuguese people were the product of this miscegenation
– which offered justification for the success of Portuguese colonization
and the ability of the Portuguese to adapt to other climes. Generally, the
Portuguese are represented as a people of discovery and colonization who
had preceded all others in this process. Portugal was comprised of many
territories, and had 'over 18 million inhabitants' (Boléo 1938: 115).
Students also learned that the overseas possessions were called 'colonies'
and together constituted the 'colonial empire'. Brazil is described as the
'work of a single White people – the Portuguese'. But this is followed by
the acknowledgement that 'to develop that area of over 8 million square
kilometres, the cooperation of Black labour was necessary', with 'successive levies of slaves' who 'set out from Angola and Guinea' (Maia 1953:
151–52). Students were informed that the Portuguese were the chosen
ones when it came to making contact with other peoples (Quintinha
1938: 254–56).

Among these peoples, those most cited are the Indians 'discovered' by
Vasco da Gama, the sorcerer *(n'ganga),* the king of Kongo, and Gungunhana. Although betrayed by the Indians on various occasions, Vasco da
Gama still manages to stand up to them (Grave 1929: 117); the 'sorcerer
of Africa', known as *n'ganga,* is described by Capelo and Ivens (1930)
with all the exoticism this almost supernatural figure can be invested
with. When his services are invoked, the sorcerer spins around in 'strange
leaps', 'stares with a bestial expression', with 'strange convulsions, nostrils flaring, foaming lips' and 'appears an authentic demon' (103–4). In
another text by Capelo and Ivens, the *n'ganga* can be either a sorcerer or
a diviner: the authors make no distinction – or fail to understand the
difference – between the two. Just as they speak of the sorcerer, so they
speak of the diviner and what he does – 'divine' the ailments affecting
people – but as if the latter were also a sorcerer who employs a 'coarse
therapeutic'. Not only that, but 'diviners are in general ugly men, defec-
tive even, and nearly always individuals [who are] biliously perverse and
enemies of their own kind' (Capelo and Ivens 1938a: 455–56). Then
there was the king of Kongo (this was the 1930s), Pedro Lenga, descendant of the Kongolese dynasty, which had been Christian since the arrival of the Portuguese in São Salvador (now M'Banza Kongo) and their
baptism of the king (Nzinga a Nkuwu, known as João I to the Portuguese) and queen (Nzinga a Nlaza/Leonor). He had ascended the throne
in 1923, taking the title of Pedro VII. He is described as a 'flesh and
bone king, sturdy and with large moustaches, quite Black, as real and as

Christian as were the kings of Abyssinia until a year ago'. He conducted his relations with others 'with the aplomb of an important Black lord'. A map of Angola, from 1846, shows regions with the names of 'noble titles offered to the Indigenous nobles'. These nobles, who despite their status were still treated as *Indígenas,* had a 'gracious monarch, educated at the Catholic mission, and a celebrated hunter of elephants', who was still a 'Black' as well as a king (Quintinha 1937b: 366–68).

Gungunhana and the Nguni make regular appearances in nearly every treatment of the African wars of occupation found in the readers. These wars were presented as a struggle for something which rightfully belonged to Portugal. They took place 'in the inhospitable wastes of Africa' where 'the soldier went to fight the insolent Black who affronted us' (quoted in U. Machado 193?: 215–16). As well as being insolent, the African as presented in descriptions of the wars was a 'rebellious Black', and tenacious too, for every day the Nguni 'received new reinforcements'. In Chaimite, 'holy place of the Blacks, where certain religious ceremonies were held to secure the fetishes' protection of the lives of the fugitives', the 'cunning chieftain' was seized by Mouzinho de Albuquerque 'at the head of 50 or more chosen men', and the 'powerful Nguni chief' was made 'to sit on the ground as a token of obedience' (Lemos 1933: 181–82). In another reader, Gungunhana is described as 'formidable' (quoted in Figueirinhas 1941: 5). Descriptions of this episode are nearly always accompanied by a picture of Gungunhana (A. Júnior 193?: 220–22), and praise for the heroism of the Portuguese, emphasizing the fact that the Portuguese were far outnumbered by their adversary: with just 270 men they vanquished 6,500 'determined' and 'fearless' 'Blacks' who acted like 'ferocious animals' and wrought 'scenes of great carnage' (Noronha 1937: 389). Gungunhana is also described in this text as a man of 'haughty' bearing and 'formidable arrogance'.

There was more to be said on the qualities and defects (usually the latter) assigned to the Natives, who were described as Portuguese but denied the rights that came with such status, depending on the individual, the subject, or the ideas to be conveyed, which were often contradictory. The Natives are depicted as furtive and deceitful (despite all the good will the Portuguese had shown them) in the description of the episode known as 'The Flight of the Ganguelas' (R. de Azevedo 1953: 214–19) during the explorations of Capelo and Ivens. Since they were depicted as servile burden carriers who frequently ran away, they were variously described as wicked, ingrates, rogues, scoundrels, accursed, injudicious, cowardly and disobedient. The African, the 'Black', had the ability 'to disguise himself in the brush like a chameleon'. The drawing reproduced below (Figure 2) neatly conveys the esteem in which Africans were held by the colonizers. It shows the explorers Capelo and Ivens (seated, in the centre) with arms and a dog to protect themselves. On the ground in front of them is a trunk and a pile of books, the symbols of Western civilization and learning. Flanking the explorers, and a little behind them, are two semiclothed Natives with glum expressions. They too are seated, but on the ground, below the explorers.

The notion that Africans were lazy was widespread. Although some texts mention that the *Indígenas* knew how to smelt iron, copper and silver and make various objects – typically personal adornments – from these metals, there is no indication of how widespread this activity was. For the *Indígenas,* silver was 'the precious metal par excellence, perhaps because it is white' and was used for making small objects 'for use by chiefs and *macotas* (dignitaries)'; it was cast and wrought in 'able' fashion by the 'heathen *mussorongo*,' despite their 'rudimentary tools' (Pinto 1938: 450–52). The physical robustness of African people was another salient characteristic. In Guinea, for instance, 'busy trading settlements' had grown up 'on which there descended, on the robust shoulders of the

Figure 2. Capelo and Ivens in Africa (Tavares 1953: 230).

Blacks, the various products of the land' (Magalhãis 1937: 209–10). As for language, the Africans spoke a 'guttural and unintelligible tongue' (Chagas 1938: 358–60).

Some content does present Blacks in a positive light. For example, 'The Little Black Angolan Boy at School' (Frias 1933: 122) is described as the best-behaved, most attentive and respectful boy in his class. This was positive discrimination, underlining the idea that the Blacks must be given opportunities and support if they are to get to the same point as the Whites. It is mainly in texts written by missionaries, however, that we find the notion that 'Natives' are capable of being civilized. A text taken from *Portugal Missionário* notes that among the inhabitants of the island of São Tomé e Príncipe we find 'good and bad: those who want to work, those who are lazy; temperate some, vicious others' (quoted in Fontinha 1938: 250–52). With these 'truths', the idea was to destroy 'the notions of those who presented the Natives of São Tomé e Príncipe as unproductive, useless and even dangerous', for in fact they were 'the colonial people with the lowest illiteracy rates' and São Tomé e Príncipe had 'fewer illiterate people than metropolitan Portugal'; the Santomeans were a 'wholly Portuguese' people and 'those who most felt the Catholic religion', to the point that 'it has not been easy, to date, for the seed of alien religion to develop, grow and germinate'. This text reflects the discourse of the missionaries who argued that Natives were capable of being civilized if evangelized first. Other missionary texts evoked the work of St Francis Xavier in India, Anchieta and Nóbrega in Brazil, and António Barroso and Fr Leconte in Angola, among others.[70]

But it is in the book directed at the Natives of Angola that the missions stand out most, for

> teaching Religion and Civilization to the *Indígenas* … is most useful, for these make civilized and worthy men out of the Blacks … When on the completion of his studies someone leaves the Missions, he should never forget what he owes them, but should always remember the education and instruction he received from them and work to teach his fellows what he learned in the Missions (Molar 1947: 42).

The missions did not only teach their pupils to read and write: they also instructed them in the gospel. For this reason, certain fetishist practices were vigorously opposed. Unlike previous books, this new book for use in Angola had no pictures, but large print and short texts with strong messages that emphasized life in the metropolis, celebrating the (White) Portuguese and their role as moral and cultural authorities. It also told

---

70. See, for example, the text by archbishop Ossirinco (Vidal 1937: 408A–408D).

history in a different way. It was written mostly in the first person singular or plural, not the conventional third person. And so we read that

> men who do not know how to read are like blind men, like animals ... The Portuguese language ... is the most beautiful of all languages. I want to learn very well, so later I can be of use to the *Pátria* and help our missionaries in civilizing my brothers of the Black race (Molar, 1947: 4).

This book provided 'instruction' second and 'education' first, as the missionaries said,[71] and its purposes were moralizing. The precepts which among the Portuguese would be transmitted from one family member to another were to be transmitted to the African via the missions. These precepts included getting to school on time and removing one's hat as a token of respect for the flag. In return, the Natives would find themselves indebted, spiritually at least:

> I love Portugal because the Portuguese ... brought civilization to this land of Angola [and] are civilizing us ... It is my *Pátria,* and every man must love his *Pátria* (Molar 1947: 28).

Another text presents the difference between 'Civilized and Savage'. The qualities for which the 'civilized man' is praised, in opposition to the 'savage' who lacked them, are: cleanliness, neat dress, the ability to read and write, good manners, keeping a clean and tidy house, cultivating large fields, having money to eat and clothe himself and, of course, paying his taxes on time. The 'History of Angola' is presented as 'the continuation of the glorious History of Portugal', with both countries represented by the same flag. Another text, 'The Missions', reveals that these had 'schools for teaching the sciences', 'workshops for teaching the manual crafts', 'pharmacies for treating the body' and 'churches for guiding the soul'; for all these reasons, the Natives should 'esteem and respect the missionaries', who taught them 'Religion and Civilization' (Molar 1947: 42). In 'Respect for Authority', the reader promotes 'unquestioning' obedience to the administrative authorities, for the latter were 'representatives of the Government of Portugal, to which the Blacks [owed] many favours' (Molar 1947: 35). Whatever their status, the Natives were expected to be obedient to the colonizers. The missions educated adults

---

71. Some theorists of the regime distinguished between 'instruction' and 'education'. The former could even act to the detriment of the latter, which was taken to designate the transmission of 'morals' and 'good manners'. So 'good' instruction ended up being limited to 'the most rudimentary intellectual skills, i.e. reading, writing and arithmetic' (Mónica 1977: 343).

as well as children, as attested by a letter sent by a nineteen-year-old student of the Catholic mission of Bailundo to the director of the Benguela school district to apply for the examination in primary education (i.e. three years of schooling) (Molar 1947: 45–46, 75).

The curriculum for the secondary school course in Portuguese as of the 1931–32 academic year, as introduced by new legislation,[72] required that among the subjects given in years one and two of secondary school be 'stories and fables' that would 'contribute to the moral education of the students', 'short descriptions of landscapes of Portugal (mainland, islands and overseas)' and 'short descriptions of the nation's usages, customs, institutions and monuments' (Lima 1932: 351). In fact, the 'usages and customs' section, as well as certain descriptions of overseas landscapes and their populations, could have been included under 'stories and fables', for they seem merely to have been invented with the aim of conjuring up exotic, fantastic and stirring images. It seems the real objective was not to create a moral, political and social consciousness at all, or to make students aware of how much remained to be done, but simply to show that these places and people existed – albeit at a considerable remove (not just spatially but temporally) from the metropolis; these societies were frozen in time in terms of development, and this difference was to be emphasized.

Only in the 'usages and customs' sections is an attempt made to actually show real practices. We learn of strange or bizarre practices relative to the body, clothing, customs and rituals. In a text entitled 'Customs of Mozambique', we read:

> Nearly all the *Indígenas* … 'illustrate' their skin with heathen designs … from head to toe, and even though this gives them, especially in the face, an extra-human appearance which is a little diabolical and absolutely ferocious, they are nevertheless a sign of beauty. There are women in certain regions, in those people known as the Makonde, who pierce their upper lip with rings of wood … until it becomes a horrific thing, making their lips look like a kind of enormous duck's beak (M. C. 1953: 206–8).

Here, the Natives are described as something completely separate and different from anything the metropolis was familiar with. But almost immediately afterwards we learn of contact between the Mozambicans and other cultures, when mention is made of the use of a nose ring by the Native women, a custom 'clearly copied from civilized peoples, Arabs or Indians, who mix for purposes of trade … with the *Indígena*

---

72. *Decreto* no. 20 369 of 8 October 1931.

of the interior' (M. C. 1953: 206). The Mozambicans are seen as an example of a people who, in their primitiveness and ingenuousness, copy what others do, since they are 'savages', have no taste, and are unable to combine things in a pleasing fashion. Arabs and Indians are described as self-seeking and opportunistic in entering into dealings with the Africans to achieve their commercial ends. In addition,

> [a] significant difference in mentality can be observed between the *Indígena* of the coast and his counterpart in the interior, the former being more intelligent, the civilization of the coast having rubbed off on him, ... and ... the latter being obtuse, a mixture of man and animal, living in the jungles like veritable kings of the animals, among the wild beasts ... they have no semblance of intellect, living according to the customs of the quasi-primitive man (M. C. 1953: 206–207).

This description reveals the key to progress by the Natives – contact with the coast, i.e. with the White man, the representative of European civilization, who offers them a way out of the 'primitive' world and makes them more 'intelligent'. Civilization brings the Africans a sense of decorum and makes them see the need to dress when dealing with other cultures. However, the African was still a long way from being able to dress 'properly', and is ridiculed for this:

> Grazed by civilization, out of a notion of modesty that came from the need to establish commerce with or serve the European, he dresses in European style, or ... wears a cloth that covers him from the waist to ... below the knee ... On his head ... a man's hat, or a lady's, as long as the European calls it a hat! (M. C. 1953: 207–8).

In these ethnocentric descriptions based on European ideas of civilization, the African is depicted as still in the 'cradle of humanity' and still, therefore, with a long way to go. But through contact with the colonizers, he might leave his barbarous world behind and reach a higher level of civilization.

Still in the realm of Native customs comes a description of a 'Black Funeral'[73] in which the Africans are portrayed as savages with a streak of madness. Their funeral ceremonies are occasions of 'pleasure' and 'festivity'. On the day of burial, the corpse was 'placed in a box (or sometimes simply tied to a branch)' and carried 'amid an infernal uproar to the graveside, to the sound of numerous gunshots', as 'the wives of the deceased ... loudly bewailed their loss'. As for the men, they were

---

73. On this subject see also Capelo and Ivens 1938b: 456–58.

'mostly drunk' and 'in their wild derangement threw themselves to the ground, rolling over and over, and getting to their feet in extraordinary leaps, making fearful grimaces'. And so 'the cortège came to its destination amid this tumultuous savagery' (Capelo and Ivens 1953: 259–61). Elsewhere, the punishments meted out to 'Blacks' by their own chiefs are criticized, while the intervention of the administration is praised for its ability to free the 'poor' Africans from their barbarous customs: the administrators 'are not normally cruel in their punishments, contrary to what occurs with the *sobas* who employ the death penalty and tremendous corporal punishment'; when the crime 'is of no importance', they use reproof; if the crime is more serious, they administer 'picturesque punishments which make the European observer laugh' (J. Vasconcelos 1937: 375–76). One of these punishments was applied to a woman:

> She was still a girl, and the other girls were insulting her … and the poor girl was reduced to tears. I felt sorry for her, and gave orders for the punishment to cease. Her crime? The theft of a chicken. After pronouncing his orders, the chief retired … to his own [hut], and a profound silence once again fell as the village slept (J. Vasconcelos 1937: 376).

Here too the Natives are seen as indulging in irrational practices, prompting the administrator to intervene. And when this happens, the *soba* loses his power and makes a humiliated retreat to his hut.[74] As for festive rituals, the most frequent was the *batuque,* performed by '*Indígenas* of a warrior race whose songs and dances have something grand and majestic about them'. The *batuques* made a 'deafening noise' and their participants included 'shapely little Black girls … with tattoos' who danced the *chibobo* with 'blandishing jiggles which to the faster and faster sound of the marimbas and drums grew faster and faster too … and dizzier still, to finish … in an epic belly dance, the sublime and ecstatic apotheosis of the curved line'. Their 'bodies of purest ebony' moved 'without putting a foot wrong' as 'all the Black rabble danced'. The Africans were seen as having a special predilection for dances with accelerated rhythms, although they were not acknowledged as having a feeling for music or harmony (Garrett 1937: 238–39).

Descriptions of 'Indian customs' include aspects of home and family life, religious practice and ceremonies. The Indian is seen as superstitious – 'the Oriental sees God in everything, even in the snake, to whom

---

74. But this did not always happen. The administrator might feel there was no reason for interfering when it was a matter of 'usages and customs'. Much as he might consider certain practices to be strange, he was more interested in ensuring that the Natives turned up for the jobs the colonizers or state had given them.

he daily offers a cup of milk and which, not rarely, kills a member of his family' – and given to revelry. Descriptions of Indian festivities, like the wedding feasts of the rich, are freighted with exoticism (T. Ribeiro 1931: 293). There are descriptions of the *ossoró* (the place where the 'Indigenous Christian brides and grooms of Goa' went to receive blessings), *pancatis* (banquets), the *sigamó* ('pagan' carnival) and the *adao* (the rice harvest feast), all of them accompanied by illustrations (Rodrigues 1930: 301–308). While the text indicates the caste to which each named individual belonged (Brahmin, Khatri, Charado/Kshatriya, Vaishya, Maratha, Shudra), it gives no indication as to how this system was organized or why the Indians used it. All the descriptions are anachronic. Finally, despite the fact that the text emphasizes the exoticism of these differences, it is absent of adjectives that might be construed as pejorative or discriminatory, or which suggest a lack of sanity, as occurs in the descriptions of African practices.

One more example from the Portuguese Orient demonstrates how an overseas territory was built in such a way as to respect the differences between two civilizations without the two actually mixing. The place we are speaking of is Macao. This colony receives no more than a cursory description of its natural and urban landscape, but it is interesting to note how the latter gives visible expression to the way the colony was run. The city's 'principal thoroughfare', Avenida de Almeida Ribeiro, running from one end of the peninsula to the other, from the outer limits of the Portuguese quarter to the outer limits of the Chinese quarter, 'shows two different old civilizations, which will never mingle, despite their long cohabitation'; after Largo do Leal Senado the city 'loses its European appearance and becomes Chinese'. In the streets of Macao we find 'boards with advertisements in Chinese and shutters and lanterns and dragons and strange figures of lacquered metal, in an immense and picturesque tumult of forms and colours'. We also see many 'Chinese emporia, Chinese fabrics, apothecaries, shops selling baubles and sequins, herbalists, eateries, gambling houses, always with the same exotic-looking congestion' (F. Castro 1953: 267–71). What we see here is a situation contrary to what was happening in Africa, where the colonizers were attempting to impose a different order: villages were dismantled and others built on adjacent land, in a different configuration; children were taken from their homes to go to catechism and mass; and attempts were made to secure external labour for work on the plantations and the construction of roads and bridges. Although the text on Macao focuses on the urban landscape, it also shows us how the city was organized in human terms. There was no change to the existing order in Macao; the 'habits' and aesthetic preferences of the Chinese were respected. The only small alteration was in the promotion of better standards of hygiene. It seems that colonization in Macao was different from elsewhere, perhaps because the colonizer acknowledged there a level of civilization which, although viewed as inferior to Europe, was superior to Africa.

Essentially, the overseas scenario depicted in these readers shows that the 'empire' is known to some extent, although all kinds of ideas exist with respect to it. The Portuguese are presented as those 'who will go on giving new worlds to the world', and for this reason the pride of 'being Portuguese' is exalted. Black people are never credited with having contributed anything to Portuguese civilization, although they are known to have been present in Portugal since the sixteenth century (Tinhorão 1988). The only acknowledged influence is that of the Arabs (Teixeira 1931: 126). Despite having been defeated, the Arabs are recognized as a culture that had left its mark on Portugal. This idea appears, for example, in a 'vocational training' reader in which the Arabic influence is acknowledged, especially on the level of words and social institutions which the Christians had borrowed from the Arabs: 'Even today the common people say that any old ruin is "from the time of the Moors", such is the impression [the latter] made on them' (Lopes 1935: 89–90).

Cinema and colonialism in action: moving pictures on colonial themes (1928–53)

To gain an idea of the image of the colonies and their inhabitants as projected in moving pictures, I viewed a number of films conserved in Lisbon's Arquivo Nacional das Imagens em Movimento (ANIM) archive. I chose to examine these films because the early decades of the Estado Novo were an extremely fertile period for the production of audiovisual material – material which involved the spectator in heuristic and meaning-construction processes which were very different from verbal text, but whose analysis yields as much if not more insight, for they were rich in information and most have not yet been properly analyzed. Film is an outstanding medium for constructing perceptions of reality. Not only does it allow us to record what we see, it also allows us to record what we want to show. In other words, it is in the fragmentation of the real, and the selection of one reality over others, that the power of moving pictures lies. Fernando Leiro wrote that there were films showing in Lisbon with 'Blacks, savanna, wild beasts and *batuques*!' but lamented that cinema was overlooking the main thing, which was the 'gigantic work of civilization' (1935: 1, 7). Some of the films I viewed did, however, highlight this aspect.

Films bring together moving pictures, text and sound; and they are as important for what they hide as for what they show – perhaps more so. After the introduction of censorship in 1929,[75] all films made after 1932 were subject to the approval of the state censorship office, the Inspecção-Geral de Espectáculos. When screened, they opened with a monogram attesting to their clearance for viewing. In the interests of the good image of the 'empire' and colonial policy, any film which portrayed maltreatment of Africans, the struggle between the 'White man' (the colonizer) and the 'Black man' (the colonized), racial segregation in the United States, the human rights struggles of the US Blacks, or which advanced a pacifist or antimilitarist agenda, was banned – or at least the offending scenes were excised (Geada 1977). One more consideration: cinema had to be economically viable.

For all of these reasons, whenever we analyze a film we have to maintain a critical scepticism in relation to the images we are seeing. Further contributing factors to the constructed nature of moving pictures include the position of the director, the effect of those filming on those being filmed, editing techniques, means of production, sponsors, market, and considerations with regard to reception and censorship. Like photographs, films brought the visual 'reality' of the colonies back home to the metropolis. But this 'reality' is fabricated right from the moment the cameraman starts filming, the shot is composed, the soundtrack plays (on many occasions this was the Portuguese national anthem), the chromatic spectrum is reduced or an intertitle is inserted. As Marcus Banks and Howard Morphy note, a distinction can be drawn between the study of visual cultural forms and the use of the visual media for describing and analyzing culture (1997: 1). This is the difference, as Sol Worth puts it, between using a medium and studying the way the medium is used (1981: 190). Therefore, to study and analyze films is also a way of analyzing the history of a society and of humanity as a whole. Marc Ferro, the historian who has dedicated most attention to the study of the connections between history and cinema,[76] views the latter as an 'agent of history', an analysis he bases on the Soviet cinema and the US anti-Nazi films of 1939–43. In Ferro's view, cinema often offers 'a counter-critique of society' (1987). As an 'agent of history', it seeks to influence the spectator, and when the film in question is a vehicle for ideology or propaganda it seeks to send the spectator a message; and in

75. Film censorship already existed in Portugal before the Estado Novo: according to Lauro António, the earliest mention of censorship dates from 1919 and alludes to a law of 1917 on the exhibition of moving pictures (1978: 25).

76. Ferro's contributions to this subject include two collections of essays, *Analyse de film, analyse de sociétés* (1976) and *Cinéma et Histoire* ([1933] 1977).

so doing it can change the course of history. Under the Estado Novo, there seems to have been a direct link between cinematic output on the one hand, and the history of Portugal and social aspects relative to colonial representations on the other. Like everything made in this period, these films carry a very strong ideological charge. Expressions such as 'in great apotheosis' and 'triumphant' abound. My analysis will focus not on the technical and aesthetic aspects of these films but on their general message, their content in terms of the way they represent the colonies, the roles assigned to Natives in colonial society and the way certain images discriminated or marginalized them.[77]

For the present purposes, three dates stand out in the history of Portuguese cinema. The first is 1926, when the avant-garde first made its appearance in Portuguese cinema, combining foreign with local influences. The second is 1931, the year the 'talkie' made its appearance in Portugal,[78] although not yet as a generalized phenomenon. The third is 1948, when new legislation[79] was passed on the protection of Portuguese cinema. This legislation addressed three areas of cinematic output: 'populist comedy', films 'in praise of the nation' (on the glories of past or present) and 'cinematographic adaptations of literary works' (Costa 1982: 183). Producing films[80] in a country of limited resources was a major undertaking. But investment was made in this new 'instrument for the diffusion of ideas', whose reach, as António Lopes Ribeiro noted, could exceed that of the newspapers and radio (1933). Not only was it useful for recording important events and facts, cinema could also be used for propaganda purposes. Writing in *A Província de Angola* (15 August 1934), Viana Costa sang the praises of cinema as an 'agent of propaganda and diffusion' and drew attention to its 'function as an agent of colonial propaganda'. But for Costa, the 'colonial films' left much to be desired, as they explored what was least important to 'the presentation of our endeavours as colonizers, like antelope hunts in the desert of Mossâmedes, Huíla, etc.'; to date (1934), no film had focused on

---

77. The films discussed in this section range in duration from short to feature length. Generally speaking, a film of 50 minutes or more is considered to be feature length, and a film of 10–20 minutes a short film. Other films of intermediate length existed.

78. The first Portuguese talkie was Leitão de Barros's *A Severa*. The soundtrack was added in Paris.

79. Law no. 2027.

80. Among the leading early Portuguese production companies were Invicta Film, which used French technology, and Tobis Portuguesa, launched in 1933 by Germans using the Tobis Klang Film system. Tobis was the first production company in Portugal to have a studio equipped for sound film. The SPN, the Sociedade Portuguesa de Actualidades Cinematográficas (SPAC) and the AGC, via the 'Cinegraphic Missions', were also active in film production.

'colonizing action'. Aspects relating to the subject populations were not what Costa had in mind, however, for he does not even mention them. For Costa, 'the primary function of cinema as an agent of colonial propaganda must be conceived from a purely economic point of view.' The important thing was to show people – Portuguese and foreigners alike – the possibilities presented by the Portuguese overseas territories, making cinema an 'accessible compendium', 'an educational medium', for the 'Portuguese populace' had only 'a few vague notions' of what Africa was. In a country which proclaimed that the future was in the colonies, the idea which most of its people had of Africa was, for Costa, 'quite ridiculous' and 'somewhat compromising'.

Conceiving cinema primarily as a medium of propaganda (Ferro 1931, 1950), the Estado Novo, in the person of individuals like António Ferro, decided to endow film production structures, and in 1935 the SPN launched its 'travelling cinema' initiative. From this moment on, Portuguese cinema was in the hands of the SPN[81] under the direction of António Ferro. When the SPN was re-named SNI (Secretariado Nacional de Informação) in 1944, it continued to sponsor cinematic output and also introduced official prizes for cinema. Ferro was assisted in his work by Lopes Ribeiro (1908–1995),[82] a 'modernist' supporter of Salazarism, and Leitão de Barros (1896–1967), the regime's official set designer at various events. For Ferro, documentaries were a 'salutary tendency in Portuguese cinema which had not yet been sufficiently developed' (1950: 65). Like the official exhibitions, films were advertised as cheap and easy ways to 'travel' (*O Planalto*[83] 1931: no. 43: 12). An

---

81. Among the documentaries produced by the SPN were two films of the presidential journeys to Africa, one of the Exhibition of the Portuguese World, and one of the journey of Cardinal Cerejeira to Africa. After its launch in 1935, '2,235 screenings attended by 2,304,570 persons' were organized from 1937 to 1947 as part of the travelling cinema initiative. Many screenings were opened by guest speakers, including '1,585 speakers from the localities which enthusiastically took up the initiative'. 'For six months in 1946, the SNI's Travelling Cinema toured the Azores archipelago, holding 116 screenings attended by 230,700 spectators, with 70 guest speakers.' The SNI issued programmes to 'all provincial bodies', such as 'syndicates, hospitals, barracks, schools, factories, parish councils' (*Catorze Anos de Política* 1948).

82. Lopes Ribeiro directed dramas on political (*A Revolução de Maio,* 1937) and colonial (*Feitiço do Império,* 1940) themes, and also made documentaries on regime initiatives with major media impact – exhibitions, state visits to the colonies and other events. *Portugal na Exposição de Paris* (1937) and *O Cortejo Histórico de Lisboa* (1947), produced by the CML and organized as part of the commemorations of the '8th Centenary of the Conquest of Lisbon', portray moments captured by a director who was au fait with the world of cinema outside Portugal and knew Soviet directors who, like him, worked in propaganda, including Eisenstein and Dziga Vertov.

83. *O Planalto* was first published on 17 May 1930 in Nova Lisboa (now Huambo), Angola.

example was *Angola,* screened by the Portuguese government at the exhibition of Seville and later shown in Nova Lisboa by the distributor Peairo. Documentary film played a significant role in the cultural and scientific agendas of many institutions. According to the AGC report of 1933–34 (Lencastre 1934: 21–22), colonial propaganda films were shown in many Portuguese cities. Films were lent to secondary schools, colleges and private guilds, and to the SGL for its 'colony week'. They were also sent to Rio de Janeiro for screening during the 'Portuguese Fortnight' organized by the newspaper *O Século.*

Like other colonial powers, since the early twentieth century Portugal had been making short films showing Natives in traditional dress performing ritual ceremonies. Their principal idea in my view was to show what colonial subjects looked like, and how they could be 'useful' to the Portuguese; the settlers were shown to respect the 'usages and customs' of the Natives, no matter how strange and eccentric they considered them to be. Ernesto Albuquerque made several such films, including *A Cultura do Cacau* (1909), which was shot in São Tomé e Príncipe, while M. Antunes Amor did the same in the 'Far East' (Matos-Cruz and Antunes 1997: 59). In 1929 Augusto Seara, working for the army cinematography department, made the documentary *Por Terras de Ébano* on the 'ethnography' and 'scenery' of Guinea and São Tomé e Príncipe. In 1930 Antunes da Mata and his cameraman José César de Sá made several films as part of the *Missão Cinematográfica a Angola* (F. Ribeiro 1973: 21). As far as I have been able to ascertain, no documentaries were made on Timor. Several documentaries on India and Macao were made prior to 1934, such as *Monumentos Históricos da Índia* and *Macau Pitoresco* (Lencastre 1934). Later in the same decade, the colonial minister Vieira Machado created the Missão Cinegráfica às Colónias de África (MCCA)[84] in an attempt to stimulate the production of propaganda and documentary films on colonization. This initiative had the support of the AGC, directed at the time by Júlio Cayolla.

With the MCCA came the first detailed and comprehensive tour of the colonies by a Portuguese film crew.[85] Between February and October 1938 its itinerary took in Madeira, Cape Verde, Guinea, São Tomé e Príncipe, Angola and Mozambique. The documentaries filmed during this tour were still being released in 1946. The aim of the mission was to make one feature-length documentary and several smaller documentaries on each of the African colonies; in these the objective was to portray

---

84. *Decreto* no. 27 859, published in the *Diário do Governo* of April 1937.

85. This film crew was headed by Carlos Selvagem – pseudonym of Carlos Afonso dos Santos – and included artistic director Lopes Ribeiro, technical director Brito Aranha and director of photography Isy Goldberger. The narrators were Lopes Ribeiro, Pedro Moutinho, Elmano Cunha e Costa and Manuel Ribeiro.

not only the landscape, the wildlife and the *batuques,* but also what was considered to be the 'civilized' side of Africa, with its large, rapidly growing cities.[86]

Two films are essential viewing for a comprehension of the political orientation of the regime: *Revolução de Maio* (1937) and *14 Anos de Política do Espírito. Apontamentos para Uma Exposição* (1948), both directed by Lopes Ribeiro and both strongly nationalist in their import. The first of these films does not even make any reference to the colonies, except for one scene in which two actors discuss a newspaper report that Salazar was going to sell a colony to Mussolini to build a bridge over the Tagus. *Revolução de Maio* showed that the regime intended to create a new order and put everything and everyone in a preordained place. It is an overtly propagandistic film which alternates between documentary and fiction. At a period when war was looming and foreign ideologies were in the air, the important thing was to preserve the national identity, or what was considered as such. The films of this period therefore sought to show what made this 'identity' unique. And they often went further, ranging over a historical heritage which was presented as a source of pride, and extending this pride to the present day and the colonial possessions. The existence and survival of the 'empire' were important, for they were the raison d'être of the Portuguese nation; and in articulating the relationship of hierarchy between metropolis and colonies they reinforced the power of the former.

Journeys to the African colonies and incentives for 'White' settlement

Some of the documentaries made during the colonial journeys merit special examination. One film, *I Cruzeiro de Férias às Colónias do Ocidente* (1936), directed by Nuno San-Payo, was made on the initiative of the magazine *O Mundo Português.* Its subject was the holiday cruise to Cape Verde, Guinea, São Tomé e Príncipe and Angola organized by the AGC. In this film we see the Natives livening up the society events of the colonists with their *batuques* and 'traditional' dances. *Viagem de Sua Eminência o Cardeal Patriarca de Lisboa,* by Lopes Ribeiro, was made in the mid-1940s. It documented the voyage of Cardinal Gonçalves Cerejeira on board the *Serpa Pinto* for the consecration of the new cathedral of Lourenço Marques (as Maputo, the Mozambican capital, was

---

86. The first of these films, produced in Portugal, was *Exposição Histórica da Ocupação,* by Lopes Ribeiro. Others included: *Viagem de Sua Excelência o Presidente da República a Angola* (1939), *Guiné, Berço do Império* (1940), *Aspectos de Moçambique* (made in 1941, but probably not premiered until seven years later), *São Tomé e Príncipe* (1941), *Angola, Uma Nova Lusitânia* (1944), *Gentes Que Nós Civilizámos* (1944), *As Ilhas Crioulas de Cabo Verde* (1945) and *Guiné Portuguesa* (1946).

then known). The cardinal's voyage took him to Funchal (Madeira), São Tomé e Príncipe, and Luanda and Lobito (Angola). He also visited several places in Mozambique. *Viagem do Chefe de Estado às Colónias de Angola e São Tomé e Príncipe* (1939), also by Lopes Ribeiro, was an account of president Óscar Carmona's visit to Angola, São Tomé e Príncipe and Madeira. This film opened on 22 May 1939 in Lisbon's Tivoli Theatre and documented the entire journey right from the day of departure on 11 July 1938. Carmona visited a number of plantations (Esperança, Sundy, Rio de Ouro, Monte Café and Água Izé, among others) and seemed happy and at ease at all times; he did not have the austere and remote bearing of Salazar and was happy to let the Natives touch him as they effusively welcomed him. An attentive viewing of this film gives the impression that every aspect of the reception given to Carmona had been prepared in advance by the settlers – the ceremonies, salutations and manifestations of 'affection and respect', in the words of the narrator. We see identically dressed children accompanied by their teacher, and the fishermen of São Tomé e Príncipe come to greet Carmona. In the cities, the streets are festooned with bunting as settlers and Natives – dressed in uniform or in suits with cravat or bow tie – wait for the president to pass. As he does so, they take off their hats to greet him. These assimilated Natives supposedly demonstrated the success of Portuguese colonialism. Indigenous chiefs and Natives of higher social standing did too, like the Kongolese king Pedro V, 'representing those who 400 years ago for ever accepted to loyally serve the sovereignty of Portugal' (in the words of the narrator). The enthusiasm with which Carmona is welcomed is given visual expression in the banners which decorate the streets; clearly the message is that the Natives wanted the colonies to be maintained. In Cabinda we see banners with slogans reading 'We won't sell, we won't give up, we won't lease and we won't share our colonies'. In Roça do Couto (Angola) one banner has a rhyming slogan which reads: 'To all of you we salute you / We are all your people / Our hearts go with you / Long live the president.' The narrator describes such rhymes as 'quatrains of ingenuous sincerity', strengthening in this way a view of the Africans as childish and ingenuous – although it was almost certainly the colonizers who had composed or commissioned the rhymes. The same motive seems to be behind the claim that 'protection of the *Indígenas*' was 'carried to the utmost extremes'. And yet the Natives do not seem overly excited by the proceedings, as they are stiff-postured and their expressions are rather distrustful. One episode, 'A sessão solene na Câmara Municipal', documents a speech given in the municipal chambers of Luanda, in a room occupied only by settlers. This speech was directed not at the Natives, who only appear in street festivities and in this instance had remained outside, but rather at the settlers, and stressed that much remained to be done locally. The religious element is much in evidence too. We see the construction of chapels and churches, and the Natives going to mass. We see the 'Chapel of Our Lady of Nazaré' and the 'Open-air Mass in the Fort of S. Miguel' (Angola) attended by Natives who for the most part are clothed and shod in European style; they are separated from the White worshippers, however, by a rope marking the line they should not overstep. Significantly, this barrier exists in, of all places, one where surely no distinction should exist. After seeing Natives greeting Carmona in the streets, Natives in the army and musical bands, Natives who work on the plantations, we now see Natives serving meals in 'Grande Hotel Terminus' and 'Lunch in Cassequel' (Angola), with Carmona enjoying a meal while (in the words of the narrator) 'the obliging *Indígenas* intoned a heathen chant'. Some Natives in white suits and shoes are seen waiting tables, while others hold straw parasols to shield the seated guests from the sun. Elsewhere in the film the Natives are described in terms of 'their extremely simple apparel and their distinctive coiffures'. But despite their 'simplicity', the Natives seem to acknowledge the 'benefits of our civilizing action', for the narrator tells us they have come thousands of kilometres on horseback or on foot, from the 'confines of the Cuamato and the Cuanhame', to take part in the 'procession of *Indígenas* of the province of Huíla'. The populations in question had only recently been incorporated into colonial rule, but the Portuguese missionaries saw in them 'exceptional conditions for assimilation', in the words of the narrator.

All this offered a justification for colonization, and a good reason for Carmona's visit to be repeated the following year. His return was documented in Brito Aranha's *A Segunda Viagem Triunfal* (1939), distributed by the SPN. This time Carmona was accompanied by his colonial minister, and his journey took in the Portuguese East African territories, Cape Verde, São Tomé e Príncipe, Angola (Luanda) and the Union of South Africa. The highlight of this documentary is the 'allegorical procession' held in Lourenço Marques in honour of Carmona. At the head of the procession we see a group of costumed Natives playing drums. They are followed by a series of allegorical floats: one with the legendary figure of Adamastor, another with Bartolomeu Dias, another still with the ships of Vasco da Gama; one float depicts 'the conquests', another the religious missions (this float is named 'The Shadow of the Cross' and is flanked by female missionaries); then comes 'Occupation', with an effigy of Mouzinho de Albuquerque, and floats dedicated to Indigenous art from the provinces of Sul do Sade, Zambezia and Nyassa, which was famous for its sculpted heads. Other floats illustrate the goods produced locally, and the income they generated. One float is dedicated to education (complete with books, many on music), with representations from the Liceu Salazar, Escola Técnica Sá da Bandeira and other colleges. After this comes a parade representing the evolution of transport 'from the old *machimba* [litter] to the modern aeroplane'. The *machimba* is carried by two Natives, and in it sits a settler on a chair, under a canopy that provides shade; this is followed by a rickshaw, with a Native pulling a White woman; a cart, again drawn by a Native; another cart, this one drawn by two oxen driven by a Native; a Boer wagon drawn by numerous oxen – all methods of transport made obsolete by the advent of the automobile. Next come a bus, with a White driver, White passengers and White pedestrians walking alongside; an almost-life-size railway locomotive, again with White passengers and flanked by Whites; a 'Michelin-type' railway carriage, with White passengers; and finally the reproduction of an aircraft identical to those used in the colony. This all associates the most recent and advanced forms of transport with the Whites.

In the Mozambican city of Beira, we see an exhibition inaugurated by the Companhia de Moçambique which reconstituted an 'Indigenous village', with barefoot, simply attired Natives busy working at spinning and weaving. The mise-en-scène indicates that unlike the Natives we see in the colonies, those who came to the exhibitions in metropolitan Portugal were specially selected, as was their clothing. Several Catholic masses are shown in this documentary: in São Tomé e Príncipe, on the seashore; in Marracuene (Mozambique), where an outdoor mass evokes the heroes of the Mozambican campaigns in the presence of Native soldiers; and in Cape Town. In Lourenço Marques, 'in the school parade that brought together thousands of White children from the schools and thousands of Black children from the missions', we see the wives of Carmona and his minister distributing packed lunches – with the exception of one or two Blacks, the recipients were White children.

Carmona also visited South Africa on this second colonial tour. From what the documentary shows us of this country, it is a world away from the Portuguese colonies of the same period in its greater wealth and development. Owing to segregation, no Natives are seen in the streets where the settlers stroll, but only on the farms or in the interior. When the Natives did walk these streets, it was at times or in places where they were unlikely to encounter settlers.

Two films, Ismael Costa's *No País das Laurentinas – Colonos* (1934) and Lopes Ribeiro's *Feitiço do Império* (1940), are interesting for their treatment of the 'White settlement' drive[87] in Africa. The first of these films, dedicated equally to old and new settlers, shows specimens of the former whose distinctive traits are their 'rude health', 'joy' and 'lucidity', their success in life and work; the setting is Mozambique, with most scenes shot in the Associação dos Velhos Colonos complex. At one point the film shows the 'Laurentinas' – European girls in identical dress, the 'Marias of Portugal', 'our faithful and … comely allies', represented by young women dressed in traditional Portuguese costumes. Next stop, as the intertitle informs us, is the 'Taj Mahal, the Raja and his court'. We now see some young people with vaguely Asian facial features and apparel, and finally 'a group of little dark girls' with Asian features, and the 'porcelains of China', as some Chinese girls are called. The constantly prowling camera seems intent on showing all the diversity of the 'types' of female beauty to be found in the 'empire', and yet there are no African women among them. The ideal of beauty is exemplified only by European and Asian women, such as *senhorinha* Suzete Neves Dias, a *Maria de Portugal* raised in the Mozambique sun' and *senhorinha* Sara Matos Ribeiro, a Venetian born and brought up in Lourenço Marques'. In a film purportedly about the colonies, there are very few references to colonial subjects: the emphasis is very much on the colonizer and on feminine beauty, a beauty which is exoticized and celebrated for its diversity, whether the women in question are European or Asian.

Feitiço do Império[88] is a fictional work which taps into the fascination for Africa and the 'empire', represented by the exoticism of the African depicted on the poster of the film (Figure 3). It was premiered on 23 May 1940 in Lisbon's Eden Theatre, in the presence of the heads of state and government, and ran for seven weeks. The screenplay was

---

87. The colonies are also mentioned in films not ostensibly on 'imperial' themes. One example is *Cantiga da Rua* (1949), directed by Henrique Campos. In this film we witness a conversation which effectively conveys the different ideas the Portuguese had of the colonies: some thought it was hard, 'back-breaking' work in the colonies, while for others the 'Whites' in Africa did nothing – and neither did they have to, for the 'Blacks' worked for them. In Africa, the one who was 'good for work' was the 'Black man': 'The overseer shouts and the Black gets down to some good hard graft' while the plantation owner watches the others working.

88. *Feitiço do Império* is one of eight feature-length dramas directed by Lopes Ribeiro between 1934 and 1959. For many years its whereabouts were unknown. Recently, a nitrate negative of the film was discovered, but this had no soundtrack and was, moreover, incomplete. The first of its fifteen reels was missing, comprising some 15 minutes (400 metres) of film. For this reason Matos-Cruz decided to publish the shooting script and the dialogues as they appear in the original manuscript. All the quoted excerpts of dialogue are from the film as viewed. There are occasional discrepancies between the shooting script and the film dialogue, probably due to last-minute changes on the film set.

by Lopes Ribeiro, based on the book of the same title which won the competition organized by the AGC (J. Júnior 1940). Its objective was to show the 'Portuguese Colonial Empire' in all its allure and fascination, and thereby to encourage the Portuguese to emigrate to Africa instead of America (and this meant the United States as well as Brazil). It also evidenced the unity of the 'Portuguese world' at a time when the country's overseas possessions were under threat from other colonial powers. *Feitiço do Império* is set in the United States, Lisbon and Africa (Guinea, Angola and Mozambique), with brief interludes in Madeira, Cape Verde

Figure 3. One of the posters for the film *Feitiço do Império* (Cinemateca Portuguesa).

and São Tomé e Príncipe. It is a mixture of fiction and documentary, as some of its footage has its origins in the work of the MCCA. We see African landscapes, big game animals and exoticized populations. The plot revolves around a character named Francisco Morais, a Portuguese immigrant in the United States who has not forgotten his love for his native country. The same cannot be said of his son, Luís Morais, who wants to become a naturalized American. But before Luís takes this step, and although he's engaged to be married to a rich Philadelphia heiress named Fay Gordon, his father convinces him to go on a hunting expedition in Angola.

His voyage takes Luís to Lisbon, Guinea, São Tomé e Príncipe and Mozambique, where his 'Portugueseness' and 'enchantment with the empire' end up making him change his plans. Contributing factors in this turnaround include Mariazinha, the daughter of the settler and bush trader Vitorino da Umbala. Mariazinha looks after Luís after he has been mauled by a lion and saved by a Native. Luís decides against taking out US citizenship, and travels to Portugal with Mariazinha to celebrate their engagement. For Luís, Portuguese colonization is good, while American colonization is bad – he observes that the Americans 'lacked in scruples what they exceeded in resources'.

Feitiço do Império depicts the Natives of the colonized areas represented in a number of guises: as employees of the settlers, running errands, carrying trunks, working in homesteads, plantations and factories, but also as participants in rituals and dances, practising military manoeuvres or taking part in wars between rival Native groups. These practices combine to paint a picture of the Natives in 'nature', in their own world, which is different from the world of the colonizer and impenetrable to the eyes of a Western observer. And yet the Natives were capable of incorporating elements of Western civilization[89] and, in this sense, of being considered good examples of the success of the colonizing mission. In illustration of the assimilation of Western culture we see Native children – some wearing bibs, others seminaked – listening to the stories Mariazinha tells them and learning their first letters in the *Cartilha Maternal*. The screenplay describes them as 'little Blacks' and 'poor children'. Their education extends to catechism, also administered by Mariazinha. Another reference to assimilation is in Catholic ritual. In Bubaque (Guinea) we witness a scene in which, to the sound of church bells, the Native girls (in tunic and veil) and boys (in suits with short or long trousers, but all barefoot) make an orderly file in the direction of mass.

---

89. These civilizing ideals cannot always be reduced to their Christian component, although they increasingly came to be synonymous with Christianity during the Estado Novo: they also had their roots in the secular evolutionism of the nineteenth century.

Luís's uncle lives in Angola and has two employees – a man and a woman who are always seen in Alentejan costume, for their employer had no love for the colonies. The male employee is named Brás. He runs errands and exemplifies the Native employee whose loyalty to his colonist employer is such that he will give his life for him. Brás is protective of Luís, and his friend Vitorino refers to him as a 'dedicated Black'. To show the Natives, the camera captures them frontally and in profile in a market in Bafatá (Guinea), for example. In general, the Natives are secondary characters who make no contribution to the plot. They are referred to as 'Blacks', 'servants' or even 'Black servants' and, with the exception of Brás, are entirely two-dimensional characters: we never learn where they are from or who their families are. But amid this undifferentiated mass of 'Blacks', one distinction is made: between the *pretos calcinhas* – Blacks who wear European clothes – and the *pretos do mato* – Blacks who live in the bush.

In the scene where Fay (whom Luís has now joined in Mozambique) and the local administrator witness a *batuque* in Marracuene, beside the monument to the dead of the 1895 'war of pacification' which culminated in the Portuguese defeat of the Nguni emperor Gungunhana, Luís recalls the intentions of the Natives before pacification, while Fay exclaims that she can't understand how 'those people' were allowed to remain in such a 'state of savagery'. The dialogue continues:

> Administrator: It's always been standard procedure … to respect the customs of others so they respect ours. We have a proverb that goes: 'To every spindle its yarn, to every land its use'.

> Luís: It's truly admirable, … the cooperation between two races so different I've been seeing in our colonies. And it's in these barbarous festivities that we can best appreciate the distance that separates one from the other, and therefore the difficulty and the scope of this cooperation.

> Fay: I really think I prefer the Blacks of Harlem.

This scene exemplifies, in a certain form, the type of colonial action which the regime wanted to display. It reveals the occupation of Africa as a success, with pacified Natives and settlers who have nothing to fear from being there. But in Fay's view, the Natives still exist in a state of savagery and the Portuguese should not be allowing this to happen. She considers Portuguese colonization to have been a failure, unlike American colonization, which sought to 'Americanize' African Americans. This is the cue for the administrator, an important figure[90] in

---

90. As a former administrator told me in an interview: 'Below the equator, the boss was the administrator!'

the colonial territories, to step in with his 'respect the customs of others' line: not interfering in certain Native practices is the best way for the Portuguese to gain respect from the Natives. *Feitiço do Império* also has a strong documentary component, with Native dances, warrior folklore, Black people at work, and 'heathen rituals'. It made a major impact on the viewing public, but for those whose knowledge of Africa extended beyond the confines of Luanda and Lourenço Marques, it must have seemed an over-romanticized fantasy.

Exhibitions and other events in metropolitan Portugal on screen

The major exhibitions and their attractions contributed to the construction of a collective memory which could be fixed in photographs, postcards and films. The presence of the Natives from various Portuguese colonies participating in the exhibitions is a major feature in the films of these exhibitions, with the Natives shown naked or clothed in animal products such as plumage, hides, furs and bones. These films served to advertise the exhibition as it was happening, to relive it once it had finished, and to document it for those who had never visited it in the first place. Some included footage from the documentaries made in Africa. Documentaries of exhibitions held outside Portugal include *Portugal na Exposição de Paris de 1937* (1942) and *Portugal na Exposição de Bruxelas* (1958), both by Lopes Ribeiro. Two films were made on the subject of the 1932 Industrial Exhibition of Lisbon: *Guiné, Aldeia Indígena em Lisboa* (1931)[91] and *África em Lisboa. Os Indígenas da Guiné na Grande Exposição Industrial Portuguesa* (1932), by Salazar Diniz and Raul Reis. In the first, we see that the Natives were confined to a makeshift village of eight huts. In this village were contained one prince, one princess, four chieftains, one *impedido*[92] and another thirty-nine people, plus chickens, pigeons, pigs, goats, a donkey and a milking cow. With this mise-en-scène the objective was to present the non-Europeans as being nearer to 'nature' than 'civilization' and urban society. The non-Europeans are nearly always shown clothed, in more elaborate dress than what we see in the documentaries made in the colonies. These Guineans were in fact Muslims, as we can see in the scene showing their morning prayers. The camera follows a sequence of activities performed by the Natives, and these activities are presented as though they were daily scenes in the life of the 'Blacks of Guinea' (as the intertitle reads). In the dancing

---

91. As the date of the documentary (1931) actually precedes the exhibition, it would seem that the film was merely an advertisement for the exhibition, but the print I viewed contains footage of the exhibition itself and therefore its date must be wrong.

92. A soldier in the private service of the chieftains, corresponding to the soldiers on barracks duty in metropolitan Portugal.

scenes, women and men participate alternately or simultaneously. Here the Natives are described as 'Black men and women, dancers, singers and players of strange instruments' who 'show off their classic *batuque*', which is described as 'a kind of crazy Charleston'. Special emphasis is given to the ceremony in which the chieftains are awarded medals 'for distinguished overseas service'. At this ceremony the chieftains appear 'in strange and richly-embroidered vestments'. Native women are introduced with intertitles such as 'young girls of characteristic beauty, the envy of many White women', 'a princess with dark eyes full of faith' and 'Black beauties'. The bare-chested Native girls we see in this scene are clearly ill at ease. They smile occasionally – perhaps the presence of the cameraman is disturbing them, or the crew's reaction to their nudity has no equivalent in their natural environment. The Natives are referred to as chieftains, princes or players, according to their social standing and the role they performed in their community. The film dedicates most of its time to the Natives, and visitors are seen only very occasionally.

The other documentary, *África em Lisboa,* opens with a picture of the map of Guinea, suggesting we have just arrived at a settlement named Aldeia Nova de Sam Corlá. The real setting of the village, however, was Lisbon's Eduardo VII gardens. This film shows young individuals from Africa who are very smartly turned out, right up to their haircuts. Everything looks premeditated: the women look at the camera as they are working, as if posing for a photograph. In the scene intertitled 'the flower of Guinea, whose faithless eyes deceive', we see girls filmed frontally and in profile. The way the camera observes them seems to intimidate them, and their postures are rather 'unnatural'. The intertitle describes 'indiscretions of the lens' as we see a bare-chested girl going to fetch water, or women getting dressed behind a folding screen or washing themselves together. This film is almost entirely dedicated to the Natives; the visitors to the exhibition are nowhere to be seen. Despite this, the individuals from Africa are never named and the emphasis is on the activities they are performing. Some women are seen milling and sifting grain or cooking rice, 'the staple food' (intertitle); others wash clothes and hang them out to dry, embroider at the sewing machine, weave and stitch fabrics; others still serve dainties on trays while a White man stands behind them, overseeing their actions. In the part dedicated to performances, the 'Natives' appear dressed 'appropriately', as the intertitle informs us; we see the 'Fula in their dances and chants full of picturesque appeal and Black colour', as the intertitle explains. These scenes demonstrate the capacities of the African people represented, including the ability to work – and if they could work, they could attain Western standards of civilization.

The unfinished documentary *I Exposição Colonial Portuguesa – Porto 1934* (1935) by Aníbal Contreiras contains no pictures of the exhibition itself but instead offers footage of Porto, other locations in Portugal and the exhibition venue, the Palácio de Cristal, all of which was designed to attract visitors to the event. The Natives participating in this film are the same ones as shown in previous documentaries, such as *África em Lisboa* (1932) and *I Companhia de Infantaria Indígena de Angola em Lisboa* (1933). Another documentary of the same exhibition is *Moçambique, Ritmos Guerreiros em Cantos e Danças* (1934),[93] again by Aníbal Contreiras. (This film is rather misleadingly titled, for it is set not in Africa but at the colonial exhibition of Porto.) The Natives are shown in sculptures and paintings, in dioramas with life-sized figures, and in their 'Indigenous villages'. In the Palácio das Colónias we see columns capped by enormous heads. These heads represent the inhabitants of the colonies and are reminiscent of the statues of Portugal dos Pequenitos. Some panels show Natives engaged in diverse activities. The Natives who participate in the exhibition are also shown performing tasks and receiving small gifts from the visitors. There is a strong religious element in this documentary, as well: inside the palace we see the cross and a series of dioramas with missionaries,[94] the symbols of evangelization. Although its subject is a colonial exhibition, this film spends less time on the Africans than on the local population, with the emphasis on Portugal's pavilions and folklore ensembles.

Another documentary of the 1930s is *Exposição Histórica da Ocupação* (1937), on the exhibition held in Lisbon's Parque Eduardo VII. No Natives from outside Portugal participated in this event, which primarily focused on the heroes of the wars of occupation. Directed by Lopes Ribeiro with text by the Arquivo Histórico Colonial (AHC) director Manuel Múrias and premiered on 11 May 1938 in Lisbon's São Luiz Theatre, *Exposição Histórica da Ocupação* is essentially a visual account of the various rooms of the exhibition and their contents: there are portraits (by Eduardo Malta) of the Portuguese heroes of the wars of occupation, sculptures of Henry the Navigator and Vasco da Gama, publications by Serpa Pinto, Capelo and Ivens, and artefacts from the wars. The subject matter also extends to other heroes of other battles as far back as the

---

93. This film too is incomplete, with lacunae and an abrupt ending.

94. In one of these dioramas we see a priest facing an altar, flanked by two kneeling boys – simultaneously an evocation of the missionaries who died in the service of colonization and the propagation of the faith, and of those who were still actively engaged in the 'salvation of souls'. In another diorama, a female missionary tends to sick Natives while another (also female) teaches a girl to sew and stitch; another shows a priest overseeing the manual work of an African.

seventeenth century, and the cross is a ubiquitous presence. The documentary devotes special emphasis to the Portuguese defeat of the Nguni emperor Gungunhana on 28 December 1895. There are references to the soldiers who marched with Mouzinho de Albuquerque to Chaimite, and their heroism is extolled. The episode is reconstructed in a scale model with 48 White soldiers, 3 officers, 207 Native auxiliaries, 76 Native porters, etc. Gungunhana, the formidable *Indígena* chief, is escorted by 3,000 of his 'warriors'. Despite this disparity in numbers, Gungunhana was defeated and humiliated in front of his army, and we see some of his personal effects: rifle, photos, hat, portraits of ten of his lawful wives, and a silver goblet. With the exception of adversary leaders such as Gungunhana, the Natives are never named, or are referred to in relation to the group they belong to; those mentioned in the film are those who took part in the battles – fighting for or against the Portuguese. Most are represented as belonging to the latter camp, and this disparity only serves to render the feats of the Portuguese more heroic still.

Two documentaries were made of the Exhibition of the Portuguese World. Both were eponymously titled. One was by F. Carneiro Mendes (1940) and the other was by Lopes Ribeiro (1941). The first film shows the interior of each pavilion and the 'Indigenous villages' of the Jardim do Ultramar adjacent to the exhibition. It opens with a colour drawing showing six women arranged in two rows. In the front row there is a woman from the Portuguese region of Minho, an Indian woman, and a Madeiran woman. In the back row there is a Macanese, a Timorese and, placed in a position further back, an African woman. This forms a tableau of the diversity of the human 'types' of the 'empire' represented, but at the same time announces the minor importance of the African woman in the drawing. In the colonial section we see an African sculpture placed on a heap of stones, African ritual masks topping columns with carved animals and other motifs based on African fauna and flora, and a sculpture of an African man in profile, with exaggerated bodily features. The Africans are always shown in proximity to nature – minerals, fauna and flora – and their great size is associated with strength and physical prowess. Some appear clothed and shod, while others are semi-naked, wearing nothing but a loincloth. The camera lingers on shots of Africans in a dugout on the pond, the tattooed face of a woman and the various activities being performed by the Natives. In the Pavilion of Indigenous Art we see African sculptures from various places, although none of the sculptors is named.

One of the most interesting scenes in the second film shows the Pavilion of Colonization, which extols the Portuguese efforts in the propagation of the Christian faith over the course of five centuries, the institution of the overseas captaincies and the foundation of the fortress of Mina. A number of models reconstruct episodes and themes such as the reception of the Portuguese in the court of the king of Kongo, the fighting at Chaimite, education, the missions, health care, means of transport by air, land and water, and roads and communication arteries. The camera lingers on giant posters depicting the Natives of Cape Verde, Guinea, São Tomé e Príncipe, Angola, Mozambique, India, Macao and Timor. The Natives themselves are found in the colonial section of the exhibition. Their lives and habitats are reconstructed using materials actually found in the colonies, and we see them kneading dough, hammering, weaving, playing instruments and dancing. Macao is reconstituted as a street with authentic elements such as restaurants, and with figures working with wood. In many sculptures, Africans are shown in larger-than-life scale, as on the door of the Pavilion of Indigenous Art. In another building, the heads of the Africans are higher than the doors, perhaps to create the impression that they were monstruous and indomitable. A gigantic representation of three African women can also be seen at the entrance of another pavilion.

Religious imagery features strongly in this film. To give just a few examples we can cite: (a) the banner with the legend 'Portugal has always been Christian' (Pavilion of the Foundation); (b) the legend of an image of Our Lady of the Conception, which apparently accompanied 'the count of Vila Flor at the battle of Ameixial' (Pavilion of the Discoveries); (c) the panel in the China room (Pavilion of the Portuguese Around the World) with its elements of religious syncretism – a Chinese goddess of mercy (clearly styled on Western depictions of the Virgin) and St Francis Xavier; (d) the evocation of the influence of popular Catholicism on the 'Empire of the Rising Sun' in the Japan room; and (e) the Chapel of Faith in the colonial centre, where every day the Natives (who have 'purposely come from the four corners of the empire', in the words of the narrator) went to mass. On their exit from mass, the (clothed) Natives file out in an orderly fashion, a visual allusion to the order that existed in an 'empire' in which all participated, collaborated and were happy. Religion is also present in the dioramas representing the work of the missions. Generally speaking, the populations represented here belong to two separate worlds: in the main exhibition hall we find the metropolitan Portuguese, while the Jardim Tropical accommodates the colonial peoples from Cape Verde to Timor. One effect of this suggestive spatial layout is the negation of cultural life of all nonmetropolitan peoples, who are all treated as *Indígenas*. Little time is dedicated to them in this film – which is probably indicative of their scant political and social power.

Native colonial subjects were also in demand in other events organized in metropolitan Portugal. One of these was the tribute to the 'Indigenous soldiers' in the film *I Companhia de Infantaria Indígena* ... (1933), which counted on the participation of the President of the Ministry, the minister for the colonies and Salazar himself. The Natives are present throughout the film, and we are told that they belong to the 'Black troop incorporated in the military parade commemorating the 28th of May'. We see a military march past, mostly composed of soldiers of metropolitan Portugal, a musical band with a few African members, a statue alluding to the Great War, and military exercises. Lopes Ribeiro's *As Festas do Duplo Centenário* (1940) documents the centenary commemorations of this year. One part of these commemorations, a procession illustrating Portugal and its history, is specifically treated in another documentary, *O Cortejo do Mundo Português* by Carneiro Mendes (1940). Ribeiro's film (which is incomplete) documents the commemorations of Portugal's 'double centenary' – the foundation and the restoration of 1140 and 1640 respectively – held in Lisbon, Guimarães, Porto, Braga, Alentejo and Sagres. In the footage documenting the Grande Cortejo do Trabalho procession in Porto we see an allegorical float named 'Colonial Agriculture', with two chairs at the front, surmounted by two busts representing Africans (big eyes, thick lips), and two columns at the back, topped by African sculptures. The Natives themselves are seen only once in this film, the part showing the Procession of the Portuguese World in Lisbon, where they are presented as symbols of the Portuguese conquests. This procession includes an Indian driving an elephant, and an allegorical float drawn by oxen and carrying an African female.

1947 was another centenary year, this time marking the eight hundredth anniversary of the capture of Lisbon from the Moors, commemorated by a parade organized by Leitão de Barros in Lisbon's Praça do Império. Two documentaries were made of this parade: *O Cortejo Histórico de Lisboa*[95] by Lopes Ribeiro (1947) and *O Cortejo Histórico com a Representação de Todas as Colónias Portuguesas em Carros Alegóricos* by Leitão de Barros (1947). The parade featured elements representing all the most important episodes and characters in the history of Portugal, such as Henry the Navigator and the mythical Adamastor, both shown flanked by Africans. There are representations of the heroes of the Discoveries and of major figures – nobles, knights and soldiers – from the sixteenth, seventeenth and eighteenth centuries. Each colony is repre-

---

95. In this film we can see the Argentinian First Lady Eva Perón on the tribune of honour, alongside Portugal's head of state, Óscar Carmona, and prime minister, Salazar.

sented by an allegorical float, on top of which (or walking alongside
it) we see representatives of its inhabitants. Each float is pulled by a
pair of oxen led by an inhabitant of metropolitan Portugal. The Natives of Cape Verde, who were seen as good examples of assimilation,
are clothed and shod. Other Natives – wearing masks or with musical
instruments – go barefoot. The float representing India is an especially
exuberant spectacle, with Indian men in turbans and Indian women in
veils and jewels. The float representing Macao carries two dragons and
a large gilded Buddha, two symbols frequently used in representations
of this east Asian colony. The Natives are generally represented in this
film as proof of the success of colonization, part of the nation and the
'empire'.

Documentaries made in the colonies and the mise-en-scène of the wars of occupation

Many of the documentaries made in the colonies[96] emphasize the potential of the African territories in human and natural terms. Some focus on the creation of structures designed to facilitate the education
and evangelization of the Africans; others seek to portray their 'usages
and customs'. This is the case of *Costumes Primitivos dos Indígenas em
Moçambique* (1928?), made by the Brigada Cinematográfica Portuguesa
and produced by the AGC. The title is significant, not so much for 'customs' as for 'primitive', a term which suggests these Africans were still
a long way from modern civilization. Filmed in Angónia, Inhambane
and Tete (Mozambique), this documentary shows the Natives pounding
grain and making fire, illustrating the scarcity of resources and high-
lighting the rudimentary and 'primitive' act of rubbing sticks on stone
to get fire, preparing food in pots made from gourds, working on plantations, doing pottery and basketwork, weaving and making clothes,
making jewellery, working cotton, and looking for gold, although no
mention is made of the gold prospectors known as *garimpeiros*. We also
see Indigenous Mozambican dances and 'war dances' by the women of
Angónia and Inhambane. Women are also shown with their children,
perhaps an allusion to their maternal side and an attempt to show that
the Africans had a 'good', i.e. emotional, aspect and were therefore susceptible to absorbing the lessons of the Christian faith. In a film totally
dedicated to Native colonial subjects, there is even time to illustrate the
polygamy of some Africans: we see a chieftain with his various wives.

---

96. As an exhaustive search of the photo archives of the Cinemateca Portuguesa revealed, there are very few still photographs from these documentaries: most photographs
are of the film crew and the various stages on its itinerary.

Another documentary, *Acção Colonizadora dos Portugueses* by Antunes da Mata (1932), is filmed in Angola. This film opens with the intertitle 'Villagers of Portugal have been settling in Angola with the assistance of the State. They have been provided with irrigated land, seed, houses and money.' As if this wasn't enticement enough, we are also shown another resource on which the White settler can count – the work of the Natives. One of the following scenes shows Natives working on the construction of a dam or bridge over a river. Yet colonization also helped the Natives, encouraging them to produce their own foods. We can deduce as much from the intertitle 'To stimulate the production of cereals, wheat seeds have been distributed to the *Indígenas*'. In another scene we see the Natives working on the grain harvest. Everything is going well and an intertitle even informs us that 'the *soba* (tribal chief) manifests his contentment to the *Maniputo* (the Portuguese overseer)'. Investment is also being made in health care – for the Natives as well as the settlers. The film shows 'the central hospital of Luanda, built last century' and still 'one of the best in Africa'. The 'hospital for *Indígenas*', meanwhile, is described as 'one of the best on the West Coast' (of Africa). Named the 'Charity Hospital', it is smaller than Luanda's central hospital, although Natives far outnumbered settlers. Livestock farming is also an object of investment.[97] In the scenes showing nurseries, cereals and milking cows being pacified by the children of settlers, the goal is to show that it was the settlers who taught these activities to the Natives. The suggestion seems to be that these structures are being organized in expectation of future Portuguese settlers. The Natives are seen in their dwellings and in scenes designed to show their 'habits'. There are references to the *chilongo* ('the dwelling of a shepherd family'), the 'dance of the shepherds' wives', 'elaborate coiffures' and a 'mock combat' by the shepherds. Then we are taken 'just a few kilometres away, [to] another dance … the dance of civilization'. The dance in question is a traditional Portuguese one, performed by the children of settlers and Natives of Luís de Camões Primary School no. 60. We are given another perspective on 'civilization' at the entrance to the secondary school of Cidade Sá da Bandeira. In this scene, a group of children are seen leaving the school: all the children are White except for one *Mestiça* – a demonstration of how far the Natives still were from education.

Most of the people we see in this film work in agriculture. The Portuguese settlers oversee the work of the Natives on the *fazendas* (plan-

---

97. These scenes take place in a *fazenda* whose buildings bear a close resemblance to the traditional houses of the Alentejo, and the herds are driven by a settler. They could easily have been filmed anywhere in Portugal.

tations) and in the schools, while the Natives are depicted as workers, plantation labourers or shepherds, or shown in connection with their 'traditional customs'. (Although portrayed as remote from 'civilization', the Natives are nevertheless presented as workers.) Native men and women alike seem reserved in the presence of the camera, and are never given names. Despite the inequalities, the world we are presented is one in which everything seems to be running smoothly and everyone is in their place.

The documentary *Angola Uma Nova Lusitânia* by Lopes Ribeiro (1944) emphasizes the economic and sociocultural potential of the colonies. Based on material filmed by the MCCA, it was given a preview screening at the Insituto Superior Técnico's (IST) Exhibition of Colonial Construction. The film extols the colonizing and evangelizing mission of Portugal and seeks to convey the idea that the Natives owed their peaceful existence to the Portuguese. In illustration of this we see the king of Kongo receiving Carmona in the company of his queen and Native bodyguard. These monarchs had led a tranquil existence for many years 'because the Portuguese with their European civilization brought peace and simplicity of customs to the Kongo' (the narrator's words) – common discourse at a time when Portugal was asserting its desire to be 'European'. The film's narrator informs us that every one of the *Indígenas,* who 'even ride bicycles around São Salvador', is 'living testimony to our civilizing action'. The narrator continues: 'This is how we proceed on all the continents, fusing Europe with Asia, Africa and America, mixing the products of their soils and the souls of their peoples, turning everything equally Portuguese.' The presence of various churches should come as no surprise, as Catholic missions had been active in Angola since the fifteenth century (although Protestant missions were to be found there too). In one scene we see Natives filing into church. When they come out, they are followed by two priests. Most of these churchgoers are bare-torsoed women; some wear dresses; all are barefoot.[98] In another church we see an African organist accompanying a Native choir. As the narrator informs us, 'all know how to read', 'they're singing in Latin', and 'only the patience and selfless effort of the missionaries could achieve such a miracle'. We are also shown a procession. Here, 'the cross presides over and blesses the work and the land of Angola', where Portugal leads the Natives from 'barbarism' to the 'light of civilization' (the narrator's words), an articulation of the idea that despite everything the Natives

---

98. This occurred at a time when, in metropolitan Portugal, women had to attend mass 'properly' dressed – they had to cover their faces with a veil, and short skirts and plunging necklines were considered unsuitable.

could be civilized with the help of the settlers. This documentary also shows the concern the settlers have for the health of the Natives. We see hospitals, laboratories, vaccination posts, the maternity hospital of São Salvador do Congo and small houses where Natives are accommodated as they recover from sleeping sickness. In addition to the scenes showing the Natives as passive recipients of the process of civilization and evangelization, others show them in more active roles: unloading goods from a ship in the port of Lobito; working in industry and manufacturing, in railway factories, a sugarcane factory and a diamond mine; and building roads, bridges, and railways. Their work is supervised by one or more settlers, who occasionally carry a stick. As the narrator explains, 'exploitation has a civilizing function'. In other words, only by civilizing the Natives could the settlers exploit Africa: this was the key to the problem of colonization.

In Lopes Ribeiro's *Gentes que Nós Civilizámos (apontamentos etnográficos de Angola)* (1944), made during the existence of the MCCA and property of the AGC, the title says it all: the Portuguese civilized the 'peoples' (*Gentes*) of Africa. This documentary focuses on different aspects of the 'mission' of the Portuguese, mainly among the Angolans. It opens with the caption 'The film you are about to see is not intended as a scientific study of the Angolan tribes and races. It is merely the first attempt to turn to account an inexhaustible treasure which deserves to be brought to fulfilment.' The 'treasure' in question is presumably human; but little else seems to be known about it. The camera gives much attention to the Native females, who are filmed frontally and in profile in a manner reminiscent not only of the 'physical anthropology' approach to photography but also of the mugshots of criminals and the mentally ill. These women are described with expressions such as: 'colour doesn't matter, a woman's not a woman if she doesn't like to make herself pretty'; while the 'Black fishwives' in the fishing port of Lobito 'add a note of colour and attest to our civilizing vocation'. Mentioning the rings that the girls wear on their ankles, the narrator tells us that 'on the ankle, a number of rings complete the outfit'. These rings are seen as just a part of the costume; there is no explanation of why these rings *(malungas)* are worn (the more the girl was valued the more rings she wore, so she would be unable to run far). Another feature of the women which attracts attention is their hair – the Kwanyama girls take three days to make their hair ready during the feast of puberty – and their tattoos, which although commonly found among the men, are even more frequent in 'the weaker sex', according to the narrator. Angolan women are presented as sexually permissive, like the Chokwe who 'dance and spin lasciviously'. But the film also shows how evangelization was suc-

ceeding. We see many Natives – men, women and children – entering
a church as a bell rings. A Native man holds a crucifix to his chest, and
a large cross stands in the open air. The Natives are also described as in-
dustrious: 'the Black women work hard'; 'the man sows, but the woman
tills the earth, gets in the harvest, threshes the grain and cooks'; 'the
Blacks have a special affection for ceramics, which is produced either
by men or women'; 'they work in the service of the White man in the
plantations that supply the sisal factories where they make rope, fishing
nets, carpets'; and they also 'cultivate cotton'. As for the Chokwe, these
'skilled artists' make masks and other wooden objects such as tables and
chairs which are 'magnificently carved' – an acknowledgement of the
artistic abilities of the Natives. The Natives of the colonies are also differentiated by their ethnic groupings and their practices, which in this
film are classified according to Western models and preconceptions.
The Cuval people are nomads, 'proud, haughty, believing themselves
superior to the White man', yet 'very primitive' and with 'an impressive
resilience'. We see members of the Cuval standing (most of them) side
by side, their arms hanging at their sides; they are filmed frontally and in
profile, as if they were human curiosities, and there are close-ups of their
sandals, loincloths, bracelets and anklets, hair, and necklaces. Another
group, the Kwanyama, are cattle farmers and skilled horsemen: 'quick
and agile [the Kwanyama man] practises sport his own way ... showing ... a wrestling technique similar to Greco-Roman wrestling' (narrator). In this scene we see a staged wrestling match between two men,
more dance than combat, which the narrator compares to boxing. In the
province of Malanje, the women dance to the rhythm of the *batuques*
with an accompaniment of voice and instruments such as the finger
piano, basket with bells and drum, which is also used to communicate
with distant villages and warn of the approach of the authorities. According to the narrator, these dances are 'a little like the traditional circle
dances of the village feasts of Portugal'. This was a comparison based
on two phenomena familiar to the scriptwriter, but with no attempt to
contextualize one or the other. Then there are the 'Bushmen', an ethnic
group distinct from the Bantu, 'who speak the Khoisan language [and]
are among the most backward, if not the most backward, of the native
peoples of Angola'. They 'make a meagre living from hunting, gathering
wild fruits and lizards', and speak with a kind of clicking noise.[99] The
Ganguela attract attention for their circumcision ritual, in which the
'masks' represent 'other-worldly figures come to cause terror and panic'
(narrator).

---

99. The same hierarchization is found in the major exhibitions (see Chapter III).

Lopes Ribeiro's *As Ilhas Crioulas de Cabo Verde* (1945) was another MCCA production. The background music for this film is not the national anthem, or classical music, but the *morna* typical of Cape Verde. Cape Verdean music is acknowledged as different from the *batuque* characteristic of other African peoples, and is described as 'languidly expressive'. Portuguese evangelization seems to have been successful, for the narrator speaks of the 'profound faith of the good Creole people'. And investment was being made not only in evangelization, but education as well. We see 'almost 400 students who strive to improve their knowledge in the colonial school', most of them Whites or *Mestiços*. Some – but not many – went 'reluctantly' to the *escolas superiores* of metropolitan Portugal. This documentary places emphasis on sports and the 'physically perfect boys, real eugenic types', who proved 'the excellence of the Portuguese colonization processes'.

Ricardo Malheiro's documentary *O Ensino em Angola* (1950)[100] portrays education in the secondary schools, technical colleges, and religious and private institutions of the colony. It was filmed in Luanda (Liceu Salvador Correia de Sá, Escola Industrial), Huíla, Moçâmedes, Tchivinguiro (Escola Agro-Pecuária), Benguela (Colónia de Férias), Bié (Instituto Liceal e Técnico), Nova Lisboa, Sá da Bandeira (Liceu, Escola Industrial) and Cuíma, Huambo region (the primary schoolteacher training college). This documentary shows the *Indígenas* receiving a 'special education ... entrusted to the Catholic missions' (narrator). We see a priest, Fr Freire, teaching the Bible in a mission in Huíla, while another priest, Fr Carlos Estermann (an ethnographer as well as a missionary), does the same. The Natives (children, youths and adults) also appear in the 'Teófilo Duarte primary schoolteacher training college', endowed by the minister who gave it its name, while in the industrial schools of Huíla and Luanda the Natives could learn carpentry, metalwork and other crafts.

Another documentary on a similar subject was *Acção Missionária em Angola* (1951),[101] by Lemos Pereira and João Silva. This film, now the property of the AGU, extols the spirit of sacrifice of the missionaries, who are described as 'heroes and saints'. These missionaries, we are told, made huts in the undergrowth which 'the *Indígenas* immediately tried to destroy by setting fire to them'. Yet the missionaries raised these same *Indígenas* from a 'primitive life to make useful men of them', to

---

100. An AGC film sponsored by the Central Office for Public Instruction Services of Angola.

101. This film incorporates scenes from the documentary *O Ensino em Angola* (the Natives coming out of church and Fathers Freire and Estermann).

'mould good workers, healthy men' who attended classes, where they chose 'vocations preparing them to face life' (narrator). These 'vocations' took markedly different forms, however. The children of settlers were oriented towards school and study, with an emphasis on knowledge, technical professions and sports; but the children of Natives were oriented towards the acquisition of craft skills. Although the missions did teach basic reading and writing skills, the 'great opportunity' given to the 'young *Indígena*' who worked hard was, as the narrator tells us, to enter a seminary.

At a time when the regime was in a position of acute discomfort there appeared a film which evoked the memory of the heroes of the 'empire' and the exploits of the Portuguese occupation of Africa. Jorge Brum de Canto's *Chaimite* (1953)[102] was an epic action film, a Western in all but setting, whose rousing soundtrack, scored by Joly Braga dos Santos, won the SNI's Grand Prize for best feature-length film. The action depicts the following episodes: a group of Nguni 'hordes' attacking the inhabitants of Lourenço Marques in October 1894; the African campaigns under António Enes and associates; the attempts by Caldas Xavier, Aires Ornelas, Eduardo Costa, Paiva Couceiro, Freire Andrade and, a little later, Galhardo and Mouzinho to liberate Mozambique; and various episodes in the wars of occupation – Marracuene, Magul, Cooela, the conflagration of Manjacaze, Chaimite (and the seizure of Gungunhana) and Macontene (where Mouzinho, now royal commissioner of the province of Mozambique, subjugates Macontene). The Portuguese troops were alarmed when they learned that the rebellious Natives outnumbered them by 6,500 compared to a little over 200. This difference in numbers between settlers/allies and Native opposition is emphasized, and the fact that the Portuguese won in spite of being outnumbered is presented as testimony of the heroic character of the Portuguese.

We occasionally see Natives on the side of the settlers in this film, while others are on the side of the rebels. They are informers or spies, or perform menial tasks for the settlers. With the exception of the leaders, they have no social status. Many had befriended the settlers, perhaps out of fear or because they felt this was the only way to ensure their survival. Thousands of Natives thought otherwise, however. They rebelled

---

102. This film drew on many sources: documents, reports, interviews and research of various kinds. Vassalo Pandayo was its historic and military consultant. It was produced by Cinematografia Nacional (Cinal), created in 1950 with Brum do Canto among its founders. It was premiered on 4 April 1953 in Lisbon's Monumental Theatre, in the presence of several high-ranking politicians. It was advertised in various parts of the sphere of Portuguese influence: the mainland, Madeira, the Azores, Angola, Mozambique and Brazil.

against the colonization and occupation of African soil and set fire to the settlers' camps. Although some Natives are depicted as faithful friends, the film generally represents them as dull-witted, lazy and pagan. The Portuguese nation, on the other hand, is shown to have the Catholic religion on its side. Christmas had gone uncelebrated due to an attack on Christmas Eve in 1894. The Natives were not Catholic and therefore had no respect for religion; with no God, they wandered lost and aimless through the world (Figure 4). This evaluation seems strange at a time when postwar decolonization was now underway among other colonial powers – although it had yet to occur in Portugal, it was nevertheless indicative of a reformulation of ideas in relation to overseas possessions. The Natives are never given individual identities; with the exception of Mambaza and Mauáua and their leaders, such as Gungunhana, they are simply designated as 'Blacks' or *'Indígenas'*. Gungunhana is played by a large, muscular African. This representation lends itself to two interpretations: either it is an allusion to the brutish stature associated with the Africans, or an attempt to ridicule Gungunhana for his obesity. After Gungunhana is found, Mouzinho gives the order to arrest the 'fugitive' and bind his hands. At this point Mouzinho says: 'Two Whites, no. Two Blacks. Can't you hear? Are you deaf? Sit down on the ground' (Figure 5). Gungunhana answers: 'It's dirty.' This exchange is representative, essentially, of the humiliation suffered by many Africans.

Another interesting feature of *Chaimite* is its use of Native languages. The character named António, for example, always speaks Landin to the

Figure 4. Natives of Mozambique (Cinemateca Portuguesa).

Figure 5. 'The capture of Gungunhana' (Cinemateca Portuguesa).

Natives, up until the battle of Marracuene, after which the Portuguese are in direct confrontation with the Nguni, and Nguni becomes the language spoken between the warring factions (Seabra 2000: 244). Another idea which *Chaimite* seeks to convey to its Portuguese spectators is that after pacification Africa was a prosperous and fertile country, and that to live and work there was to enjoy happiness and wealth (Figure 6).

The purpose of these films was to disseminate propaganda (for the regime and the colonies) rather than convey information. Neither did they have much to do with 'geographic tourism', to echo the expression of Luís de Pina (1977), or with ethnography. Their objective was to cultivate a colonial consciousness and their tone was apologetic. The 'seventh art', was used, therefore, as a weapon in defence of the regime and its colonial policy. In its representations of Africa, the regime sought to project a national consciousness of a single, undivided Portugal. Its general message takes the form of a product created for dissemination among the people of Portugal, foreign – mainly Western – countries and (last of all) the colonized populations themselves. In the films with sound, orchestral arrangements, musical accompaniment (epic music which legitimizes and stages the power of certain characters) and the 'folklore' and 'rituals' of the Natives reinforce this message. Some documentaries evidence the capacity for work of the African Native, and the importance of the role of the Native in the construction of Africa's

Figure 6. In a fertile land and with the work of the Native, the settlers could prosper (Cinemateca Portuguesa).

promising future. Yet this work is always overseen by a White, metropolitan Portuguese – African labour at the service of 'White' know-how. As for the images depicting the development and modernization of the colonies in the form of cities such as Luanda, Lobito, Lourenço Marques and Beira, the lives of the Native inhabitants of these cities were very different from what the films show us. In the documentaries filmed at the exhibitions, the camera – operated by a White metropolitan Portuguese male who occupies a position of strength by virtue of his possession of the machine that can film and construe – is invariably drawn to the exotic, the different, the picturesque. All this effort is at the service of documenting 'Overseas Portugal' and its peoples with their 'usages and customs', the civilizing work which was being carried out there, and the role of the missions. Most of the Natives who came to the exhibitions were chieftains, princes or princesses in their communities of origin, or youths carefully selected for their appearance. Many wore Western clothing and shoes – their companions in the group wore matching outfits – and rarely appeared naked, as they do in the documentaries filmed in the colonies. In both cases, however, their identities are represented by the role or status they enjoy within their communities, not by their names. The Natives are housed in makeshift villages built with the help of the Natives themselves; they are incarcerated in 'nature', denied any identity other than that which the colonizers label them with on their arrival in metropolitan Portugal: there is no process of negotiation here, but rather an imposition and a removal of identity. The way the Natives look at the camera, turn their backs or smile, looks rehearsed, although on many occasions they seem distinctly ill at ease. And we can detect a certain voyeuristic pleasure on the part of the cameraman – a pleasure which at bottom is expressive of the power relations between camera-man and subject. The Natives are represented as instances of a single indivisible whole (all are indiscriminately called *Indígenas*), but among this undifferentiated whole some attempt is made to identify distinct characteristics.

In the final analysis, all the films we have discussed here have more things in common than differences. The differences are largely a ques-tion of context. Not only that, but documentary makers also made dra-mas, and some films borrowed documentary passages from others. The resulting montage may form a coherent sequence for the spectator, but there is little chronological continuity in terms of the footage. Under the Estado Novo, colonial policy cohabited with a defence of the postulates of Christianity, according to which all people are equal; and yet a certain racism is pervasive in these films, and expressions of a belief in Western superiority (cultural but not racial), or a combination of both attitudes, are not unusual.

Portuguese cinema increasingly turned its attention to Brazil in the 1950s, perhaps due to the rise of Luso-tropicalism and the idea that Brazil was a living and positive example of the 'Portuguese way of being in the world', in the words of Adriano Moreira. Examples of this new-found interest in the ex-colony include *Gloriosa Viagem ao Brasil* (1957), *Viagem Presidencial ao Brasil* (1957) and *Comunidade Luso-Brasileira* (1958), all made by Lopes Ribeiro. As the 1950s drew to a close the regime sought to project the image of a multiracial Portugal, a change which is evident in films like *Nossos Irmãos, os Africanos* (1963) and *Catembe* (1965). Films on the 'overseas possessions' continued to appear through the '60s and up to 1974. By now, however, and despite censor-ship, these films began to incorporate a degree of social criticism of the regime's colonial policy, or to address aspects such as forced labour. But this criticism had to be made with much subtlety, for the censors would typically make more than one hundred cuts from a single film. This ten-dency towards a certain 'redressing of the balance' and the denunciation of discriminatory practices continued into the 1980s.[103]

---

103. Appendix I lists some of these films by year and director.

Recurrent images and prejudices

In written discourse, the ideas and prejudices associated with 'Native populations' often contain a racial component. The various formulations of this discourse give us an insight into how the Portuguese elites presented the Native populations, the views, images and descriptions their presentations contained, and the ideas they conveyed – how some are expressions of discriminatory and racist attitudes, some subtle, others flagrant. The texts I shall be examining here are the work of people from various walks of life – not just missionaries[104] and administrative staff, but also politicians, anthropologists, doctors, military men and journalists. The latter, for example, treated different data in the same way, and the absence of a critical spirit is immediately evident. It is important to remember, too, that although they will be examined sequentially here, the basic assumptions of these texts, and their principles, objectives and opinions with regard to colonization, vary greatly. If we ask whether the 'colonized populations' were the targets of discrimination, the answer will be yes, for as soon as there exists a relationship of power between colonizer and colonized in which opposing but uneven forces are set against each other, a relationship of discrimination is likely to emerge between the stronger and weaker parties, with the latter disadvantaged from the outset. The dominant group, the one which holds power, reveals ethnocentric tendencies and considers itself to belong to an exemplary 'race'. And the subordinate group, in this context the Blacks, considered globally as a 'race', are viewed as inherently inferior. This racism can manifest itself in various forms, including different systems of classification, the criteria employed to arrive at these classifications, and the scant knowledge of the origins and ways of life of the subjugated populations. Sometimes, distinctions are made only on the basis of a region or a distinctive sociocultural characteristic. In missionary texts, the Africans are associated with the 'infernal' *batuques* – sometimes lugubrious, sometimes frenetic – and with paganism, fetishism and cannibalism; they are seen as amoral, demonic, or childish creatures. This view of Africans as childish led to the use of diminutives such as *engraçadinhos* (from *engraçado,* cute) and *pretinhos* (from *preto,* black).

Preconceptions of the backwardness, laziness, lasciviousness and carelessness of the Africans were current as early as the 1920s. Fr Faustino

---

104. See Valverde (1997) for an account of observations on Africans, based mainly on bodily characteristics, by missionaries in the Portuguese African colonies from 1930 to 1960.

Moreira dos Santos writes in an article[105] on the *Indígenas* of the enclave of Cabinda, 'unimproved by the light of civilization', that:

> [t]he *Indígena* ... is lazy and indolent, detests assiduous work and it costs him untold effort to leave his township to go and work. As for the woman, an authentic slave, she toils in the fields [while] the man drinks, eats and does nothing. Their dwellings are very basic, without hygiene and without cleanliness. Their nutrition is generally deficient. The conjugal tie is unstable ... Most of the chiefs are polygamous ... Up to the age of 11 or 12 the child is quite active, intelligent and lucid of spirit [but] at 16 turns brutish, and is incapable of further learning ... The dress of the Black, man or woman, is no more than a tiny loincloth (1925: 214–15).

In a text published in 1946 (but written in 1926), Brito Camacho[106] lists a series of ideas commonly associated with Blacks:

> It has long been established that laziness is a quality of the individual in Whites, and an attribute of the race in Blacks ... They build their houses, thatched huts with no furniture ... Any rag serves them for covering their natural modesty, and many do not even use this rag but use instead the bark of certain trees ... In good years they live well; in bad years they are as hungry as the beasts. If he did not have to pay taxes, [the Black man] would grow strictly what is necessary to feed himself ... He buys his wives in exchange for cattle ... If he falls ill, he pays his physicians, his sorcerers, in kind, and Nature is the dispensary which provides ... all kind of medicines. He enjoys himself in the *batuques,* which are free and public spectacles, and for those which are held in honour of a White man he is paid in food ... The Black man ... loves to dress up. He can imitate like a monkey and his model, naturally, is the White man (1946: 191–93).

Álvaro Montenegro (1928), who although a supporter of colonization never formulated any feasible proposals on colonial policy, cites various authors, principally Le Bon, in his attempt to justify the inferiority of Blacks. One of the questions addressed by Montenegro seems especially pertinent: 'Can they [the Africans] prosper without mixing and inter-breeding?' In Montenegro's view, Africans should be subjected to forced labour; even when in contact with superior civilizations, argues Mon-

---

105. Published in the monthly *Missões de Angola e Congo,* founded in Braga in 1920.

106. Manuel de Brito Camacho was a leading republican figure. A military physician, journalist, author and deputy of the Constituent Assembly, he sat in the Câmara dos Deputados from 1910 to 1926 and was Minister of Progress in the Governo Provisório da República in Mozambique.

tenegro, they are incapable of evolving. In support of this argument he cites Le Bon, who pointed to the fact that 'a lofty civilization had fallen into the hands of the Black race' in Haiti, and had been 'reduced to a miserably inferior form' (quoted in Montenegro, 1928: 65). For Montenegro, the 'Black race', with its 'poorly developed intelligence, attested by studies of physical features', was 'unable to create a civilization' and would therefore end up disappearing, along with its institutions. The 'Negro' is a 'beast of burden, who rarely rises from his extreme humility' (Montenegro 1928: 7, 65, 67, 83). But for Montenegro the future of Angola did not lie in the elimination of the 'Black race', 'for extermination would in a certain way annul a righteous past of protection, in addition to the fact that it would be impossible to achieve'. And yet he argues:

> To educate them, at a time when illiteracy persists in Portugal due to the lack of regular schooling, is absurd. To make them strong, when due to neglect sickness spreads to more and more people, is more than absurd, it is insane. To call them to civilization would not only involve an expense we would be unable to maintain, but would also lead us into serious difficulties if they were to become our competitors, unless they integrated in the life of the Nation, which in a sense is pointless to speculate about, given the variety of characters that constitute their soul (1928: 99).

Discriminatory attitudes abound in the following decade too. One of the most common of these attitudes was that there exists an innate inequality between the African and the European, the former living in an earlier state of civilization than the latter, and only capable of evolution through contact with the latter. The speeches[107] given at the Imperial Conference, which opened on 1 June 1933 and lasted for one month, offer good material for reflection on this subject. The conference was attended by the governors of India, Mozambique, Angola, Cape Verde, São Tomé e Príncipe, Macao, Guinea and Timor. Armindo Monteiro's opening speech claims 'the nation is the same in every part of the world' and that 'sons of the same flock, emerging from the same history, covered by the same flag' pursued the same collective ideal, with 'no antagonism'. Monteiro then proceeds to contradict himself[108] in his attempt to demonstrate that these supposed 'brothers' were very different from each other. The 'Black' had 'limited horizons' and it was necessary to

---

107. Published in the *Boletim Geral das Colónias*, no. 97, June 1933.

108. In addition to their contradictions, the speeches of Armindo Monteiro are among the most hypocritical and the most difficult to summarize in terms of the ideas they contain.

'elevate' his life 'to increasingly high levels of moral and material necessity', and this would only be possible via 'contact with the European'. Not only this, but the Natives, 'dogged ... by a thousand diseases', were 'abandoned to the scant resources of their own wherewithal' and 'would quickly perish, if European science did not come to their aid' (*Álbum-Catálogo Oficial* 1934: 74, 86, 88). As in other speeches, no mention is made of what settlers could learn from Natives. It is always the Native who can learn from the settler: *perhaps.*

In other speeches, accounts of the 'colonized populations' describe 'stupid', 'uneducated', 'backward' beings who live in an inferior state of civilization. Over and over again we hear that the Natives live in appalling domestic conditions, that their villages are disorganized, that they have no technology in their transport – only *tipóias*[109] on earth and dugouts on rivers and lakes, or vehicles which used animals as their motive force. Scientific and pseudo-scientific evidence is produced in demonstration of this 'backwardness', such as the work of Alfredo de Athayde (1953) on the physical and psychological tests carried out on *Indígenas* in Guinea and Angola. These tests determined the psychological characteristics of their subjects by exercises of association, comprehension, combination and concentration. Tests of physical strength were carried out to determine and compare mental and physical faculties, which were seen as standing in opposition to one another: *Indígenas* with superior mental faculties were presumed neither to enjoy nor be capable of heavy physical labour. Yet, as with IQ tests, these physical tests were influenced by factors not so much physical as sociocultural. The idea that some Black people had uncommon physical strength is found, for example, in a series of advertisements for the *Ovomaltine* brand published in the periodical *O Planalto,* where an African swimmer is used to illustrate the sporting qualities associated with physical robustness, and in caricatures allusive to boxing. In the West, the idea that a robust body means a feeble mind has a long pedigree. To attribute Herculean strength to Blacks, then, was also to justify the view that they were 'good for labour'. This idea is articulated in a paper on the aptitudes of the 'colonial races' presented by Mendes Correia at the Colonial Anthropology Congress of 1934. Correia ends his paper with the conclusion that the Bantu were suited for labour, but showed scant regard for the future, and the same could be said of the inhabitants of Guinea and Timor (1934c). It was probably this same prejudice that led the lawyer Marques Mano, in a speech given at the inaugural session of the Imperial Economic Conference on behalf of the colonial delegations, to observe:

---

109. A litter for one or more persons.

The lot of the Black race is labour, necessarily and exclusively; of the White race, supremacy in administrative functions; and of both, the discharge of intermediary activities (1936).

Although they were viewed as 'suitable' for work (Figure 7), Africans were also commonly conceived as lazy and work-shy, or willing to work only to satisfy their basic needs, or even prone to quitting work when other commitments – social or personal – called. Speaking at a conference at the SGL, the former governor of Timor, Captain Teófilo Duarte, argued that the *'Indígena* should not be allowed to give himself up to inertia and the *dulce far niente* he is so fond of, on the pretext that his work is poorly paid' (1936: 37). Meanwhile, we find various images depicting Africans working on the plantations or in other menial tasks, serving the elites and the middle and upper classes (the Whites). Another common idea was that in many African regions, women worked in agriculture and on domestic tasks while the men did nothing; however, this was a notion that some elements of the colonial administration sought to counter.[110]

Figure 7. Caricature of a final-year student of the ESC (*Álbum dos finalistas da ESC* 1941–45).

The idea of laziness sometimes extended to the lack of hygiene and health care. The missions and the expansion of colonial medicine played a fundamental role in this respect and the combat against tropical diseases is illustrated in many texts and images. Elsewhere, the 'colonized populations' are described as occupying the fringes of rationality, in a near-bestial or animal state, or as a species between the animal and the vegetable. Among the politicians of the regime, they were often seen as lacking in social and economic structures, living 'in a kind of natural state', rather like Rousseau's 'noble savages'. Another common preconception was that although they were committed by Natives and settlers alike, certain crimes or offences, such as theft, occurred more frequently in one race

---

110. This was at a time when most men in metropolitan Portugal preferred their wives to remain at home, confined to the domestic orbit: that African women worked the land while the men did nothing would have been inconceivable to them. But in both cases, women were the victims of discrimination – either they were imprisoned in the home, or forced to do the agricultural and domestic work unassisted.

than the other. Some commentators argued that certain vices and crimes were more common among the settlers, and others among the Natives (Mello 1937: 18). The idea that the Natives were violent, with belligerent tendencies or ferocious tempers that had to be tamed in the name of peace, was also frequent. In an article in *Panorama* magazine we read: 'The agitation of the Black world prevented Mozambique from finding her feet quickly, and the European scramble for Africa ... found the Colony without frontiers and convulsed by tribal wars.' It had been necessary, therefore, 'to grievously subjugate the tribes and liquidate the imperialist aspirations of the Blacks' (Lobato 1952).

The Africans were frequently associated with dancing and music (essentially rhythmic, not melodic, music, based on membranophones, idiophones and cordophones). The origins of this musicality were located in the war dances of pre-occupation Africa, and perhaps for this reason too the music of the Natives was seen as unclean, lacking in art or aesthetics, and monotonous, although there was some appreciation of its cadenced rhythms (*O Planalto* 1931: no. 82, 8). Just like the Portuguese peasant, the Native was 'folklorified'. Writing on the 'dances and music' of the Cape Verdeans, Mello defines the *batuque* as a gathering with 'Indigenous music' similar to the Portuguese *modinhas,* and mentions various local musical genres: the *coladeira,* the *taca,* the *landum* and the *morna,* the latter being more characteristic of the higher social classes (1932: 81). In another text the same author writes:

> Weddings, as indeed like ... other festivities, always include dancing, music and other merry-making. It is difficult to imagine another people ... so inclined to revelry (1936: 62).

There is also the question of anthropophagy or cannibalism. Henrique Galvão was governor of Huíla (1930) and a senior inspector in the colonial administration (1945). In 1947, as an independent deputy representing Angola in the National Assembly, he denounced the conditions of Indigenous labour,[111] and was a late opponent to Salazarist policy. Galvão had earlier published a book containing a selection of texts from the 1930s and '40s, based on a number of apparently authentic documents compiled by administrative staff. The title of this book was *Antropófagos.* According to the accounts contained in this book, cannibalism was widely practised by various Angolan groups, especially

---

111. With its allegations that only the dead were not forced to work, Galvão's report raised a furore. The 'Report on the Problems of the Natives in the Portuguese Colonies Presented by H. Galvão to the National Assembly Meeting in Camera' (1947) was included in a book, *O Assalto ao Santa Maria,* published in 1974 (after the revolution of 25 April). It was published in English in 1961 (see Thomaz 1997: 285).

in the north of the country, but due to the influence of the missions it was now believed to be dying out.[112] Cannibalism was seen as a natural psychosomatic tendency. The need to eradicate it, however, helped legitimize the presence of the colonizers in Africa. The belief that some Africans practised cannibalism was widespread in other quarters, too. Images illustrating cannibalism can be found in several publications. In the 'Ecos e comentários' section of issue no. 93 of *O Planalto,* we read:

> Tell us ... what you eat and we'll tell you whether your flesh tastes ... of pork or venison. It depends on your diet. That's ... the conclusion of an American explorer in a survey of ... cannibals ... all over the world (1932: 2).

We have already seen, as Jahoda (1999) too observed, that the Africans were viewed as infantile, as overgrown children, or in the 'infancy of humanity'. This attitude may well have informed a certain paternalism on the part of the colonizers, and the use of expressions which described Native populations as living under the protection or 'in the custody' of the colonizer. To legitimize this idea of the childishness of adult Africans, the evidence of science was enlisted. At the Colonial Anthropology Congress of 1934, a paper was presented containing the conclusions of a study in which school tests were administered to fourteen Natives who had been educated in the missions and were present at the colonial exhibition. (Among the examinees was the son of the Guinean chieftain, Abdulai Sissé.) One of the conclusions of this study was that the mental age of the '*Indígenas* of Angola' 'corresponded to that of European children aged between 6 and 13' (M. Costa 1934: 403). In a conference held at the University of Coimbra in 1937, Mello affirmed that the 'lumpen colonials' formed 'the great mass of the *Indígenas* of the Portuguese colonies, with the exceptions of India and Macao'; the Native populations occupied a 'degree of semi-civilization, with those African *Indígenas* comparable with children in their psychological impulsiveness and their levels of ignorance'. Not only that, they were 'childishly improvident'. In educating the Africans as if they were children, it was 'essential' that the Europeans were, 'in the colonies, the only ones to mete out punishment', to show that they were 'the only ones with the power to govern' (Mello 1937: 6, 9, 16–17). While some saw them as 'noble savages' or as ingenuous and careless, others considered these 'overgrown children' to be 'very crafty', and sometimes compared this craftiness with that of monkeys. The more overtly racist aspects of attitudes towards African

---

112. On this text by Galvão and its inclusion in what Pina-Cabral calls the 'emotional constitution of colonial power', see Pina-Cabral (2001).

colonial subjects were occasionally softened by this vision of Blacks as children, but they were not at all eliminated.

Although children are typically viewed as nonsexual beings, the Africans – those same 'overgrown children' – are frequently depicted as oversexed. Images of the sensuality, lasciviousness, and insinuating or unbridled sexuality of Black people are commonly invoked in references to the their nudity, immodesty and virility. We can even detect a distinction between the sexuality of men and women. Female sexuality seems to be better tolerated, and is referred to in an 'erotic' register which would probably not have shocked most authors or readers. Male sexuality is depicted in terms of physical prowess, and is assigned a wild, uncontrollable and untamable nature. In the descriptions I have examined, the tone is now one of attraction, now one of repulsion. At the Imperial Conference of 1933, Armindo Monteiro asserted that the 'external nudity' of the Black person was 'the reflection of his moral nudity'. Having settled that, Monteiro then asks: 'Is there still time for the European to save these societies from death, which is all they seem to be waiting for?' Another remark by the colonial minister reveals that the idea of natural selection first proposed by Darwin in the nineteenth century was still in vogue: 'In my view, selection will go about its work and, within a few decades, the Black races which were unable to ascend the gruelling paths to civilization will have disappeared' (*Álbum-Catálogo Oficial* 1934: 86). Some discourse on Native women reveals the relationship between the imagining subject and the imagined 'object'. On many occasions the Native woman was seen as an erotic object, although not always overtly. Some recent authors have described the colonies of European countries as the 'harems of the West'[113] (Young 1995). The language used in reference to Native women often suggests that they were 'easy women', always available. Their dress and jewellery – necklaces, bracelets and hair – are often described at length, in attempts to show that Native women take care of their appearance just as Western women do. Yet these descriptions are based on Western standards of beauty. In his account of the settlement of Cape Verde, which was the outcome of the intermarriage of the Balanta, Papel and Bijago groups of Guinea with Felupe and Jalofe stock, and of intermarriage between women of the aforementioned groups and male Portuguese and Jewish settlers expelled to Cape Verde, Mello describes Cape Verdean women as 'tall, slim, svelte, pretty', with 'elegantly proportioned bodies' and 'big and beautiful eyes, of languid expression and ardently sensual'. Some of these women were

---

113. Robert Young's (1995) book examines the White settlers' obsessive, but not always overtly acknowledged, desire for interracial sex.

like 'statues by Phidias torn from a Greek museum, coated in chocolate, and awakened to sensual life by the tropical sun'; they needed only to go around in the nude for the 'illusion to be complete'. Their dances

> provoke in these distinguished dancers a veritable kinaesthetic frenzy, especially when they dance the *coladeiras,* whose movements are of the most suggestive and immodest lasciviousness (1936b: 60–63).

African women were frequently depicted with their children, the intention being to show that they also possessed a (positive) maternal instinct. Yet they were also seen as lacking in many of the basic skills needed for looking after children. Only by domestication – by being civilized – could they learn the basics of hygiene, how to treat their children better, how to look after their bodies, develop a sense of modesty and dress decently. This reference to hygiene included sexual conduct. The Native woman had to be inculcated with a sense of moral hygiene by the promotion of monogamy, family ideals and Christian principles, in work which was usually carried out by the missions.

On another front, the enemy was superstition and fetishist practices. Cape Verde was cited as an example of the successful propagation of the Catholic religion, although much still remained to be done. According to Mello, 'the Cape Verdeans profess, in their near-totality, the Roman Catholic and Apostolic religion' (1932: 77). The same author also maintains that 'although widely superstitious and still preserving certain fetishist practices', the Cape Verdeans were 'fervently practising Catholics, and as such, monogamous marriage' was 'without exception, the rule among them' (1936b: 60–61). Speaking at the Imperial Conference of 1933, Armindo Monteiro contended that 'Black societies, for centuries organized on the lines of superstition, ideas and forms of discipline', were beginning to be 'shaken' and therefore had 'considerable potential for adapting to a better life' (*Álbum-Catálogo Oficial,* 1934: 86). However, the influence of 'civilization' might also create new elements which, as hybrids, would cause perplexity, as occurred with the languages of the 'colonized populations'. When mixed with Portuguese, these languages – already considered odd in themselves – were dismissed as a 'Black man's babble', full of incomprehensible words. According to Mello, the creole language of Cape Verde was a cocktail of 'dialects of the Blacks of Guinea' and 'the Portuguese language, seasoned with a varied condiment of Brazilianisms, Anglicisms and Gallicisms; and spiced with [other features from] multiple linguistic sources'. Significantly, when mixed with other dialects like 'the Creole of Cape Verde and Guinea, or Macanese', Portuguese was considered to become less masculine (Mello 1936b: 63).

Mestiços[114] themselves were seen as occupying a realm that was neither Black nor White. This ambivalence led many authors to consider them as a phenomenon which could not be clearly located or circumscribed; and this was at the source of great debate on the health and fertility of *Mestiço* offspring. *Mestiços* were described as having unclean or polluted blood, or a higher concentration of melanin.[115] Some of the stereotypes associated with Blacks were extended to *Mestiços* too. If a White father did not recognize a *Mestiço* child as his own, the child would be treated as Black, a bastard who belonged neither to the world of White people or the Black community. But if a White father did recognize a *Mestiço* child as his own, the child might be upgraded to 'Assimilado' status, with the right to move in the circles of the civilization which his father represented. In theory, and if he received an education, he might even aspire to a job in the service of the Portuguese state. Visual representations of the Assimilated *Mestiço* depict individuals whose dress shows they are capable of being civilized – they are usually clothed, most but not all wear shoes – accompanied by a symbol attesting to their redemption (a cross or a statue) or education (a book). And yet the Assimilated *Mestiço* was a figure of ridicule: for not knowing how to match his clothing properly, or for wearing a suit and tie but no shoes, or for wearing only one shoe at a time, to save them. Despite the ridicule he received, he might nevertheless be held up as a good example of assimilation, proof that the ascent to Western civilization was possible. More frequently, however, the *Mestiço* was associated with a raft of negative ideas, as in the following description:

> Instead of being a mixture of the virtues of ... Blacks and Europeans, the Mulatto is a repository of the defects of the two races ... Most of them die while children, but ... many ... grow up ... corrupted by vices ... The *Mestiço* hates the European because he sees in him the intelligence and learning that he himself lacks, and he hates the Black because it was the latter's blood that made him different ... For the consolation of the Whites, I would say that ... there are exceptions, and there are even some *Mulatas* – but these are rare cases – who are only unfaithful ... once a week!!! (Saccadura 1928).

At the Colonial Anthropology Congress, Mendes Correia noted that *Mestiço* numbers had increased considerably, while research on hybrid-

---

114. The term *Mestiço* designated an individual of mixed European and Asian descent. Similar terms were *Mulato* and *Cabrita* (the daughter of a *Mestiço* woman and a White man).

115. The liking for melanization was for long held in disdain by European Albinos. Melanism is the term used to designate darker skin pigmentations.

ism among the Blacks of Cape Verde and the Chinese of Macao had shown that physically the results were closer to the 'Blacks' and 'Yellow men' than the Portuguese (Correia 1934a: 331–49). And 'in view of the supreme interests of the nation and of humanity', Monteiro argued that hybridism should not be encouraged (Correia, 1934a). The *Mestiço*, then, did not belong to any predefined human type. With regard to phenotypical characteristics, however, he is described according to the characteristic features of Blacks. It was through 'culture', the acquisition of knowledge and social ascent, that the *Mestiço* could gain access to the civilized world – not the fact that he was fairer-skinned than a Black person.

In the case of women – *Mestiças, Mulatas* and *Cabritas* – the discourse is very fertile. The *Mestiça* is viewed as oversexed; she is believed to have the power – invested in her beauty, or in a fetish – to cast spells over the White man (this is a clear allusion to the African side of her descent). Images of the *Mestiça* emphasize both her nudity (and thereby her proximity to the untamed, natural world) and her dress – clothing and 'accessories' such as headgear, wraps and shawls. The *Mestiça* is also frequently depicted performing tasks typical of the Western woman. One of the albums published as part of the Exhibition of the Portuguese World contains a photograph of a Cape Verdean woman with the caption 'Creole woman doing crochet' (Galvão 1940). This evidenced contact between the *Mestiça* and the civilized world. Thus, both *Mestiço* and *Mestiça* are represented as a mixture, not only biologically, but also in sociocultural terms.

All of the representations we have examined here have been based on Western standards of evaluation, and thus they reveal the prejudices of their authors. White people are generally associated with power in one form or another, while the Natives, especially the Africans, are bereft of it. Since these representations were not generally questioned in their day, racial discrimination was not a subtle or obfuscatory process but an explicit one, with supposedly scientific data cited to buttress certain ideas. This is the case, for example, of many of the studies in 'physical anthropology'. On the nonacademic level, there was a tendency in sketches and cartoons to heap ridicule on the Black person. Not only are 'Negroid' characteristics such as dark skin, thick lips, curly hair and flattened nose exaggerated, the discrimination is also in the setting. Blacks are invariably depicted in a position of servility relative to White people; they are shown as being poor, and unlikely to escape from this historically inherited station any time soon. It seems some of the Natives themselves felt this discrimination. Their facial expressions are usually unhappy, wearied, melancholy, remote. And what if Natives stopped being 'primitive' and became *Assimilados* with access to civilization? Would they stop being childish, would they lose their innocence and idleness and rise to a position of importance in Portuguese society? The Natives are frequently seen as incapable of organizing themselves collectively or as lacking the power to confront the colonial authorities. But they also had no public representation in government,[116] and neither did they have access to the jobs available to settlers. For Portugal to remain in Africa it was necessary that certain groups, viewed as inferior, lacking in evangelization and civilization, should continue to exist. Had the Natives become civilized citizens with full rights, it would no longer have made sense to talk of civilizing them.

The production of 'anthropological knowledge' of the colonies

In this section we will see how anthropological studies in the Portuguese colonies generated certain representations of the 'colonized populations', and examine the underlying relationship between anthropological studies and colonial power. One of the texts that provided great inspiration for this book was by Mendes Correia (1918), a work based on notes taken by Fonseca Cardoso during his research in Angola at the end of the nineteenth century. The following excerpt from Mendes Correia makes reference to many of the metrics that were used to produce colonial anthropological knowledge:

> Skin colour was: in 2, from no. 28 on the Broca scale, i.e. a chocolate tone; in 1, from no. 29 on the same scale, i.e. a lighter tone, reddish brown; in 1, from nos. 29–30, i.e. between dark yellow (no. 30) and the previous … The Cassequel woman, a native of Culuio … was of skin colour no. 44, old parchment yellow, dark brown eyes, mesaticephalic (ceph. ind. 78.8), hyper-platyrrhinic (nasal ind. 109.1), almost *dolicopsida* (anterior ind. 60.4), total facial index 101.6, Cuvier facial angle 69°[117] (M. Correia, 1918: 292–293; 317).

---

116. The idea that the Native element should be represented in the governments of the colonies originates in the Administrative Code for the Colonies, drafted in 1881 by Júlio de Vilhena. It contained the proposal that the colonial governments or *conselhos* be composed only of appointed members, 'two of which should obligatorily be selected from among the Indigenous element, without distinction of race or religion'. But the code was never enacted and as late as 1935 the colonial governments were dominated by state clerks and other appointees, with no Native representation.

117. From research by Fonseca Cardoso, published after his death.

From the 1870s to the 1950s, Portugal could not properly lay claim to any tradition in social and cultural anthropology in its colonies – this despite defining itself as a colonial power. The anthropological research conducted within Portugal mainly focused on popular, essentially rural, culture. This research was probably the reflection of a desire at the time to seek and affirm a supposed national identity. Yet studies of the rural, indigenous population of Portugal and of the colonial populations 'were carried out separately' (Pina-Cabral 1991: 15). By the start of the twentieth century, there were increasing calls for scientific research in the colonies. Yet the colonial powers of Europe remained remote from the British model of indirect administration, which was based on knowledge of the colonized societies.[118] There was no great investment in scientific projects – by state or private enterprise – in Portugal. As late as 1940 João F. Rodrigues observed in a review of the groundwork legislation that 'the cultural and higher educational institutions of the colonies ... were not coordinating their efforts as they ought to be' (1940: 71). The first moves towards the creation of museums of ethnography and anthropology (and the institutions responsible for running them) had come at the close of the nineteenth century. Significantly, they tended to operate alongside (or as part of) disciplines such as zoology and natural history. Thus, the Museu Bocage (the 'national museum of natural history') brought together zoology and anthropology, while the Faculty of Science of the University of Porto had a Department of Zoology and Anthropology, and the Museum of Anthropology of the University of Coimbra operated under the aegis of the university's Museum of Natural History, which had sections devoted to zoology, mineralogy, geology and botany.

It was in Coimbra, too, that anthropology was first officially studied in Portugal. The chair of Anthropology, Human Palaeontology and Prehistoric Archaeology, part of the Faculty of Philosophy, was created by

---

118. In the British context, however, the development of anthropology was inseparable from the political and ideological issues of the interwar period (Goody 1995). While on the one hand anthropologists worked in the service of political interests, on the other they documented the social and cultural realities of the populations they studied, and in their appreciation and dissemination of these realities they clearly contributed to the affirmation of anthropology as a discipline. Goody (1995) examines the way the different views of a nascent discipline were influenced by the institutions that cultivated it. In the 1930s, for example, one anthropological study was financed by an American foundation, not the British colonial powers. Goody also attempts to ascertain whether the discipline based its affirmation on contemporary determining factors such as colonialism, the continuing subjugation of the African territories to British rule, anti-Semitism or communism. Goody discusses these issues in light of the work of anthropologists such as Malinowski, Fortes, Radcliffe-Brown and Evans-Pritchard.

Bernardino Machado (1851–1944) in a charter dated 2 July 1885.[119]
In the early years of its existence, the chosen areas of research were
mainly in the field of 'physical anthropology'. For the academic year
1887–88, the recommended manuals were the *Manuel d'anthropologie*
by Paul Topinard (188?), *Instructions cranéologiques et cranéométriques,
de la Société d'Anthropologie de Paris* by Paul Broca (1875) and *Le Préhistorique, antiquité de l'homme* by Gabriel Mortillet.[120] Dissertations for
anthropology were on subjects ranging from osteology, ethnography
and sociology, to anthropometry and human ecology. Between 1907
and 1950, Eusébio Tamagnini[121] (minister for education from 1934 to
1936), the successor to Bernardino Machado (twice elected president
of Portugal), was the professor who held the chair of Anthropology,
managing the Anthropology and Prehistoric Archaeology section of
Coimbra's Museum of Natural History. Anthropology was now divided
into two separate areas: 'Zoological Anthropology' (Tamagnini's designation), which was designed as a general introduction to 'Primatology',
and 'Ethnological Anthropology', whose focus was the study and char-
acterization of the 'human races' (Areia and Rocha 1985: 17–18). The
University of Coimbra also created a course in colonial ethnography,[122]
whose programme, drawn up by João Gualberto de Barros e Cunha in
1912–13, stressed the importance 'for the colonizing peoples' of 'accurate knowledge of the ethnography of the *Indígenas* of their colonies'.[123]
Practically the whole course was dedicated to the peoples of Africa, their
social organizations and the objects they produced, although the populations of India, Macao and Timor were also taken into consideration.
Another component of anthropological study was the course in criminal
anthropology, officially introduced in 1908–9 and designated a 'Course
in Anthropometry'. 'Ethnological Anthropology' never evolved beyond
the incipient phase, despite the many collections of 'material culture'
that were assembled. However, the ethnological anthropology module,
whose programme described it as a 'general introduction to racial studies', did continue to be administered to students of the Faculty of Arts.
For the academic year of 1929–30, its study programme included such

---

119. Published in no. 149 of the *Diário do Governo*, 9 July.

120. See the *Anuário da Universidade de Coimbra*, 1887–88: 173.

121. On the work of Tamagnini in the Instituto de Antropologia of Coimbra, see
G. D. dos Santos (1996).

122. The University of Coimbra had introduced a colonial course in its Faculty of Law
as early as December 1901. This course was directed by Rui Ulrich and Marnoco e Sousa
between 1905 and 1910.

123. One of the introductory topics to the course programme, cited in Areia and
Rocha (1985: 18).

subjects as 'Ethnology and Ethnography – General Considerations', 'Notions of Species and Race', 'Distinctive Characters of the Races', 'Skin Colour, Melanins etc.', 'Diverse Anthropometric Indexes', 'Classification of the Human Races', 'The Classification of Topinard', 'The Classification of Deniker', 'The Classification of Strats', 'The Classification of Schertz, Ruggeri, Haddan'. Under these headings, Tamagnini and his disciples carried out research in somatometry and osteometry, physiology and biodemographics. Coimbra's perspective on anthropology was similar to the *Rassenkunde* approach of the German school. For the 1939–40 academic year, the anthropology course continued to include in its programme modules such as 'Comparative Morphology of Present-day Hominids', 'Anthropometry', 'Osteometry', 'Craniometry', 'Morphological Types in Present-day Hominids' and 'Notions of Species and Race in the Light of Genetic Principles' (Areia and Rocha 1985: 21, 52).

The programme for 1929–30 had cited melanin as a possible basis for racial classification; by measuring pigmentation, it was possible to establish a tonal spectrum on which comparisons could be based. This same thesis was upheld by José Antunes Serra[124] at the National Congress of Population Sciences, where he argued that 'pigmentation is the basis for classification of the major races' (1940). In the nineteenth century, certain authors had attempted to establish standards according to which different skin tones could be classified; to do so, they established tables or scales designed to accommodate a broad chromatic spectrum, such as those of Fischer or Fischer-Saller for hair, Martin or Saller and Schultz-Hesch for eyes, and the printed colours suggested by Broca (1879). But as Serra pointed out, there was no numeric correspondence between one scale and another: different researchers used different scales, and there was no objective correlation between one author's scale and another. Not only that, some scales were better suited to certain population groups and less well suited to others. Serra argued that it was preferable to use these scales rather than vague terms like 'fair', 'ash-coloured', 'red-headed' or 'brown'; yet, since differences in skin colour were essentially due to different levels of melanin, in-depth study of pigmentation required the use of quantitative metrics and the appropriate colorimeters. The 'international colour nomenclature' was already being used in colorimetry, according to which the perception of colour as associated with

---

124. Having obtained his degree and doctorate in biological sciences from the University of Coimbra in 1936 and 1939 respectively, Serra went on to participate in congresses and submitted papers for the International Scientific Exhibition organized by UNESCO in 1946.

a 'standard' observer was always the same, regardless of the colorimeter being used. Therefore, argued Serra, it was better still to use 'truly quantitative' methods for determining colour, instead of scales.

The School of Anthropology of Porto also played a major role in developing anthropological knowledge. Among its leading figures were Mendes Correia, Santos Júnior and António de Almeida. Of the three, Mendes Correia's work was probably the best known, and the most influential. Correia also founded the University of Porto's Instituto de Investigação Científica de Antropologia, and was president of the SPAE (founded in 1918). Correia published several texts on the 'race' issue, including *Raça e Nacionalidade* (1919b)[125] and *Raças do Império* (1943). But he also wrote on groups considered to be deviant or abnormal, such as criminals (in the tradition of Lombroso) and children, and on subjects such as prehistoric archaeology and geography. In the 1930s, António de Almeida and Santos Júnior began to gain a reputation with the articles they published on physical anthropology and the colonial populations, as we can see by the papers they presented at the Colonial Anthropology Congress of 1934.

Another significant event was the creation of anthropological missions in the colonies (initially confined to Mozambique) with the task of compiling anthropometric data. These missions were given the official seal of approval in legislation introduced in 1935 by Vieira Machado.[126] As the text of this legislation[127] stated, the objective of these missions was to gain 'knowledge of the ethnic groups of each of our overseas dominions, i.e. the compilation of their respective ethnological charts' (S. Júnior 1956: 6). Missions were sent to Guinea, Angola, Mozambique, São Tomé e Príncipe and Timor. In 1937, further legislation[128] introduced by Vieira Machado authorized a second campaign for the furtherance of anthropological, archaeological and ethnographic research in Mozambique (*O Século* 1940b: 49). The first mission to Mozambique had been in 1936; others were dispatched in 1937, 1945, 1946, 1948

---

125. This book is no longer to be found in the library of the University of Porto's Faculty of Sciences.

126. The anthropological missions were 'dependent on the Council of Geographic Missions and Colonial Research' and each was constituted by: 'a leader (an anthropologist of recognized competence)'; 'one or more adjutants and helpers (appointed by the leader)'; 'personnel from the local colonial administration'; and any 'European or Indigenous personnel' that the mission leaders considered necessary ('Anthropological and Ethnographic Missions to the Colonies', *Decreto-Lei* no. 34 478, 1951: 146–47).

127. *Decreto* no. 34 478 of 3 April 1935.

128. *Decreto-Lei* no. 27 922.

and 1955. All were headed by Santos Júnior,[129] assistant lecturer in the Faculty of Science at the University of Porto, who held a scholarship from the Instituto para a Alta Cultura and the Junta de Missões Coloniais and had studied under Mendes Correia. The work of the later missions was more sociocultural in scope, with studies on the diet and material culture of the Natives (housing, apparel), but no attempt was made to insert this research into a systematic framework and nowhere do we find descriptions of social structure. The anthropological missions to Mozambique produced '44 studies, of which only 14 address ethnographic topics' (R. Pereira 1986: 193) – although 'ethnography' was not understood in the same way then as it is now. For Moutinho (1982), the explanations and justifications produced by Portuguese colonial ethnology were ultimately utilitarian: they supported colonialism by underpinning its ideological structure.

The Centro de Estudos de Etnologia Peninsular (CEEP)[130] was created in 1945, under the direction of Mendes Correia. The CEEP did include an ethnological dimension in its work (ethnology at this time was the poor relation of anthropology, which essentially meant physical anthropology). Mendes Correia invited Jorge Dias (later appointed the centre's director) to organize the centre's ethnographic section. Dias was accompanied by a team of assistants (Margot Dias, Fernando Galhano [1904–95], Ernesto Veiga de Oliveira [1910–90] and Benjamim Pereira) who worked with him on research in Portuguese ethnology and ethnography – a different field from the SPAE, whose remit was centred on physical anthropology. Among the junior members of Dias's team were António Carreira (1905–88), Fernando Quintino and Viegas Guerreiro (1912–97). In 1949, the centre was divided into various sections: prehistory (directed by Mendes Correia), physical anthropology and human biology (directed by Alfredo Athayde), and ethnography (directed by Jorge Dias). The work of Dias and his assistants marked a renaissance in ethnological studies in Portugal, after the original generation of Leite de Vasconcelos, Adolfo Coelho, Teófilo Braga, Consiglieri

---

129. For a full list of the works published as part of the Anthropological Missions to Mozambique, see S. Júnior (1956). On the missions to the colonies, see M. Correia (1945) and S. Júnior (1937a, 1937b, 1938a, 1938b, 1944a, 1944b).

130. This was followed in 1954 by the creation of the Centro de Estudos de Etnologia do Ultramar (CEEU), with the assistance of the Instituto Superior de Estudos Ultramarinos (ISEU) and Junta de Investigações do Ultramar (JIU). The overseas front was part of the CEEU's brief, and its mission was to encourage 'not exclusively biological study of the dominated populations'; and yet 'research of an eminently anthropobiological nature continued to be encouraged' (R. Pereira 1986: 194).

Pedroso and Rocha Peixoto. Now, however, ethnology was an independent discipline, with its own methods and practices (R. Pereira 1989: 66). In 1956 Dias and his team began working from Lisbon.

Anthropological knowledge of the Portuguese colonies still lagged a good way behind the trends then emerging in Europe, in which the importance of sociocultural aspects was increasingly recognized. The scientific anachronism was evident. While social anthropology in Britain, for example, was by now more sensitive to the study of social life, Portugal – and in a similar fashion Germany – continued to insist on the study of somatic features. This approach was a holdover from the early years of the twentieth century, when anthropology went to great lengths to define and classify the physical nature and origin of the 'races' – and by extension their culture – in its attempts to ascertain their respective degrees of development. Many of these racial classifications established a fundamental distinction between 'White', 'Yellow' and 'Black'. Within the 'White' – or Caucasian or European – category, subdistinctions were drawn between Alpine, Nordic, Mediterranean and Dinaric. These classifications were arbitrary, and depended upon the ethnocentric perspective of their inventors. Furthermore, the evolutionist ideas that had made their mark in every sphere of thought and fuelled the emergence of racial classifications continued (despite a few 'signs of crisis') to exert an influence on European thought until the end of the nineteenth century, and in Portugal were current well into the early years of the twentieth century. Until the Holocaust, 'scientific' theories on race, eugenics and racial purity rose to their highest pitch of expression, and in so doing reinforced existing colonial practices. It was in this phase that anthropology and politics mutually reinforced each other to such an extent that it is tempting to say that one was at the service of the other. There was little fieldwork in Portuguese anthropology at this time: instead of going into the field (Africa, Asia), Portuguese anthropologists preferred to let the field come to them, in the form of data collected in situ by others, which they then used in their laboratories for observation and analysis. One person gathered the materials, another elaborated the theories, and the former often lacked any academic training, relying solely on the instructions of others. Data was often ambiguous and the conclusions of questionnaires of little use, or even wrong.

However, some anthropologists believed that by knowing the Natives physically, they could better contribute to the 'colonial venture' by making it more rational; because not all Natives had the same physical characteristics or the same abilities, they argued, some were better suited to certain tasks than others. One way of bringing the field to the laboratory was to bring colonial Natives to Portugal, as occurred in the exhibitions of 1934 and 1940. Measurements made on the Natives on show at the 1940 exhibition formed the basis for the compilation of a 'Somatological and Somatometric Register' (Jorge and Sueiro, 1942). Under the guidance of Ricardo Jorge, director of the Museu Bocage, one hundred and fifty *Indígenas* (one hundred and nine men and forty-one women) classified by 'colony', 'tribe' and 'sex' – the race parameter was absent – were subjected to a battery of 'anthropological observations'.[131] Thirty-seven examinees came from Guinea (fifteen Bijago, eight Fula, ten Mandinka, four Saraculé), thirty-eight from Angola (five Bushmen, five Nzinga, eight Muchicongo, seven Sosso, thirteen Tchipungo), sixty-one from Mozambique (thirty-nine Bachope, twelve Basenga, two Machanga, six Makonde, two Vanhais), eight from Macao, and six from Timor. There were no representatives from India and no mention is made of India in the resulting report. The measurements were filed in the museum's archives and each Native was assigned a dossier[132] containing four 'bulletins': bulletin A – somatological examination and blood group; bulletin B – photographic record (individual nude, anterior, posterior and lateral [right and left] views, head, individual 'with characteristic garments and adornments', special bodily features, such as 'tattoos and somatic anomalies'); bulletin C – prints of hands and feet (palmar and plantar surfaces, fingerprints); and bulletin D – anthropometric examination. A fifth category, bulletin E, recorded indexes (on the basis of category D) and compiled canons. In the 'somatic examination' (based on Rudolf Martin's *Textbook of Anthropology*), examinees were appraised on the basis of elements such as bone structure, musculature, state of nutrition, skin, eye colour, hair, distribution of body hair, 'asymmetries, defects and deformities', tattoos, 'ethnic mutilations (head, nose, ears, upper lip, lower lip, teeth, breasts, genital organs, hands, feet)', face ('general shape of face', cheeks, eyes, nose, mouth, ears), torso, breasts ('degree of development', size, shape, firmness, areola, nipple), back, shoulders, abdomen, navel, genital organs (penis, testicles, clitoris, labia majora, labia minora), upper limbs and lower limbs. The somatometric bulletin (also based on Martin) contained around 150 measurements of head and body, taken using models developed by Broca and other anthropobiologists.

---

131. These 'observations' were conducted by Ricardo Jorge (somatic examinations), Manuel Barbosa Sueiro (head measurements), Fernando Portela Gomes and Eduardo Côrte Real (body measurements).

132. The identification profile of each Native specified: colony, district or municipality, tribe, name, sex, age, place of birth, extraction or parentage, offspring (for women), parents' birthplace – name of father and mother, tribe of father and mother – profession, language, religion, and habitual place of residence.

It is tempting, in fact, to conclude that ideas from the other side of the Atlantic – those of Boas and other anthropologists of the American school, as well as Malinowski (1884–1942),[133] who was one of the first anthropologists to keep a field diary,[134] and other representatives of British social anthropology – had made no impact in Portugal, which remained isolated from emerging trends in anthropology that primarily valued the social and cultural aspects of humanity. These ideas did not make their appearance in Portugal until the 1950s, in the work of Jorge Dias in particular, who, after conducting fieldwork in his research in Portugal, took a scientific expedition to Mozambique to study the Makonde (1956–60). By taking his work to the field,[135] Dias united two previously separate practices: the collection of field data and the formulation of theories based on its analysis and interpretation. And yet although Dias's work consummated the break with physical anthropology, anthropobiology continued to flourish through the 1950s and '60s. Theoretically, and despite its emphasis on measurement and classification, anthropobiology was not necessarily a tool for racial discrimination. And yet many of the conclusions drawn from the studies conducted in the name of anthropobiology were superfluous, often pejorative in tone and in many instances seemed merely to exalt the status not of the group under examination but of the examiners themselves. Mendes Correia had mentioned Boas, who replaced the concept of race with the concept of culture, attacked the methods of classical 'physical anthropology' and argued that humans were influenced by their environment and 'culture', in a text of 1919. But for Correia, human variations were to be explained mainly in terms of internal, innate causes:

---

133. Malinowski was the first anthropologist to keep a field diary in the modern sense of the term; contrary to the standard practice of the late nineteenth and early twentieth centuries, when anthropologists relied on travellers, missionaries and traders to collect data and distribute questionnaires for them, Malinowski worked directly in the field.

134. See *A Diary in the Strict Sense of the Term* (1967), with observations collected between 1914 and 1918.

135. This was the principle behind the creation of the Ethnic Minorities Study Mission to Overseas Portugal (MEMEUP) in 1957. Other members of the team assigned to this mission were Viegas Guerreiro and Margot Dias (the wife of Jorge Dias). This team travelled to Mozambique on various occasions between 1956 and 1960. The group selected for their research were the Makonde of northern Mozambique. The research findings were published in a series of field reports and in the four-volume monograph *Os Macondes de Moçambique*, published from 1961 (vol. 1) to 1966 (vol. 4). The first volume was republished in 1998 by the Comissão Nacional para as Comemorações dos Descobrimentos Portugueses (CNCDP) and the Instituto de Investigação Científica e Tropical (IICT).

Through heredity, the types persist down the generations ... Modern, determinist science cannot but prefer neo-Lamarckism which, thus conceived, is the application of the determinist criterion in explaining evolution ... All who from Hippocrates to Buffon, and from Buffon to the present day, have sought to explain the differences between the human races by the influence of climate, temperature, humidity, light ... have almost always placed the value of these influences higher than skin and hair colour ... We are well acquainted with the claims of Franz Boas that the physical type of immigrants to America underwent, from one generation to its immediate successor, modifications attributed to the influence of the environment and perhaps of selection ... Adaptation is a universal process of evolution ... but that does not mean that the subjection of living beings to external conditions is absolute and binding. Adaptation also involves subordination to the internal conditions of ... interorganic affinity, which only certain morphological states make possible (1919a: 1–30).

We can conclude that Mendes Correia incorporated some of the new ideas, but not others; and that this attitude was deliberate. In over a hundred texts by Mendes Correia known to me, further reference to Boas is found in only one, from 1962. By this point Correia accepts that racial hierarchies make no sense, but continues to uphold the validity of raciology:

> Racism is worthy of combat, but raciology ... is something else. This is a legitimate [field of] study, unlike racist exaggerations, [or] the generalizations at which we have supposedly arrived with regard to the classificatory value of the races from the point of view of a socio-political hierarchy (M. Correia 1962: 153, 222).

Leaving out the ethnographic work of the colonial agents and missions, ethnological research in Portugal's overseas colonies properly began with the work of Jorge Dias and his team. Dias may be seen as an exception, as R. Pereira (1986: 231) notes, for his ethnological research was more rigorous, exhaustive and scientifically valid than earlier work in the same field. And yet it was not totally independent; it was still influenced by the imperatives of colonial policy and even certain contemporary anthropobiological research. Dias himself claimed that to study the populations was to analyze their somatic characters. And as late as 1961 he wrote:

> The so-called *human races* ... all belong to the same species ... Deriving from a common origin, they gradually became differentiated through their adaptation to different natural environments, thanks to a selective process and via genetic mutations and regroupings, which in turn are subject to natural selection ... It was to us Portuguese that befell the

prodigious task ... of roaming the seas, making contact with the wildest peoples (1961: 150, 157).

Nevertheless, as stated above, Dias's work did have positive qualities, and it was clearly influenced (in the 1950s) by the American cultural anthropology of Boas and his disciples.[136] Later, Dias was to celebrate the diversity and ethnogenealogical pluralism of the Portuguese, which he attributed to their special capacity for miscegenation:

> The ethnic unity of the Portuguese, which resulted from the mixture of various sub-races of the Caucasoid race, to which at a later stage were mixed ... Negroid and Mongoloid elements ... [contributed] to give the Portuguese enormous human plasticity and an unusual ecumenical sense (1971).

The fact that these themes are addressed together was perhaps a consequence of Dias's assimilation of the Luso-tropicalist theories of Gilberto Freyre.[137] And then there was the subject chosen by Dias for his research – the Makonde of Mozambique. At a time when rebellion was beginning to ferment among the Natives of this country, it was political rather than sociocultural interest that informed his choice. It is important, therefore, to remember the context in which Dias's work was produced. Things would certainly have been different had this work taken place at another time.

Also active in colonial studies was the ESC. Founded in 1906 as the Escola Colonial, it introduced a course in colonial ethnology with the reorganization of its curriculum[138] in 1919. The Escola Colonial changed its name to Escola Superior Colonial[139] in 1927, and kept this designation until 1954–55, when it was renamed the Instituto Superior de Estudos Ultramarinos (ISEU). Another name change came in 1961, when it was rechristened the Instituto Superior de Ciências Sociais e Política Ultramarina (ISCSPU). At present it is called the Instituto Superior de Ciências Sociais e Políticas (ISCSP), a name it has had since 1974. The names of the courses it administered also changed. The 'Colonial Course' became the 'General Colonial Course' in 1919, which in turn was renamed the 'Higher Colonial Course' in 1927. The study programme of the ESC was again altered in 1946. The legislation[140] under

---

136. The American school of anthropology had its roots in Germany, for it was Boas's formative years in Germany which were the key influence in the emergence of American cultural anthropology.

137. On the reception of Freyre's work in Portugal, see Castelo (1998).

138. See *Anuário da Escola Colonial,* ESC, 1919–20 (vol. 1) to 1923–24 (vol. 5).

139. See *Anuário da Escola Superior Colonial,* ESC, 1924–27 (vols. 6–8) to 1953–54 (vol. 35); see also *Estudos Coloniais: Revista da Escola Superior Colonial.*

140. *Decreto-lei* no. 35 885/46.

which the programme was changed introduced an innovation, 'the investigation of scientific problems connected with the valorization of the overseas territories, European settlement of tropical Africa and the study of Native populations and their languages', into the work of the ESC. The ESC now offered two colonial courses: colonial administration and higher colonial studies.[141] Graduates of these courses could look forward to careers as colonial district managers, secretaries or administrators, and could even aspire to a post as governor. At this time there existed a desire – shared by Norton de Matos – to found a colonial university in which the 'colonial mentality' could be 'created and consolidated' via 'ethnographic museums, photographs, aspects of the people and things of the colonies, a colonial garden, and everything that would familiarize the future functionary as much as possible' (1944: vol. 1, 180). This desire never materialized. The ISCSPU (the successor of the ESC) came closest to embodying it.

The instruction offered by the ESC was by no means restricted to anthropology. However, the Higher Colonial Course did include a component on colonial anthropology,[142] as part of the course in Colonial Ethnology and Ethnography directed by António de Almeida. Almeida had previously collected some 'anthropological' material in Angola, but in view of the difficulties in sending scientific missions to the colonies, he favoured training functionaries in the collection of anthropometric and ethnographic data to obtain 'better knowledge of the anthropology of the various peoples of our great Empire'. Furthermore, the lack of 'individuals born in the colonies' in metropolitan Portugal made it difficult to conduct descriptive and somatometric examinations[143] with students. Announcements placed in the Lisbon daily newspapers succeeded in mustering a few Natives of Cape Verde, Guinea, Cabinda and Mozambique. Attempts were also made to recruit the assistance of Angolan cattle drivers on their visits to Lisbon. Word got around, and many reported to the ESC 'to be measured'. Almeida asked the Instituto para a Alta Cultura to pay these Natives for taking part in anthropological examinations. For Almeida, it 'was worthy of notice that individuals of considerable intellectual formation submitted themselves to so time-

---

141. The new legislation also called for philological and linguistic study of the languages and dialects spoken in the colonies, and the creation of an 'Institute of African Languages'.

142. The programme included subjects such as 'human morphobiology', 'anthropometry in practice', 'analysis and interpretation of the psychological manifestations of peoples of backwards civilization', etc.

143. Somatometry is the branch of physical anthropology which deals with measurements of the body, while somatology is the study of the anatomy and phsyiology of the human body.

consuming and inconvenient an examination': 'Of the Brahmins examined, one is a doctor and two are students at higher colleges in Lisbon;
the Macanese of Portuguese extraction also attend higher institutes of
education in the capital' ([1937] 1940a: 71–72).

Among the texts and treatises generally prescribed by the ESC were:
Lições de Antropologia by Mendes Correia (this book was also required
reading in the anthropology course offered by the Faculty of Sciences
at the University of Porto); *Lições de Antropologia* (also prescribed for
the anthropology course at the Faculty of Sciences at the University of
Lisbon); *Les races et les peuples de la Terre* by J. Deniker; *Lerhbuch der
anthropologie* by Rudolf Martin; *Éléments d'anthropologie générale* (1885)
by Paul Topinard;[144] *Etnologia e Etnografia Coloniais* by Lopo Vaz de
Sampaio e Mello; and *Populações indígenas de Angola* by Ferreira Diniz.
In his *Lehrbuch*, Rudolf Martin defined anthropology as the study of
the 'races' based on measurements – a definition close to that of the
French tradition represented by Broca and Topinard. In a text by A.
Almeida enumerating the studies on 'colonial anthropology' carried out
in the ESC – research which principally belonged to the sphere of physical anthropology, and whose objective was to differentiate, classify and
hierarchize – we find the interesting idea that Portugal was a civilizing
country 'without distinction of race or of colour, through the ages, in
the past and in the present' ([1937] 1940a: 7).

The findings of the anthropological research conducted at the ESC
were published in the ESC yearbooks of the 1930s and '40s, and these
give us a good picture of the themes and topics addressed. Professo-
rial research included[145] an 'Ethnographic Sketch of the Population of
Cape Verde' by Mello, which addressed aspects such as demographics,
religious practices, diet, 'matrimonial customs', 'dances and music' and
'linguistic features', with specific data on each island of the archipelago.
The author concludes that the Cape Verdeans are 'peaceful, rather indo-
lent, fond of revelry and very superstitious, something that stems from
a not too remote ancestral fetishist tradition' (1932: 82). Examples of
research by students include: 'Mestiços (Mulattoes of Mozambique)' by
Judah Bento Ruah, which concludes that 'the colony of Mozambique

---

144. Some of these texts were half a century old at the time, an illustration of just how
out of date the ESC's anthropology course was in terms of its bibliography.

145. Other titles: 'Anthropological and Ethnographic Investigations in Angola' by
A. Almeida ([1942–43] 1944); 'Savage and Civilized' by José Gonçalo de Santa-Rita
([1944] 1945); 'Contribution to Anthropological Research on the Population of the
Dembos (Angola) on the Vital Capacity of the Adult Male of the Mahungo and Luango'
by A. Almeida ([1943–44] 1945); and 'Socio-economic Basis for a Policy of Contact
Between Races' by Matoso Pio ([1944–45] 1945).

... is an environment hostile to mulattoes' and 'the *Mestiço* ... is a being physically weaker than his progenitors and is therefore possessed of all the defects inherent to the weak' (1932: 410); 'An Ethnographic, Ethnological and Anthropological Sketch of the Colony of Mozambique' by Leopoldo José Ródam Trindade (1937), based on the features and somatometric data of three Mozambicans – one Landin, one Bitonga and one Makua – who had lived in Lisbon since adolescence; and 'Contributions to a Research Programme on the Study of Indigenous Education and Instruction Processes in our Colonial Empire' by Francisco Ferro Murinello ([1940–41] 1942). All in all, the output is scant, given the number of students attending the school. The professors themselves produced only a limited amount of work. Probably the most significant contribution was made by António de Almeida, who was better acquainted with colonial realities.

Racial fixity and the invention of 'human types'

One notion frequently found in the study of race is that of fixity. Although it was strongly monogenist in its views of the origins of humanity, evolutionism also took on board certain polygenist notions, especially that of the fixity of the races, an idea which acquired importance with the emergence of the idea of fundamental racial 'types' in racial classification. From the mid-nineteenth century onwards, the abstract concept of 'racial type' began to be seen as something concrete, palpable and visible. 'Type' now became a standard by which one could identify various individuals of the same provenance, and establish parameters for identifying the members of a given 'race' (Edwards 1990: 240). The evaluative emphasis was placed not on the context in which the subject lived, but on his or her physical characteristics. With the idea of 'racial type', the apparent, phenotypical, difference was explained on the basis of internal, biological data, which could not be seen but were believed to be there. As Mendes Correia argued:

> As in biology the physical characteristics are the most stable and the easiest to observe with accuracy, it is in these characteristics that the notion of race is founded. Race can be described as a 'hereditary physical type' (1915: 13–14).

Thus humanity could be classified and placed on different levels of the evolutionary ladder, and comparisons drawn between the different levels. As an anonymous concept, 'type' nullified individuality, identifying only the group, or the place, to which he or she belonged. For example, expressions such as 'Cape Verde type', 'Biafada type' and 'Bijago type' were used to designate the members of certain groups. Every person belonging to a 'type' was assumed to behave in the same way, and to have the same habits and beliefs.

The paper entitled 'The Constitutional Morphological Type of the *Indígenas* of Angónia (District of Tete)' presented by A. Liz Ferreira at the Colonial Congress of 1940 shows the influence of the classical taxonomies of human 'types', as do other studies in human morphology from the same period. Kretschmer (*La Structure du Corps et le Caractère,* 1927), for instance, classified the 'types' as leptosomic, athletic, squat or abnormal-dysplastic, while C. Sigaud (*Traité Clinique de la Digestion,* 1908), his disciple Léon Mac-Auliffe (*Les Tempéraments,* 1926) and others proposed a division between respiratory, digestive, muscular and cerebral types. To these four categories Mac-Auliffe added two more, the 'round types' and the 'irregular types'. The 'round types' were characterized by harmonious development; they represented the ideal of beauty, were seen as superior and could be exemplified by the statues of ancient Greece and the Renaissance. At the other end of the scale were the 'primitive types', examples of inferior humanity found in different parts of the globe or represented by criminals and other socially excluded groups. What we have here is not only an example of the theories formulated on the basis of the evolutionist ideas still current in Europe (Darwin, Lamarck, Morgan), but also an example of how the Renaissance ideal of beauty influenced the way beauty and superiority were associated with Europeans.

Morphology sought to determine the illnesses and predispositions which were associated with each of the 'types' defined in this way.[146] At the Colonial Exhibition of 1934, the Anthropology Institute of Porto used the method devised by Giacinto Viola[147] to determine the comparative dimensions of the torso and limbs of Native examinees. Another objective of the classification of biological diversity by 'types' was to determine which physical, mental and psychological capacities were associated with each type. By the proper mapping of these capacities to their respective types, Natives could be assigned the work for which they were most suited, making it easier to 'domesticate' them. This was scientific racism, similar to what we encountered in the nineteenth century.

---

146. On these topics see, for example, Baudet et al. (1977).

147. This method was based on measurements taken on an 'anthropometric balance' on which the individual was made to lie down. It distinguished between two human types: the 'brevilinear' and the 'longilinear'.

However, the concept of 'race' was gradually losing its typological connotations and moving closer to the concept of 'population group', and the emphasis now fell on aspects such as 'variability' and 'dynamism'. The initial concept was not abandoned, in other words, but rather re-formed, the better to fit with neo-Darwinian evolutionism, which was a major influence on the physical anthropology of the mid-twentieth century. The work of Darwin and other evolutionists[148] of the second half of the nineteenth century constituted what Mayr (1982) designated the 'first Darwinian revolution'. According to Darwin ([1859] 1968), all species descended from common ancestral stock and had evolved over time via a process of natural selection. But Darwin's theory was not actually embraced as an orthodoxy of modern biology until the 1940s, the period Mayr (1982) terms the 'second Darwinian revolution'. The neo-Darwinian paradigm brought together previously disparate strands, ranging from Mendelianism and its explanation of the transmission of hereditary characteristics to Darwinism itself, in its attempts to determine the origin and evolution of the species; and it also employed bio-metric studies, which attempted to map genetic data to morphological characteristics. With its emphasis on change, Darwinism offered little support to existing racial theories based on fixed racial types. And yet from the 1950s, in its attempts to examine human variation at a biologi-cal level, physical anthropology persisted with a type-based approach. Physical anthropology[149] was dominated by authors working with ele-ments which reinforced the idea of type to the detriment of variability. In statistics, it privileged 'centralizing' metrics such as the mean and the median, rather than 'dispersive' indicators such as standard deviation and variance (R. V. Santos [1996] 1998). For those who practiced this kind of anthropology, the arguments of Franz Boas[150] (a critic of the idea of fixed racial types who contended that classical racial markers such as the cephalic index were neither fixed nor stable, but were subject to environmental influence) were clearly not persuasive enough (Boas [1940] 1982).

---

148. Darwin was not the father of evolutionism (Mayr 1982). Other evolutionist models existed in Europe before Darwin's, such as Lamarckism. And both sides of the monogenist-polygenist debate drew extensively on evolutionist ideas. Some of the evo-lutionist thinking of the late nineteenth century was actually anti-Darwinian (Stocking 1968).

149. It was probably the combination of physical anthropology, which saw race as a fixed category, and neo-Darwinism, with its emphasis on dynamism, that spawned the discipline designated 'new physical anthropology' or 'biological anthropology'.

150. See *Changes in Immigrant Body Form* (1908) and *Instability of Human Types* (1912).

Racial purity, miscegenation and the appropriation of myths

We saw above how science joined with state power to secure the progress of the nation; calls to promote 'racial hygiene' among the Portuguese were designed to ensure the biological superiority of a population group which aspired to hegemony. The weak and the incapable were not welcome, as they constituted a risk to its survival. To ensure the sovereignty of the dominant group, therefore, it had to be 'purified'. Opinion on this matter was not unanimous, however. For some, it was a question of explaining the dangers of miscegenation[151] between the Portuguese and the 'colonized populations'. One way to ensure 'racial purity' was eugenics, an influential theory in the United States and Europe now chiefly remembered for its influence on Nazi policy. The Portuguese Society for Eugenic Studies was founded by Eusébio Tamagnini in 1937, although its statutes had originally been approved in 1934. It never carried the principles of eugenics to their logical conclusions: no one was actually exterminated on its account, as occurred in other countries. Neither the colonial governors Norton de Matos and Vicente Ferreira nor the writer Gastão de Sousa Dias favoured mixed-race reproduction, although they did call for the 'social elevation of Blacks and Mulattoes' (O. Ribeiro 1981: 155). At the Colonial Anthropology Congress of 1934, Tamagnini encouraged the Portuguese to emigrate to the colonies but also warned of the dangers of mixed-race reproduction: 'Miscegenation ... is a risk for all human societies, from the Family to the State ... As no one can foresee its results, it should be advised against' (1934: 63). Discussing miscegenation between colonizer and colonized, Tamagnini argued that, generally speaking, colonizing nations had a degree of 'moral and civil perfection' higher than that of the 'colonized populations', whose 'cerebral development [was] generally more backward'. Therefore, they had serious difficulty in learning the language of the colonizer, a situation which led to a 'corruption of the forms and alteration in the meaning of most words'. Thus, the creole of São Tomé e Príncipe was to be considered a degenerate form of the Portuguese language (Ta-

---

151. This issue was also debated in countries such as Brazil, Mexico, Peru, Argentina and Venezuela. Some late-nineteenth-century authors such as Justo Sierra (Mexico), Alejandro O. Deustua (Peru), Sílvio Romero and Nina Rodrigues (Brazil), and José Ingenieros (Argentina) saw miscegenation as an obstacle to national progress. Writing in the 1890s, the Venezuelan positivist Gil Fortoul maintained that the mixing of the races would lead to a *stronger* racial type. Fortoul's perspective was over thirty years ahead of similar ideas advanced by José Vasconcelos in Mexico, and almost forty years ahead of the Luso-tropicalist theories of Gilberto Freyre.

magnini 1902: 13). Only after the elimination of hybridism from the Portuguese population was Tamagnini willing to admit the Portuguese into the group of racially superior Europeans, in opposition to their non-European inferiors.

Mendes Correia, a contemporary of Tamagnini based at the University of Porto, argued in exactly the same vein. At the Colonial Anthropology Congress of 1934, Correia called for research into the 'biological and social problems of miscegenation, whose 'grievous and dramatic intensity' ought to be a source of concern to researchers, for these problems had been overlooked since 'the golden age when the great Afonso de Albuquerque encouraged the crossbreeding of Portuguese men with Indigenous women'. On efforts to 'juridically and religiously' legalize such unions, Mendes Correia cites a rather unlikely and comical episode, 'a banquet at which several weddings were celebrated at the same time' and which 'ended in the confusion of couples the ones with the others, in an enormous pagan orgy' (1934d: 27–28). A doctor and anthropologist, Correia did not support miscegenation, for in his view the *Mestiço* was 'an unplanned being in the plan of the world' (1934a: 332). In the commemorations of 1940, Correia appealed to the 'vigour' and 'germinal purity of the Race' for the 'historical continuity of the Nation' (1940a: 20). Elsewhere, Correia stresses that 'general miscegenation ... can only lead to a confused melting pot, from which there will emerge a humanity biologically comparable ... with the typeless and starving mongrels of the street' (1940b: 122). He also pointed to the 'benefits to the nation of restricting interracial reproduction':

> The more intense and varied the miscegenation and the more active the social and political interference of the *Mestiços* in Portuguese life, the faster and more drastic the disfigurement of the traditional physiognomy of the *Pátria* and the disappearance of what is most noble and unique in Portuguese values (1940b: 130–31).

Correia then goes on to conclude that 'like naturalized foreigners, [the *Mestiços*] should never occupy senior political positions in the country, except in ... highly exceptional and unforeseen circumstances' (1940b: 132). In another paper presented at the 1940 conferences, Correia pointed to miscegenation as a 'possible degenerative factor', while also speaking out in defence of the 'purity of metropolitan Portuguese blood' – not because the *Mestiço* was necessarily inferior, but because the mixture of heterogeneous elements could generate unexpected and unfortunate results (1940c: 587).

Another speaker at the Colonial Congress was José Gonçalo Santa-Rita. He too opposed miscegenation:

The percentage of White blood [in *Mestiços*] makes them less resistant
to mesological conditions ... Others manage to procreate and are ...
the worst of social elements, looking down on the Blacks and hating the
Whites ... Worthless elements in the economic development and social
elevation of the colonies (1940b: 20–21).

Although influential, these authors did not have a monopoly on
the discourse; other commentators, especially after the appropriation
of Luso-tropicalist theory, argued the opposite. Yet among the negative
critiques of miscegenation produced at this time, a number of works
actually attempted to prove the purity of the Portuguese people. Investigations into the origins of the Portuguese had been ongoing since the
nineteenth century. Some authors, such as Leite de Vasconcelos in *Mulatos de Alcácer do Sal* (1895), acknowledged that the Portuguese were
the result of a mixture of various peoples, and even that certain parts
of the country had an evident African influence. In *O povo português*
(1885), Teófilo Braga concluded that the Portuguese were the outcome
of the combination of various groups, and that this was an example of
their superiority. Others, such as Alexandre Herculano in his *História de
Portugal*, acknowledged the Arabic influence on the Portuguese. Writing in 1914–15, Mendes Correia pointed to the 'flagrant vestiges' left
by the Germanic groups, while understating the Semitic influence. He
makes no mention of the possible influence of sub-Saharan Africa. At
the same time, Lusitanian integralists such as António Sardinha in *O
valor da raça* (1915) would not even countenance the existence of Arabic blood in the national pedigree. Although it was a historical fact that
the Portuguese were descended from various ethnic groupings, this fact
was not always accepted. Some authors insisted on proving the 'racial
purity' of the Portuguese, while others argued that no matter how much
they interbred with other people the Portuguese would never lose their
unique essence. The assimilation of Native stock would not dilute the
originality of the Portuguese, for their eugenic potential supposedly enabled them to retain this originality even in contact with exotic populations. At the Conferences on Higher Colonial Culture of 1936, Mello
argued that in contact with other groups the Portuguese would always
remain Portuguese, citing Brazil – the 'inescapable demonstration of
the great eugenic potential of Portuguese stock' – as a good example
of his thesis. In 'inter-racial reproduction', therefore, the 'Portuguese
chromosomes' would prevail, and the same dynamic would be found
'in the field of pigmentation' and 'the psychic field': 'The child of a Portuguese man and a woman of any race is still Portuguese' (1936a: 52).
Writing in the 1930s, Mendes Correia acknowledged the 'many infiltra-

tions, historically ascertained, of African blood' in reference to the work of Leite de Vasconcelos, but did not consider 'such contaminations to have persisted in the somatology' of the Portuguese (1936: 10). As for Tamagnini, in 1939 he published a demonstration that the noses of the Portuguese were very different from African noses, of whose influence they denoted nothing, despite the importation of African slaves to Portugal in the sixteenth and seventeenth centuries.

At the conferences of 1940, J. A. Pires de Lima maintained that the Portuguese were a synthesis of Lusitanian, Romance and German elements, ruling out all other influences. And as for Africa, Black people, he argued, should be 'modest helpers' of the Portuguese; they should not be encouraged to desire independence, nor should they be allowed to come to metropolitan Portugal, to maintain the 'purity of the race and prevent miscegenation' (1940: 99). Another paper presented at these conferences was Aires de Azevedo's 'The Biochemical Purity of the Portuguese People', which concluded that 'the influence of the colonial races (namely Hindu and Black) on the biochemical purity of the Portuguese people is practically nil' (1940: 563). Germano Correia (1940a) presented his findings on somatic measurements and haematological analyses of the Indo-Portuguese population, concluding that in regard to general somatic characteristics, the descendents of the Portuguese 'of pure European race' differed very little from the average type of the European Portuguese. From the somatological point of view, Germano Correia saw 'neither degeneration nor racial diversification in the descendants of Portuguese'. The only difference, a result of the tropical climate, was 'the lower degree of organic robustness' (Germano Correia 1940a: 663–78).

Various figures in the history of Portuguese colonization have proposed a policy of mixed marriage. One of these was Afonso de Albuquerque, governor of Portuguese India,[152] who encouraged the men under his command to marry women of 'Aryan' origin who had converted to Christianity, although he also emphasized he did not want his men to 'marry the Black women of Malabar' (Boxer 1967: 98). As the references to the physical and moral inferiority of the *Mestiço* in the correspondence of the viceroys of Goa reveal, racial discrimination did exist, and it favoured the European-born Portuguese (Boxer 1967: 104).

---

152. Where colonization did not occur in the same way as it did in Africa. When the Portuguese arrived in India they found complex and well-organized societies. Portuguese commoners could ascend to the nobility; and the medical school of Goa was a very well-organized institution. Although the Indians followed a different religion, their social and cultural development was considered superior to that of the Africans.

Nevertheless, the views of Afonso de Albuquerque were to serve as the inspiration for and forerunner of the ideas which Portugal tried to put into practice in its colonial domains in the twentieth century, although they failed to produce any significant results.

It was a common assumption that the Portuguese did not erect racial barriers in their colonies and that their ready miscegenation with other ethnic groups gave them a certain specificity (Boxer 1967: 35). This idea is a precursor of Luso-tropicalist ideology,[153] the foundations of which were laid in 1933 with Gilberto Freyre's *Casa-grande & senzala*. In this book, Freyre cites the readiness with which the Portuguese engaged in fraternal contact with tropical populations[154] – due, in Freyre's view, to their own indefinite ethnic and cultural origins, which lay somewhere between Europe and Africa (Andrews 1991). Freyre also argued that Portuguese men saw the 'Enchanted Mooress' of their folk mythology in the Native women of Indian and Africa, and that this explained the sexual attraction they felt towards them. An article by the right-wing intellectual Manuel Múrias records that in the Conferences on Higher Colonial Culture of 1936, the colonial minister Vieira Machado did not hesitate in designating Portugal's colonization policy as one of 'assimilation'. For Vieira Machado, 'in opposition to the policy of segregation adopted by other countries', 'we have not created unsurpassable barriers between the Native population and ourselves, on the contrary we have established close contact, absent of prejudice, with them' (*O Século* 1940b: 7–8). This 'policy of assimilation' signified integration in the *Pátria* by the transmission of language and religion, so that one day, maintained Vieira Machado, 'all the Portuguese' might have 'equal rights and obligations'. It is difficult to determine, however, whether Vieira Machado's 'policy' was favourable to miscegenation or whether he was simply referring to it as a thing of the past.

In the postwar period, when anticolonial pressure was rising and other European countries had already given independence to their colonies, Portugal found itself forced to reformulate its posture towards its overseas territories and their inhabitants. The United Nations, the anticolonial Afro-Asian conferences – principally Bandung (1955) – and the abolition of the Colonial Act (1951) all contributed to this shift in position. In Asia and Africa, new nationalist movements emerged, while

---

153. Even today, many people find it difficult to lend credence to the theory of Luso-tropicalism. Only Jorge Dias, thanks to his practice of working 'in the field', was able to form a critical vision of Luso-tropicalism that differed greatly from its conception as appropriated by the regime.

154. Some recent authors, such as Boaventura de Sousa Santos (1993), have argued in favour of the special predisposition of the Portuguese for adaptability and their 'multicultural availability'.

others grew in strength. When the United Nations Charter came into effect on 24 October 1945, Portugal found itself under pressure as a colonial power. The reaction was first a change in the tone of discourse, and second a change at the official level. This makeover of the imperial image (not, incidentally, restricted to Portugal, as France, Britain and the Netherlands reacted in similar fashion) can be exemplified in a number of initiatives, such as the 'special imperial edition' of *O Século* published in 1948, which ran to nearly two hundred pages. The colourful cover of this special edition (Figure 8) is dominated by a group of

Figure 8. Cover of the 16 October 1948 edition of *O Século*.

five persons: in the centre is an African, flanked by a missionary (on his right) and a settler (on his left). Behind them stand an Asian and a soldier. Beneath this group of five, under the feet of the African, is a lion, the symbol of the dangers of the wild. To the left of the central group we see an illustration of the feats of Correia de Sá in Angola, and to the right is a depiction of Mouzinho's exploits in Mozambique. What we have, in short, is a compendium of the iconic figures of the 'empire'. Inside, there are articles which proclaim the equality of metropolitan and colonial Portuguese under the same flag; others report the efforts of the government to secure the progressive assimilation of the Natives.

Taking a closer look at the actual texts, however, we see that the Africans continue to be designated simply as 'Blacks', 'savages' and *Indígenas,* and that they are still a long way from 'civilization'. In an interview with *comandante* Gabriel Teixeira, the governor-general of Mozambique, we read:

> The upward march of the *Indígena* to civilization has to be slow and gradual, for it is outright folly to expect peoples who only two generations ago practised cannibalism to assimilate, in one go, the principles of our civilization. We must … remember the centuries it took the White race to move from cave to house. And we still have relapses, like wars (109).

On page 151, in an article entitled 'Education in Manica and Sofala', the caption of a photograph (Figure 9) explicitly states that 'in our empire', 'there is no racial prejudice. In a school in Beira, five boys happily pose for *O Século:* a Chinese, an Indian, a *Mestiço* and two Europeans, one blond and one dark.' This photograph was supposed to illustrate the absence of racial prejudice and the equality of all children, but curiously, it does not include a Mozambican child. The article informs us

that the *Indígenas* were 'educated and instructed', but in 'rudimentary schools', almost all of which were run 'under the direct guidance and supervision of the Diocese of Beira, as stipulated in the Missionary Statute'. The Natives, then, received a 'different' education designed to cater to the social role in store for them ('brief instruction in reading, writing and arithmetic, manual and agricultural

Figure 9. Pupils of a school in Beira, Mozambique, from the special imperial edition of *O Século* (1948: 151).

work') while they continued to be represented as indebted to Portugal. Here, as elsewhere, the importance of acknowledging the equality of the 'races' shines through. Albeit with the proviso that equality between them is possible, the belief in the existence of 'races' persists.

Notwithstanding the United Nations Charter, racial classifications persisted into the 1950s and beyond. One issue of *Panorama* noted that in 1950 the population of the province of Mozambique was divided into the 'non-civilized Native' ('i.e. peaceful and obedient, but yet to assimilate European customs') and the 'civilized', comprising 'Whites', 'Yellows', 'Indians', 'Mixed-race' and 'Blacks'. The same article distinguishes between 'non-civilized Blacks' and 'civilized', the latter in opposition to *Indígenas* (Lobato 1952). In some places, populations are broken down in different ways in the same year, due to different criteria of classification. But although the classifications persisted, ideas on the relative superiority and inferiority of the 'races' were beginning to fade from the discourse: for the important thing was for the Western world to retain its colonies. Some countries opted to gradually concede autonomy to their colonial dominions, and thus the decolonization process got underway. Portugal did not follow this strategy. Instead, it chose to bring its overseas territories into the national fold, calling them 'provinces'[155] – provinces which were as Portuguese as the Minho or the Algarve – instead of 'colonies'.[156] This decision was formalized in the Constitution of 1951, which now extended the *Indígena* statute to the Natives of Angola, Mozambique and Guinea, who were considered not to have reached the 'level of culture and social development of the Europeans', unlike those of 'Cape Verde, Portuguesa India and Macao' (F. Santos 1955: 159). And as a census of 1950 revealed, only a tiny percentage of the colonial population enjoyed 'civilized' or 'assimilated' status (R. Pereira 1986: 214). The expression 'colonization' was gradually replaced by 'integration' (although the actual principle of integration dated from the *liberalismo* period of post-1820). The discriminatory precepts of the Colonial Act began to be abandoned too, and the regime adopted the 'scientific' theory of Freyre,[157] which viewed Portuguese colonization as *different*. Under the new ideology, Portuguese colonization was dis-

---

155. The expression 'overseas provinces' was already current in the nineteenth century. The Estado Novo replaced it with 'colonies' before reverting to the earlier designation in the 1950s.

156. The Ministry of the Colonies was renamed the Overseas Ministry, while the *Boletim Geral das Colónias* became the *Boletim Geral do Ultramar* (although in 1951 the two designations were used interchangeably).

157. On Luso-tropicalism and miscegenation in the colonial and postcolonial contexts, see Vale de Almeida (2000).

interested, driven by Christian ideals and the attempt to integrate the 'colonized populations' into Western civilization. The *Indígena* was now referred to in more neutral terms, although some archetypes persisted. A similar shift occurred in the discourse on Portugal's 'imperial vocation'. This now proclaimed a pluricontinental nation, comprised of Portuguese of all 'races' who identified with the nation. The new vision was reflected in the literature of the period,[158] such as Alberto de Andrade's *Muitas raças, uma só nação* (1953). And yet the inequality which existed between these 'races' still transpired in official speeches. In the Overseas Week commemorations of 1952, Moreira da Silva argued that 'autonomy' and 'independence' made no sense, for the objective was

> not only the welfare of the populations, but their progressive integration in our customs; the learning of our language, the forsaking of primitive ways; the subordination to our civil, commercial, labour and criminal laws … And let it not be said that the effort is worthless or that no useful results have been obtained. In Cape Verde, India and Macao, there are no *Indígenas*. In São Tomé, Guinea, Angola, Mozambique and Timor, the number of *Assimilados* is rising (1952: 226).

For Moreira da Silva, colonial policy at this time was not a question of the emancipation of the overseas populations, but of their relinquishment of their 'primitive' ways and their subjection to the institutions of civilization as represented by metropolitan Portugal. Some discourse in favour of greater tolerance of Black Africans did begin to emerge, however. The administrative officer Manuel Dias Belchior, for example, called for 'comprehension of the Native as an instrument of Indigenous policy':

> When it comes to evaluating the qualities of the Black man, it is not logical to measure them … by our own standards, expecting the *Indígena* to be impressed by the same facts as we are (1951: 19).

The *Indígena* statute, which barred most of the colonial population from access to citizenship, remained intact despite the revision of 1954. Taking the statute together with the text of the Constitution of 1951 on the assimilation process, what we have is an oxymoron: the 'Assimilated *Indígena*'.

The legislation on obligatory agricultural work and forced labour was also changed, and effectively abolished. Natives were now frequently referred to as 'Portuguese of the colonies' or 'Coloured Portuguese'. The

---

158. Many texts speak not of race but of a nationality, territory, multicoloured society or language shared by many people of different values, religion, etc.

discourse produced by the ESC reveals a certain reluctance to use the word 'race', along with a tendency to exalt the qualities of the Africans, and an emphasis on the need to treat them humanely if the success of colonization was to be ensured. Speaking in the National Assembly, Mendes Correia called for the success of 'White colonization' in Africa and referred to the Natives in more benevolent terms. The following is an example of the softening of his discourse:

> We cannot and must not consider the problem of overseas colonization without taking into account ... the interests and rights of the *Indígenas* ... Yet some, sadly, insist on the supremacy of the interests of the White man. They are the ones who do not understand the real value of the Black, they are the ones of whom we can say what André Gide said: 'The less intelligent the White man, the stupider the Black man seems to him' (1952: 20–21).

In colleges and universities, some professors began advising their students to replace the word 'race' with 'ethnic group'. Yet their students considered the term 'race' to be more appropriate to what they had learned in the manuals of Deniker and Topinard. We find one example of the new orientation in a paper of 1953 entitled 'Contribution to the Study of the Blood Groups with Ethnological Characteristics' (Barreto and Alberto 1953). The initial wording of the title was '... Ethnological Characteristic of Human Races'. In the text, from the front cover onwards, the word *raças* ('races') is scored out in blue. Who did this, and when, is unknown, and neither do we know why the book was allowed to be consulted in this form. But it seems likely the title was changed in the 1950s, at a time when the existence of 'races' was beginning to be questioned and the use of the term 'race' to cause a certain discomfort.

Orlando Ribeiro writes that miscegenation 'flourished' right up to the 1950s in Angola. But with the arrival in Angola of White women from metropolitan Portugal and the envy they came to feel in regard to the 'Coloured girls', there was a certain 'hardening of racial oppositions', just as Jorge Dias had shown in the case of Mozambique. Although the official line was to defend the existence of pluriracial overseas societies, Ribeiro notes that miscegenation began to decrease after the 1950s, and that 'between the world of the Blacks and the world of the Whites an ever-wider chasm is opened' (1981: 153). On the propaganda level, 'photographs proliferated of White and Black children side by side on school benches and in playgrounds' (Ribeiro 1981: 154). Some Black coffee traders began to enjoy a degree of prosperity. But there was no Black elite in Angola, 'as much due to poverty as the prejudice that excluded Coloured people'. Not until Portuguese sovereignty came under threat were *Mestiço* delegates sent to the UN and Cape Verdean and Hindu deputies 'elected' to the National Assembly (Ribeiro 1981: 165). Even in the postwar period, then, the discrimination and hierarchies persisted, despite an apparent change in discourse. In 1960, the UN Declaration on Decolonization, which recognized the right to independence of colonized countries and peoples, was approved by a majority vote. However, it took the outbreak of war in Angola in 1961 for the *Indígena* statute to be finally laid to rest and for Luso-tropicalism to be taken up in earnest as the ideology which had always guided Portuguese colonization.

Chapter III

Exhibiting the Empire, Imagining the Nation

*Representations of the Colonies
and the Overseas Portuguese
in the Great Exhibitions*

The age of the great exhibitions

From the middle of the nineteenth century, the industrial world put it-self on display in exhibitions held in major cities all over North America and Europe. Most of these exhibitions celebrated or commemorated a special event, historic or not, or showcased the latest developments in science and technology. They were ephemeral creations, purpose-built and later dismantled, and lasted for no more than six months. On show at these exhibitions were the resources and raw materials yielded by the colonies, archaeological artefacts, the latest styles and innovations in architecture, and the arts in general. Progress was celebrated on every level. The products on show were therefore organized in such a way as to evidence a hierarchy in terms of economic, technological and racial development. This ordering was designed to show how industrial societ-ies were more advanced than agricultural societies. A major exhibition involved considerable financial outlay, but participants and organizers could normally expect a return on their investment. As a selective presen-tation of reality, every major exhibition had an educational component and imposed some kind of order on its exhibits. Some exhibitions were stages for the mise-en-scène of models of colonial administration, where supposed 'tribes' and their 'usages and customs' were put on display. Here too the 'cultures' on display were organized and exhibited as if on a scale of evolution ranging all the way from savagery to civilization, in a spectrum of colours extending from the blackest 'Blacks' of Africa to the yellow-skinned and almost-White peoples of Asia. The evolutionary ideas often associated with this spectrum of skin colour were reproduced not only in the great exhibitions, but also in anthropological theory and the popular consciousness. And it was in this packaging that the people of Europe and America were invited to come and see – almost without leaving their own homes – the Native peoples (colonized or not) which previously they had known only from books, if at all.

Although the roots of the World's Fair phenomenon went back to the Middle Ages at least – often in association with religious festivals – it is generally accepted that the modern exhibition age opened with the Great Exhibition held in the Crystal Palace (designed by the architect Joseph Paxton) in London in 1851. The Great Exhibition was followed in 1853 by the New York Exhibition, which, like its forerunner in London, was housed in a specially constructed 'Crystal Palace'. Other cities followed suit: Paris, Philadelphia, Chicago, St Louis, Buffalo, San Francisco, Seattle, Atlanta, New Orleans, Nashville, and many more. Some exhibitions had international renown; others were national, or even regional, affairs. Some exhibitions left a legacy in the form of museums.[1] The World's Fair survived until after the Second World War, and each major exhibition drew on the input of scientists, politicians, senior church dignitaries and other prominent figures. Taking his cue from the classic text of Marcel Mauss, Burton Benedict (1983) compared these World's Fairs with enormous potlatches, ritual feasts of wealth and power in which the participants gave away or even destroyed their own possessions to gain prestige and outdo their rivals (competitors, nations, cities, countries, colonial empires). And there was much in common between the potlatch and the World's Fair: both were ritualized competitions, in which the idea was to gain prestige and maintain reciprocal relations between parties of comparable calibre who at the same time were rivals; and both were costly events organized on a lavish scale, with social, economic, political, legal, moral and aesthetic aspects that added up to a total social fact.

One variant of the World's Fair was the colonial exhibition, which was designed to showcase the natural and human resources of the imperial power that organized it. The first international colonial exhibition was held in the Netherlands in 1883. This was followed by the Colonial and Indian Exhibition of 1886, held in London. Later came the

---

1. For example, the Musée d'Ethnographie du Trocadéro, after the Exposition Universelle of Paris (1878); the Musée du Congo Belge, after the Brussels exhibition of 1897; and the Field Columbian Museum, after the Chicago exhibition of 1893.

Exposition Nationale Coloniale of Marseille (1922), the British Empire Exhibition of Wembley (1924–25) and the Empire Exhibition of Glasgow (1938), the Exposition Internationale Coloniale of Antwerp (1930), and the Exposition Coloniale Internationale of Paris (1931). Other exhibitions not specifically on a colonial theme also included elements related to colonialism, or explored ideas on how to bring other cultures to civilization and economically exploit the resources of distant lands. Some authors use the terms 'world's fair' and 'exhibition' interchangeably.[2] However we choose to designate them, all these events share certain characteristics, with a certain continuity of intent; and a shared vision can be detected in them all.[3] As Rydell (1992: 27) noted, the American exhibitions were similar to the European ones, and like their European counterparts, American organizers combined imperialism and the supremacy of the Whites in the design of their exhibitions. The physical settings for the exhibitions can be compared with places of popular diversion such as zoos or botanic gardens or circuses, or the exhibitions (temporary or permanent) organized by missionary societies or natural history museums – all of them stages for the display of other 'races' or species. The members of these *Naturvölker* were seen as closer to nature than civilization, and were therefore exhibited in zoos, behind barriers or in wire enclosures – but also in fairgrounds or public parks like the Jardin d'Acclimatation of Paris, created in 1859 by Geoffroy Saint-Hilaire for the study and exhibition of exotic plants and animals, but later a frequent venue for 'ethnological exhibitions'. Not the animals but their human companions became the principal or even exclusive attraction for visitors fascinated by alterity and exoticism. From 1877 to 1890, the Jardin d'Acclimatation hosted exhibitions of human beings for periods of weeks or even months.[4] These inhabitants of remote territories were put on display just as the resources and raw materials of the colonies were. After capturing their potentially dangerous 'exhibits', the exhibition organizers put them in a safe and confined place which

---

2. At a conference held in Paris in 1928 attended by delegates from forty-one nations (Portugal was one of the signatories of the resulting convention), a body of regulations for future world's fairs was established. Exhibitions were defined as instruments of 'education and teaching', like 'temporary museums with educational and technical purposes'; world's fairs, on the other hand, had 'commercial purposes'. And the former were accompanied by 'congresses, ceremonies, solemn sessions, official visits, inaugurations … festivals and other events' directed at a diverse public (F. Cunha 1933: 10–11), with greater attention lavished on display.

3. On the different approaches to these events by different nations, see Benedict (1991) and Coombes (1991).

4. On the exhibitions held in the Jardin d'Acclimatation, see Coutancier and Barthe 1995.

was 'open' to the visiting public. This confinement usually took the form of a replica of a Native village, with elements which were characteristic and representative of the particular culture on show, and inhabited by groups of performers from African societies.

This practice of putting human beings on display appears to date from the 1870s, when agents and functionaries were dispatched to remote regions with the mission of bringing back specimens of 'exotic types' to the West. The ethnographic spectacles that were organized in Germany, for example, went by the name of *Völkerschau* and became common events after 1874, when Carl Hagenbeck, a wild animal trainer and merchant from Hamburg and later the director of a zoo and a circus, began exhibiting humans from remote reaches of the globe in various cities of Germany and Europe, including Paris and London[5] (Corbey 1993: 345). The formula was a success on various levels. It was educational, but it also had curiosity and entertainment value, and it began to spread. It was not only inhabitants of remote places that were put on display, but also beings seen as indomitable, human monsters and the insane; some provoked fascination in the visiting public, others, repulsion. When the Centennial Exhibition of Philadelphia (1876) put Indigenous Americans on display, the phenomenon went truly global. In 1878, Paris hosted the first international exhibition of non-Western humans, in specially built pavilions and 'Indigenous villages'. Four hundred Natives of the French colonies of Indochina, Senegal and Tahiti went on display at this exhibition. The Exposition Universelle of 1889, also held in Paris, also featured 'ethnographic villages', while the Chicago Exhibition of 1893 put Natives of Java, Samoa, Dahomey, Egypt and North America itself on display.

Otis Mason, curator of ethnology at Washington's National Museum of Natural History, was impressed by the 'educational power' of the 'life groups' on show at exhibitions like these (Hinsley 1991: 346). By bringing dwellings, everyday work and rituals to life, cultural history could be taught in a way that would attract many visitors.[6] Enthused, Mason set about bringing life groups to the Chicago exhibition of 1893, which was to commemorate the fourth centenary of the colonization of the New World. From Fort Rupert in British Columbia, Franz Boas brought fourteen members of the Kwakiutl group as representatives of

---

5. After 1901 it became difficult to recruit Natives from the German colonies, at first due to new laws and later with the onset of the Great War. The National Socialists banned the *Völkerschau* in the 1930s, in the belief that the Natives might awaken the sympathy of the Germans for other 'races' (Corbey 1993: 342, 358).

6. The Great Exhibition of 1851 attracted 6 million visitors, the Paris Universal Expo of 1878 16 million, and the 1900 Expo, also in Paris, 50 million.

the pristine conditions of pre-Columbian life on the continent. Their 'job' was to perform various ceremonies and simply to live as normally as possible. Some of the rituals the Kwakiutl were requested to perform had fallen into disuse some time previously and had to be relearned especially for the exhibition. The motto of the Chicago exhibition was 'To See is to Know', an expression which was later to become associated with it: for to see the exhibition was to know about other places and other peoples. The life group formula which Boas used at the exhibition was an attempt to show other societies in their own contexts. By displaying scenes of everyday life, the life group brought exhibition visitors into contact with the specificities of a particular culture and geographic region.[7] But there were disadvantages as well as advantages to this formula. The life group involved the visitor directly in the spectacle and was visible from all sides, without props such as painted backdrops or diorama effects. Normally, each life group took the form of 'a family or several members of a tribe, dressed in their native costume and engaged in some characteristic work or art illustrative of their life and particular art or industry'.[8] Yet when the group on display was very big, it became difficult to create an illusion of reality (and it was very expensive too). The life group also turned 'tribe' into a static concept and was itself associated with tribal notions. Although the life group was intended to integrate spatial and temporal dynamics, it also, paradoxically, attempted to present the life group in a timeless, frozen and unchanging present. However, with Boas and the emergence of relativist anthropology, the emphasis shifted towards the placing of the objects of study in living contexts. The cultures put on show in this way were presented either as part of an evolutionary sequence or as dispersed in a synchronous 'ethnographic present' (Clifford 1988: 228).

The age of the great exhibitions extended well into the twentieth century, reaching its height in the period between the two World Wars.

---

7. Boas had previously experimented with the life group format, which had first been used in Paris in 1870. On his arrival in the United States in 1887, Boas criticized the evolutionist classifications and the 'limits of the comparative method' then in vogue, calling instead for 'cultural relativism'. According to this relativist approach, every cultural object had to be understood within the context of its production and use. This entailed carrying out 'fieldwork' (Boas 1887: 61–62). While in the evolutionist, type-based system culture was viewed as a unified whole, in the 'geographic' approach advocated by Boas we must no longer speak of culture, but of cultures (Stocking 1974). For authors such as Mason and Powell, the objective of the exhibition was to demonstrate progress – of anthropology, science and culture; for Boas, it was to demonstrate that civilization was a 'relative' concept (see Jacknis 1985: 83).

8. American Museum of Natural History, Department of Anthropology, Accessions, 1894–95 and 1901–36, New York (quoted in Jacknis 1985: 100).

After the First World War, with widespread economic crisis and attacks on imperialism, many European governments decided to use their exhibitions to promote their empires. These exhibitions were designed to show the supposed benefits of colonialism (for colonizer and colonized alike) and of imperialism, which was projected as an essential condition for modernity and progress.

Portugal joined the international exhibition circuit in the nineteenth century, and not, as some authors have claimed, in the period between the two World Wars. Official exaltation of Portugal's 'imperial exploits' also dated from the late nineteenth century, a time when the discourse referred 'nakedly and openly to empire and colonies – the Portuguese were the representatives of Western civilization, of Christianity, of science – and to race'. This discourse evoked figures such as Vasco da Gama and other heroes of the past, who were viewed as 'a way of popularizing the narratives of national identity' and could 'condense in a single figure the representation of an imperial past' (Sobral 1999: 71–72). The tricentenary of the death of Camões (1880), for instance, was commemorated with a 'triumphal procession' whose allegorical floats included one float portraying the colonies.

Portugal participated in foreign exhibitions[9] and organized some of its own. Examples of the former are Paris (1855, 1867 and 1879), London (1862), Vienna (1873), Philadelphia (1876) and Amsterdam (1883), and of the latter Porto (1861 and 1865), Lisbon (1863 and 1882), Coimbra (1869 and 1884) and Guimarães (1884). The first international exhibition to be held in Portugal was the 1865 exhibition in Porto, at which the city's own 'Palácio de Cristal' was inaugurated. Participant countries included Spain, Belgium, France, Britain, Italy, Austria, Brazil, the Netherlands, Switzerland and Denmark. Other major exhibitions held in Portugal included the Portuguese Insular and Colonial Exhibition of 1894, held in Porto's Palácio de Cristal as part of the commemorations of the fifth centenary of the birth of Henry the Navigator; the Universal International and Colonial Exhibition, held in 1897 in Lisbon to commemorate the fourth centenary of the 'discovery' of India;[10] and the Colonial Exhibition of Cotton, Rubber, Cocoa and

---

9. Lisbon's Museu Colonial, which was founded in 1871, was instrumental in the Portuguese participation in some of these. It was responsible for organizing the Portuguese colonial representations at the Vienna Weltausstellung of 1873, the International Geographic Exhibition of 1875, the Amsterdam International Colonial Exhibition of 1883 and the Paris Exposition Universelle of 1889. It was also active in the organization of the Industrial Exhibition of Porto in 1891 (see Roque 2001).

10. At a time when the colonial powers were endowing scientific expeditions to Africa, it is significant that one of the allegorical floats participating in the commemorations featured a group of singing and dancing Nguni – no doubt a major attraction at the time.

Coffee of 1906, organized by the SGL. In 1915 came the celebrations of the centenaries of two key events in Portugal's colonial adventure: the conquest of Ceuta and the death of Afonso de Albuquerque, events which respectively 'marked the beginning and the apogee of the feats of the Discoveries' (Catroga 1996: 568). These exhibitions were the opportunity for the country to 'set out its stall' with exhibits from metropolitan Portugal and its colonies, including raw materials, the products obtained from these raw materials, and maps and graphic information.

With these events, Portugal wanted to project itself as a respectable colonial power whose empire was economically productive if managed and exploited properly. After the First World War, however, criticism of its African policy began to be levelled at Portugal. The Portuguese government reacted with a programme of decentralization, creating a new administrative model based on the appointment of high commissioners (1920) whose mission was to improve policy on the occupation and development of the colonies. With the publication of the Ross Report of 1925, commissioned by the League of Nations and exposing the practice of forced labour in the Portuguese colonies, the country again came under fire. Portugal therefore had to clean up its image as a colonial power, and the colonial exhibition, as a way of legitimizing colonialism, was one way to do this. The Darwinian idea of the power of the strong over the weak was still evident in these exhibitions, but now the emphasis was on showing that the objective of domination was the elevation of the colonized peoples – colonialism was a humanitarian mission, in other words. Curiously, by the time the exhibition wave reached its peak in Portugal in 1940, the phenomenon was on the decline elsewhere in the West.

It was not, then, with the advent of the Estado Novo that Portugal began to organize and participate in exhibitions, although the Estado Novo did put its weight behind such initiatives. Beginning with the Exposition Universelle of Brussels (1935), which the SPN supported right from the outset, and followed by the Exposition Universelle of Paris (1937) and the New York World's Fair (1939), Portugal lost no opportunity to transmit propaganda for the policy of the regime. As successor to the SPN, the SNI played an important role in the centenary commemorations of 1940 and 1947, and also contributed to the Portuguese representations in international exhibitions. Since the images of the colonies projected at these exhibitions had to be positive, they were selected and adapted to display only what the regime wished to display. The literature on the exhibitions which Portugal organized or participated in from the nineteenth century onwards is extremely limited in Portugal itself. Several studies exist in the fields of art history (Acciaiuoli 1998; França 1980; Portela 1982; Neto 1995; R. A. Santos 1994) and the history of science and technology (A. Silva 2000), as does a study by a Brazilian anthropologist (Thomaz 1997). My examination focuses on the exhibitions[11] held between 1924 and 1940 and the ways they depicted the colonial question, with special consideration of their representations of Natives. I will also examine these exhibitions as cultural constructs, including the pictorial material in which Natives appear, and the discourse produced around them.[12] Essentially, as places where everything seemed to have its 'proper place' (F. Cunha[13] 1933: 15), these exhibitions were a representation of the country and everything which was a part of it, colonial territories included.

Representations of the Portuguese colonies, 1924–31

In 1924, Portugal participated in the Exposition Internationale of Brussels. Its participation was commemorated in a special edition of *O Século,* which described Portugal as the world's third colonial power, possessor of a vast territory, charged with a civilizing and humanitarian mission regarding the conservation, protection and struggle for progress of the 'Aboriginal races'. The population of Cape Verde in particular was mentioned as having been raised to a high degree of civilization, and therefore as potentially a valuable work resource. India was described as the 'most Portuguese' of the colonies, where with their education and their love of work the Portuguese Hindus spread the Portuguese language and customs all along the coast, from the China seas and the Indian Ocean to Port Said. The populations of the other territories were mentioned only in relation to their value as labour, as symbols of the wealth their work generated. This was the case of the *Indígenas* of Mozam-

---

11. I cannot fully agree with some authors who define these exhibitions as specifically dedicated to industry, the colonies or the celebration of the achievements of the Estado Novo. All had elements of each, and it is impossible to separate one aspect from the other; at least the organizers were unable to do so.

12. My sources include official publications and regulations, guides, reports, postcards, posters, interviews, press articles, letters, telegrams and films. These materials are often dispersed, with frequent lacunae, and are often contradictory. The Arquivo Histórico Ultramarino (AHU) contains more material than I have cited here. The fact that its catalogue is incomplete, and that its materials are stored at random and unsystematically, did not help. The former Arquivo Histórico Colonial participated in various international colonial exhibitions, and presumably has many important documents among its holdings. Lisbon's Biblioteca Nacional (BN) has copious amounts of materials which are subject to restricted access due to their age and poor condition.

13. Francisco Carmo e Cunha was a doctor of economic science, law graduate and departmental chief at the Ministry for Trade, Industry and Agriculture.

bique, for instance, who were described as good mine workers. At the Exposition Internationale des Arts Décoratifs et Industriels Modernes held in Paris the following year, the emphasis was on the importance of the natural produce of the colonies, such as exotic woods which were ideal for decorative arts. The same year (1925), Portugal also participated in the Interallied Colonial Exhibition, also in Paris. To mark the Portuguese presence in this exhibition, a manual based on the yearbook *Anuário da Guiné* was published. Some of the ideas expressed in this manual are summarized in Table 1. According to its author, Armando Castro,[14] Guinea was the richest of the African colonies 'in its potential for agricultural production', while its population was a 'bizarre and multicoloured hotchpotch of eleven races and diverse sub-races, forming a significant body of approximately eight hundred thousand inhabitants'. And, Castro continued, across all these peoples the somatic features were 'so flagrantly' confused that it was impossible 'to determine . . . which were the earliest settlers of the Province' (1925: 8, 31).

Table 1. Ideas associated with the people of Guinea (Castro 1925).

	Name of group	
	Men	Women
Conduct		
Good natured	Fula, Mandinka	
Ill natured	Banhun, Nalu, Balanta	
Hardworking	Manjaku, Banhun, Balanta	Banhun, Biafada
Lazy	Felup, Balanta	
Dishonest	Mandinka, Banhun, Balanta	
Warlike	All in general, especially the Balanta	
Lasciviousness/polygamy	All are polygamous	Bijago
Incomprehensible 'customs'	Fula, Papel, Manjaku, Balanta, Nalu, Bijago	Fula, Manjaku
Power of concentration	Fula, Papel	
Expansive	Mandinka	
Crafty	Papel	
Physiognomy		
Not very robust	Fula	
Robust	Felup, Papel, Manjaku	
Beauty		Manjaku

14. Armando Castro was an employee of the Colonial Ministry and a member of the Colonial Council for the province of Guinea. He was appointed to represent Portugal at the Interallied Colonial Exhibition of Paris.

Castro divides the Guinean population, which he collectively designates as *Indígena,* into different 'races': Balanta, Banhun (Brame or
Mankanya), Manjaku, Cassanga, Bayot, Felup, Fula, Mandinka, Papel,
Biafada, Bijago, Nalu, 'diverse' and 'unknown'. He then offers a précis
of the presumed relationships between the 'character' and the physiognomy of each 'race'. Thus, the Fula are 'good-natured', 'not very robust',
'prone to illness'; and they wear tattooes, which Castro considers an
'absurd practice' that causes 'deformities in the lips' of the women. Like
the Fula, the Mandinka are 'good-natured'. They are 'happy, expansive,
hospitable and obedient', practise trade and agriculture, but are dishon-
est and 'thought the only good trader was a trickster'. The Felup are
described as 'robust, muscular, healthy and resilient', but 'when it comes
to work do not exert themselves: they produce only what they need to
eat and pay their taxes'. The Papel are 'very quick-witted and alert, well
built, muscular and resilient', and with good 'power of concentration'.
They 'deform their teeth by sharpening them'. The Manjaku are 'a sub-
division of the Papel, whom they resemble physically and in their customs'; 'seafaring by temperament, they are the ones who provide most
personnel for the crews of ships'. As for the Manjaku woman, she is
'reasonably slim and pleasant'; she 'adores brightly-coloured fabrics and
ornaments herself, like the idols, with bracelets and bizarre necklaces of
beads'. The Manjaku, Castro tells us, have a penchant for trade, 'since
they are very hard working'. The Banhun (Brame or Mankanya) are
considered 'the hardest working, after the Balanta'; but are 'cowards and
oafishly underhand in their dealings, do not believe in the soul or even
know what it is, but believe in transmigration'. For them, 'the woman is
not so much a being as a *thing,* a despicable rag with no will of its own,
which the men trade as they would trade a cow or a goat'; and yet they
are 'always ready to have her at home and to take her in, even if they
know that the children she brings with her are not theirs'. And while 'the
man is in charge in the constitution of their *ménage,* it is the woman who
produces more'. While 'the man sells the product, the woman carries it
on her back'. The Balanta have bellicose instincts, are shrewd and hard-
working, with a propensity to theft: they say they will only stop thieving
'the day the White man stops writing'; 'as soon as their children are born
they are washed and left to cry to their heart's content, for no one takes
any notice'; they practise circumcision and 'select the women they are to
marry when the latter are still young children'. The Biafada 'are veritable
lovers of drums and dancing'; 'it is the woman who works ... while the
man sleeps to his heart's content'. The Nalu 'also practise circumcision';
their women 'are generally considered as slaves, and no care is shown
them when pregnant, when sometimes their husbands even beat them'.

The Bijago 'are the only *Indígenas* who do not practise circumcision; they take 'no care in their personal hygiene' and 'do not know what soap is'; they are 'good swimmers, which greatly helps them when fishing'; 'they live on monkeys, mice, boa, dogs and other domestic creatures; they eat cows, goats and hens when these animals die of illness or when a funeral takes place, not bothering to remove the hide or pluck the feathers' (1925: 34–39). One characteristic common to almost all groups is 'their warlike tendency, their combative nature', 'a reminiscence, which they continue to keenly feel, of the strife and butchery of days gone by' (1925: 32–33). As for polygamy, Castro observes that all the 'heathens' practise it. His description of the Bijago woman provides an example of the lasciviousness often associated with the Africans:

> She chooses her companion, rules over him and drives him out of the home ... Off he scurries like a dog, and in comes his replacement ... who knows that ... the same fate awaits him. Heaven help the man who is perfect in the eyes of the Bijago woman and whose physique embodies what for them is the ideal type of man! He knows there's not enough of him to go round ... And if he doesn't want to die, overcome by exhaustion, he must flee far from the greedy eyes of these insatiable Eves (1925: 39).

In 1929, Portugal took part in the Exposición Ibero-Americana of Seville, where it sought to protect the image of a metropolitan, colonial and pluricontinental country. This was an exhibition of 'art, history, industry, commerce and agriculture' in which participated 'the two nations of the Iberian peninsula and all the republics of the Americas' (*Regulamento da Exposição Portuguesa em Sevilha* 1929: 3). It was an optimistic Portugal that took part in this exhibition, embracing modernism and exalting the riches of 'metropolis' and 'colonies' (*Guia oficial da Exposição Portuguesa em Sevilha* 1929). The colonies themselves were represented collectively, with the exception of Macao, which had its own pavilion. No 'life groups' of Natives were on show. Instead, there were catalogues, monographs, diagrams, maps, films, statistics, graphs, products, works of art and illustrated postcards. Some of the films had been made in the African colonies (Angola, Mozambique, São Tomé e Príncipe and Guinea) as propaganda for the Portuguese colonial effort. Despite the colonial focus, however, most exhibitors were in the 'metropolitan' section. The Portuguese pavilion was designed by Carlos and Guilherme Rebelo de Andrade, who had earlier designed the Portuguese pavilion for the Rio de Janeiro exhibition of 1922. The official catalogue of the Portuguese participation (*Exposição Portuguesa em Sevilha* 1929) is divided into two parts. The first part is devoted to the 'Metropolis' and the second to the 'Colonies', with each overseas domain given its own section. Information about the inhabitants of the colonies is restricted to population numbers; no data at all is given for Angola and 'Portuguese India'.

Portugal was also present at the Barcelona exhibition of the same year, but not as an official exhibitor and with a smaller representation.[15] The aim of this exhibition was to showcase the industrial might of Europe, but the Portuguese stand did no more than illustrate its backwardness as an industrial nation. Its colonial vocation, however, was proclaimed in no fewer than seven sections (agriculture, colonies, trade, industry, administration, tourism, arts) and a reception room which gave pride of place to Portugal's imperial exploits.

The following year (1930) came the Exposition Internationale Coloniale, Maritime et d'Art Flamand, held in Antwerp, Belgium. As well as showcasing Belgium's African conquests, this exhibition also featured colonial representations from countries including France, the Netherlands, Britain, Italy and Portugal. It included live representatives of the colonized peoples, who were confined to mock villages built specially for the event. The Antwerp exhibition was overtly colonial in its intentions, and a demonstration of the importance Belgium attached to its overseas possessions, the activities connected with these possessions, the investment they attracted and the wealth (diamonds, hardwoods, etc.) they contained. It was one of a set of three exhibitions[16] which, along with other initiatives, had been organized to mark the centenary of Belgian independence. Parallel events included congresses and conferences on colonial themes, with an emphasis on activities conducive to the emergence of civilization. Portugal's commissioner to the Antwerp exhibition was Armando Cortesão, at the time agent-general for the colonies. The Portuguese pavilion, designed by Ventura Ferreira, contained a display of raw materials and products of colonial origin, as well as maps, graphs and photographs designed to illustrate aspects related to colonial administration, political and economic development, agriculture and industry. It was a summary, in other words, of the colonial life of the nation and of the colonizing methods of the Portuguese.

---

15. A representation was deemed 'unofficial' when the government of the exhibiting country did not accept the invitation of the host country for political or economic reasons. Some governments nevertheless allowed their nationals to participate in a private capacity.

16. The other two exhibitions were the Exposition Internationale de la Grande Industrie, Science et Applications et Art Wallon Ancien (Liège, 1930), and the Exposition Universelle (Brussels, 1935). Portugal was invited to participate in all three exhibitions.

In one of the catalogues for this exhibition,[17] written by Jaime Cortesão (1930), Portugal is presented as a country of natural qualities and vast territories, with emphasis on the success of colonization, the medical and moral succour given to the *Indígenas,* the combat against tropical diseases, the diffusion of professional and academic instruction, the organization of regional works and the endeavours of missionaries. On the inhabitants of this 'Overseas Portugal', we learn that in Angola there were people of 'White race' and *Indígenas.* The latter belonged to the Bantu group, which was composed of numerous 'races': the Kabinda, the Mussorongo, the Mbaka, the Chokwe, the Ginga, the Kisama, the Libolo, the Bailundu and the Mandomba, to name just a few; each name designated a supposedly different 'race'. These Natives were generally described as very robust, of medium height, and capable of performing all kinds of agricultural and industrial tasks – contact with the Portuguese presumably having allowed them to acquire work habits. The inhabitants of Cape Verde were classified as 'Whites', 'Blacks' or *Mestiços,* with no further information offered. In Guinea there was a whole mosaic of 'races' and it was difficult to trace the origins of the different customs and religions. To this 'list of races' were added the *grumetes*[18] and other groups of *Indígenas* 'more or less assimilated' into European civilization. The total number of *Indígenas* in the colony was 350,000. In 1925 there were 768 Europeans and Syrians in Guinea (Cortesão, 1930: 10–2). Despite the division of the populations in this way, no specific characteristics were assigned to the particular groups. Their principal quality was their capacity for work, which was seen as an encouraging sign, for *contratos* were on the increase. The inhabitants of Portuguese India were subdivided into those of Goa, Damão and Diu, where the 'diverse races' lived in articulation with the castes:

> There are Europeans, descendants of the old Portuguese families, Christian Hindus, Pagans and Muslims, and Africans. Among the Hindus ... we find numerous castes, from the Brahmin, who are proud of their intellectual superiority, to the wretched Pariahs (Cortesão 1930: 13).

The only information offered on Macao is the population, which had grown enormously since 1920. For Mozambique, the latest census information (up to 1930) is given. The Mozambican population was divided into 'races and sub-races of the Bantu group'. The *Indígenas* were

---

17. *Exposition internationale coloniale, maritime et d'art flamand – Antwerp, 1930, Catalogue officiel de la section portugaise,* Commissariat de l'Exposition Portugaise à Anvers, Lisbon.

18. An apprentice in the navy.

mainly 'tall and svelte', and provided the Portuguese with 'soldiers of the very first order, like the Landin' who had proved their loyalty during the Great War, and 'workers for the agricultural and industrial operations of the Portuguese, and for the mines of the Rand'. The rest of the population consisted of 'Whites' (all foreigners were included in this category), Asians and *Mestiços*. As for Timor, its 'Indigenous' people were Malayans, and were described as belonging to a still 'very rudimentary' state of civilization. They were not physically robust, but were intelligent and adroit. According to the most recent census of 1930, the population consisted of 'Malays', individuals of the 'Yellow race', the 'Black race', *Mestiços,* the 'White race' and Asians (Cortesão 1930: 11–12, 19). In São Tomé e Príncipe, the population had been divided into *Indígenas,* 'hired labour' and 'Europeans' at the most recent census. Attention was drawn to 'the delicate problem of the labour shortage in São Tomé, with labour having to be imported from the [African] continent, for the *Indígena* of the islands flees from work as much as possible'. Labour was therefore 'imported from Angola, Mozambique, Cape Verde, etc.'.

1931 was the year of the International Colonial Exhibition of Paris, which ran from 6 May until the end of October. Commissioner-general of this exhibition was Maréchal Lyautey, an emblematic figure of the French colonization of Morocco. The exhibition was located in the Bois de Vincennes on the outskirts of Paris, with Lake Daumesnil at its centre. In addition to the host nation, other countries present at the exhibition were Belgium, Denmark, the United States, Italy, the Netherlands and Portugal. The exhibition included a zoo with specimens of the fauna of the various colonies. In the six months it was open, the exhibition attracted 33 million visitors (Grilo 1932: 5–7), although not everyone in France was happy to see it taking place.[19]

---

19. A counterexhibition, *La Vérité sur les Colonies,* was held at the same time. Organized by a collective of surrealists, communists and intellectuals, it attracted five thousand visitors. The surrealists, for example, recognized the value of African sculptures, praising the ability of their creators to represent abstraction and seize the essence of what was fundamental in art. *La Vérité sur les Colonies* was a 'mini-exhibition' featuring photographs from the colonial wars and information designed to refute the supposed benefits of colonization and the work of the missions. It was designed to divert potential visitors from the other exhibition, or if they still went, to make them see things with different eyes. Its prospectus was signed by André Breton, Paul Éluard, Benjamin Péret, Georges Sadoul, Pierre Unik, André Thirion, René Crevel, Louis Aragon, René Char, Maxime Alexandre, Yves Tanguy and Georges Malkine (Orsenna [1988] 1989: 380–81). This prospectus was allowed to circulate because France was a democratic republic; in France, therefore, unlike Portugal, people were free to speak out against colonialism. In addition, within France colonialism was opposed by a Native elite of individuals from various regions of the French empire.

The official exhibition poster was designed by Desmeures, with the title 'Around the World in a Day' (Figure 10). This poster shows four figures, each representing a colonized people, given visual unity by the frame which contains them. The starkly contrasting skin colours of the four figures evidence the phenotypical differences between the groups represented in the poster, and make clear allusion to colour as a differentiating factor. Another significant detail is the clothing worn by each figure. The Black man wears a metal neck band which is vaguely reminiscent of the neck shackles worn by slaves (although whether it was the artist's explicit intention to make this association is unclear), but besides this neck band and the colour of his skin, nothing else which might suggest his status or occupation is to be seen. The Native American wears a large necklace, the North African is fully garbed and the Asian, also clothed, wears a hat. Each figure evokes a different state of civilization. But this poster is much more than just a representation of the French colonies as a multiracial em-

Figure 10. Poster for the 1931 Paris Colonial Exhibition by Desmeures, Biblioteca Nacional, Lisbon.

pire. The brown-skinned figure alludes to the Natives of North Africa, the yellow-skinned figure to those of Indochina (or of Asia in general), the black-skinned figure to those of what was then called 'Black Africa'. But if these three figures represent the *Indígenas* who constituted the French empire, united under the national flag which flies in the background, the red-skinned Native American is a curious inclusion, for as far as I have been able to ascertain nowhere else does a Native American appear in the official posters and documents of the exhibition. In the official guides, he is replaced by French traders in the Indies. Of course, although the poster's designer may have taken his primary inspiration from the French colonial empire in particular, its slogan – 'Around the World in a Day' – perhaps suggested a more all-embracing intent.

The Portuguese section of the exhibition[20] opened on 27 May. Its commissioner-general was Silveira e Castro. A number of conferences were held during the exhibition, and a group of students from the ESC visited it. However, according to Grilo (1932), a delegate from the colony of Mozambique, Portugal's section offered next to nothing in terms of research and information on its colonies. With its art deco style denoting the encroaching influence of avant-garde trends in European art, the poster designed for the Portuguese representation shows just one figure: an African woman. The other imperial 'types' are nowhere to be seen (Figure 11). This may have been because at the time of the exhibition, most of Portugal's investments in its colonies were going to Africa. The poster was by Fred Kradolfer (1903–1968), a Swiss designer who had been based in Portugal since 1927.

Figure 11. Poster for the 1931 Paris Colonial Exhibition by Fred Kradolfer, Biblioteca Nacional, Lisbon.

The four Portuguese pavilions at the exhibition were designed by the architect Raul Lino. Two of these pavilions were dedicated to historic themes and the importance of colonization in Portugal's history, and were designed in the late Gothic Manueline style specific to Portugal. These pavilions celebrated the colonial ventures of the Portuguese in a context of exploration and discovery, the exploits of the country's heroes in the maritime expansion and the dissemination of European civilization. There was also a 'metropolitan' pavilion (with an exhibition of the natural and industrial resources of the colonies), and one dedicated to Angola and Mozambique. A smaller, fifth pavilion offered wine tasting. The Angola and Mozambique pavilion was the largest of the pavilions of the Portuguese representation, perhaps a reflection of the importance of the two

20. A bibliography of colonial knowledge presented by the AGC, the AHC, the exhibition commissariat, the Museu Agrícola Colonial of Lisbon, the SGL, the University of Porto and the colonies themselves was published as part of Portugal's participation in the exhibition (see *Exposition coloniale internationale de 1931 à Paris. Bibliographie* 1931).

colonies in terms of their size and natural resources (*Exposition coloniale internationale de Paris [section portugaise]* 1931). On exhibition here were natural products, objects manufactured by Natives, specimens of local fauna, maps, tables, diagrams and other printed matter. Mozambique was also represented in one of the historical pavilions. The central pavilion was dedicated to Portugal and the colonies of Cape Verde, Guinea, São Tomé e Príncipe, Macao and Timor. The metropolitan pavilion featured exhibitions on the 'Catholic Missions Overseas' and 'Colonial Education in the Metropolis and Education in the Colonies', this latter with the participation of the Arquivo Histórico Colonial. Guinea was described as a country with great agricultural potential and an abundant labour supply. Its delegation included a pirogue in which *Indígenas* offered visitors rides on the lake, which must have been a great attraction. On São Tomé e Príncipe, the official catalogue (*Exposition coloniale internationale de Paris [section portugaise]* 1931) stressed that two doctors from the Faculté de Médecine de Paris had examined the *Indígenas* and found that, contrary to suspicions, they enjoyed good health, and that Portugal's *Indígena* policy was exemplary. The catalogue also drew attention to the natural and human resources (i.e. labour) of Angola. Timor received less attention than the other colonial possessions.

The one country that stood out from the others was Mozambique. Of this colony, and its capital city Lourenço Marques especially, we learn that the population was composed of *Indígenas* and European settlers from Portugal and elsewhere. Among the *Indígenas* there was a great variety of 'races', including the 'finest types of the Black race', such as the Makua, Tonga, Zulu and Landin (*O Século* 1931: 29). The Mozambican representation included a number of large canvas posters. One of these, designed by Rocha Pereira under the guidance of the exhibition commissariat, divided the population of Mozambique by 'race', using the following classifications: 'Blacks', 'Whites', *'Mestiços'*, 'Indo-Portuguese' and 'Yellows' (Figure 12). The poster does not give numbers for the Native population, but to judge by the relative size of the figures it clearly con-

Figure 12. 'Population of Mozambique by race' (Grilo 1932: 35).

stitutes the majority. Colonial education in metropolitan Portugal and education in the colonies were illustrated in four diagrams based on statistics from 1929, separating the data on the *Indígenas* from the data on the *Assimilados*. There were separate figures for primary, secondary and vocational education, the latter combining data from various branches of instruction. The fourth diagram, which is reproduced in Figure 13, gave account of the numbers of 'European' and *Indígena* students, with

breakdowns of expenditure by each branch and parcel of state and municipalities, the Companhia de Moçambique and private initiative. As for vocational training, here we find a representation of a society ordered by 'natural' hierarchies: the White man sits at a typewriter and wears a suit and tie, while the Black man stands in front of a machine and wears overalls. As Table 2 shows, although in terms of school enrolment Blacks (9,833) outnumbered Whites

Figure 13. Colonial education in numbers (Grilo 1932: 38).

(360) by over 27 to 1, investment in education for Whites (1,465,177 escudos) was three times higher than it was for *Indígenas* (589,140 escudos). For each European student, expenditure was 67.93 times higher than it was for each *Indígena* student. The disparities are significant in primary education too, where 3.73 times more was spent on each European student. This occurred in a context in which the number of *Indígena* students was six times higher than the number of European students. In secondary education, expenditure on each European student was 6.9 times higher than on his or her *Indígena* counterpart – this in a context where the *Indígenas* constituted less than half of the total number of students.

Another publication on the same exhibition (Melo and Zysset 1931)[21] contained a chapter on 'public instruction' in Angola. In this we can see that the kind of education directed at the *Indígenas* was essentially vocational, and given by the missions. According to Melo and Zysset, the delegate for Angola at the exhibition, the primary education

---

21. A joint effort of the official colonial services and the translator Frédéric-Léon Zysset.

Table 2. Disparities in expenditure on colonial education.

	Indígenas (I)	Europeans (E)	I/E	E/I
Students	30,122.0	5,021.0	6.00	0.17
Primary expenditure	2,606,811.0	1,620,603.0	1.61	0.62
Exp./student	86.5	322.8	0.27	3.73
Students \	76.0	182.0	0.42	2.39
Secondary expenditure	46,261.0	763,964.0	0.06	16.51
Exp./student	608.7	4,197.6	0.15	6.90
Students	9,833.0	360.0	27.31	0.04
Vocational expenditure	589,140.0	1,465,177.0	0.40	2.49
Exp./student	59.9	4,069.9	0.01	67.93

given at nursery and primary schools was directed at the 'White race' and *Assimilados*. There were sixty-eight such schools in the colony at this time. As for Angola's two secondary schools or *liceus*, their objective was to allow the children of settlers and 'civilized' others – 'Blacks' or *Mestiços* – to acquire the learning necessary for their admission to Portuguese universities. Vocational education was intended for the *Indígenas*. It was administered in twenty 'rural schools' and thirty-seven 'workshop-schools'. The teachers in the former institutions were *Indígenas* with Escola Normal Rural (i.e. locally acquired) qualifications. The teachers of the 'workshop-schools' were European, with qualifications gained in metropolitan Portugal. Melo and Zysset also name a number of Catholic missions operating in 1930, all of them with adjoining rural schools – for boys, girls, or coeducational – or trade workshops offering apprenticeships with carpenters, smiths, stonemasons, bookbinders, typographers, cobblers, tailors and tanners. Some of these workshops operated alongside rural estates, dispensaries and livestock installations. There were also missions run by various Protestant denominations in Angola, some of which are cited (Melo and Zysset 1931: 37, 39–40, 43–45).

As for the 'social economy of the colonies', Grilo observes that 'the coloured man' should not consider himself 'dishonoured or downcast for being [coloured]' in regard to the record of Natives who deposited money in banks, since it was important to monitor the proportion of the Native population which made deposits: this was an important indicator for evaluating its 'degree of progress' and 'evolution', a 'matter of primordial importance' for Portugal's 'colonial functions'. In the section 'Sport in the Colonies', we read that a 'measurement system' had recently been adopted for 'the *Indígena* military contingent' under which Indigenous soldiers were classified according to Pignet's formula. This was the pretext for a display of 'watercolour diagrams' which evidenced the presence of 'physical anthropology' in these events. Some *Indígenas* had been brought from the Portuguese overseas territories, at the request of the exhibition commissariat, the previous September. This contingent included 'twelve Landin to guard the pavilions in Vincennes', but 'some of the soldiers who had distinguished themselves in the recent sports events belonged to other sub-races'. These *Indígenas* were to participate in 'sports events or tournaments that the presence of Indigenous groups of other nationalities would make possible', while 'the organization of the group into a football team would be greatly appreciated'. Perhaps for this reason, the visiting Landin were required to be of good physical constitution. The '10th Indigenous Company' received 'special instruction in the perfection of skills such as music, choral singing, *jogo do pau,* etc.'. And as in all similar events, their every movement was monitored: 'In Portugal as in France, they were directly and fully subordinated to the General Commissariat' (Grilo 1932: 62–64, 80–81).

A 'Guinean village' at the Lisbon Industrial Exhibition (1932)

In 1932[22] came the Lisbon Industrial Exhibition, organized by the Associação Industrial Portuguesa. It was this event that inaugurated the Palácio de Exposições of Lisbon's Parque Eduardo VII.[23] The exhibition ran from 3 October to 30 December 1932. According to reports in the press,[24] the exhibition drew visitors in their thousands – by some estimates, fifteen thousand visitors every day. The colonies also participated in this exhibition, at the instigation of the AGC and its director. This cooperation was to have been beneficial for both parties, for in metropolitan Portugal there was still much ignorance about what went on in the colonies, especially where industry was concerned. The exhi-

---

22. In this same year, the Colonial Ministry organized the colonial produce fairs of Luanda and Lourenço Marques (Figure 14), accompanied by two colonial conferences organized by H. Galvão. A declared intention of these fairs was to attract settlers and influential 'Indigenous chiefs' to Luanda and Lourenço Marques. In May, the SGL held an exhibition on Guinea including a 'curious graphic' with 'the types of the various Native races, strong and adaptable to work' (*IP* 1932, no. 52: 50) (see *Exposição da Colónia da Guiné. 1932, Catálogo* 1932).

23. This palace had earlier been used at the International Exhibition of Rio de Janeiro in 1922. It was reerected in Parque Eduardo VII and was inaugurated to mark the official opening of the exhibition.

24. I have primarily drawn on figures from the review *Indústria Portuguesa (IP)* published between March and December 1932.

Figure 14. Poster advertising the 1932 colonial produce fairs of Luanda and Lourenço Marques, Biblioteca Nacional, Lisbon.

bition was a reaffirmation of the power of fairs and exhibitions to raise the 'level of civic education of the population' (*IP* no. 52: 17). In the words of lieutenant-colonel Garcez de Lencastre, agent-general for the colonies, it would be 'interesting and unusual to divulge' the colony of Guinea 'among the population of Lisbon and outsiders who are naturally attracted by the Exhibition', by its proximity, by the 'valuable elements' contained among the Guineans and their 'industrial activities and customs'. Acting in the name of the AGC, Lencastre suggested the organization of an 'Indigenous village', a 'typical settlement, where artists, such as weavers, tailors, smiths, saddlers, etc., would exercise their crafts and go about their daily lives' (*IP* no. 51: 39).

As the reigning ideology proclaimed a single, indivisible Portugal, it made no sense to make distinctions between industry in the metropolis and industry in the colonies: all was Portuguese industry. And as if in corroboration of this apparent unity, we learn that various metropolitan firms and companies had industrial concerns in Angola, Mozambique,

Macao and India, where 'hundreds of Whites and thousands of *Indíge-nas*' worked (*IP* no. 52: 28). The colonial part of the exhibition comprised an official section and a private-sector section. The former hosted a 'demonstration of the tendencies and prospects of the *Indígenas* in the exercise of various industrial skills' (*IP* no. 53: 56–57). The upper galleries of two rooms to the rear of the pavilion of honour exhibited 'the primitive industries of the *Indígenas* and the regular work of the students of the Catholic missions', the objective being to show how 'the *Indígenas* and the little Blacks, educated in the missions', worked. As a complement to this section, an 'Indigenous village' was mocked up with living, working, performing 'Guinean *Indígenas*', and was 'one of the biggest attractions'. This 'village' was proclaimed by Lencastre as a 'first' in Portugal, a must-see attraction which was also designed to 'make the chieftains, leaders, and some among their people, see the beauty of Portugal, of the Metropolis, seat of the Empire' (*IP* no. 52: 27). The man responsible for 'supervising' and 'guiding' the *Indígenas* during their stay was António Pereira Cardoso, a senior employee of the Curadoria dos Negócios Indígenas da Guiné. The exhibition was to be advertised in cinemas and in documentaries, the TSF, press and regional guilds. In addition to the film shows, the exhibition featured concerts, illuminations (billed as 'spectacles') and other 'diverse and varied' events among which were the programmes of 'Colonial Demonstration' (*IP* no. 56: 25). Various articles in the magazine *Indústria Portuguesa* are informed by recurring ideas. One such idea is that Portuguese colonization was 'different', and that therefore Portugal was unique in the world: it was a country where people born in territories under its dominion had the same rights as those born in metropolitan Portugal and those of the 'White race'. (As we know, in reality this was not true. There were differences. There was the Colonial Act and the *Indígena* statute. And then there were the distinctions made between *Indígenas, Assimilados* and *Civilizados*.) Another idea was that Portuguese sovereignty over the colonized peoples was based on very strong moral ties, so strong that a Portuguese could travel anywhere in the colonies and be welcomed wherever he went, without the need to carry a weapon. The claim, in other words, was that the Portuguese empire was not so much about *colonizing* as *assimilating* and *civilizing*.

Another intention of the organizers of the Lisbon Industrial Exhibition was to show 'the common people of the metropolis' how 'the people of Africa' lived, 'just like the folklore groups of the Portuguese provinces, with their chants and dances, their habits and speech, their apparel – typical, characteristic, traditional and clean'. The AGC had brought

[c]raftsmen full of ingenuity ... and Blacks of a certain learning, intelligent and deserving of ... respect. All demonstrate their state of progress, although they are subject ... to their own ways of living (*IP* 1932 no. 56: 56).

Although these Blacks were subject to the constraints of their own way of life, *Indústria Portuguesa* considered them as worthy of respect. Four of them were chieftains *(régulos)*, while others formed part of their retinues or performed various tasks – in crafts, industry or folklore. The chieftains tend to be referred to in a different register relative to other Natives. Most articles give emphasis to the chieftains and the prince (the son of one of the chieftains). Their names are given and their ranks indicated:

Four African chieftains ... and a real prince, the son of one of them – His Highness Abdulbalder, heir to the chieftain Branjalmebalder. The other chieftains are called Boncoassanha, Sambeiçufe and Dembadanejo, and are officers in our army, four of them lieutenants and one, Mr Dembadanejo, a second lieutenant, as we can see by the gilt emblems of rank they exhibit on their shoulders ... They have brought in their private service a *regular,* whose rank corresponds to that of the orderly of the metropolis, and with them have come 39 Black men and women – dancers, singers and players of the strange and noisy instruments which accompany the classic *batuque* of the African feast (*IP* 1932 no. 56: 53).

The chieftains came as representatives of the 'Indigenous authorities' and were 'chosen from those of greatest prestige [and those who had performed] the most relevant services to the administration of the colony'; they understood Portuguese and spoke it 'fairly well', they had 'excellent bearing', were 'very intelligent' and had come 'decked out in their best costumes and finery', bringing the 'saddles and trappings' (*IP* 1932: no. 56: 55–56) which they used for riding. When the Portuguese president, Óscar Carmona, visited the exhibition on 4 October, his attention was directed towards the chieftains and Prince Abdulbalder, 'dressed in their gold-trimmed gala *cabangas,* displaying on their epaulettes the stripes of ensign and second lieutenant in the colonial army'. As for the remaining Natives, they were collectively referred to as 'Blacks' and in their 'gaudy apparel' they welcomed the president 'with warrior chants and marches', playing 'heathen instruments'. Inside one of the Native cabins, General Carmona announced that he felt 'great pleasure in seeing such loyal servants of the *Pátria,* which protects them and holds them in affection' (*IP* 1932 no. 56: 44). According to Lencastre, the chieftains were 'among the bravest and most loyal in Guinea'. They had 'sacrificed themselves for the sovereignty of Portugal' and been 'educated by Europeans who instilled in them a spirit of love for Portugal'. When the minister for the colonies, Armindo Monteiro, visited the exhibition, the chieftains 'expressed their satisfaction and gratitude for the good treatment' they had received. The twenty-eight-year-old Prince Abdulbalder was described as most engaging, with 'shining eyes' and 'teeth of a dazzling whiteness' (*IP* 1932 no. 56: 53). The (unnamed) *IP* journalist related that the prince was 'much in demand' and that 'White ladies' were making insinuations at him and even sending him letters with 'words more than friendly' (*IP* 1932 no. 56: 62). As the journalist put it, 'bursting with health and vigour at 28 years of age', he was attracting 'certain attentions' (*IP* 1932 no. 56: 62). Perhaps also because he was the son of a chieftain, and spoke and understood Portuguese, and was a 'winsome and articulate young man', he was invited to 'visit the houses of rich people' who lived near the park (*IP* 1932 no. 56: 54). And yet in celebrating the 'youthful joy of the thatched-hut "prince"' (*IP* 1932 no. 56: 62), the journalist encloses the word *prince* in inverted commas. Because he was not a real prince? Because he was Black? For, as the journalist noted, this prince's domain was not a castle but a thatched hut. *Indústria Portuguesa* described the *Indígenas* as representatives of the Native elites of Guinea. Members of the elite they may have been, but few could speak Portuguese. The prince's sister and the 'Black girls who accompanied her, the daughters of other chieftains', did not understand Portuguese. And in an interview he gave to the editor of *Novidades,* Prince Abdulbalder is described as speaking consistently good Portuguese, although he made the odd grammatical error and used the occasional verb in the infinitive, a habit 'so much to the predilection of the Blacks who speak our language' (*IP* 1932: no. 56: 53, 62, 54, 60).

On 7 November 1932 the chieftains (Boncó Sanhá, Samba Iussufo Baldé, Bram-Dj'Ame Baldé and Demba Danejo) received silver medals for 'Distinction In Overseas Services'. At the end of the award ceremony, Lencastre announced that because the minister for the colonies had given them the opportunity to behold the greatness of Portugal and its people, they should increase their respect, loyalty and faith 'in the destinies of Portugal'. Lencastre also reported that the government intended to make an effort to 'create in Guinea the schools appropriate' to the education of the *Indígenas* (*IP* 1932: no. 57: 65–66). Here again the idea transpires that it was the metropolitan Portuguese who had elevated the overseas Portuguese, and that the latter should be eternally grateful to the former for continuing to administer to their educational needs. Although the chieftains were named, the members of their retinue were simply referred to as 'Blacks'; they wore the same white tunics with turbans, which made a stark contrast with the 'inky black' of their faces. As individuals, they were mentioned only in connection with the particular roles they played in the exhibition. Thus the group included 'two weavers, one tailor-embroiderer, one shoemaker, one blacksmith and one goldsmith'; its performing artists numbered 'one gourd player, one fiddler, one marimba player, two Jews (a man and a woman), dancers and musicians, one *caifás* (a dancer and acrobat), four Futa-Fula dancers and two wrestlers'. Then there were 'ten young girls, of characteristic beauty, [who had come] to sing as a choir and take part in the dances' (Figure 15). In all, the retinue numbered '39 *Indígenas,* belonging to various tribes of the Fula race' (*IP* 1932: no. 56: 56). During Carmona's visit the cloth, footwear and embroidery produced by the *Indígenas* – all made with 'primitive machinery' (*IP* 1932 no. 56: 45) – were admired.

Before the exhibition opened its doors, the Natives were busy building the village they would live in: the men built the huts, while the women took care of the cooking and other chores. The village was named Sam Corlá, after the Guinean chieftainship to which the Natives belonged. It comprised eight 'hovels' or 'huts' in which the thirty-nine Natives were billeted, the women on one side and the men on the other. The village also had its own animals, which were kept in a special corral. In the interview he gave to *Novidades,* Abdulbalder noted that not only the 'mere servants' but also the chieftains had worked on the construc-

Figure 15. A camera operator from *O Século Cinematográfico* filming the 'beauties' of the village of Sam Corlá (*IP* 1932: no. 57, 69).

tion of the village, the latter in a supervisory capacity. According to the prince, it had been necessary for the chieftains to impose their authority, for in the view of the Natives they had not come to build villages: 'the tailor said he came to make suits; the musician to play; the weaver to weave; the dancer to dance' (*IP* 1932 no. 56: 55, 60). A little persuasion was needed, therefore, and the Natives were treated to a visit to the theatre as a reward.

The Natives were also seen as opportunistic. During Armindo Monteiro's visit he was treated to a *batuque,* at the end of which 'the dancer, reaching out to shake the hand of Armindo Monteiro, proffered his left hand to ask for change' – but 'two fat silver coins made him dance with contentment' (*IP* 1932 no. 56: 52). Elsewhere we are informed that during the *batuques* the dancers made a 'good collection of coin' (*IP* 1932 no. 56: 59). As in many situations, Natives and *batuques* went together. For example, in the *batuque* held during Carmona's visit, the *caifás* dancer showed off 'his remarkable choreographic gifts, amid the war chants and yells and the clamour of heathen instruments' (*IP* 1932 no. 56: 46). The artistic performances of the Natives were viewed as a 'curious and picturesque exhibition of Black dance, music and song' and were witnessed by 'many people who had come along out of curiosity' (*IP* 1932 no. 56: 58).

The behaviour of the Natives was a source of curiosity and amusement, too. When Linhares de Almeida's film of the 'heathen village of Parque Eduardo VII' was shown to the Natives, 'it was impossible to describe their amazement and enthusiasm when they saw themselves reproduced on the screen'. They 'laughed uproariously, jumped up and down in their chairs like lunatics' and 'found motive for amusement in [their] poses, a single expression, a grimace, even the *batuque* itself' (*IP* 1932 no. 56: 52). The childishness and laziness of the Natives were also mentioned: 'Among themselves, the Blacks have fun, laugh, sing and play' (*IP* 1932 no. 56: 54). When a photographer showed Abdulbalder the photographs he had taken of him, the prince's reaction was described as follows: 'The "prince", just like a child who had been given an expensive toy, goes around delightedly', 'showing his picture to everyone' (*IP* 1932 no. 56: 61). This is a reaffirmation of the perceived similarity of Natives with children, or the idea that the Natives were overgrown children and represented the part of the adult that remained a child, and neither princes nor chieftains were immune to this perception.

The beauty of the Native women was a major allurement: the exhibition featured 'a certain number of types of female Indigenous beauty'. The Natives were also seen as deeply superstitious. Just as they had been in the sixteenth century, the Fula and Mandinka were 'faithful to their infidel religion'. Prince Abdulbalder noted that the Natives continued to observe their religious practices during the exhibition, praying five times a day (morning, noon, after lunch, afternoon, sundown and midnight). They customarily ate whenever they felt like it, not at fixed hours like the 'gentlemen' of the metropolis. As Muslims, the Fula could eat nothing that had not been prepared by fellow Muslims; and back in Guinea their 'priests' would not be pleased to hear that they had drunk wine, for example. And so, for the duration of the exhibition, the Fula observed a diet similar to their diet back home in Guinea, but served in three daily meals:

> At 8 in the morning, milk from a cow which has been hired to them; white bread with sugar and kola nuts; at noon, fish or meat, except pork, which their religion does not allow; and at 6 in the evening, any of the aforementioned victuals, with potatoes and fruit (*IP* 1932 no. 56: 54).

Discipline was imposed not only by the strict mealtimes ordained by the organizers of the exhibition, but also by the village chiefs: the Natives had to live 'in good composure and discipline, maintained, of course, by their chiefs. Any misdemeanour would be punished by the chieftains.' The insistence on regular mealtimes is significant, for by controlling time we control people. As Foucault noted, 'time penetrates the body and with it all the meticulous controls of power' (1977: 152). Discipline was imposed, and power asserted, via control over the Natives' bodies. The Natives were allowed to leave the exhibition precinct, but only with authorization and – just like big children – only when properly accompanied. The Guinean chieftains and prince Abdulbalder visited southern Portugal during their sojourn in the country, 'with the proper authorization' of the minister for the colonies and the administrative committee of the exhibition, accompanied by AGC representative António Pereira Cardoso and various journalists.

The inhabitants of metropolitan Portugal, and visitors to the exhibition in particular, showed great curiosity about the Natives. When the Fula of Guinea made a boat excursion on the Tagus to Boca do Inferno and Trafaria, stopping in the bay of Estoril, a multitude took canoes or swam out to take a closer look at them. In their visits to various towns and villages many people came to admire them (*IP* 1932 no. 57: 63). Within the exhibition, the public initially showed 'extraordinary curiosity' towards the *Indígenas,* but this 'unbridled curiosity led some persons to the practice of excesses which obliged the authorities to intervene'. It was the 'desire to see the *Indígenas*' that led to the village being 'stoned by curious onlookers who, in so unorthodox a manner, wanted to force them out of a shack where some of them were lodged, so they could see them'. Such acts were 'distressing for the Coloured Portuguese [and] would end up … giving them a deplorable notion of the manners of their White brothers'. And so 'to prevent the public from invading it, the settlement of the *Indígenas* was … put under the guard of the Police and some army recruits' for a few days. Without pronouncing further measures, the exhibition committee resolved to expect 'moderation from the public of the capital' in their manifestations of curiosity, which was nevertheless considered to be 'understandable' (*IP* 1932 no. 56: 56). But if their curiosity was understandable, surely their behaviour towards their 'Coloured Portuguese' conationals was not. In another issue of the *IP* published after the end of the exhibition, we are informed that it had attracted over forty-five thousand visitors, and that the populace had been 'orderly and disciplined at all times'. The whole event had gone off 'without the slightest disturbance or disorder', and at no point had 'the civil police had reason to intervene' (*IP* 1932 no. 58: 34). Just two months later, the stoning episode seemed to have been forgotten. For the behaviour of the visitors there was only praise.

The Portuguese Colonial Exhibition of 1934

Concept and objectives

The first Portuguese Colonial Exhibition took place in Porto from 16 June to 30 September 1934, closing with a grand colonial procession. The venue was the Palácio de Cristal, which had hosted previous exhibitions and was renamed 'Palace of the Colonies' especially for the event. With over four hundred pavilions that took five months to build, the exhibition attracted 1 million visitors. According to the exhibition's commissioner, Henrique Galvão, 'the average daily number of visitors was 12,000.' Among the 'illustrious foreigners' to visit the exhibition were the Prince of Wales, the Belgian colonial minister Paul Tchoffen and the editor in chief of *Le Temps,* among other foreign journalists. According to the report Galvão drew up after the event, a total of 1,799,000 escudos was invested in the exhibition (1935: 19, 37). A colonial exhibition was not exactly a new idea in Portugal at this time. Support had been voiced for an exhibition of this type as early as the Colonial Congress of 1901. And as far as its organization was concerned, it had precedents to draw on, such as the exhibitions of Spain (1929), Belgium (1930) and France (1931). As Armindo Monteiro wrote, the exhibition of 1934 was 'not something that can be appreciated in isolation' (1934: 353).[25] It

---

25. As we saw in Chapter II, the Colonial Anthropology Congress ran in parallel to this exhibition. A number of other conferences were held on the subject of the Portu-

was also the pretext for a colonial literature competition, whose second prize went to *Terras do Feitiço*, a collection of stories by none other than Henrique Galvão, the exhibition's commissioner.

The purpose of the 1934 exhibition was to showcase colonization in its different aspects, such as the natural and human resources of the overseas possessions, and economy and industry in the colonies – with the emphasis on the 'utilitarian' character of the event and on the investment being made in the religious conversion and education of the colonized populations. Displaying these achievements would be a demonstration of the didactic nature of the event, and a way of exercising more effective sovereignty over the colonies.

The leaflet published as a guide to the exhibition (Figure 16) proclaimed a modern Portugal where order reigned, a country that had given 'new worlds to the world' using 'highly original colonial methods'. By putting on show the vastness of its possessions Portugal was no longer 'a small country'.[26] And as centuries of rule confirmed, Portugal's power over its foreign domains was legitimate. Curiously, however, for all its centuries of familiarity with them, Portugal did not have any great knowledge about

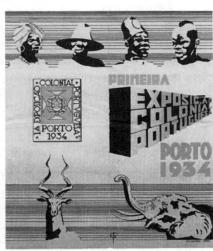

Figure 16. Leaflet from the 1934 Colonial Exhibition.

these territories or their populations, and neither had any great investment been made in them. Therefore, the exhibition was intended to stimulate research, encourage colonial studies and promote economic, material and technological expansion. It was also designed to serve as

guese colonies. In one of these, Galvão presented a paper suggestively titled 'The Colonial Function of Portugal – the National Raison d'Être'.

26. An allusion to the famous exhibition poster. As its title, 'Portugal is Not a Small Country', proclaimed, this poster was an attempt to show that the surface area of the 'Portuguese empire' was larger than the whole of Europe. In other words, a direct comparison was being drawn between the 'empire' and other European countries, most of them bigger than Portugal, without actually taking into consideration the colonies that some of *them* possessed. The 'Portuguese empire' was only bigger than Europe because no distinction was made between metropolitan Portugal and its overseas possessions, which were conceived in this context as a single, indivisible, united entity.

a reminder that the colonies were Portugal's raison d'être as a nation, and that the period of the maritime discoveries was a source of national pride. Finally, it was designed to give 'a lesson to the masses: with simplicity, with emotive and pictorial power, with occasionally ingenuous elements' which would impress and educate them, for the exhibition was, and had to be, for the masses (Galvão 1934a: 32). According to Galvão, this event 'was the first lesson in colonialism given to the Portuguese masses'; and if all the Portuguese could have gone to the colonies, they would have received a 'complete lesson' (Galvão 1934a: 16). Galvão himself alludes to the idea that the exhibition offered the opportunity to take a journey through the expanses of the 'empire', expanses which together constituted 'a whole' (1934a: 16). Those who made the journey would undergo a 'spiritual transformation' (1934a: 27). Circulating on foot or on the 'colonial train', visitors could enjoy the sensation of travelling around the world as they marvelled at its diversity of architecture, landscape and, of course, inhabitants.

'Order' was a watchword of the Estado Novo regime, and here too order was everywhere to be seen, with clear demarcation of the official area, the private sector area, and another area containing attractions and diversions,[27] distributed around the Palace of the Colonies, the gardens and the street leading from the palace to the barracks of the No. 3 Battalion of Machine Gunners. All the streets and avenues in the exhibition precinct were named after regions of the 'empire'. The official section included one part dedicated to history, and another to the 'colonial achievements of the Portuguese in the last forty years'. This section also featured a military and various ethnographic exhibits. Outside the entrance to the exhibition was Praça do Império: 'Empire Square'. At the centre of this square was the 'Monument to the Portuguese Colonial Effort',[28] at the base of which were six sculptures of the figures considered emblematic of this effort – the woman, the soldier, the missionary, the trader, the farmer and the doctor. Two illuminated fountains adorned the square – decorative features which were also symbols of progress and technology in metropolitan Portugal. Another salient feature was the 'Monument to the Fallen of Portuguese Colonization', which celebrated the major role played by the Portuguese in this process and to a certain extent gave them some legitimization, backed up in part by their endeavours. Inside the palace, and part of the official section, was an installation designated 'Ethnography, Class XLVI, Usages and Cus-

27. These diversions included a zoo (with specimens of African fauna), 'Luna Parque', a 'colonial train', theatre, 'heathen spectacles', a cable car, a cinema and a 'colonial bookshop' (Galvão 1935: 25–26).

28. This monument, designed by Sousa Caldas, has now been moved to the neighbourhood of Foz, Porto.

toms'. This installation was disposed along a 'central aisle' and illustrated Portugal's colonial activity over the previous fifty years.[29] In addition to the part showcasing 'European Settlement', the exhibition also sought to 'show the liberal and humanitarian models on which "Indigenous Policy" was based'. A diorama showed an 'Indigenous tribunal' and the 'diploma of appointment of a tribal chief'. This part of the exhibition also featured 'photographs of Indigenous chiefs' which, according to the exhibition's organizers, spoke volumes of the respect for 'the customs of the peoples' shown by their Portuguese rulers – 'the acknowledgement, within certain limits, of the authority of their chiefs, the guarantee of their property and their freedom to work as they saw fit'. But these limits were often imposed by the colonizers, not by the 'Indigenous chiefs'. As for 'Education in the Colonies', the idea was to show the expansion of education in primary, national, higher and vocational schools, and in central *liceus* (*Guia Oficial do Visitante* 1934: 7, 13–17).

Another installation was 'Medicine and Hygiene', where a 'group of life-sized mannequins' recreated the 'exact idea of an encampment where victims of sleeping sickness are treated'. The 'Medicine and Hygiene' area included an exhibit of work in the field of 'scientific anatomy and anthropology' (*Guia Oficial do Visitante:* 17–19), and replicas of African and Asian heads made from moulds and skulls. This area was organized by two institutes. The Anthropology Institute of the University of Porto exhibited 'ethnographic and anthropometric studies', 'documentaries of anthropology' and 'masks and skulls of Natives of the colonies, a bibliography and photographs'. The Anatomy Institute of the Faculty of Medicine of the same university contributed with 'anatomical studies of Natives of the colonies', as well as a bibliography and photographs. This show of diversity was designed to encompass all the 'racial types' of the empire. Following evolutionist theory, each exhibit was designed to exemplify the place of each 'type' in the empire and humanity in general. Next came 'Spiritual Assistance', which showcased the 'action of the religious missions', including catechism, medical care and vocational training, in five groups of mannequins together with maps and photographs. According to the doctrine of the regime, the missions were one of the principal reasons for the presence of Portugal in the colonies, as they were key components of the colonizing 'vocation' of the Portuguese. The missionaries themselves were described as the 'champions and benefactors of the progress and prosperity of intellectually and morally backward peoples' (V. de M. 1935: 153). Another area was dedicated to 'Indigenous Art' and offered a collection of the 'artistic expressions' of

---

29. There seems to have been no clear consensus on this number, as other sources give forty years, not fifty.

the Natives of the colonies. The 'rudimentary' manifestations of 'culture' on display were intended to demonstrate the inferior state of civilization of those who had produced them.

The Ethnographic Pavilion belonged to the 'Ethnography' group, which featured, as the official guide informs us, 'a curious[30] collection of ethnographic artefacts from the colonies'. Here we find the 'allegorical pavilions of S. Tomé, India and Macao' and 'heathen villages inhabited by Natives of Angola, Mozambique and Guinea'. In Rua da Beira stood the 'Pavilion of the Mozambique Company', with four plaster busts of Indigenous types, an 'ethnographic map of the Territory', 'photographs of Indigenous types of thirteen sub-races', 'photographic reproductions of Indigenous types and customs' and 'huts in which … a goldsmith, a turner and a weaver work' (*Álbum-Catálogo Oficial* 1934: 440–41, 447). Over on 'Macao street' was the pavilion of the same name; this featured a 'teahouse' with a resident orchestra of Chinese musicians. On the same street was a Hindu temple 'garrisoned with dancing girls and *Indígenas*[31] of the State [of India]'. There was also an 'evocation and representation of the military occupation and pacification of the colonies in the last fifty years', in which there participated 'an Indigenous company of Mozambican soldiers' (Galvão 1935: 25). Neither was Brazil forgotten. One of the commemorative publications (*Portugal através do tempo* 1934) informs us that 'the formation of colonial Brazil was highly troublesome', for 'there was no organized, established empire like that of the Incas in Peru or the Aztecs in Mexico, but only dispersed tribes which the newcomers had to defeat one by one.' But with the arrival of the Portuguese came Christianity, as the colonizers 'preserved the Native Indian population', 'developed the colony for agriculture' and 'covered the country in cities and fine buildings'. Brazil was the 'glorious standard' by which the value of the 'extraordinary qualities of the Portuguese people, when placed at the service of Civilization', was to be measured, and was now the 'emancipated, rich and happy' child of the empire, where Portuguese was spoken.

Natives as 'living artefacts'

In a place where a certain order was imposed, what status was assigned to the Natives? Various sources inform us that 324 Natives were present

---

30. The adjective 'curious' was applied to objects of which little or nothing was known, neither their purpose, nor by whom they were used; and no attempt was made to present them in a systematic fashion.

31. As appears in other sources, the people who participated in the exhibitions could be classified as *Indígenas* indiscriminately, despite not having this status, as happened with the people of the State of India (who never had it).

at the exhibition. However, a report compiled in 1934 by the agent-general for the colonies mentions that the AGC 'gave assistance to 185 *Indígenas* from the Colonies'. This is unclear. Did only 185 Natives require assistance? Or did only 185 actually travel to the exhibition? Were the remainder already in Portugal? Writing on the 1931 Colonial Exhibition of Paris, Mendes Correia noted how French scientific reviews had revealed that 'many of the supposed ethnographic demonstrations' held at this exhibition were 'mere showman's contrivances'; and that the 'threatening gestures' of the New Caledonian dancers which 'fearfully brought to mind their not-too-distant cannibalism, were uncharacteristic pantomimes accompanied by religious canticles taught to the *Indígenas* by peaceable missionaries'. And while his French colleagues had not been authorized to study a single *Indígena,* writes Mendes Correia, in Porto it had been possible 'to exhaustively examine over 300 *Indígenas*' (*Trabalhos do I Congresso Nacional* 1934, vol. 1: 28–29).

Various publications emphasized the 'different' character of Portuguese colonization and the special treatment given to the Natives, under 'a regime of equality and freedom'. In political terms, the Constitution and the Colonial Act considered

> all Portuguese, born in the Mainland, in the adjacent islands or in the overseas provinces, to be Portuguese citizens ... Only a policy of unity would bring ... civilization to the *Indígena,* and the expansion of the language (*Portugal através do tempo* 1934).

'Equal' they may have been, but when the Natives of Africa, India, Macao and Timor came to the exhibition they aroused a great deal of curiosity.[32] For the metropolitan Portuguese, it was their opportunity to see '*Indígenas* from all the Colonies in an environment as close as possible to their own' (Galvão 1934b: 30). Various articles noted that the 'Blacks' were one of the biggest – if not the biggest – attractions. But this was not so much because any great attempt was made to exhibit the interest and originality of these peoples, but rather because they were invested with an exoticism with which the inhabitants of metropolitan Portugal were unfamiliar; they were the 'primitives' (many went naked,

---

32. Of the many events and manifestations organized as part of the exhibition, those in which the Natives participated were: the 'colony days', marked by conferences and popular/cultural events; manifestations designed to exalt the 'colonial spirit', such as the colonial procession; sports events such as the First International Shooting Competition between colonial nations, 'sports competitions between *Indígenas* of the colonies' and 'aviation day and the demonstrations of gymnastics and military exercises by the soldiers of Mozambique' (Galvão 1935: 24–25, 32).

spoke no Portuguese and were not Catholics) who justified Portugal's ongoing presence in the overseas territories. Although they were 'primitives', however, they had been pacified, and therefore they were now ready to evolve and become civilized, i.e. genuine citizens. Galvão relates how many visitors would enthusiastically exclaim: 'Let's go and see the Blacks!' (1934a: 27).

In an exhibition whose 'manifestations were unanimous and harmonious', where 'all men of all political persuasions and all ideologies came together' (Galvão 1935: 40–41), the conduct of some visitors was rather less than correct: some men acted provocatively towards the Native women, particularly the African ones, while some of the female visitors seemed enthralled by the naked bodies of the African men. In fact, the sensuality and sexuality of the Natives were topics which generated much discussion during the exhibition. The sensuality of the African women was frowned upon by female visitors. But their own behaviour came in for criticism in press reports and oral accounts: the way they lingered in contemplation of the beauty and physical vigour of the Native men was not appropriate to their status as women, it was argued, and only denigrated the image of the women of metropolitan Portugal. The Natives were believed to be oversexed, a view illustrated in a text on Mozambique which made a point of noting that 'polygamy is legitimate among the *Indígenas*' (*Álbum-Catálogo Oficial* 1934: 329).

Not only were they physically put on show, the Natives were also captured in images. The artists invited by Galvão to make portraits of the Natives were of a conservative stripe. One of these was Eduardo Malta (1900–67), whose portraits of members of each of the groups ('races') on show at the exhibition were published as a collection of picture postcards. These postcards would have circulated in metropolitan Portugal, serving as reminders of the exoticism and diversity to be found in the colonial empire. Malta was known as a painter of society women, and the fact that he was painting pictures of 'Black women' gave some cause for comment. In some of his portraits we can detect a certain distress, boredom and remoteness on the faces of the Natives. Clearly they were not enjoying the 'party' – an impression which the realism of the portraits did little to mitigate. As for photography, one firm, Fotografia Alvão, had the exclusive rights to take photographs of the exhibition. The photograph album published by Alvão reveals a marked contrast between the photos showing modernity and progress and others showing the rustic character of the colonies. There are no reports of complaints from the subjects about having their photos taken and distributed. As with the films, the idea conveyed was that the Natives were happy to see pictures of themselves.

The demographic data on the colonies given in the *Álbum-Catálogo Oficial* is often vague, revealing the deficiencies in intelligence on the colonial populations. On various occasions we are told that population figures are 'estimates' or that no 'precise population figures' (*Álbum-Catálogo Oficial* 1934: 308) exist. Of the 'Indigenous races' of Mozambique we are informed that they belonged to 'the great Bantu family', of which 'all the people of equatorial and southern Africa were members, with the exception of the Bushmen and Hottentots' (*Álbum-Catálogo Oficial* 1934: 329). The Bantu themselves were subdivided into 'Landin, Nguni, Muchope, Tonga, Ngoni and Makua' (*Álbum-Catálogo Oficial* 1934: 329). The *Indígena* of Mozambique was 'rarely ... deep or light black' but instead usually '*pardo* tending to dark'; he was described as 'markedly dolichocephalic, with narrow forehead, thick lips, flat nose, wide nostrils, thick woolly hair, thin beard, late in greying'; he legitimately practised polygamy, and was hospitable; the 'mothers ... were affectionate towards their children' (*Álbum-Catálogo Oficial* 1934: 329). Of all the Natives, the 'Ronga, Ngoni, Adjao and the Makua' were the bravest, and made 'good soldiers' (*Álbum-Catálogo Oficial* 1934: 329). Many had 'won the *Cruz de Guerra* in the Nyassa campaign (1917–18)' (*Álbum-Catálogo Oficial* 1934: 329). The text of the catalogue makes a distinction between the 'Indigenous' and 'non-Indigenous' populations. In the case of the former, their numbers were 'annually estimated' on the basis of the *palhota* tax levy. The latter were 'diluted among the Indigenous population' and probably constituted 'a hundredth' part of it. Since 1928, the non-Indigenous population had been censused via family records, using the same procedure as metropolitan Portugal. These 'non-Indigenous' inhabitants comprised Europeans, Indians, Chinese[33] and *Mestiços*. And in Mozambique there was an important distinction to be made when speaking of 'Indians': there was the *monhé* – the name given to the 'Mohammedan or Hindu Indian, almost invariably a British subject' who 'traded with the *Indígena*' – and the *canarim*, an 'Indo-Portuguese Goan' who had come to the colony in 'public employment'. Other population classifications were Indo-British and Indo-Portuguese. The Europeans were either Portuguese or foreigners. The latter group included Britons, Greeks, Germans, Italians, Swiss and French (*Álbum-Catálogo Oficial* 1934: 326–29).

---

33. More accurately, Cantonese, i.e. from Guangdong province. It was from here that 'in 1887 about a thousand workers were imported for the construction of the railway linking Lourenço Marques and Ressano Garcia'. By 1934, however, the Cantonese community did not even number four hundred.

As for India, its population was constituted, 'according to the latest census', of 'Whites, Blacks and *Mestiços,* Yellow men and *Índios'.* The syntactic pairing of 'Blacks and *Mestiços'* is significant, isolating both groups from the metropolitan Portuguese, the inhabitants of Portuguese India and the other colonies, and foreigners, nearly all of them of Hindu-British origin (*Álbum-Catálogo Oficial* 1934: 364). The population of Cape Verde was mainly formed of 'Natives produced by the mating of our settlers with *Indígenas* from Guinea', and 'according to the latest census' was comprised of 'Whites', 'Blacks', *Mestiços* and 'foreigners' (*Álbum-Catálogo Oficial* 1934: 266–68). Guinea is described as a 'repository of valuable ethnic and moral examples who from the Orient shaped a migratory course for the north of Africa'. It is home to a 'chequerboard of races, all of them full of unusual usages and customs', although 'our authorities' had had to introduce 'the principles of civilization' (*Álbum-Catálogo Oficial* 1934: 279). Population density, 'according to the latest census', was broken down by 'race' – 'Whites', 'Blacks', *'Mestiços'* and 'Yellows', as well as 'foreigners' (*Álbum-Catálogo Oficial* 1934: 280). Although a new category – 'Yellows' – is introduced here, it is unclear what criteria are used in defining it. Perhaps these 'Yellow' people were the result of the interbreeding of Asians with Europeans? Or with Arabs?

In Angola, the population was comprised of *'Indígenas, Assimilados* and *Mestiços';* 'foreigners' were classed as 'White'. The catalogue also informs us that in Angola 'most *Indígenas* were hard-working and suited to the exercise of all professions'. The population of São Tomé e Príncipe was divided between 'Europeans' and 'Natives', with the latter further divided into an 'autochthonous race designated the *forros'* and the 'remaining labourers who had come [here] from other colonies to work in agriculture'.

The text on Timor was written by Júlio Garcez de Lencastre, who had been in Timor during the war of the 1910s and had remained there until 1922. This is the first text in which the emphasis is on the inhabitants of a colony, not its 'natural riches'. The 'origin of the Timorese people' is given as the result of the 'successive migration of the Batak peoples of northern Sumatra and of the Alfuro from the Celebes, both already miscegenated during waves of immigration from island to island as far as Timor'. And so the Timorese population had a mixture of Melanesian and Indonesian blood, in combination with Papua blood to various degrees, with the Papua component more accentuated on the eastern tip of the island. There was also 'some miscegenation between Europeans and Indians, and much [miscegenation] between Chinese and Africans'. 'Hindu and Mohammedan civilization' had not reached Timor. Among the peoples of Timor were found 'the qualities and defects proper to the amalgam of races which entered their admixture, further subject to the influence of environment, climate and diet'. Data from one of the last censuses before 1934 indicated that the inhabitants of Timor were divided among Europeans, Chinese, Africans, Timorese and *Mestiços,* with the latter two groups included in the same category. Work was an important factor, for military colonization had had 'a significant civilizing and educating function'.

Then there was Macao, the 'pearl of the East', one of the most densely populated places on the planet. Its inhabitants, according to the 'latest census', comprised 'Yellows,' 'Whites', 'Blacks and *Mestiços*', with the latter two again paired in the same category. Distinctions were also made between metropolitan Portuguese, 'White' and *Assimilado* Portuguese born in the colonies, 'individuals of Chinese origin naturalized as Portuguese', and 'foreigners' (*Álbum-Catálogo Oficial* 1934: 385–86, 371).

All these classifications tended to differ from one census to the next, especially where the Africans were concerned. This phenomenon is illustrated in census figures for the Mozambican region of Beira between 1897 and 1928, which were published to coincide with the exhibition. In 1897, the population of Beira was broken down into 'Africans' and a motley of nationals from various continents.[34] The following year, 1898, the census had three population categories: Africans (classed as *Indígenas*), Europeans and Asians. By 1900, the non-Native population was classified by its country of origin,[35] while the Indigenous population was divided into *Indígenas* and *Mestiços*. No further information is advanced with regard to these *Mestiços;* we are informed neither of the origins of their parents nor of the reasons for their classification as *Mestiços*. By the time of the most recently published census before the 1934 Portuguese Colonial Exhibition (31 December 1928), new categories had been introduced, with the population of Beira classified by Europeans, Indians, 'Yellows', 'Mixed-bloods' and *Indígenas* (*A cidade da Beira* 1934: 32, 67).

Some of the ideas about the Natives current at the time of the exhibition are significant, too. Here as elsewhere, they were seen as 'overgrown children'. Under the Colonial Act and the Organic Charter, the state guaranteed 'the protection and defence of the *Indígenas,* according to

---

34. 2,714 Africans, 540 Portuguese, 216 Britons, 46 Germans, 43 French, 40 Greek, 20 Spanish, 11 Dutch, 11 Italians, 14 Swiss, 11 Swedish, 10 Americans, 165 Indo-English, 110 Indo-Portuguese, 85 Chinese and 5 Arabs (*A cidade da Beira* 1934: 30).

35. 649 Portuguese, 242 Britons, 68 Italians, 61 French, 46 Germans, 30 Turks, 20 Austrians, 17 Americans, 7 Spanish, 11 Swiss, 13 Russians, 13 Egyptians, 10 Dutch, 8 Romanians, 2 Norwegians, 5 Brazilians, 4 Belgians, 1 Mexican and 297 Asians (*A cidade da Beira* 1934: 32).

the principles of humanity and sovereignty'. 'All authorities and settlers' had the duty of 'protecting the *Indígenas*'; and a further obligation was to 'accommodate and uphold initiatives' designed to 'civilize the *Indígena* and increase his love for the Portuguese *Pátria*' (*Álbum-Catálogo Oficial* 1934: 70). The Natives of the colonies were also described as 'natural riches'. As an article entitled 'The Indigenous Wealth of Angola' revealed, this wealth was in the form of raw materials. Its author, Ralph Delgado,[36] quoted the latest census of the 'Indigenous population' (this census was complete by August 1934), which recorded '2,972,587 individuals, male and female, not including Assimilated Blacks' (Delgado 1934). For Delgado, this 'phalanx of Natives' constituted 'one of the biggest and most protected riches of the Colony'; and he pointed out the 'value of the cooperation of the Indigenous masses in the transformation and occupation of the African territories, which legitimately belong to us'. Delgado considered the 'ignorant Blacks' to be 'conscious individuals' who were 'susceptible to progress', but lived in territories which belonged not to them but 'legitimately' to the colonizers. He also contended that with 'our rational colonizing methods ... racial barriers are destroyed [and] basic, immutable principles of humanitarianism ... emerge, proud examples of a pacifying equality' (Delgado 1934). At bottom, what these views and classifications tell us is how colonized populations were seen under Portuguese rule. Secular and Christian ideologies both acknowledged the equality of human 'nature', but emphasis was also placed on the inequalities that existed in terms of civilization, and it was the job of the settlers to redress the balance.

The Colonial Procession and the scale of civilization

The Colonial Exhibition of 1934 closed with the Colonial Procession of 30 September. This procession illustrated the various episodes in the history of the Portuguese discoveries and colonial expansion, and its participants included inhabitants of the overseas territories. The procession was divided into four thematic categories: the historic, the political, the economic, and the 'moral and spiritual'. It covered a six-kilometre route from Foz to the Palácio de Cristal, and each of the four categories was represented by a number of allegorical floats. In the historical section were the Knights of Ceuta, Gil Eanes, the Discoveries, the Captains of the Indian Conquest, the Scouts of Brazil, the Colonial Army of the

---

36. As secretary to the Provincial Commission for the Commemoration of the Double Centenary, Ralph Delgado (1901–?) had the job of reporting on the festivities held in the province of Benguela in commemoration of the foundation and restoration of Portuguese rule. He was the author of several books, including *História de Angola* [D. L., 1973-D. L., 1978] and *A famosa e Histórica Benguela. Catálogo dos Governadores (1779–1940)*.

Eighteenth Century, and a float dedicated to the *funantes, aviados* and *pombeiros,* the traders of the African interior who first made contact with the Indigenous populations'. The political section included the Imperial Banner, representations of the colonial forces, the old settlers and the residents of the colonies, and children as the 'colonizers of tomorrow'. The float dedicated to Cape Verde was drawn by oxen, driven by 'Natives' of the colony in European dress; its Guinean counterpart carried the Mandinka chieftain Mamadu Sissé, who participated in the exhibition and was accompanied by Balanta and Bijago *Indígenas* carrying agricultural produce. The float representing São Tomé e Príncipe was decorated with 'stylized heathen motifs' and was accompanied by *Indígenas* from Cape Verde, one of the colonies which provided São Tomé e Príncipe with migrant labour; the Angolan float was accompanied by 'Black warriors', although the guide omits to mention that these warriors were not 'actors' but in fact *authentic* warriors, or their descendents. Two floats were dedicated to 'Mozambique and the territories of Manica and Sofala (Mozambique Company)', both accompanied by Natives. The first depicted the prowess of the Nguni in the form of two large African heads, but also the downfall of the Nguni empire, extolling the pacification of Mozambique and the role played by Mouzinho de Albuquerque in this pacification; the second depicted a colony in an 'advanced state of civilization' rising from the ruins of the 'Nguni Empire'. The India float, again accompanied by 'Natives of the colony', featured an Indian temple and a golden caravel; the Macanese float carried a miniature Chinese pagoda flanked by four dragons, and was again accompanied by Natives of the colony; and the Timor float illustrated the rugged terrain of the colony and a 'typical Timorese dwelling' with decorative motifs such as coffee plants and buffaloes (*O Cortejo Colonial no Porto* 1934).

The 'economic section' of the procession featured floats dedicated to fauna and transport, with live specimens of African fauna – these animals, like the Natives themselves, were symbols *par excellence* of the exotic – and traditional African means of transport, such as the camel, the litter, the rickshaw, the hartebeest, the donkey, the Boer wagon (drawn by ten pairs of oxen), the palanquin and even the Ford automobile. The floats dedicated to commerce and industry and the 'group representing agriculture' featured figures representing the regions of Portugal, whose inhabitants, like those of the colonies, were classed into various groups. Six floats made up the 'moral and spiritual' section of the procession: the Catholic missions (accompanied by priests and nuns from the overseas missions); Portuguese flags from the fifteenth century to the present day; colonial propaganda (organized by the daily newspaper *O Século*); the Navy; the Metropolitan Army; and the 'Black troop', a tribute to the 'services rendered in the military occupation of the colonies' (*O Cortejo Colonial no Porto* 1934: 10, 16).

In this procession, the Natives were all described as Portuguese. But in addition to the various classifications assigned to them, the fact that some were paid to participate while others did so for nothing suggests differential treatment. The emphasis in this procession was not on ethnological diversity, but on the fact that all participants were part of a single entity under Portuguese sovereignty. And yet to visit the exhibition and witness the closing procession would have been inescapably to remain with the impression that distinctions were drawn among the Natives, despite the fact that they were indiscriminately referred to as *Indígenas,* and that each group was assigned to its own level of civilization according to its way of life, dress, social status, education and occupation. The Angolans, Mozambicans and Guineans occupied the lowest level on this scale of civilization. In a 1934 issue of *A Província de Angola* published in honour of the 'Restoration of Angola' of 15 August 1648, a photograph of a Native woman with the caption 'A Black woman of Mucancala' is contextualized thus:

> A family of this curious tribe, a branch of the Bushman people with characteristics similar to the Mucubal, Bacanisses, and Bacassequeres, came to the Portuguese Colonial Exhibition ... It is one of the lowest species on the scale of humanity. It is ignorant of the existence and usefulness of metals, does not practice agriculture, and lives in caves and dens. It lives on roots, plants, insects, reptiles, molluscs etc. Its language is curious and unique.

Although referring in particular to the 'Bushmen', the above description to some extent exemplifies the way Angolans were viewed in general. Command of the Portuguese language varied greatly, but this aspect does not seem to have been influential when it came to establishing the hierarchy. Natives (with the status of *Indígena*) were almost always represented in a 'natural' setting; what few articles of clothing they wore did not denote high social status, with the exception of the chieftains and their offspring. As for their 'usages and customs', these were invariably manual tasks, such as carving (the so-called *manipanços*) or weaving, while their musical performances were described as *batuques* or 'strange dances'. Chieftains were evaluated differently, owing to their more sophisticated and ornate clothing, and the fact that certain of their adult offspring wore Western clothing or spoke Portuguese, and were held to be good examples of colonization. One level higher on the scale of civilization were the Cape Verdeans. Most were *Mestiços* and, as such, were more like the Whites. Their apparel, style of dressing and command of the Portuguese language supposedly indicated that they were superior to the inhabitants of Angola, Mozambique, Guinea and even São Tomé e Príncipe.

Higher on the scale than any of the African peoples were the Timorese. There was a reason for this. The Timorese were considered as superior to the Africans because they were more organized and commanded respect. Here, too, it was similarity with the European that counted – the more hierarchized the society, the more 'civilized' it was considered. However, most Timorese did not speak Portuguese well. Also, there were certain warrior practices associated with the people of the Malay Archipelago, of which Timor was part, and because of these practices the Timorese were seen as lacking the social sophistication and elegance of manners found in the Natives of Macao and India. Two families of Timorese chieftains came to the Portuguese Colonial Exhibition. Both had been handpicked by the then agent-general for the colonies (who had previously lived in Timor); and from the way we see them being treated, and the time dedicated to them in a documentary film made at the exhibition, their superior status relative to the Africans seems clear. Perhaps the agent-general for the colonies (who had married a Timorese woman) wanted to project a different image of Timor in Portugal, and therefore his selection of these families was not a casual one.

At the top of the hierarchy came the Macanese and the Indians, whose more sophisticated and ornate dress was held to indicate a higher degree of social and cultural development. In keeping with their status, they were accommodated in pavilions whose more complex architecture evoked the golden years of the 'first Portuguese empire'. From India came snake charmers and dancers who were put up in a pavilion whose architecture was a collage of Indian and Portuguese styles. From Macao came an orchestra whose music, by all accounts, visitors to the exhibition found more palatable than the African *batuques*. All of these aspects combined to place Asian colonial subjects closer to the Europeans on the scale of civilization.

Representations of the Portuguese colonies, 1934–39

After the Portuguese Colonial Exhibition in Porto, Portugal participated in the Exhibition of Colonial Art in Naples, held in the same year (1934). In February of the following year, the Portuguese colonies were again on display at the 9th International Fair in Tripoli. In these exhibitions, Portugal's intention was to show its support for Mussolini's Italy and its colonial policy. Also in 1935, Portugal participated in another exhibition in Libya (where its objectives were commercial, but also imperial) and was also present at the Exposition Universelle et Internationale of Brussels, although not as an official participant. Among the attractions of the Brussels exhibition were an 'Indian village' and 'Arab souks'. Portugal was present with a stand dedicated to its colonies, and the AGC redeployed some of the elements that had been on display at the previous year's colonial exhibition in Porto. Relative to previous exhibitions, however, the Portuguese presence at Brussels was fairly muted.

In 1937, Portugal participated in the Exposition Universelle of Paris, which was dedicated to the 'Arts and Techniques of Modern Life'. Here too the Portuguese colonies were on show. The Portuguese representation[37] was organized by the SPN. Its 'Pavilion of Order' faced the Seine and included among its various sections[38] an 'Overseas' room with diagrams on the work of the missions, medical assistance for Natives and the construction of roads. Pride of place went to the role of Portugal as a civilizing nation. As this was a universal, not a colonial, exhibition, relatively little space was dedicated to the empire, a situation reflected in the commemorative issue of *O Século*. The colonies were essentially presented in terms of economic and political issues, and of the human and natural resources offered by a vast and wealthy empire. Only a small part of the Portuguese pavilion was dedicated to the 'spiritual interests of the Indigenous populations'. How far these 'interests' actually reflected the needs of the colonial subjects is debatable anyway, as they were selected not by the Natives but by the Organic Statute of the Portuguese Catholic Missions. The idea projected was that public order was a given, that the period of the Indigenous revolts was a thing of the past and that even in the remotest regions of the interior the 'Blacks' respected Portuguese sovereignty (*O Século* 1937: 6, 18).

Visitors to the Pavilion of Order were offered various SPN publications on Portugal on their way out. Some of these publications were on colonial and imperial themes, with suggestive titles such as: 'Portugal, the country that has contributed most to geographic knowledge of the world', 'The Portuguese Colonial Empire', 'Portuguese Domination in Morocco' and 'Big Game Hunting and Tourism in Portuguese Africa'. Also on offer were sets of picture postcards. These included a set on 'Portuguese Costumes' (with photographs by Mário Novaes) and a series entitled[39] 'Types from the Portuguese Empire' (with drawings by Eduardo

---

37. The members of the organizing committee were António Ferro (commissioner-general), António Eça de Queirós (deputy commissioner-general), Paulo Mendes Osório (press secretary) and Keil do Amaral (architect).

38. 'State', 'Achievements', 'Public Works', 'Folk Art', 'Riches', 'Science' and 'Tourism'.

39. This collection had originally been compiled for the Portuguese Colonial Exhibition in Porto (1934). It was republished as part of the Portuguese participations in the

Malta). The first series showed human figures, each in a certain type of apparel illustrating the different regions of the country. The second series extended the idea to the overseas territories, with drawings by Malta representing each of the 'human types' found in the territories and held to be distinct from all the other types. To drive home the distinction, emphasis was given to the more representative characteristics of each.

Despite its intentions, the Portuguese pavilion seemed to show a fantasy world, which prompted one journalist to comment 'how it must be fun [in Portugal] to build roads and break rocks' and 'how it must be fun to be Black in the Portuguese colonies' (quoted in Acciaiuoli 1998: 64). And yet the 'entertainment factor' which António Ferro attempted to inject into the programme, following a warped logic which somehow contrived to convert the discharge of duty into pleasure and fun, was in many ways alien to the realities of Portugal, and would certainly not have been looked upon lightly by the Salazar regime.

Still in 1937, the Historic Exhibition of the Occupation was held on the initiative of the AGC. The organizer of this exhibition, Júlio Cayola, recruited the services of Manuel Múrias, a journalist, member of parliament and director of the AHC, and Luís de Montalvor, a writer. In a poem published to mark the exhibition, the colonizer was composed of two groups which together made a 'strong and earnest whole' and were responsible for the 'possession and colonization of the Empire'. These groups were the 'soldiers of the sword' and the 'soldiers of the cross'. Both are described as 'pioneers of Africa', brave volunteers who had faced the 'unknown dangers of regions teeming with different peoples', and who in fighting 'to civilize' the Africans had become 'heroes'. The colonial subject was the 'Negro': 'intractable', 'warlike', 'hostile', 'cunning', 'injudicious', 'barbaric', 'fearless', 'lawless and faithless', sick in body and soul, uneducated, 'savage', 'coarse', pagan (unbaptized) and uncultured (S. Tavares 1937). The object of this exhibition[40] was to show the 'endeavours of the Portuguese to assimilate the *Indígenas* and defend overseas Portugal, from the 19th century until the campaigns of the Great War' (*Catálogo da Exposição Histórica* 1937, vol. 1: vi). It opened on 19 July in the Palácio das Exposições in Lisbon's Parque Eduardo VII (Carmona, Salazar and Machado 1936: 94). Running in parallel with this exhibition was the Congress on Portuguese World Expansion. Among the visitors to the exhibition were students who had

---

Paris exhibition of 1937 and the Historic Exhibition of the Occupation of the same year.

40. One of the publications released to coincide with the exhibition was *Exposição Histórica da Ocupação no Século XIX, Principais Factos da Ocupação Ultramarina (Séculos XIX e XX, até à Grande Guerra)* (1937).

been born in the colonies of Angola and Mozambique and were visiting metropolitan Portugal for the first time (*BGC* 1937: no. 144, 70). The exhibition was recorded in a documentary. Although this exhibition was ostensibly about events of the past, its catalogue was firmly rooted in the present, as illustrated in the speech it published by Vieira Machado: 'We have a great empire which we are developing; we have many millions of subjects, whom we educate and civilize' (1937 vol. 1: xviii). The present was also very much in evidence in the room dedicated to the Colonial Act,[41] where visitors were informed that 'the Nation continues to operate Overseas, according to principles consistent with its humanitarian and civilizing tradition' (xix). Other rooms were dedicated to various colonial and military themes,[42] with the emphasis on the Portuguese heroes of the campaigns of the nineteenth century. The exploits of Mouzinho de Albuquerque were especially celebrated. In an article by the journalist Guedes de Amorim (1940: 71), we read how the sword of Mouzinho subjugated the 'treacherous and seditious *Indígenas*'. Gungunhana was variously dubbed the 'invincible enemy of the Portuguese', a 'runaway Black', the 'Lion of Gaza' and an 'artful Black emperor'.

There was no 'live' participation by colonial Natives at this exhibition, contrary to what had occurred in 1931, 1932 and 1934. Natives did, however, participate in fairs and exhibitions held in Portugal's overseas possessions, such as the Angolan exhibition–fair of 1938. The provinces of Luanda, Malange, Benguela, Bié and Huíla were represented in this exhibition, which featured produce, photographs, maps, graphs and objects of 'Indigenous art' on show in over a hundred pavilions and stands. The *Indígenas* themselves were confined to a separate paddock where they performed their 'characteristic songs and dances', which were described as the 'most interesting spectacle'. The work of the missions was also on show (*Guia da Exposição – Feira de Angola* 1938).

The following year, 1939, Portugal participated in the New York World's Fair. As with the Exposition Universelle of 1937 in Paris, the Portuguese representation was organized by the SPN. The architect selected by SPN director António Ferro was Jorge Segurado. The theme of the New York World's Fair was 'the world of tomorrow'. Portugal chose not to emphasize its industrial sector, preferring instead to extol the vir-

---

41. The catalogue *Exposição Histórica da Ocupação* published by the AGC tells us that the Colonial Act room was to be the first at an exhibition to be held in 1947 'to show nationals and foreigners what the Estado Novo has accomplished in its colonies' (xix). Was an exhibition planned for 1947? It seems unlikely that the event in question was the great exhibition of 1940, preparations for which would already have been underway in 1937.

42. These included the rooms of 'The Coats of Arms', Morocco, Literary Monuments, Brazil, The Orient, Faith, and Seamanship.

tues of the small and humble *casa lusitana*. The only imperial reference was to be found in the 'Room of Honour' in the Hall of Nations, which was reserved for official functions and concerts. Here the colonial empire was evoked in paintings illustrating the development of the colonial administration, with the emphasis on Angola and Mozambique.

Portugal also took part in the International Exhibition of San Francisco held in the same year. The same architect, Jorge Segurado, designed its pavilion, but the Portuguese presence was more subdued here than in New York. The San Francisco exhibition celebrated the explorers of the Pacific coast, and as such was another opportunity to evoke the Portuguese maritime voyages, the achievements of the Estado Novo, folk art, Portuguese agriculture and industry, and the activities of Portuguese residents of California.[43] Neither of the US exhibitions featured 'live' Natives, although the colonial component was present at both.

The Exhibition of the Portuguese World (1940)

Concept and objectives

The colonies and the Portuguese discoveries returned to the limelight in 1940. This pairing of the 'glorious destiny' of Portugal with its maritime discoveries went back to the sixteenth and seventeenth centuries. Celebrating them was a way of producing identities – collective identities, in the present case – and as José Manuel Sobral (1999: 83) noted, 'the production of identities is the production of memories, not only oral and written, but those which are circumscribed in a space [such as] national territory'. For Sobral, this space is 'a foundation of memory, a symbol of identity, and a wellspring of resources' (1999: 83). The act of celebration is also a way of preserving the social cohesion of a group, of creating a social memory: in short, of creating a community – real or imagined. As Hobsbawm and Ranger ([1983] 1985) noted, the invention of traditions has a fundamental role in the construction of nationalist ideologies.[44]

In 1940, while most of Europe was at war and Spain was just emerging from its own turmoils, Portugal staged a great nationalist commem-

---

43. Insufficient information on this exhibition prevents me from giving a more detailed account.

44. Writing in the late nineteenth century, Ernest Renan argued that it was necessary 'to forget the historic horror to create a nation': the emergence of a collective consciousness was conditional upon forgetting certain events of the past. Only when it had a certain amount of common cultural traits, argued Renan, could a country call itself a 'nation' ([1882] 1992).

oration of not one but two centenaries. This commemoration was part of a set of propaganda initiatives organized on behalf of the country and the regime. Chairman of the exhibition's executive committee was Júlio Dantas. The exhibition marked the centenaries of the foundation of nationhood (1140) and the Restoration (1640), and it was also designed to glorify the Estado Novo as an entity capable of organizing an event of this scale. The celebrations included a series of congresses,[45] a 'Historic Exhibition'[46] (inaugurated on 23 June) and the Imperial Procession of 30 June. The exhibition represented a huge investment in material and human terms. With expenditure on the event topping 35 million escudos, several commentators have described it as the biggest political and cultural 'happening' ever organized under the Estado Novo.

The celebrations ran for six months, from 2 June to 2 December 1940, and were divided across several venues. Lisbon, the national capital, became an imperial capital. Over these six months, some 3 million people visited the exhibition, some of them European émigrés who had come to Lisbon in the hope of finding a place on a transatlantic liner. The exhibition was filmed for posterity by Lopes Ribeiro and Carneiro Mendes. Although it was styled on previous international exhibitions, this was an overtly nationalist event which was not really directed at foreign visitors. And as the host nation was one of limited resources, it could hardly hope to compete with the events organized by larger, richer nations.

The procession,[47] organized by Henrique Galvão,[48] was divided into three sections: Portugal Past, Portugal Today, and Portugal Tomorrow. Its route took it down Lisbon's Avenida da Índia and into the exhibition enclosure. Portugal Past was in turn divided into seven periods: Foundation, Consolidation, Peace, Expansion, Empire, Splendour, and Colonial Occupation, this last including an allegorical float dedicated to the colonies. Portugal Today included a parade of figures representing the twenty-one provinces of Portugal: eleven from the mainland, two from the islands and eight from the overseas possessions. The participants wore the costumes typical of their region or province, including the Natives who had travelled to Lisbon from the colonies. Portugal Tomorrow consisted of a parade by the Mocidade Portuguesa youth movement,

---

45. See Chapter II for the issues addressed at these conferences.

46. See *Mundo Português: imagens de uma exposição histórica* (1957).

47. See *Cortejo do Mundo Português* (1940).

48. Although not a member of the Executive Committee for the Commemorations, Galvão was in charge of the colonial section, the organization of the procession, the preparation of the foundation celebrations in Guimarães, co-organization of the Colonial Congress and the propaganda radio broadcasts for the 'Centenários'.

whose members were seen as embodying the future of the country and the continuity of the Estado Novo.

Attention has often been drawn to the fact that modernist artists willingly participated in an event organized by an ultraconservative state.[49] As secretary of the executive committee, António Ferro was instrumental in securing the participation of the modernists. Perhaps the only exception to the dominant modernist style of the exhibition's architecture was its colonial section, which was not modern at all. Despite the political and ideological objectives of the commemorations, they seem to have mobilized artists and intellectuals from all shades of the political spectrum, many of them with views diametrically opposed to those of the regime. That figures such as Jaime Cortesão and Norton de Matos participated in the conferences, for example, was an illustration that the colonial component of Portuguese nationalism was not incompatible with their democratic and republican views – or indeed with the views of the republican camp as a whole. And the exhibition met with a generally good critical reception, even from opposition quarters. In an interview with the Portuguese daily *O Público*, Francisco Igrejas Caeiro – an actor, stage director, producer, announcer, television presenter and member of parliament whose political and above all cultural views earned him the opprobium of the Estado Novo – remembered the exhibition thus:

> Very pretty. Even all those Blacks who came, we accepted that as natural. There was no talk of decolonization in those days. More than that: men like Keil do Amaral – and other anti-regime architects of the time – worked for the exhibition (Leme 1999: 26).

The interviews I conducted revealed a similar insouciance with regard to the presence of the Natives. Of all the people I spoke to, only one person – who had lived in the colonies previous to 1940 – stated that they had not visited the exhibition because they disagreed with the policy of the regime. The exhibition mobilized thousands of people, and it was covered by the state broadcaster Emissora Nacional, which in collaboration with Companhia Rádio Marconi broadcast the inaugural sessions of the commemorations to all the colonies.[50]

---

49. In reality, many seem to have worked at the exhibition because they saw it not as an initiative of the regime but as a nationalist manifestation, with which they could identify and which transcended the regime.

50. Emissora Nacional had been directed by Henrique Galvão since its inception in 1935. Its broadcasting schedule included programmes directed at the colonies and countries with large communities of Portuguese migrants, like Brazil.

As the *Roteiro dos Pavilhões*[51] tells us, the exhibition was divided into four sections: (1) the Historical Section,[52] with the Casa de Santo António and a Seventeenth-Century Neighbourhood designated the Commercial and Industrial Quarter; (2) the Regional Centre[53] and a 'mound of Portuguese villages';[54] (3) the Colonial Section, with a garden offering a 'colourful ethnographic evocation of the overseas provinces', a pavilion and a 'jungle'; and (4) a section given over to 'diverse attractions', including restaurants, a funfair, a pond and lake, the Telecommunications Pavilion and the Ports and Railways Pavilion. The layout of the exhibition followed a chronological sequence. Visitors entered through the 'Foundation Gate' in Praça Afonso de Albuquerque, and then proceeded to the historical section.[55] At the centre of the exhibition was Praça do Império, between the river Tagus and the abbey of the Jerónimos. In the Portuguese Around the World Pavilion, visitors could marvel at how far Portuguese explorers had ventured, reaching places as remote as Japan, Abyssinia and Canada. For the 'Portuguese World' on show at this exhibition encompassed not only the territories which in 1940 were actually under Portuguese rule, but others which had previously been part of the Portuguese sphere of influence, such as Malacca, Ceylon and Japan. These were evoked as if they remained eternally connected to Portugal, and so the 'historical city' which this pavilion contained was also a fantasy city.

---

51. This guide was published in three versions, A, B and C. The 'C' series was dedicated to northern Portugal, as a tribute to the city of Porto. Its author was the journalist Rollin de Macedo.

52. This section included the following components: the Foundation Pavilion (architect: Rodrigues Lima), the Formation and Conquest Pavilion, the Independence Pavilion, the Discoveries Pavilion (Pardal Monteiro), the Sphere of the Discoveries, the Colonization Pavilion (Carlos Ramos) with its shrine to 'Faith and Empire', the Portuguese Around the World Pavilion (Cottinelli Telmo), the Pavilion of Honour and Lisbon (Cristino da Silva), the Padrão dos Descobrimentos (designed by Cottinelli Telmo, with sculptures by Leopoldo de Almeida), and a period galleon called the *Nau de Portugal* (a recreation of a sailing ship in the style of a seventeenth-century galleon, designed by Leitão de Barros and Martins Barata).

53. The Regional Centre included the Folk Life Pavilion (architect: Veloso Reis) and the 'Portuguese Villages'.

54. Despite the poverty in which the rural Portuguese lived, the regime trumpeted peasant life as noble and virtuous. As the Guinean independence leader Amílcar Cabral noted, if the Colonial Act and the *Indígena* statute had been applied in metropolitan Portugal many Portuguese would themselves have been *Indígenas,* for like the *Indígenas* of the colonies they had to work to survive and did not know how to read or write.

55. Chronologically, the exhibition cuts off around 1640, although there was no obvious reason for this. Some historians contend that later periods were deliberately omitted, such as the African wars of occupation (Catroga 1996).

Next to the Colonization Pavilion[56] and a good example of the civilizing endeavours of the Portuguese was Raul Lino's pavilion of Brazil, the
only official foreign participant at the exhibition. Portugal's 'great sister
nation' was represented at the exhibition in its colonial and postcolonial phases: the former in various rooms of the Portuguese Around the
World pavilion, the latter in 'its own', i.e. Brazil, pavilion (*Pavilhão do
Brasil* 1941). In the room depicting Brazil's colonial period, no reference
was made to the African element, the slave trade or the coffee plantations (although there was a stand offering Brazilian coffee). Slavery was
an issue that was well-nigh absent from this exhibition, as it had been
from the colonial exhibition of Porto: it was a theme that was difficult
to depict at a time when the objective was to transmit a good image of
Portuguese colonization. Brazil's own pavilion, inaugurated by Brazilian
president Getúlio Vargas, depicted a modern nation which was a synthesis of Portuguese and Brazilian elements. There was no reference to Africa or Africans. Although the emphasis was very much on the modern,
the lobby of the Brazil pavilion featured two statues of naked 'Indians',
their backs turned to one another: an oblique reference, perhaps, to the
origins of the country.[57]

In a way, the 'successful' colonization of Brazil served as a justification
for the continuation of Portuguese colonial rule elsewhere. This was the
line taken in a publication commemorating the centenary celebrations,
in which the journalist Luiz Figueira argued that the Portuguese had no
'racial prejudices' and that the *Indígenas* were 'potentially our equals';
the only difference, in fact, was in the respective 'colours' of the Portuguese of 'other races' (1940: 53). On several occasions we are reminded
that Portugal was the first colonial power to declare in its Constitution
and Colonial Act that metropolis and colonies constituted a single, indivisible territory. Salazar himself, in an interview with António Ferro
some time around October 1938, stated that Portugal would broach
no discussion on its sovereignty over its colonies and that 'the criticism
generally levelled' at its overseas administration was 'tendentious' and
'ill-intentioned' (Figueira 1940: 54). For Salazar, from the beginning,

> With the efforts of the first kings, our frontiers were defined and estab-
> lished in the Iberian Peninsula. Wars, there were many; but neither inva-
> sion nor confusion of races nor annexation of territories ... From first to

---

56. See the guide to this pavilion, compiled by its director, Júlio Cayolla, agent-general
for the colonies in 1940 (Cayolla, 1937?).

57. The centenaries were also commemorated in Brazil, with events such as the Festa
de Santo António and the Festa da Raça celebrated in the Gabinete Português de Leitura,
complete with speeches (see *Comissão executiva das festas centenárias*, 1940).

last the chiefs had the same Portuguese blood in their veins (quoted in *O Século* 1940a: 360).

And so the centenary commemorations were a celebration of 'race' – the Portuguese race that many believed to have survived intact over the course of the centuries. As we can readily appreciate, the term 'race' could here take on various meanings, including 'nation'; and the same author would often use the word in different acceptations in different contexts.

The colonial section

If the Exhibition of the Portuguese World was to 'ordain Portugal as an Empire' (Catroga 1996: 598), the inclusion of a section which show-cased Portugal's overseas presence was fundamental. And while the intention was clearly to represent the colonies as a unified whole, a certain pluralism can also be detected. The desire to include a colonial section in the exhibition had first been voiced when Salazar presented his plans for the centenary commemorations.[58] Several families of Natives had arrived in Lisbon by the end of May, where they were met as they came off their ship by the minister of the colonies and a crowd eager to see for themselves the 'peoples of the empire'. Fewer Natives were present than at the Portuguese Colonial Exhibition in Porto, however. It seems their numbers were restricted to the bare minimum necessary for showing the variety of human 'types' contained in the empire. This and other limitations seem to have exasperated Galvão, who lamented the lack of resources and seems to have had less enthusiasm for this exhibition than he had had for the earlier event in Porto. This perhaps explains why the catalogue written by Galvão focused exclusively on the colonial section. Unlike other texts which touched only briefly on colonial issues, Galvão examined them in some depth. One of the exhibition visitors I interviewed remembered that:

> [t]he 1934 exhibition was more interesting … [looks at photos] and the Exhibition of the Portuguese World was very dark [and] secluded … That in itself was a political idea, you understand? … Everything's in the dark … There were some lights … but the place was all twilight (April 2003).

---

58. Salazar wanted a 'grand historical exhibition' which exemplified the 'civilizing action' and traced 'every footstep and vestige' of Portugal around the world; he proposed the reproduction of the 'characteristic architecture of each of the twenty-one Portuguese provinces … in houses whose inhabitants, in their typical apparel', busied themselves with the 'usages and customs of their regions' (*Diário de Notícias* 27 March 1938).

If the colonial section was shrouded in twilight, perhaps this was an attempt to reproduce the darkness of dense forest (the catalogue tells us that UV lighting was installed), or a scenographic device designed to underline the secondary nature of the colonies in relation to metropolitan Portugal by muting their visual presence. The colonial section did indeed contrast with the brightness of the Praça do Império and its 'monumental luminous fountain'. In the layout of the exhibition, the representatives of the overseas possessions were banished to the margins, with the centre comprising the abbey of the Jerónimos and the Praça do Império. In these margins were some of the most 'strange' and 'exotic' human specimens known: among the *'Indígenas'* of the colonies, with their exotic festive dress' were the 'Kipungu women with their bizarre and elaborate hairstyles, with rings and necklaces around their necks, and a group of musicians that elicited odd and barbaric drones from their strange instruments' (*Diário de Notícias* 28 June 1940).

The colonial section offered visitors the chance to discover, 'in two hours', the whole Portuguese empire 'from Africa to the Pacific', and it was Galvão's desire that it should become a permanent attraction as a museum of the colonies. Inaugurated on 27 June, it was 'an ethnographic document of three continents: Africa, Asia and Oceania', across which there were 'genuinely Portuguese lands' (*O Século* 1940a: 382). It was installed in the Jardim Colonial with its lush tropical plants,[59] with a series of artificial subenvironments designed to give visitors the sensation that they were actually in the heat of the tropics, among their inhabitants and their natural riches. As one interviewee told me:

> No one knew much about the overseas possessions, so the visitors laughed at the Blacks and the Arabs, at these guys walking around dressed in white who ... must have been the Fula or the Mandinka of Guinea ... It was very impressive seeing all those people and the Black women with their tits on show and stuff (April 2003).

The colonial section was divided into seven sectors. The first sector contained the pavilions of the overseas provinces. Galvão wished to project the idea that these provinces were each components of a single reality – the Portuguese colonies – and so the differences between them were

---

59. This 'colonial garden' was in the former grounds of the palace of Belém. It was maintained by the Instituto Superior de Agronomia, which operated with funding from the Ministry of the Colonies, and was used for teaching agriculture to would-be colonial settlers. It was later renamed the Jardim do Ultramar ('Overseas Garden'); its present name is the Jardim-Museu Agrícola Tropical, and it belongs to the Instituto de Investigação Científica e Tropical (IICT) and the Ministry for Science and Higher Education.

played down while the similarities were stressed, collectively distinguishing them from the colonies of other countries. This was done without
neglecting to convey what gave each environment its unique 'character'
and made it different from the others, although little attention was paid
to this uniqueness. The Angola and Mozambique pavilion was designed
by António Lino and built as a permanent structure. It featured an exhibition of photographs documenting the 'ethnography' of the two colonies, including a documentary by Elmano da Cunha e Costa. At the
entrance to this pavilion were 'six statues of corpulent Black *Indígenas,*
and in the ground around the pavilion, wooden columns topped with
sorcerer masks' (*O Século* 1940a: 382). The pavilion was painted 'hot red'
and its roof was thatched (*O Século* 1940a: 382). In the Guinea pavilion
(architect: Gonçalo de Melo Breyner) was a photomontage illustrating
the 'races of Guinea', with busts of the 'various races' that inhabited
the province and 'maps showing the distribution of cultures' (Galvão
1940: 273–74). The Island Colonies pavilion, which represented Cape
Verde, São Tomé e Príncipe and Timor, was designed by Vasco Palmeiro
and featured a series of dioramas illustrating 'Indigenous life'. Here too
the exhibits included heads and busts of the various 'races', designed
to illustrate the variety of 'human types' found in Portugal's overseas
possessions. The strong colours and the decor of the colonial pavilions
exoticized the lives of the inhabitants of the colonies. Note that Timor
was placed alongside Cape Verde and São Tomé e Príncipe, and not in
the Asian part of the colonial section as might have been expected: the
reason, perhaps, had less to do with the fact that Timor was classified as
an 'island colony' and more with its ranking on the scale of civilization,
according to which Timor was considered to be closer to the two Atlantic archipelagoes than to India or Macao.

As at the Portuguese Colonial Exhibition in Porto in 1934, all the
streets were named after regions of the empire. Rua da Índia, designed
by Vasco Palmeiro, was lined with buildings 'typical of Portuguese
India'[60] with nooks where 'Portuguese influence' was always 'distinct'
(Galvão 1940: 276). There was no attempt to recreate Goan life here;
the idea was simply to display examples of typical architecture. Rua de
Macau (designed by Saúl de Almeida and Raúl Campos) reconstituted
life in Macao with its pavilion, lottery houses, emporia, fan-tan (a popu-

---

60. The church of São Francisco Xavier, the Arco dos Condenados, the palace of the
viscount of Bardim and the Arco da Conceição. The buildings representing Portuguese
India formed a kind of architectural palimpsest, a hotchpotch of different periods and
overlapping elements that came together in a *coincidentia oppositorium*. Similarly, the
recreation of a Macanese street was nothing more than a pastiche of the so-called typical
elements thereof.

lar game) dens, pagoda and houses of Native Macanese. The whole scene was tricked out in gaudy tones, with scarlet the predominant colour. These representations of India and Macao are examples of what Edward Said (1995) called 'Orientalism': the representation of the 'Orient' in all its facets, from literature to science to the arts, according to Western constructs and idealizations.

In the second sector of the colonial section we find a number of pavilions and installations: the Catholic Missions pavilion (architect: Vasco Palmeiro), which was located near the 'Indigenous villages' so that the missionaries could continue to exercise their activities[61] during the exhibition; the Portuguese House for the Colonies (Vasco Palmeiro); the Imperial Tourism and Hunting pavilion (Gonçalo de Melo Breyner); the

Indigenous Art pavilion[62] (Melo Breyner), with one gallery of African and another of Asian art; and the Peoples of the Empire wing, with sculptures by Manuel de Oliveira of the 'heads' of the 'most representative races of the Empire', an attempt at the 'first major gallery of Imperial peoples ever rendered in sculpture' (Galvão 1940: 284). Made to larger-than-life scale, these busts depicted the various 'Indigenous types' with the attire and phenotypical characteristics which distinguished them. There were busts of Africans, Timorese and Indians, both men and women (Figure 17). The figures of Natives which appear in these contexts are often dispropor-

Figure 17. Bust of an African in the Jardim Botânico Tropical, from the Exhibition of the Portuguese World, 1940.

---

61. On 7 May 1940 the Estado Novo signed a Concordate and Missionary Agreement with the Vatican, which reinforced Portugal's overseas missionary activities. The Concordate marked the end – on paper at least – of a conflict between church and state which had first broken out in 1910. On 27 June, Cardinal Cerejeira celebrated a 'Pontifical Mass' in the church of the Jerónimos in Lisbon. This mass was officially included in the centenary commemorations and was designed to glorify the role of the missions in bringing Portuguese civilization to 'pagan' and 'uncultivated' peoples. It may or may not have been a coincidence that this mass took place on the same afternoon as the inauguration of the colonial section – the part of the exhibition which documented colonization and its civilizing mission.

62. The exhibits – made in advance or at the exhibition itself – were described with adjectives such as 'Native', 'Indigenous', 'primitive', 'Black', and 'heathen'. How the contemporary artists and advocates of modernism who participated in and helped build

tionately large, and are typically placed on the floor, with one or more arms or their lower limbs missing, and with a contemplative or passive expression on their faces, their gazes fixed on infinity.

The third sector comprised the 'Villages and Dwellings of the Indigenous Peoples – A Document of Usages and Customs'. In this compound there 'lived' 138 Natives. The settlements it contained were: villages of the *Indígenas* of Guinea (Bijago, Fula and Mandinka); Angolan villages (including the house of the king of Kongo); the villages of the Muchope and Makonde peoples of Mozambique; a village of the peoples living in the territory of the Mozambique Company; replicas of 'typical' Cape Verdean and Macanese dwellings; a village of Timorese *Indígenas* on top of a cave; a 'house of the Natives' of São Tomé e Príncipe; typical Indian dwellings; and the Village of the *Muleques,* where the 'Indigenous' children could play. From this it is clear that Galvão took pains to differentiate between the colonial populations. The children of the colonial subjects who had come to the exhibition were classed as *Indígenas,* as were those who had come from Guinea, Angola, Mozambique and Timor. Those from Cape Verde, India and Macao, on the other hand, were classed as *Naturais* (Natives).

In the fourth sector, the principal attractions were the Monument to Portugal's Colonial Achievements and the Monument to Portuguese Expansion,[63] both by Melo Breyner. The fifth sector contained 'private pavilions and showcases', while in the sixth sector were the 'official art exhibitors'. For the seventh and final sector, Galvão included catalogues of Fausto Sampaio, a painter whose works – representations of the 'human types' of the empire – were on display at various locations throughout the exhibition precinct, and of the painter Chiu Shiu Ngon, whose works were exhibited in 'Macao Street'. Chiu Shiu Ngon was probably the first artist to actually travel to the colonies to document the empire in painting.

In the album dedicated to the colonial section, Galvão's classification and qualification of the inhabitants of the colonies is based on a raft of criteria, not always sharply differentiated. What is immediately evident is that no single differentiating criterion is operative. Popula-

---

the exhibition viewed this art remains unknown. We do know that an exhibition of 'Indigenous decorative art' organized by the SGL in 1929 attracted the attention of the modernists. And in 1925 the magazine *ABC* noted the influence of 'Black art' on modern sculpture (see França 1974: 215–16).

63. This monument was in the form of an armillary sphere surrounded by eight columns, each of which held a clock showing local times in the colonies relative to noon in Lisbon. Clearly the idea was to illustrate the vastness of an empire on which the sun never set.

tions are classified by 'race' and 'colour', although not always following the same principle. What Galvão's sources were, or whether he in fact knew all the territories he mentioned, we are unable to determine, for he rarely provides references. But even if he was drawing on the work of earlier authors (of the late nineteenth and early twentieth centuries), four decades later Galvão continues to describe the colonial subjects of Portugal as if nothing had changed. Here and in other texts, in fact, the exhibition is replete with anachronisms.

Galvão divides the population of Angola into three 'races': 'Black', 'Mixed' and 'White' (this latter category comprising fifty-eight thousand Portuguese and foreigners, 5 per cent of the total population). For the many 'races' which made up the 'Indigenous populations', Galvão proposes a classification based on their 'ethnic characteristics'. In terms of skin colour, he reduces them to two 'types': the Bantu and the Bushman. The Bantu comprised three subtypes: the 'quasi-ink-black person', who lived in the lowland regions; the 'bronze-skinned man', who occupied the plateau regions with no large vegetation; and the 'light brown man', who lived in the forest and plateau regions. Skin colouring was to some extent reflected in the 'colour of the eyes and hair', 'ranging from tawny to black in their usually woolly hair'; baldness was very rare, and 'red or white hair' was not greatly in abundance. Viewed in profile, the Bantu 'type' had a 'prognathous face, with salient jaws, thick and outturned lips'; viewed frontally, he was 'low-browed, [with] prominent cheekbones and deep-set eyes'. While foreheads did vary, the nose was the 'most uniform characteristic of the physiognomy'. It was 'flat and broad, almost an equilateral triangle in shape'. In terms of 'ethnological and ethnographic information', Galvão informs us that 'the Aborigines of Angola' were ignorant of agriculture, 'living on roots and berries, leading a primitive and errant life, the representatives of a decadent race, repelled and vanquished by the Bantu invaders, a mixture of the Black and Hamitic races' which occupied 'sub-equatorial Africa'. In their 'body care' they were 'commonly conceived as being ignorant [of] the most rudimentary precepts of hygiene and cleanliness', although 'some hygienic practices are to be found', not only 'as a result of their contact with the European' but also 'according to their own usages and customs'. After a brief account of some of these practices, Galvão goes on to describe other practices which would doubtless have provoked laughter in more ethnocentric Westerners (1940: 26, 31).

Galvão describes the population of Cape Verde as the result of miscegenation between 'Portuguese and Jews and women of Negroid descent from the coast of Guinea'. Other incoming populations included 'racial elements of various provenances of the kingdom, the Azores, Madeira and later Asia, America and above all Brazil'. The census (taken some time before 1940) classified the Cape Verdean population as 'White', 'Black' and '*Mestiço*'. As for 'anthropological data on the Natives of Cape Verde' (and for 'anthropological data' read *physical* anthropological data), Galvão cites ESC professor António de Almeida to the effect that little research existed. The available data was limited to the measurements of six individuals taken by Almeida at the ESC, and the measurements of another thirteen individuals taken by Mendes Correia. 'Usages and customs' and 'material and social life' revealed ancestral African influences, as well as 'significant assimilation caused by colonization'. Cape Verdean creole is described as 'very attractive when spoken by women, who use it with a certain elegance and gentle flamboyance, employing half-words and terminations with an adorable childishness' (1940: 61–62).

The population of Guinea is described as a mixture of peoples from 'Ethiopia, Yemen, the upper Nile, Egypt, the Libyan desert and the Atlantic'. It is classified into seventeen 'ethnically different' groups, listed in order of population numbers: Balanta, Fula (Blacks, *forros* and Futa-Fula), Manjaku, Mandinka, Papel, Brame or Mankanya, Bijago, Felup, Biafada, Kunante, Bayot, Nalu, Sosso, Kassanga, Kobiana, Banhun and Sarakole. In terms of its origins, the population is divided into three main categories: Fula, Mandinka, and coastal Blacks. After identifying the different groups, Galvão goes on to describe the qualities he sees as characteristic of each. The Balanta, for instance, have an 'admirable physical constitution', and are 'energetic and intelligent'. The Felupe are 'endowed with exceptional strength, agility and stature'; they are also 'the most primitive people of Guinea', and still use the bow and arrow as weapons; their 'attire, besides the cache-sexe', includes 'adornments in great profusion and variety'. Interbreeding, observes Galvão, had adulterated the 'primitive type' of the Biafada, described as 'fetish-worshippers, highly Islamized even in their apparel', which they had copied from the Mandinka. The Biafada are also 'remarkable for their indolence, idleness and approach to work'. On the Nalu, Galvão writes that 'their population heartland' was shrinking, although there was some 'extremely curious information' about them. The Nalu were accused of practising anthropophagy and indulging in 'strange and diabolic rites possibly dedicated to the deity Moloch'. Yet the 'Nalu, Biafada and other races' were now dying out, and Galvão observes that 'a careful *in loco* ethnological and ethnographic study [of them] would be of great interest'. Another group, the Bijago, could not be 'classified by somatic characteristics' due to the 'diversity of types' which the group encompassed, 'from the purest Black type to regular features, revealing constant cross-breeding and degeneracies from what would have been the primitive type'. Note here the persistence of nineteenth-century discourse in terms such as 'race' and 'type'. Galvão also connects degeneracy with reproduction between different groups (1940: 87–95). He does, however, seem to be aware of the need for direct ethnological research of the populations he is describing.

Galvão describes Portuguese India as 'part of the great museum of races and ethnic groups' that the Indo-Gangetic peninsula had been when it was populated by the following 'racial groupings': 'Negrito – Pre-Dravidian (Australians, Vedaic, etc.) – Dravidians (displaying somatic similarities with Indo-African-Ethiopic man) – White Dolichocephalic (Indo-European man)'. The 'Pre-Dravidians, Kolarians and Mundas together with the Vedaic Negrito' were 'the autochthonous peoples of India, driven out of the best locations by the successive invasions of other peoples, by Dravidian, Caucasian and many other racial groupings'. And it was in India that the 'greatest variety of [human] types' was to be found: those of 'tall stature, with straight or wavy hair, prominent or slender nose, dolichocephalic head', and those of 'short stature, all tones of dark complexion through to Black, with wavy or woolly hair, broad and flat nose, rounded face'. Depending on their state of civilization – and many Hindus were 'highly advanced in culture and intelligence' – they could exercise a number of professions. Their languages – Konkani, Gujarati, Marathi and Hindustani – were derived from Sanskrit. Contrary to what he noted for Africa, Galvão reminds his readers that when the Portuguese first made contact with India they encountered 'civilization and intellectual development demonstrated by vestiges that Indian culture has left over the centuries'. The Indian population is also differentiated by religion and caste. It comprised Europeans and their descendants, Christian Hindustanis, pagan Hindustanis, Mohammedans, Parsis, and Africans and their descendants. Under the caste system and the Indo-Brahminic mentality, which sought 'to avoid the miscegenation of the dominators with the Aboriginals' and demarcate the 'progressive stages of culture, manifested by the professions', the population could be divided into Brahmins (priests and wise men), Kshatriya (soldiers and administrators), Vaishya (farmers and traders), Sudra (servants of the higher castes) and Pariahs (casteless, unclean and 'without rights of humanity'). Galvão also considers the *Devadasi* or 'dancing girls' a caste in their own right. These *Devadasi* were 'dancers of the Gods' and were 'detailed to the different temples (*diulas* or *devalayas*)', commonly referred to as 'pagodas'; they were 'the singing and dancing slaves of the divinity [and danced] accompanied by music played by the men of their caste (*Gaecas* and *Mordangueiros*)'; most were 'courtesans to the Brahmins of the temple' (1940: 119–26).

In Macao, the 'homogeneity of slanted eyes' prevailed, but there was a 'multiplicity' of 'Chinese types', from the 'tall stature and light skin of the northern Chinese to the darker, shorter southern type'. Despite the Chinese influence, however, the Macanese were the result of 'racial interbreeding in which Portuguese features predominated'. Galvão describes the 'Chinaman' as having 'a great tendency for acquiring superfluous habits, but his three principal vices [were] tobacco, opium and gambling', with fan-tan the game of choice. Few people now understood 'the serried patois of other times', claimed Galvão, and the Portuguese spoken in 1940 Macao was good, metropolitan Portuguese. Galvão describes Macao as having an intense social life, with a variety of activities which were the mark of a 'civilized and cultured people'. The predominant local religion was Roman Catholicism, the result of long-standing and diligent missionary activity. Galvão makes no mention of it, but to any supporter of colonization this religious aspect would have been one more indicator that the Macanese were to be seen as 'civilized' (1940: 142–55).

Moving on to Mozambique, its population belonged to the eastern and southern groups of the great Bantu family of which all the peoples of equatorial and southern Africa were a part, with the exception of the 'Hottentot Aboriginals' and the 'Bushmen' 'expelled and scattered by the various invasions' of the Bantu. Of the twenty-three thousand Europeans included among the 'non-Indigenous population', writes Galvão, twenty thousand were Portuguese; and of its thousand 'yellow-skinned' members a further two hundred and forty were Portuguese. Of the thirteen thousand 'Mixed-race' members of the 'non-Indigenous population', no fewer than twelve thousand were Portuguese.[64] Perhaps Galvão is counting all *Assimilados* as Portuguese citizens. Galvão draws on the work of the leading nineteenth-century anthropologist Joseph Deniker in classing among the oriental Bantu the numerous mixed-blood peoples of Ethiopic descent from the banks of the Nile to fifteen degrees south, between the east African coast and the African Great Lakes. Miscegenation with the Arabs had led to the emergence of a mixed population which spoke Swahili, a language strongly influenced by Arabic. In Mozambique, writes Galvão, there were various 'groups or sub-races' which could in turn be divided into tribes. Examples of these 'sub-races' (Batonga, Vachopi, Bashenga, Makua) and 'tribes' are given. Galvão then proceeds to generalizations. The *Indígenas* of Mozambique are 'dark *pardo* in colour, the deep black and light black tonalities are uncommon [and they] possess the features characteristic of the Bantu race to which

---

64. I have rounded these numbers to the nearest thousand.

they belong'. Among the Baronga and Landin, 'more correct features and tall stature are common, with perfect types', while the Makua are described as 'shorter, with more accentuated racial features, especially in the interior of the region' they inhabited. As interracial reproduction was on the increase, the 'defined type' was disappearing. The three principal languages, all Bantu, were Ronga, Sena and Swahili. Other languages included Tswa, Chopi, Tonga, Nyungwe, Chuwabu of Quelimane, and Yao. Superstition and sorcery among the *Indígenas* was dying out, writes Galvão, as a result of the work of the Catholic missions, while some had become Muslims as a result of Islamic influence. He notes that Arab blood was still evident, albeit in diluted form, in the *Indígenas* of the coastal regions, especially in the north (1940: 191–209).

Of São Tomé e Príncipe, Galvão writes: 'There is not, and never has been, a characteristic race of São Tomé e Príncipe', whose population was a mixture of 'the most varied types'. More precisely, it was the result of interbreeding between European colonizers[65] and various African peoples, and between the latter among themselves. Therefore it was difficult, writes Galvão, to study the 'ethnic makeup of this population', which had 'reached a most remarkable degree of refinement' and was 'abandoning its vagabond ways and beginning to understand the need to collaborate in the progress of its land' (1940: 23–28).

Finally, Timor. According to the last census taken before 1940, its population was comprised of five 'races': 'White', 'Mixed', 'Black', 'Yellow' and 'Native'. By nationality, the population of Timor comprised metropolitan Portuguese, colonial Portuguese, Portuguese nationals from other colonies, and foreigners (1940: 257–58). In general, writes Galvão, the people of Timor were *Mestiçados,* i.e. of mixed blood. When it came to classifying the different peoples of Timor, the most 'disconcerting chaos' reigned. This 'chaos' was:

> [e]thnographic, anthropological and ethnological, the evident outcome of the disparity of races which interbred long ago ... producing a wide range of types from the pale European and Chinese complexion to the darkest of African types, from the characteristic woolly hair [of the African] to the straight hair of the Malay, from the robust type of the tall and athletic highlander to the delicate and weak type of the marshlands (1940: 255).

Various languages and dialects were spoken in Timor, the most common being Tetum, in which Malay[66] and Portuguese loanwords predomi-

---

65. São Tomé e Príncipe was already frequented by Castilian, French and Genoan traders as early as 1522.
66. The name *Timor,* for example, is of Malayan origin and means 'East'.

nated. Galvão rejects the view that the 'Indigenous society' of Timor was 'a band of barefoot ragamuffins', arguing instead that it was 'organized down to the smallest detail' and had 'a hierarchy of authority with well-defined functions'. However, it was governed by 'usages and customs … without the traditional "style"' (1940: 263–64). Here again, Galvão's text reveals the need to classify the colonial populations, to make every group fit a predefined 'type'. He carries this 'type'-based discourse to the point that a single Native of Timor is held to represent all the inhabitants of the territory. To each 'type', certain behavioural characteristics could be assigned. This discourse belonged to the nineteenth century, and yet it remained current to the extent that it shaped the information given to visitors to the exhibition and anyone who wished to learn more about it from the catalogue. The census data cited here is not reliable, and should be interpreted merely as elucidatory of the classifications used and the relative proportions of the populations which inhabited the colonies.

Natives as merchandise

My research in the AHU revealed how and by whom the Natives considered as representative of the colonies they inhabited were selected to go on show at the Exhibition of the Portuguese World. To establish what form the selection process took and how the Natives were supervised and accommodated, I consulted letters, telegrams and reports which passed through the office of Vieira Machado, Portuguese minister for the colonies at the time of the exhibition. I also attempted to determine why, since they did not represent the majority of the population of a given territory, or did not even belong to it, certain individuals were chosen rather than others, and whether there was any discrimination in the choices made. My research also revealed that the transport and installation of certain Native groups was not trouble-free, contrary to what Omar Ribeiro Thomaz (1997) appears to suggest when he emphasizes mainly the festive aspects of the exhibition.

According to a letter sent to Vieira Machado and dated 27 July 1940 (AHU, process no. 4/64, subject: 'Exhibition of the Portuguese World'), the 'Angolan representation' comprised 'thirty-seven *Indígenas*', divided among 'civilized', *Assimilados* and 'heathen'. Six members of the group were classed as 'civilized', and were either Catholic or Protestant. The Catholics were the king (aged seventy-five), queen (aged thirty-two) and princess (aged twenty-three months) of Kongo, as well as their secretary (aged forty) and a minister to the king (aged forty-eight). The sole Protestant was another of the king's ministers (aged twenty-five). The *Assimilados* included two Catholics: the king's servant (aged eighteen) and the maid-in-waiting to the princess (aged eleven). The 'heathens' were the remaining Natives, who were divided into 'tribes'. The Sosso 'tribe' provided weavers and contributed with seven members: three men, two women, a boy (probable age: four) and a baby girl (probable age: seven months). The Nzinga 'tribe' contributed five marimba players – three men and two girls. Three men, two women, one boy and seven girls came from the Cipungu 'tribe'. The Cipungu girls were described as 'curious specimens of Angolan ethnography, with their adornments and extremely elaborate hairstyles', for which a hairdresser had been specially called in. Unlike the above groups, the 'Bushmen' were classed not as a 'tribe' but a 'race'. They supplied one man, one boy and two girls. The names of these Natives are never given, regardless of their social status. They are described only in terms of their place of origin and the activity they have come to perform. And they came accompanied by the guardian 'chosen ... to wait upon them'. Special emphasis is placed on the supposedly good relations which existed between the monarchs of Kongo and the Portuguese government. Yet even as monarchs they seem to have been treated as little better than merchandise – items that could be ordered, shipped and delivered. Only the king of Kongo and his retinue were authorized to leave the exhibition whenever they wished;[67] the other members of the representation could only leave with prior permission.

From the contents of a briefing[68] sent to Vieira Machado, we can conclude that initially all colonies were to be represented, with the sole exception of São Tomé e Príncipe, whose presence at the exhibition was to be limited to the Island Colonies pavilion alongside Cape Verde and Timor, with no 'Indigenous representation'. And yet there *was* a Native representation of São Tomé e Príncipe at the exhibition; at least, the colonial section included a Native house of São Tomé e Príncipe, but whether its 'inhabitants' were actually from the island is unknown. São Tomé e Príncipe was also represented in the Historic Procession. In a telegram of 19 March 1940 (AHU process no. 4/64, subject: 'Exhibition of the Portuguese World'), the governor of Cape Verde announced that he had 'procured' a group of ten Cape Verdeans, and that moves were now afoot to collect 'folk songs', 'legends' and 'adages' and to

---

67. During their stay in Portugal the Kongolese monarchs and their retinue visited Caldas da Rainha, where they took part in the centenary celebrations held in that town, and Porto, at the invitation of the ethnographic exhibition and harvest fair being held in the city's Palácio de Cristal. On this visit they were accompanied by the guard in chief of the colonial section. They also travelled freely around Lisbon, in a car placed at their disposal by the wife of President Carmona.

68. Briefing no. 734 of 23 February 1940 (AHU process no. 4/64, subject: 'Exhibition of the Portuguese World').

compile 'anthologies of popular and erudite Cape Verdean poetry'. All
these elements would show off Cape Verde as a good example of 'assimilation'. Then there was the 'Indian representation', in whose 'order'
were included a snake charmer, a conjurer, a 'sorcerer or astrologer' and
'two *Bayaderes*'. In a dispatch of 20 November 1939 (AHU process no.
4/64, subject: 'Exhibition of the Portuguese World'), however, the delegate reported difficulties in meeting this order, a situation which for
the governor-general of Nova Goa was only to have been expected, as
the same difficulties had been encountered during preparations for the
Portuguese Colonial Exhibition of 1934:

> The colony took then, and continues to take, a very dim view of the in-
> clusion of *Bayaderes* [*Devadasi*] in its representation. These women were
> [originally] servants in Hindu temples. They exercised sacred prostitu-
> tion. Special legislation has put an end ... to this tradition. Thus, today
> the term *Bayadere* simply means prostitute ... When a group is to be
> organized for one of the large religious festivals, the *Bayaderes* have to be
> brought from British India. The *Bayaderes* sent to the Porto exhibition
> were recruited from those who exercise the public profession of prosti-
> tute, but even so it was very difficult ... to persuade them to come ...
> Snake charmers, sorcerers and conjurers, there are none in the Colony.
> Those who went to Porto came from British India. It will probably be
> necessary to have them sent from there again. The ethnographic rep-
> resentation would no longer be of Portuguese India, but of India as a
> whole. I know it caused some surprise in Porto that the sorcerer spoke
> English, understood some French (as he habitually exercises his profes-
> sion in Pondicherry and other French establishments in India) and knew
> nothing of Portuguese.

Significantly, this so-called representation included no aspect indicative
of Portuguese influence on the Indian element. We are tempted to think
that the objective of the organizers of the exhibition was to make it as
attractive as possible for a diverse public (cultured and educated or otherwise), and the inclusion of more exotic elements would guarantee this.
And as it was to be held in the capital city, the exhibition had to outdo
the success of Porto. To achieve this, the Natives on show had to include
figures which, even if they had no direct connection with Portugal's
overseas territories, would constitute a significant attraction for visitors,
and especially tourists. This seems to be the only explanation for the
organizers' demanding the participation of people who were not from
the overseas territories or could not properly be said to represent them.
In a later dispatch (20 March 1940), the governor-general of India announced that he had 'managed to find a conjurer-snake charmer and
his assistant, and an astrologer'. He also mentioned that the former two

individuals were foreigners, i.e. not from Portuguese India, and spoke only Hindi Gujarati. Not only this, but the astrologer demanded a fee of 250 rupees per month, from the date of embarkation in Goa to the date of disembarkation in the same port. Clearly the Indians were more demanding than the Africans. And in a dispatch dated 1 April 1940, the exhibition's assistant commissioner, Manuel Sá de Melo, noted that he did not feel it necessary to escort the Indian representation, for it did not include many *Indígenas*. I was unable to find out whether the Indian representation had a guardian, or whether its members required authorization or an escort to leave the exhibition compound. A letter from Vieira Machado's office to the exhibition's commissioner-general, dated 20 August 1940 (AHU process no. 4/64, subject: 'Exhibition of the Portuguese World'), states that it had been impossible to recruit the elements requested for the 'Luso-Indian ethnographic representation' and that 'the shortage of transports[69] due to the international situation also contributed to this impossibility'. Representatives from India are known to have been present at the exhibition, however, as photographs[70] and drawings of the event show. Note the nuance in the use of 'Luso-Indian' rather than just 'Indian': some members of the representation were not from Portuguese India, after all, but the preferred expression suggests some kind of mixture of 'Portuguese' with 'Indian'. What really makes this expression stand out is that it has no parallel in references to other colonial populations – expressions such as 'Luso-African' or 'Luso-Timorese' are nowhere to be found. Was no one aware of these groups? Or were they looked upon less kindly?

The 'Guinean representation' was comprised of thirty-seven Natives of Guinea. It came to Portugal under the escort of the second class administrator Augusto Monteiro. In Bolama, Monteiro had to sign a declaration of liability (dated 11 August 1940) in the presence of the 'Curator general of the *Indígenas*' in which he pledged to 'oversee and assist' his charges (AHU process no. 4/64, subject: 'Exhibition of the Portuguese World'). He was given a dispatch note in which the representation was broken down by 'race': fifteen Bijago, twelve Mandinka and ten Fula. The Guinean representation was met in Lisbon by Mimoso Moreira, assistant director of the colonial section of the exhibition, into whose custody the thirty-seven *Indígenas* were officially delivered. Moreira had

---

69. The 'elements' in question were those mentioned in the briefing of 20 November 1939. By now the Second World War was under way and transport routes out of India may have been under British control.

70. The album photographs of the Colonial Section are in sepia tone, a technique developed after black and white photography, which had been used in the albums of the 1934 exhibition.

the job of supervising the *Indígenas* on a daily basis; he was 'not a director, but rather in charge of assisting and overseeing the *Indígenas*'. And
so not only were they delivered like so much merchandise, the Natives
were 'overseen and assisted', a verbal formula that we encounter again
in a letter dated 30 October 1940 (AHU process no. 4/64, subject:
'Exhibition of the Portuguese World') from Augusto Monteiro in which
he discharges himself from his functions as escort to the 'Indigenous
representation'.

According to the report on the 'Timor representation' sent to Vieira Machado by the delegate João da Costa Freitas on 15 August 1940
(AHU process no. 4/64, subject: 'Exhibition of the Portuguese World'),
this representation 'comprised a *suco* leader [a *suco* in Timor is roughly
equivalent to a parish] named Francisco, his wife, two of their children,
a male servant named Moisés and a female servant named Herminia'.
All were 'Natives of Hato-Udo, in the Civil District of Suro', and 'happily represented one of the many characteristic types of the Indigenous
population of Timor'. With the exception of the king of Kongo, this
is the first time the names of members of the 'Indigenous representations' are given – and here even the servants are named. With regard to
their command of Portuguese, Costa Freitas makes no mention of the
women, but states that all the men spoke Portuguese, although with 'a
certain difficulty' in the case of the *suco* leader and the servant Moisés.
The leader's oldest son, João, spoke Portuguese perfectly and had been
educated in the missionary school of Ainaro (Suro) – making him a fine
example of assimilation. 'All the *Indígenas*', noted Costa Freitas, were
Catholics, as well as 'sensible, respectful, and perfectly disciplined'. For
this reason, they honoured 'in remarkable fashion the action of the administrative staff of Timor'. Indeed, the deputy director of the colonial
section described them as 'the best thing' to have appeared among the
Indígenas.[71] Despite this praise, Costa Freitas also noted the credulous-
ness of these *Indígenas*, whose 'primitive mentality' was so easily impressed. Although they were a *suco* leader and his family, in the eyes
of the delegate they were '*Indígenas*' nonetheless – 'primitives' with an

---

71. The Timorese seem to have been treated differently from their co-colonials. This
was perhaps because the Timorese in question occupied positions of authority in their
homeland. Then again, it may be a reflection of the different status enjoyed by Timor
relative to Africa. The colonization of Timor seems to have developed along rather different lines: for over two centuries, the island was controlled by the Topaz, a *Mestiço* group
which claimed Portuguese descent. The Timorese offered resistance to incomers, and
were fiercely autonomous in their polity. Almost the whole military force of Timor was
comprised of Natives. Finally, the Timorese were not 'Blacks': they were part Malayan,
and Malayans were held in higher regard than Blacks.

infantile mentality, specimens of a civilization inferior to the European. As for their dress, they wore 'in addition to their *lipas*[72] and warrior costumes, some outfits of European cut'. In metropolitan Portugal, Costa Freitas had heard calls for the *Indígenas* to be 'dressed strictly in Indigenous fashion'. But in his opinion, these were senseless appeals by people who were 'looking for the curious and picturesque in everything', for 'European dress ... has entered the customs of a considerable part of the Indigenous population'. Yet this permissiveness was not extended to the Africans, who had to wear what they were told to.

According to Guilherme Cunha, delegate of the 'Mozambican representation', the latter comprised 'a group of forty Chopi formed by thirty men who were *timbila* (marimba) players and dancers, five women and five children' (G. Cunha 1940). For Cunha, 'the *timbila* orchestras of the Chopi' were 'the purest expression of Indigenous music' and the inhabitants of their territory who best embodied the 'musical spirit of the Bantu'. Six members of the Makonde people of Nyassa also came. The three men clearly displayed 'their tribal markings in their tattoos'. One was a member of 'the famous *fúndi uá machanano*', Makonde craftsmen specializing in ivory and wood carvings. The delegate comments that this group was 'formed of two of the most representative Bantu sub-races'. During the exhibition, wrote the delegate, of 'all the characteristic dances' performed by the Natives, 'those of Mozambique [were] rightly the most interesting', while 'their garments and well turned out appearance' were much appreciated (from the report by Cunha, now in the AHU).

The Macanese delegate who wrote the report on the 'Indigenous representation'of Macao describes himself as a 'manager and director'. His report, dated 11 August 1940 (AHU process no. 4/64, subject: 'Exhibition of the Portuguese World'), details the members of the representation: 'one female singer and her attendant, two coolie carters who doubled as bankers in fan-tan, and three camphorwood carvers'. Of these craftsmen and coolies, only three spoke Portuguese. And the journey of the Macanese representation was not a peaceful one:

> On their arrival in Hong Kong it was found that the representation was installed in horrific conditions on board the ship which was to take them to the Dutch Indies, for the tickets bought for them in Lisbon were deck tickets, which did not entitle them to a bunk ... As the passengers were not *Indígenas* of primitive and rudimentary civilization but persons accustomed to the common conveniences ... it was necessary to find a solution to the matter. The singer and her attendant were given berths in

---

72. A cotton skirt worn in Timor.

2nd class ... and the men were berthed in a sectioned-off part of the hold equipped with newly-purchased camp beds.

As we can see, people were treated differently according to their origins or social status. Only when the Macanese representation arrived in the Dutch Indies was it transferred to a cargo ship, where it was berthed 'in an enormous cabin with ten beds, the ship's hospital'. On their arrival in Lisbon the Macanese were met by Mimoso Moreira, who installed them in the Jardim Colonial. Although they occasionally took walks outside the exhibition enclosure, they were always 'accompanied by persons of the utmost reliability'.

The need to detail an escort to the Macanese representation was questioned. Vieira Machado initially felt this measure was unnecessary. But he eventually decided to the contrary, and the escorts sometimes had to sign a declaration of liability in the presence of the curator of the *Indígenas,* pledging to fulfil their duties of 'overseeing and assisting'. The governor-general of Mozambique, Joaquim Nunes de Oliveira, suggested that the escort of the 'Indigenous representation' from Mozambique be someone familiar with their 'habits' and 'customs' (27 March 1940), while the government appointee in charge of Timor, António Jacinto Magro, proposed that the escort be a member of the administration who knew 'at least a little' of the language, customs and psychology of the *'Indígenas'* (20 April 1940). All the Natives brought to the exhibition received medical assistance when necessary – during the journey, at the exhibition, or in hospital. None of the children born at the exhibition seems to have survived. Only in the report for Guinea and Cape Verde were the names of sick individuals given. The names of servants were also included in the report for Timor. In all the other reports, only chiefs were named.

It wasn't just the health of the Natives that was kept under close watch. Their behaviour was, too. However, by late August, one of the exhibition's most hotly discussed topics was the marriage of two Africans in the colonial section and the later baptism of two 'Indigenous' children. All of the *Indígenas* took part in these ceremonies. But instead of serving as good examples of the success of the civilizing and evangelizing efforts in the overseas territories, they in fact generated controversy, not only for the circumstances in which they occurred, but also because various national newspapers carried stories on these episodes, which the exhibition organizers had not planned. Vieira Machado revealed he was 'very surprised to have learned of the marriage of two African *Indígenas* only from the newspapers', and considered the episode 'so shocking that I ought to have been warned about it beforehand' (27 August 1940). None of the delegates, however, accepted responsibility for the episode.[73] Although the Natives were 'overseen', certain phenomena escaped the control of their 'guardians'. This is more than a case of resistance by the weaker party, the one that despite its subjugation and supervision proves capable of turning the situation to its own advantage; it also attests to the ability of the Natives to organize themselves secretly, within a confined space subject to permanent observation, opposing the instituted discipline by holding a wedding and a procession: neither had been expected, and both events were of interest only to those who participated in them. Forms of resistance can emerge from power relations, and as such should not be viewed as independent of them.[74] In the case of the exhibitions, the power of the Natives also lay in their ability to organize themselves (an ability not normally acknowledged by the colonizers) and to hold these unplanned ceremonies. As Foucault observed, where there is power there is resistance; and this resistance never exists in a position of exteriority relative to power (1978: 95–96). But this form of resistance put up by the Natives was not appreciated by those who wielded power within the exhibition enclosure.[75] On the contrary, the fact that the Natives had organized themselves in this way was seen as a threat to the smooth running of the exhibition and the 'order of events'.

Here as elsewhere, the term *Indígena* is indiscriminately applied as a descriptor of 'Native populations', even when the people in question did not in fact have *Indígena* status. And discriminatory attitudes are not always rooted in the idea of 'race', but rather articulated in terms

---

73. The wedding was between '*Indígenas* who had lived in the Metropolis for years', in the words of the delegate for Mozambique. The bridegroom was a native of Guinea, and had lived in Portugal for eighteen years; his bride was from Benguela, and had lived in Portugal for twenty-eight years. They were '*civilizados*', employees in the colonial section, and 'before the ceremony, had lived as concubines', in the words of the Angolan delegate. The delegates only learned of the wedding from the newspapers, and as these *Indígenas* were not under their charge, they (the delegates of Guinea, Timor and Macao) refused responsibility; their duties were merely to monitor and maintain 'vigilance and assistance' over the *Indígenas* they had brought with them. And the groom, although a natural of Bolama and a member of the 'Brame or Mankanya race', did not belong to this group (so the delegate of Guinea claimed).

74. Lila Abu-Lughod (1986, 1990) has observed a similar phenomenon among Bedouin women. These women were subject to the impositions of their menfolk with regard to marriage – they were forced to wed with patrilineal parallel cousins – and morality, under a system which defined men as superior. So to negotiate power and gender relations they resorted to stratagems – resisting power by using their own power. The social subordination to which women were subjected was not irreversible, and they could exploit existing power relations to their own advantage.

75. The same cannot be said of the poetry produced by the Bedouin women, which was accepted by those whose established system it served (Lila Abu-Lughod 1986, 1990).

such as *colonizado* or 'under Portuguese sovereignty'. All the colonized groups were 'non-Europeans', however, so 'race' could serve as a factor of discrimination. African/not-African was another major line of distinction (the Africans themselves being classed as *Indígena, Assimilado* or *Civilizado*), as was relative proximity to the European, as in the case of the Natives of India and Macao; here the 'civilization' factor and social status played fundamental roles. The fact that all these 'representatives' were at the exhibition together was not only a demonstration of how different they were from each other, it also projected Portugal as a country with many diverse peoples from distant territories under its wing. In other words, Portugal had the gift of leading different human groups scattered all over the world, groups which thanks to the Portuguese could now aspire to a higher level of 'civilization'. However, there is a contradiction here: although the objective was to put the differences on display (as witness the efforts made to bring individuals who were representative of diverse social and cultural milieux), all were lumped together in the same place, all were considered *Indígenas,* and little or nothing was in fact known about them; some were even assuming a false identity for the benefit of the exhibition. What the colonial section ended up recreating was a fiction which was based on reality but was contrived to show only what was intended to be seen. Galvão himself, in the foreword to the catalogue for the colonial section (1940), alludes to its irreality in writing that the different materials brought together and organized there according to a preestablished rationale had the objective of creating a 'fiction'. What the colonial section really celebrated was not the knowledge of the daily, ritual, social and cultural lives of the populations represented there, but the civilizing mission of the Portuguese.

Colonial representations in Portugal dos Pequenitos

Portugal dos Pequenitos ('Little People's Portugal') is a representation of Portugal created especially for children. As such, it is clearly educational in purpose. Unlike the other exhibitions of the period, Portugal dos Pequenitos has survived, and can still be visited today. In this section I propose to identify the colonial images that Portugal dos Pequenitos projected to its young visitors, and how these images were constructed.

Portugal dos Pequenitos was conceived in the late 1930s by a doctor from Coimbra, Fernando Bissaya-Barreto,[76] and built to plans by the

---

76. On the life and work of Bissaya-Barreto, see Sousa (1999). This edition includes the documentary *Rumo à Vida: A Obra de Assistência na Beira Litoral* by João Mendes.

architect Cassiano Branco.[77] 'Since 1940, [it has been] an educational/ fun park directed essentially at Children' (Portugal dos Pequenitos [PP] 2000: 4). The origins of Portugal dos Pequenitos have to be understood as part of a series of children's homes built by the Provincial Council of Beira Litoral, of which Bissaya-Barreto was president.[78] It was perhaps in recognition of the responsibility for the formation of young individuals that Bissaya-Barreto sought to develop an infrastructure directed specifically at children, the 'men of tomorrow', which could perpetuate the values of 'nation' and 'race' (Bissaya-Barreto 1940); for Barreto, children, as 'national human capital', were 'extremely malleable material' (Bissaya-Barreto 1970: 212). In the documentary *Rumo à Vida: A Obra de Assistência na Beira Litoral,*[79] the narrator proclaims that Portugal dos Pequenitos contains 'the whole of Portugal on this and the other side of the sea, a simple and outreaching Portugal which fills childish souls with waves of joy'.

Construction of the 'little people's village' ('aldeia dos pequenitos' was the original designation) in Coimbra, far from Lisbon, can also be seen as a riposte to the centralism of the capital. The year of its creation, 1940, was the year of the 'grandiose' Exhibition of the Portuguese World in Lisbon. Initially, a number of parallel events had been planned in other parts of the country, such as a work procession in Porto, an exhibition of jewellery in Coimbra, and an exhibition of Baroque art in Porto (Bandeirinha 1996). Bissaya-Barreto was therefore striking a blow for regionalism by devising a project which, like the Lisbon exhibition, celebrated the centenaries of foundation and restoration, but whose home was the provincial university town of Coimbra. Significantly, when the Lisbon exhibition closed, some of the materials used in it were transferred to Portugal dos Pequenitos.

---

77. Cassiano Branco's contributions to Portugal dos Pequenitos range between 1937 and 1962 (Neves 2000: 10). Why Bissaya-Barreto chose Cassiano Branco as architect remains unknown, especially as he associated with opposition circles. Bissaya-Barreto was active in the masons, and perhaps had known Cassiano Branco for some time already. Cassiano Branco's involvement is especially interesting if we consider that he had made a name for himself as an architect of modernism, and with the commission for Portugal dos Pequenitos he found himself working in more traditionalist, regime-friendly architectural idioms.

78. Bissaya-Barreto had ties to the União Nacional and the state apparatus; he was close to the regime and to Salazar himself. His principal interests, however, were medicine and social assistance.

79. A film on the work of Bissaya-Barreto in the field of 'social medicine', with text by Henrique Galvão. It was not funded by the SNI, and is now considered lost by the Cinemateca Portuguesa; the only extant copy may be in the Fundação Bissaya-Barreto (FBB).

My intention in visiting Portugal dos Pequenitos[80] was to examine it as a construct and to determine what part the colonies and their inhabitants played in the complex as a whole. Portugal dos Pequenitos is divided into five main sections: Overseas Portugal,[81] Monumental Portugal, Coimbra, Metropolitan Portugal, and the Children's House (Figure 18). Together, they were designed to represent Portugal in all its aspects, to illustrate the lives and 'culture' of its inhabitants, their activities and the artefacts they produced – all objectives which were similar to those of the great exhibitions of the day. The objective of Portugal dos Pequenitos was to tell the history of the 'nation' to children, and in this respect its buildings are to be interpreted 'as objects of the same cultural unity – the nation' (Porto 1994: 7). Included in this 'unity' is the Overseas section, representing the former Portuguese colonies of Africa (now countries with Portuguese as an official language), as well as Macao, India, Timor, Brazil and the island groups of the Azores and Madeira. As the plan of Portugal dos Pequenitos shows (Figure 18), Monumental Portugal occupies the centre of the complex, together with a smaller section dedicated to Coimbra and its monuments. With the exception of a few small alterations to the Brazil pavilion, the original park remains largely unchanged. That so little has changed reinforces the idea that although the years have passed and the national and international context has shifted, the basic purpose of Portugal dos Pequenitos remained the same for a quarter of a century (1937–62). The reason for this is quite possibly that, despite changes elsewhere, there have been no changes either in the educational component of the project nor in the colonialist and nationalist perceptions that informed its construction.

When we enter Portugal dos Pequenitos, we pass under a mock battlement and come first to the Overseas Portugal section. In the centre of this section is a square, with a life-sized bust of the creator of Portugal dos Pequenitos, Bissaya-Barreto, in the centre. Flanking this bust – one might even say acting as its bodyguard – are six large sculptures of muscle-bound African men, their arms crossed. These sculptures are unnamed and untitled (Figure 19). On either side of the bust of Bissaya-Barreto and his African 'bodyguards' run two avenues which lead to another square, this one containing a map of the world showing some of the sea routes covered by the early navigators. Next to this map is a life-sized, full-body sculpture of Henry the Navigator (1394–1460)

---

80. I visited the park on several occasions in April and May 2002.

81. The original designation was 'Portugal de Além-Mar'. Today this section is known as 'Portugal Insular e de Além-Mar' ('Insular and Overseas Portugal') and 'Países de Expressão Portuguesa' ('Portuguese-speaking Countries'). I have opted to use the original, shorter designation.

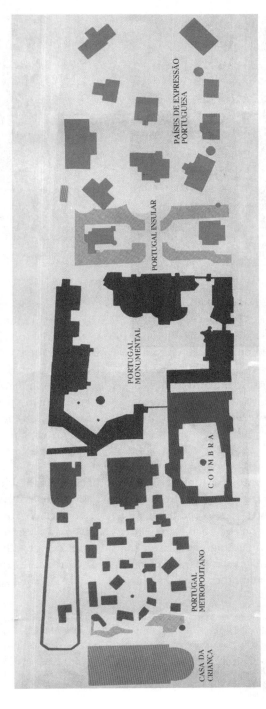

Figure 18. Map of Portugal dos Pequenitos, from a leaflet published in the 1970s.

Figure 19. African figures at the entrance to the Overseas Portugal section
(1940s).

– like the exhibition of 1940, Portugal dos Pequenitos was designed to
showcase the great 'Portuguese empire'.[82] Along the two avenues stand
various pavilions. The pavilions on the avenue to the right represent the
territories located on the Atlantic route: Angola, São Tomé e Príncipe,
Brazil and Cape Verde. The avenue to the left contains the pavilions of
the territories on the Indian Ocean route: Mozambique, India, Timor
and Macao. The two avenues converge in front of the map of the world,
after passing between the pavilions of the Azores (on the left) and Madeira (on the right). Between the two avenues, along an axis connecting
the entrance square with the map of the world, are the Guiné-Bissau
pavilion and the 'Mission Chapel'.

In illustrating the epic exploits of the Portuguese, the buildings of
this section take us back in time to a mythical past and to a differentiation between Portugal and the populations it colonized. Examples of
this are the pavilions of Angola and Mozambique, whose exteriors are
reminiscent of the Portuguese forts of the sixteenth century, although
tree trunks and thatch were used in their original construction. The dec-
oration of these and other pavilions evinces a certain 'Orientalism' and

---

82. The guide also indicates that this part includes 'Island Portugal' (the Azores, Madeira and Macao), the 'Portuguese-speaking Countries' – those now known as PALOP
(the group of African countries which have Portuguese as an official language) – and Brazil, Timor and India. At the entrance to the Macao pavilion we can read: 'The Portuguese
presence [in Macao] survived until the 20th century. Portuguese administration of the
territory ceased on 31 December 1999.'

'Africanism', deliberately contrived to transport the observer to remote, and completely different, places.

One scene in João Mendes's documentary *Portugal dos Pequenitos* (1968?) shows the African sculptures of this section: the narrator describes them as 'the image of overseas', which is 'perhaps vague in their imagination' (i.e. the imagination of children). Also in this section we find 'different types of houses from the overseas provinces' and learn that 'there are Portuguese in India, Macao and Timor too'. As the narrator tells us, they are in 'another university, the one that teaches them to be Portuguese'. The use of the officially sanctioned terminology of the 1950s and '60s ('overseas', 'overseas provinces') is a constant throughout this documentary, as are the scenes of metropolitan Portuguese children playing with children from Africa and elsewhere, projecting an image of sharing and harmony despite their diversity of origins. In the words of the narrator, these children are 'Portuguese of all grades and races'.

The Portugal dos Pequenitos guidebook (titled *Portugal dos Pequenitos*) describes the Brazil pavilion as 'a document of that great sister nation' (*Portugal dos Pequenitos [PP]* 1966: 84), 'sistered in the family environment, where the colour of the inhabitants doesn't count'. In the square at the far end of the park is the Mission Chapel, which in the words of the guidebook represents the 'great and at the same time ... modest ... efforts of the Portuguese missionary who, with the soldier at his side, through the ages has given new Worlds to the World'. It symbolizes, then, the missionaries and their bringing of civilization to inhospitable lands. In front of the chapel, beside the map illustrating what the guidebook calls 'the routes that furrowed the seas' and 'flew over [the seas] with glorious wings' (*PP* 1966: 81), the statue of Henry the Navigator is the 'incarnation of the soul of the race, discoverer of the unknown, of this Race which marshalled races, civilizer of peoples, enlightened in letters, daring in struggle, untiring in work, persistent in its ventures' (*PP* 1966: 81). The map of the world is a tiled panel set into the wall of a mock fortress, from whose battlements four cannon point at the Overseas Portugal section. At its foot is an ornamental moat, which divides the Overseas world from the Monumental and Metropolitan worlds.

Lining the avenues of Overseas Portugal and flanking the entrances to each of the pavilions in this section are small stone pillars, or *padrões*, bearing carved inscriptions. The inscriptions on these *padrões* are not the originals: they were altered by Luís de Albuquerque in the early 1990s. The original *padrões* are now inside the pavilions. The inscription for the Macao pavilion was modified in 2000; alterations to the inscription for Timor were postponed pending the results of the 2002 elections, and have now been made. It is the wording of the original inscriptions that most concerns us here; the circumstances which dictated the changes are of secondary importance. In some cases, however, comparison with the revised versions[83] can shed extra light on the originals.

The original inscription for Angola informs us that the 'civilizing action of the Portuguese' occurred 'peacefully' through negotiations with the 'Black king of the Kongo', whose son was brought to Portugal by King João II to be baptized and educated. There is no acknowledgement of the existence of 'African civilization' prior to the arrival of the Portuguese,[84] and the expression 'Black king', a colour-based descriptor, is used to describe the African. The natural, objective use of this expression is an encoded reference to the abstract and supposedly more scientific term 'race'. And there is also the suggestion of 'exchange' in the fact that Portugal's King João II brought the son of the king of Kongo to Portugal to show him the path to 'civilization' via baptism and 'learning'.

The original inscription for Guinea describes the colony as a 'province ... still containing many Black races'. Guinea was harder to subjugate than Angola, it tells us, for it was populated by *Aazenegues* and 'Blacks' who used 'poisoned spears'. However, the 'primacy of our discoverers and the valour of their endeavours' eventually subjugated the Natives.[85] With its references to 'Black races' and 'Blacks', this inscription also suggests that the latter were dangerous 'savages' with their 'poisoned spears' – hence the 'effort' required to subjugate them.

For India, the original inscription makes reference to the negotiations of the Portuguese to 'buy the greatly valued spices'; yet due to 'the intrigues of the Moors' it had to be 'by force' that the Portuguese secured 'the command of the seas' and their trading routes. The inscription adds that the Portuguese had to defeat 'the Turks, Egyptians and Indians' to establish an 'empire' in India. And while it describes the 'Moors' as intriguers, the inscription also recognizes the need to come to an agreement with them, since spices were highly valued.

São Tomé e Príncipe and Cape Verde were uninhabited when the Portuguese first arrived there, and so the original inscriptions for these

---

83. See Appendix II.

84. In the revised inscription, the expression 'Black king of the Kongo' becomes 'king of the Kongo', while 'the civilizing action of the Portuguese began peacefully' is replaced by 'established friendly relations with African civilizations'.

85. The terms *'Azenegues'*, 'Blacks' and 'Black races' are replaced by 'populations' in the revised inscription. While the original inscription tells us the navigators 'died pierced by poisoned spears', the revised text informs us simply that the Portuguese 'made contact with the populations'. The revised text also informs us that after its independence Guinea had become a 'new country' and 'one more member of the Luso-African-Brazilian community' – now on a par, that is, with countries which had earlier reached a higher level of civilization.

island groups naturally make no mention of encounter, war, or negotiations, limiting themselves to physical descriptions of the islands. The inscription for São Tomé e Príncipe does, however, tell us that the Portuguese cultivated these islands and 'colonized them in such a way that they now produce excellent coffee and the most highly-prized cocoa in the whole world'. No mention is made of the fact that this process of colonization was initially, and for centuries thereafter, based on slave trafficking.[86] The inscription for Cape Verde tells us that the islands of this archipelago were 'colonized by Whites and Blacks'. As with the inscription for Angola, this text uses a classification based on colour, and again the use of terms like 'White' and 'Black' is a veiled reference to 'race'. When it comes to the language spoken in Cape Verde, however, the local creole is described as 'somewhat different' from Portuguese, the result of a mixture of various linguistic influences, of which the dominant one was Portuguese. Interestingly, creolization is mentioned only in regard to language, and not people. Are the children who visit Portugal dos Pequenitos being told that miscegenation in Cape Verde only occurred on the level of language?

After Overseas Portugal, we come to Monumental Portugal, with its replicas of national monuments from various periods, and Metropolitan Portugal, with its traditional Portuguese houses built in a miniature, child-friendly scale. Beyond these, at the opposite extremity from the entrance, is the Children's House, originally designated the 'Ninho dos Pequenitos' or 'Nest of the Little People'.[87] To the left of this building is a garden with a globe of the world showing the maritime routes sailed by the Portuguese, and statues of Camões and Queen Isabel of Portugal, the patron saint of Coimbra. As someone wrote in the visitors' book of Portugal dos Pequenitos, 'here metropolis and overseas form a marvellous truth ... the solidarity which must unite all the parts of the Portuguese world.'[88] The purpose of the park finally becomes clear – to tell the history of Portugal to all the 'little people' who identify with it. For republicans like Bissaya-Barreto (who later aligned with the Estado Novo) or for those who were close to the regime, history was one of the fundamentals of education, as it was the subject best suited to disseminating the values of nationalism. And when Portugal dos Pequenitos was

---

86. Slavery in Portugal was abolished by the Marquis of Pombal in 1761–73 (see Boxer 1969).

87. This house was the original nucleus of Portugal dos Pequenitos. It was built as a home for young children from impoverished families.

88. The visitors' book is in two volumes (from 1950 to 1984 and from 1951 to 1982). There is now a visitors' book in the Casa-Museu Bissaya-Barreto, where various distinguished visitors have recorded their impressions of the park.

being built, the idea of the 'nation' was inseparable from that of a 'vast empire'. The history it tells is one whose heroes – Bissaya-Barreto, Henry the Navigator, Afonso Henriques and Luís de Camões – are Portuguese. In another part of this history are the 'others': the colonized peoples, relegated to a past which predates the history of the Portuguese, who belong neither to Europe or Brazil (the example of prosperity) and merely represent a stage in the evolution of humanity. The descriptions of the pavilions in Overseas Portugal offer no description of the countries they represent, or their cultures.

This placing of the 'other' in a remote past has its analogies in the discourse and practice of the early anthropologists. To endow anthropology with scientific status, its subject matter underwent a process of objectification predicated on spatial and temporal distancing. The 'other' as an object of study had to be distinct from, and preferably remote from, the anthropologist who studied him or her. And so the early anthropologists did not 'find' savagery in the 'savage', or primitiveness in the 'primitive': rather, they placed their objects in these conditions (Fabian 1983: 121). In Portugal dos Pequenitos, the various 'others' are placed in a remote past which predates the advent of the Portuguese, and in a remote place, via a mise-en-scène which creates an 'illusion of the primitive'[89] (Kuper 1988) and makes them exotic and strange to European eyes. As Adam Kuper (1988) argues, when we study constructions of the 'primitive' we are actually studying mirror images of those who made these constructions, images which oppose what their creators believe themselves to be or represent – the modern society of which they are a part and which has evolved from its antithesis. Gustav Jahoda (1999) also observes that the content of the images we construct of the 'other' says much more about us than about the people the images supposedly depict. This process is associated with a universal tendency to differentiate between those who belong to a given group or society and those who do not belong – ethnocentrism, in other words. When we differentiate between human groups, the emphasis falls on identity – one group is positively evaluated, in opposition to the 'others' who do not belong to that group. We can also establish degrees of alterity, extending from our closest circle of relations to those who are totally alien to us (Jahoda 1999: xiv).

In the case of Portugal dos Pequenitos, there is a clearly evolutionist perception in the representation of the relationship between the Portuguese and the peoples they colonized. This perception is grounded in

---

89. According to Jahoda (1999), after 'savages' fell into disuse the term 'primitives' was used as a way of classifying non-Europeans; it occurs extensively in modern anthropological and historical literature.

an ideology which places the Portuguese at the centre of the world and in command of history, and is built via a discourse on the colonized peoples which simultaneously seeks to legitimize colonialism and sees the subjugated peoples not as possessors of an interesting ethnological diversity but as lacking the civilization which only the Portuguese can bring them. In similar fashion to the great exhibitions, Portugal dos Pequenitos takes its visitors on an itinerary which embodies a gradual evolution from the Africans to the Portuguese, with Asians located at the halfway point.

This suggestion of a process of evolution is evident not only in the organization of space, the direction of movement imposed upon the visitor and the inscriptions on the *padrões,* but also in the decorative elements found on the exteriors of the pavilions of Overseas Portugal and the objects contained in their interiors. The devices used for creating a sensation of being 'elsewhere' and making the lives of the Native inhabitants of this 'elsewhere' more exotic are various: vegetation typical of the tropical regions; the architecture of the pavilions, with their abstract designs alluding to African art (also designated 'primitive art') in their strong, contrasting colours; flora and fauna in combination with human elements; the use of thatched roofs in the original pavilions of Angola, Mozambique, Guiné-Bissau, Cape Verde and Timor (Figure 20); and representations of human figures in close association with nature. For example, we see African figures represented in larger-than-life scale,[90] seminaked, without legs and wearing what appear to be loincloths. This representation of unclothed Africans is a construct of the European imagination (Jahoda 1999). In some of these statues the arms are partly missing. The representation of Africans in the form of busts or torsos may have been a solution to the problem of the exhibition of the genitals. In the full-body statue behind the Guinea pavilion – a seminaked African holding a spear (a symbol of hunting and defence), the figure wears a small loincloth. The statue is set on top of a rock with carved plant motifs, a solution which suggests a certain continuity between nature and the African hunter-gatherer, who is thereby relegated to an earlier stage in the evolution of humanity (Figure 20). Elsewhere we find stone pillars with carvings of African faces, monkeys and other hybrid representations combining diverse animal and plant features. The entrances to several pavilions – Angola, Mozambique, São Tomé e Prín-

---

90. See the drawings of Cassiano Branco (Viegas and Vale, 2000). All the African figures in Overseas Portugal are in larger-than-life scale. For Cassiano Branco, Portugal dos Pequenitos could be divided into three 'lessons': the first, on a scale of 1 to 200, is intended for infants; the second and the third, on a scale of 1 to 40, with greater detail and more extensively documented, are intended for older children (Viegas e Vale 2000: 26).

cipe, Guiné-Bissau and Cape Verde – have columns topped with busts of Africans. These busts are painted black, with red lips which produce a striking contrast. This representation has much in common with caricature, and is intended to evidence the phenotypical traits of the African. It suggests a vision of Africans as immodest and oversexed,[91] associated with strange or frightening rituals and practices, savage beings[92] from a distant and inhospitable world to which the Portuguese, with their courage and good intentions, brought civilization. Inside the pavilions, too, the furnishings evoke the mythical and magicoreligious world of the Africans, with objects used in rituals representing a dangerous paganism. African religion is viewed as irrational, incompatible[93] with the religion represented by the Mission Chapel.

The inferiorization of the non-European is also evident in the pavilions of the Asian colonies, where the emphasis is on their exoticism. This is conveyed in decorative elements and motifs which evoke the animal kingdom or the realm of the supernatural. But these pavilions also contain elements which point to a stage of 'civilization' more advanced than the Africans, and to acculturation. Asia had formerly been considered as the cradle of Aryan civilization, until it was later replaced in this role by Europe. Examples of Asian acculturation can be found in the photograph of the Liceu Nacional Infante D. Henrique – a symbol of Portuguese civilization and the Portuguese presence in the colony of Macao – and the mock-ups of Macanese streets whose trade signs – 'dentist', 'inn', 'apothecary', 'tailor', 'contractor' – are the symbols of a society more advanced than that of the African. In the India pavilion, there are Indian motifs and religious figurations of the Christian 'holy family' in miniature, or painted on porcelain – a medium which suggests a certain degree of acculturation or the existence of traits in common with Western society. At the very top of this tree of evolution is the Mission Chapel – the symbol of evangelization and civilization, whose entrance faces the map of the maritime voyages (i.e. civilization) and whose back

---

91. An idea that has existed for centuries and reached maximum currency in the nineteenth century, when it even gained some scientific respectability. Vestiges of the idea persist today, especially in popular culture (Jahoda 1999).

92. The Enlightenment considered savagery as the 'infancy of humanity'. This idea was later given visual expression in the depiction of 'savages' as children. According to Jahoda (1999), savagery was a state attributed regardless of skin pigmentation, and the more remote inhabitants of Europe were included in the early classifications of 'savages'. Changes within European society itself produced the later distinction between 'European' and 'savage' societies.

93. Here we see a restatement of the idea that 'primitive' man was illogical, with a special propensity for magic; and yet over time he developed more sophisticated religious ideas (Kuper 1988: 5).

Figure 20. The Guinea pavilion and sculpture of an African, in a photograph taken in the 1940s and now in the collection of the FBB.

is turned away from the Overseas Portugal section. Inside this chapel are photographs illustrating the links between the missions, schooling and vocational training. Outside is a statue of an African woman carrying a child on her back. This is an allusion to the 'good' sentiments awakened by maternity and, by analogy, to the 'good' sentiments of the mission-

Figure 21. Maternity sculpture at the entrance to the Mission Chapel (1940s).

aries, whose dedication brought colonized peoples to civilization (Figure 21).

A visit to Portugal dos Pequenitos therefore offers us a view of humanity according to which distinct groups exist at different stages of evolution. At the lowest stages we find the inhabitants of Angola, Mozambique and Guinea. A little higher come the inhabitants of São Tomé e Príncipe and Cape Verde: uninhabited islands which the Portuguese made productive. One level higher and we find the inhabitants of India, Timor and Macao, whose trading relations with Portugal have brought them closer to the latter; and in India, Western and Indian elements had mixed. At the top are the Portuguese themselves, propagators of civilization.

The story that Portugal dos Pequenitos tells us brings to mind Lévi-Strauss's reading of myth. For Lévi-Strauss ([1971] 1981), mythical thought operates via a process of transformation, for every myth is modified by its narrator: certain elements are eliminated and others added, changes are made to the sequence of events, and the structure is constantly modified. Yet these changes still belong to the same mythical whole. It is *because* it changes that the myth continues to exist. What we find at Portugal dos Pequenitos is exactly this combination of different elements which, converging on a single ideology, are spatially regrouped in such a way that connections are established between them – connections which make them belong to the same whole. In addition, the belief in a preexisting myth conditioned the perceptions of those who devised and designed this park. Portugal dos Pequenitos was built from scratch as testimony to an ordered 'nation', to project the idea of a 'Portuguese world' that was vast, diverse, scattered all over the globe and with ancient roots. It is therefore a representation of what 'being Portuguese'[94]

94. The expression 'being Portuguese' was used by Augusto de Castro (1940) in his humorous account of the visit of two 'provincials' to the Exhibition of the Portuguese World.

meant in the 1930s and '40s, and of the country's relationship with its overseas possessions. The 'agents of this history' (Fabian 1983: 154) were those who held the political, economic and technological power, i.e. the Portuguese.

And yet the Portugal we find in Portugal dos Pequenitos is essentially a rural, unindustrialized country, closed in upon itself yet consciously European despite being 'proudly alone'. With its medieval castles and reproductions of national monuments, Portugal dos Pequenitos gives pride of place to history; Overseas Portugal is relegated to the periphery. The inscription at the entrance to Portugal dos Pequenitos announces that it was due to the 'great adventure' of the Discoveries that 'the modern world was born'. Modernity, then, is overtly associated with discovery and expansion – and this also means the incorporation of the periphery, i.e. the overseas possessions. Yet the enduring image of the overseas subjects is of people who do not have a history similar to the Portuguese. Portugal dos Pequenitos is a construct which articulates an evolution of humanity from the Africans, in the primordial stage of development, to the Portuguese, who are a part of Europe and the great civilizations in general. This construct is bolstered by the elements on display, and it is motivated by the idea of 'race' – the concept that relegates the colonized to lower levels of civilization.

The status of the colonized populations at the exhibitions: the exotic vs. the familiar

All of the exhibitions I have examined in this chapter were attempts to articulate and give material expression to ideas, and therefore they were organized in such a way as to be deliberately instructive. These ideas concerned the nation, the colonial empire and its inhabitants. Their construction involved the objectification of values such as nationality; and the empire was part of this construction.[95] The representation of the empire enabled visitors to imagine the nation. Portugal was construed as an 'imagined community', to borrow a phrase from Anderson ([1983] 1991). Every image was designed to elicit 'colonial emotion', to awaken in the Portuguese a profound feeling for the 'empire'. The 'colonies' as a category acquired a homogeneous character, and what was taken from each colony and put on show at the exhibitions in a certain sense identi-

---

95. Unlike the Portuguese empire, in the British empire the colonies led a separate existence from the metropolis, and could not therefore constitute a threat to the idea of nationhood.

fied the 'nation'. And so the nation itself became an object of devotion, and was celebrated alongside the glory, endeavours and exploits of the colonizers.

Exhibitions were places where noises, smells and colours came together in cacophony; they were places of pilgrimage for a capitalist society.[96] But in these cases the pilgrims came to shrines of shared devotion to the state. As they left, visitors felt they had accomplished a mission, and experienced an emotional communion with the other visitors – just as authentic pilgrims 'say they feel better, comforted and gratified' (Fortuna and Ferreira 1993: 60) after they have completed their pilgrimage. But what these visitors were seeing was not colonial reality per se, but a construction deliberately conceived as distinct from the Western, urban, bourgeois and industrial world. As Corbey has noted (1993: 340), it was not the natural elements of the colonies which were celebrated but those which had been transformed by man. And it would seem that the Natives were included among these natural elements. The civilization and progress of the nation were celebrated in opposition to the inhabitants of the colonies. This process involved an evolutionist vision of history in which Portuguese or European hegemony was projected as the outcome of a natural and desirable process of development. According to this version of 'history', humanity had developed through different stages of civilization, from savagery to barbarism to the Caucasian, civilized 'White race'. In the visual staging of this 'history', each of the Natives on display was expected to play a certain role, regardless of whether he or she was fit for playing it, as in the case of the Indian courtesans who came to play the role of dancers at the 1940 exhibition. And in the diverse entertainments offered by the exhibitions, the cultural practices of the Natives were limited to *batuques,* dancing and snake charmers, without the slightest effort made to put any of these phenomena into context.

As with plays in theatres, the exhibitions manipulated time and space in their efforts to conjure up 'reality'. In constructing a history of civilization, they banished the colonial Natives to an earlier time, confined to the past and spatially confined too, in such a way that they could always be observed as they performed the tasks assigned to them. The negation of contemporaneity examined by Fabian (1983) existed not only in the origins of anthropology, but also in the political ideology

---

96. Exhibitions can be considered as similar to pilgrimages in that in both instances there occurs a levelling of status (that of pilgrims and visitors); both accommodate participation in an individual or collective mode, and both are voluntary acts and temporary escapes from everyday life. Some authors hold the view that every pilgrim is half-tourist, and every tourist half-pilgrim (Turner and Turner 1978).

of imperialism, at the world's fairs, in the discourse on missions, and in certain photographic methods. The decontemporizing gaze operates when a phenomenon in the present is observed as if it belonged to the past, as an event worth recording since threatened with disappearance; it lets us travel back in time and visit earlier stages of 'civilization'. In these exhibitions, the Portuguese brought to the present (and to modernity) colonial peoples who still belonged to the past.

The manipulation of space was also fundamental. If the exhibitions were like huge encyclopaedias, then their visitors, who could open the encyclopaedia at any page they wanted, were not just visitors but pan-optical observers. The Natives, in addition to being observed by the visitors, were also overseen and monitored by their delegates or guardians, who kept files on the tasks performed by their charges, their state of health and any incidents of incorrect conduct; these files were later sent to the minister for the colonies. Wherever the Natives found themselves, they would always have felt that they were being observed. It was this phenomenon of 'seeing without being seen' – or being observed without seeing one's observer – that Foucault described as the panopticon effect:[97] 'Whenever one is dealing with a multiplicity of individuals on whom a task or a particular form of behaviour must be imposed, the panoptic schema may be used' (1977: 205). Foucault's account of the panopticon principle in buildings whose occupants live in isolation from the outside world seems equally to apply to the compounds in which the Natives on show at the Portuguese exhibitions were confined. As in Foucault's panopticon, these compounds were places where power was staged. One author, Tony Bennett, has analyzed the relations between power and knowledge in the development of what he calls the 'exhibitionary complex'. This complex can be found in 'history and natural science museums, dioramas and panoramas, national and, later, international exhibitions'. Its importance lies in the fact that it has contributed to the 'development and circulation of new disciplines (history, biology, art history, anthropology) and their discursive formations', 'the development of new technologies of vision' (Bennett 1988: 73) and manifestations of power, as in the exhibitions.

The way the Natives were accommodated in 'villages' also brings to mind Appadurai (1988), who argued that Natives are not merely people who belong to certain places, but that they are somehow incarcerated in, or fated to occupy, these places. For Appadurai, this confinement has

---

97. Jeremy Bentham wrote his *Panopticon; or, The Inspection-House* in 1787 as an architectural blueprint for buildings such as prisons, factories, workshops, asylums and schools.

moral and metaphysical dimensions. In the Portuguese exhibitions, the Natives were confined both to their place of origin and the exhibition precinct. At the 1940 Exhibition of the Portuguese World, this place of confinement was the colonial section, which was located on the periphery of the exhibition enclosure and which itself was clearly demarcated by natural and ideological boundary markers. This was another way of controlling the Natives and keeping them subject to the power of the metropolis which had taken them there, to civilization. Close as they were to the heroic history of the metropolis and the world of technology, they formed no part of it.

When visitors were confronted with the sight of the Natives, their reactions ranged from repugnance and disdain to fascination and sympathy. These reactions were based on deeply rooted stereotypes about the supposed 'primitiveness' and 'barbarity' of the Native populations of the colonies. The organizers of the exhibitions did intend to encourage a certain engagement with the exotic, and elicit some interest in the habits of the Natives; yet, at the same time, a clear and sometimes even ironic distance was often maintained with regard to the people on show there. Visitor accounts, press reports and visual representations all reveal a curiosity or fascination with the Native men which stems from their supposed sexual prowess. But this fascination occasionally degenerates into depreciation of beings whose supposed bestial lasciviousness makes them repugnant. As Hinsley wrote of the 1893 World's Columbian Exposition of Chicago, 'the exotic and forbidden erotic merge as commodity' (1991: 354). There were explicitly sexual overtones at the Portuguese exhibitions in the interest shown by White males in seminaked Black women, and by White females in lean, healthy Black men. Speaking of the 1934 Portuguese Colonial Exhibition, one of my interviewees commented:

> Then they said some funny things ... about Black men with the ladies ... It was because they were Black, they were different and the ladies ... wanted to try them out and they liked it ... You know, things [smiles]. It was the novelty ... The Black women with their tits out ... in loincloths ... People were surprised ... but it wasn't the sex ... there was no sex, it was like going to the zoo (April 2003).

These African women wore little clothing or were naked from the waist upwards, and were commonly described with expressions such as 'black Venus', 'beauties', 'fruits of the earth' and 'black beauty'. And yet, although they were described as pretty, good-natured and erotically permissive, African women were also considered as *lacking* in beauty.

Other images of Natives elicited sympathy: the photographs of the king of Kongo with his queen and baby daughter at the 1940 exhibition, for instance, or pictures of children and babies, who were invariably described as *simpáticos*. It was frequent practice at the exhibitions for visitors to give the Natives money for their performances, or when they were asked. The Natives who actually worked at the exhibition may have received gratuities. Yet despite the sympathies they may have awakened in the visitors, at every Portuguese exhibition the Natives were subjected to salacious comments, and at the Lisbon Industrial Exhibition of 1932 the visitors even stoned them.

While official discourse viewed the Natives as lazy, at the exhibitions they almost always appeared busy at some task or other, just like the craftsman of the metropolis; and those who performed these tasks were considered to be on the right track as far as their ascension to civilization was concerned (Figure 22). Yet the metropolis seems to have seen little potential for enrichment in the objects they produced, for the question of investing in them was never raised. The Natives represented a natural wealth, and their principal value was as labour for the plantations or as manpower for the construction of bridges, roads and hospitals in the overseas possessions.

The Natives were reified by the gaze of those who organized and visited the exhibitions. This process of reification deserves further examination. The Natives came to the Portuguese exhibitions just as exotic

Figure 22. 'The two Makonde woodcarvers at work in the Exhibition village' (G. Cunha 1940).

objects and tropical plants had earlier been brought to Europe for exhibition in cabinets of curiosities. As Krzysztof Pomian observed:

> All such objects, whatever their original status, in Europe became semiophores, for they have been selected not for their use value but for their significance as representatives of the invisible: exotic countries, different societies, other climates (1984: 77).

What was really on show was not the Natives and how they organized themselves socially, how they lived or what they ate, but rather the political and scientific perceptions of those who wielded power. The way the Natives were selected, and what was intended to be put on show at the exhibitions, said much more about the colonizers and their relationship to the overseas possessions than it did about the Natives themselves. And the primary emphasis was on Portugal's past, the Discoveries and the great navigators. Portugal's right to the territories it had conquered in the past was upheld, and their continuing occupation legitimized. But this was a process of affirmation which denied the populations of these territories any pretension to civilization. Where they had arrived at some degree of civilization, it was an inferior stage relative to the Portuguese. Curiously, although concerted efforts had never succeeded in effectively occupying the colonies, although the desires of the 'Native populations' were ignored, these same populations were expected to remain in a state of eternal debt to the Portuguese, their colonizers (and saviours). At the 1934 Portuguese Colonial Exhibition, the colonial Natives were the only living exhibits. At the 1940 exhibition, visitors could choose between the 'inhabitants' of the Colonial Section and the metropolitan Portuguese of the Regional Centre; however, even this arrangement was designed to show how Portuguese peasants were superior to the 'colonized populations' in terms of 'civilization'.

There seems to have been a certain tension between the different elements on show at these exhibitions: a tension to be found in all colonial encounters, in fact. On the one hand, the objective was to illustrate the difference between 'civilized' and 'uncivilized', the diversity of the 'races', and (assuming that this diversity and the 'races' existed) to arrange these 'races' in a hierarchy of civilization, illustrating the distance between the Portuguese and the overseas peoples. On the other hand, the objective was to celebrate the adoption by the colonized people of Portuguese models[98] of language, dress and religion (Figure 23). The stories told in

---

98. Not all colonial powers operated similar models with regard to assimilation. While imposed assimilation was typical of the US and French colonial models, it was not as important in the British empire. In the exhibitions, the Natives of the French and American

Figure 23. 'Good' examples of colonization. 'The chiefs of two Indigenous representations: on the left the chief of the Makonde and on the right the chief of the Bachope' (G. Cunha 1940).

this context of tension can therefore be seen as mediators between two opposing states of humanity. They bring to mind Lévi-Strauss's ([1971] 1981) interpretation of myth as a dynamic which embraces contradictions or paradoxes. As with myths, their propagation depends on the survival of the contradictory or even diametrically opposed forces they embrace. Concord of the opposing forces can never be fully achieved; they can never exist in harmony. The discordance between 'civilized' and 'primitive', 'White' and 'Black', 'Christian' and 'heathen', almost, but never quite, resolves. And the discordance is in fact necessary if the 'story' – one which exoticizes and familiarizes at the same time – is to continue (Karp and Lavine 1991).

With regard to the selection of Natives we saw, for example, that the Exhibition of the Portuguese World in 1940 proposed to show people from a state of civilization inferior to that of the metropolitan Portuguese. But the Natives were selected according to their status in their communities of origin – and the higher their status the better, especially if they had a command of (written and/or spoken) Portuguese, no matter how difficult it was to find such people. However, the fact that not all the Natives knew the language of the colonizer only served to make them

empires were displayed as positive examples of assimilation (with their Western clothing and knowledge of Western culture), while British imperial subjects were presented as still very remote from the Western world.

seem more exotic. This leaves us at an impasse. On the one hand, the emphasis was on the works at the service of 'civilization'; but these works could not be seen to be obtaining the best results. It was important, too, that some Natives appeared seminaked (Figure 24). Their presence was evidence that Portugal still had much work to do; and this in turn reiterated the need for colonization. Yet the Natives occupied what was essentially a stage set, where they were presented as different because, in most cases, they had been urged to act as such. There were episodes, for instance, when due to 'cast' shortages the organizers recruited residents of metropolitan Portugal to play certain roles. But the inclusion of human beings engaged either in recreations of daily activities or representations or formal performances created the illusion that the activities on show were real, not representations, and this in turn created an illusion of authenticity, as Kirschenblatt-Gimblett notes (1991: 413, 416). The roles most in demand were those of dancer, carver and craftsman, with other vacancies including magician, snake charmer and 'Indigenous soldier'. Other Natives, especially Africans, were employed as restaurant waiters or tasked with rowing canoes on the lake. These events idealized a fictitious empire in which the exotic, the picturesque and alterity were exaggerated, often on the basis of the idea of 'race', to intensify the message. Regardless of the roles they played, all subjects of Portuguese sovereignty were considered as examples of other 'races' at various stages on the road to 'civilization', as represented by the Portuguese.

Figure 24. 'The Colonial Section of the Exhibition of the Portuguese World – Double Centenary 1140/1940. Photograph by Cunha e Costa. Angola – Brides and Bridesmaids'.

Conclusion

In this book I have shown how the racial theories current in the late nineteenth and early twentieth centuries were influential in Portugal. 'Race' is a polysemic term, a word with multiple meanings which can vary according to context and the author using it. The meanings ascribed to it in philosophical discourse vary depending on whether the author is a rationalist, empiricist or utilitarian, for example. Although its exact meaning varies, underlying all acceptances of the term is an ethnocentric (as well as Eurocentric and nationalist) outlook, according to which writers who conduct these analyses place themselves in a superior position, that of their own 'race', which is at the top of the classification of 'races' identifiable in social, cultural, scientific and aesthetic terms. Not only is there no consensus among the various theories which have proposed the existence of 'races', the racism with which these theories are associated lacks a 'founding father', in the words of Mosse (1992: 250), and it is in this that one of its greatest strengths lies.

Portugal was a colonial power, and some of these racial theories were applied to the 'Native populations' of its overseas possessions in an attempt to justify the power it wished to exert over them. By the late nineteenth and early twentieth centuries, Portugal had begun to invest in the production of 'knowledge' on its overseas possessions. Issues relating to the colonial populations began to be debated in various congresses, from the first National Colonial Congress of 1901 through to the Exhibition of the Portuguese World of 1940. It was above all the research of the anthropologists and biologists of the nineteenth century, which employed the concept of race as a factor of human differentiation – and not the emerging studies which placed the emphasis not on race but culture – which influenced the development of anthropology in Portugal. Thus, the standard against which the Natives of the overseas territories were measured – their physical characteristics, their colour and their conduct – was the 'White man' (and city dweller). Anthropological knowledge, produced in the surgery rather than collected in the field, was essential to colonial practice and the subjugation of the colonies, as it conferred legitimacy on theories which characterized subject populations in terms of their belonging to distinct and hierarchically ordered states of development. But some of the racial classifications used in this context were already obsolete for anthropologists such as Franz Boas, for example. How could this have happened? There were two reasons. First, the ideas of many contemporary British and American anthropologists whose work focused on sociocultural aspects of anthropology would have been unknown in Portugal, due to the country's isolation and its limited scientific field of vision. Second, some scientists continued to think in racialist terms, and continued to believe that the race factor was a valid explanation for social and cultural differences. We should remember that the period we are referring to here – which lasted until the end of the Second World War – was one in which the explanatory value of the racial factor was increasingly being called into question. However, its detractors made its supporters more vociferous.

The defence of colonial Portugal brought together figures as diverse as the authoritarian, corporatist and Catholic Oliveira Salazar and the republican, democrat and mason Norton de Matos. Portuguese colonial ideology was associated with the idea of Portugal's civilizing mission. The Colonial Act of 1930 formalized the idea of an already centuries-old empire, gave official expression to the guiding principles of colonial policy, which legitimized the possession of the overseas territories and the bringing of civilization to their populations, and established differences between citizens, *Assimilados* and *Indígenas*. According to the official discourse, because the Portuguese nation included the colonies, solidarity among all its constituent parts was an obligation. But 'solidarity' did not mean 'equality': far from it. The *Indígena* statutes served to some extent to illustrate the contradiction between proclaimed equality and manifest inequality. The Colonial Act of 1930 assigned *Indígena* status to the Natives of Angola, Guinea and Mozambique, while those of São Tomé e Príncipe and Timor received the same status in 1946. *Indígena* status was never imposed on the Natives of Cape Verde, Macao or Portuguese India, who had always been accorded a higher social position. We can detect this hierarchy in the congresses and studies whose subject matter was the colonized populations under Portuguese administration, in school readers and in the exhibitions. Although supposedly inferior to the Europeans, Asians (Indians and Chinese) were also supposedly superior to the Africans. Significantly, however, at the Portuguese exhibitions all colonial subjects, without exception – Angolans, Timorese and Indians alike – were referred to as *Indígenas*.

Various initiatives were promoted during the Estado Novo years to encourage the formation of a 'colonial conscience', and these initiatives had the support both of institutions and individuals, attached to the former or not. Although distorted by censorship, the discourse and images propagated in the period under review were a mine of information for me. References to the colonies were practically nonexistent in school readers, and efforts to integrate a colonial component in education were limited to a few initiatives, such as the 'colony weeks' and school exchange programmes between students from the metropolis and colonies. Although Portuguese history and Portuguese heroes were the principal themes of the readers, some reference was made to colonization and its success – which was partly explained by the fact that the Portuguese people were the result of extensive miscegenation themselves (although only the Arabic influence is acknowledged, not the African) and therefore had a propensity for adapting to other places and establishing dialogue with other peoples. These readers emphasize the distinction between the 'savage' and the 'civilized', a distinction based on the exaltation of the positive aspects of Western society to the detriment of all that is not Western, and the association of 'religion' with 'civilization'. The idea that it was possible to civilize the Natives was mainly found in missionary texts, and this was obviously an attempt to confer meaning on their work. In films, what we find is a representation which embraced the colonies (of Africa and Asia) as part of the nation, but nothing approaching cultural interaction is to be found. The Natives are essentially depicted as secondary characters, or in roles of subservience relative to the settlers. There is no depiction of ethnological diversity either in the school readers or the films, and neither does this intention appear to have existed.

In the written discourse of the Portuguese elites we repeatedly encounter ideas associated with the 'Native populations' which are underpinned by notions of an inferior 'race'. The ideas most commonly evoked are backwardness, laziness, lasciviousness, negligence, polygamy, groundless superstition, excessive revelry, proximity to the animal world and/or resemblance to the monkey, irrationality, warlike nature, cannibalism, robustness, childishness and abnormal sex drive. Certain 'physical anthropology' studies sought to validate some of these stereotypes, such as the physical robustness of African adults and their supposed childishness, but other stereotypes, such as cannibalism, were ignored by Portuguese anthropology. Although often considered as sexually permissive, African women could also be associated with maternity and the positive sentiments which this condition awakened. Another common idea was that the Natives could only evolve – socially, materially and morally – through contact with the European. And yet contact with civilization could also have supposedly destructive effects, as it led to the emergence of new elements on the linguistic and human levels. The *Mestiço,* for instance, was viewed as an ambivalent being who belonged neither to the White nor Black worlds. For some academics the *Mestiço* represented a threat, and therefore, they argued, miscegenation was to be avoided. Essentially, representations of the 'Native populations' revealed the evaluation criteria, and the prejudices, of the observer.

Some 'Natives' were put on display to the metropolitan population in the exhibitions of 1932, 1934 and 1940, as discussed in detail in Chapter III. In every instance they were depicted as being closer to 'nature' than urban society and its 'civilization'. The catalogues produced for these exhibitions frequently classified the Natives in terms of the colour of their skin. Colour, seen as an objective and natural differentiator, again invokes the idea of 'race' – a more abstract and, supposedly, scientific idea. In many cases the classifications which divided the colonial populations into categories such as 'White' and 'Black' are veiled references to 'race'. These categories were often found in the censuses of colonial populations, although they varied according to the year or the territory to which they referred. In the case of the population of São Tomé e Príncipe, it is interesting to note that one of the categories in the 1930 census, alongside *'Indígenas'* and 'European', was 'hired labour' – a category based not on 'race' but on occupational status.

The process by which the Natives were brought to the 1940 exhibition involved first their selection and then the negotiation of the conditions in which they would travel and be accommodated. Throughout these procedures the Natives themselves were treated like merchandise which was ordered, shipped and delivered into the custody of those charged with keeping them in good condition. The selection process was designed to assemble all the human 'types' contained in the empire; but this variety of 'types' was all but absent at the Exhibition of the Portuguese World in 1940, with Angolan or Timorese 'types' replaced by the 'Indigenous type' in general; the emphasis was now on the characteristics, qualities and defects the various representatives of the 'Indigenous type' shared. Despite their obvious diversity, the Natives were held to be part of a single, indivisible whole. They could be exhibited, classified and confined to an enclosed space because they were part of nature, the same unchanging nature that long ago Linnaeus had attempted to organize. Only 'culture', represented by Western civilization, could bring order to this 'natural' chaos.

Although in general the Natives were indiscriminately treated as *Indígenas,* some differences were acknowledged. For instance, depending on their social status in their community of provenance or the tasks they had come to perform, they might be assigned to different levels of civilization. The lowest of these levels was occupied by the Angolans, Mozambicans and Guineans, and it was among the Angolans that the most backward and decadent 'race', the 'Bushmen', were to be found. On the next level were the inhabitants of São Tomé e Príncipe, who despite their mixed-blood descent (which placed them, potentially, nearer to the Whites) were considered work-shy, meaning labour had to be imported from the other colonies. Up one more level were the Cape Verdeans, mostly *Mestiços* who had absorbed some elements of 'civilization' (language, dress, Catholicism and other habits symptomatic of their assimilation). Ranked higher than all the Africans were the Timorese, whose society of provenance was more hierarchical in its organization (and hierarchy was a marker of superiority in the West). However, the Timorese and other colonial subjects from the islands of southeast Asia also had a reputation as fierce fighters, which placed them at odds with the elegance and sophistication associated with the peoples of India and Macao. The music played by the orchestra of Chinese musicians which came to the 1934 Portuguese Colonial Exhibition was presented in aesthetic terms which were never employed in reference to the *batuques* of the Africans, for example. The people from India were represented as every bit as exotic as their fellow colonial subjects, but they wore clothes of richer fabric, elaborate ornaments and gold – a substance found not only in their apparel but also in the allegorical floats of the exhibition processions. The people from Macao and India were made to seem exotic and remote from the Europeans; yet, perhaps because the Africans were seen as even *more* remote, not least in terms of colour, these Asian subjects were nevertheless depicted as slightly closer to the Europeans. A mutual influence was considered to exist between Indians and Portuguese, as illustrated by the use of the term 'Luso-Indian representation' by the minister for the colonies, Vieira Machado, at the Exhibition of the Portuguese World of 1940 – expressions such as 'Luso-African representation' are nowhere to be found. This same idea can be detected in the use of decorative elements which attest to a certain degree of culture, such as the dishes with paintings of the Christian 'holy family' in the India pavilion of Portugal dos Pequenitos. This acknowledgement of a mixture of cultural elements serves as a kind of metaphor for the biological 'mixture' of Portuguese men and higher-caste Indian women, a practice which was both acknowledged and accepted.

At the heart of the stated objective of civilizing and evangelizing these 'exotic' and 'backward' populations there lies a paradox. For if on the one hand the official discourse proclaimed the need to protect the 'usages and customs' of the Natives, on the other hand it proclaimed the need to assimilate the Natives – a process which would naturally entail the disappearance of those same 'usages'. Yet miscegenation was never (or almost never) proposed as the solution to the problem of assimilation; the *other* was viewed as a human being capable of being 'elevated' (Portugal, after all, was a Catholic country), but the mixing of different biological worlds was not exactly encouraged. The exhibitions provided a good example of this. The individuals selected by the organizers of the exhibitions to form part of their national contingents were required to be of a certain degree of civilization, as recognized not only in their communities of origin (e.g. the African chieftains) but also by the Portuguese (i.e. the European dress they adopted). But they were *also* required to reveal a degree of civilization different from and inferior to that represented by the Portuguese, not only because they were seen as more backward (because they did not speak Portuguese or did not wear clothes) but also because they were exotic (thus, the *balayeres* and conjurers). In both cases they were seen either as symbols of the wealth of human diversity, or as the representatives of beings who were inferior to the Portuguese. The way they were represented at the exhibitions was designed to illustrate how much still remained to be done in the overseas possessions, especially in Africa. Colonization found its justification in evangelization and civilization – it was necessary and desirable. What the exhibitions put on show were 'fabricated' Natives, 'actors' whose roles were to represent the practices of a social and cultural order which the 'White' man had the job of civilizing. The Natives were put on display in their difference and inferiority for the benefit of a population united in its belief that it belonged to a superior 'race' which wielded the political and scientific power: metropolitan Portugal. Placing the Natives on display objectified this superiority by dividing people into two groups: the observers and the observed. And this was the way the exhibitions – as well as Portugal dos Pequenitos and other initiatives of the early decades of the Estado Novo, essentially devised for the benefit of a largely illiterate population – brought the 'Portuguese world' to the Portuguese people.

The exhibitions were ephemeral events. Today, the pluriracial Portuguese nation celebrated at the Exhibition of the Portuguese World survives in just a few isolated vestiges, like the black busts originally put on show as representatives of 'overseas Portuguese' and now in Lisbon's Jardim Botânico Tropical. Few observers would now see these busts as

Portuguese, and even fewer would relate them to the exhibition of 1940. Portugal dos Pequenitos remains open to the public, but has been continually renovated and modified over the years. The inscriptions on the *padrões* at the entrance to the pavilions representing the former Portuguese colonies have been changed, and the park now features more attractions for children. It continues to attract high numbers of visitors.[1] Lisbon's Praça do Império still contains certain elements from the 1940 Exhibition of the Portuguese World, such as the Padrão dos Descobrimentos, rebuilt after the event and now a popular attraction among visitors to the city. For if it is ideological and political 'functions' which usually justify the persistence of myths (Kuper 1988) and images[2] – such as the widely disseminated idea that Portuguese colonization was 'different' from other colonization initiatives – it is the changes (even minor changes) which these images undergo over the course of the years which enable them to survive.

---

1. On 19 January 2000 the Portuguese government awarded *Portugal dos Pequenitos* the Medal for Merit in Tourism.

2. Jahoda (1999) sees the centuries-long persistence of images of the 'other' as fulfilling psychological 'functions'. While they no longer enjoy scientific or political currency, such images do persist in the popular imagination.

Film

Films on colonial themes

1. *Angola, Aspectos Históricos,* date unknown.[1]
2. *Angola, Exposição Provincial, Agrícola, Pecuária e Industrial 1923,* 1923.
3. *Costumes Primitivos dos Indígenas em Moçambique,* Brigada Cinematográfica Portuguesa, 1928(?). Type: documentary. Sound: no. Duration: 9 min 15 s. Credits – directors: Brigada Cinematográfica Portuguesa; producer: AGC.
4. *Guiné. Aspectos industriais e agricultura,* Brigada Cinematográfica Portuguesa, 1928.
5. *Festejos em Lourenço Marques pela Passagem dos Territórios do Niassa para a Posse do Estado,* 1929. Type: documentary. Sound: no. Duration: 3 min 47 s.
6. *Aspectos do Rio Quanza. Quedas do Lucala,* 1930.
7. *Quedas do Dalla – Angola,* 1930.
8. *Guiné, Aldeia Indígena em Lisboa,* 1931. Type: documentary. Sound: no. Duration: 7 min 47 s. Credits – director unknown; producer: AGC.
9. *Planalto de Huíla,* António Antunes da Mata, 1931.
10. *Acção Colonizadora dos Portugueses,*[2] 1932. Type: documentary. Sound: no. Duration: 13 min 37 s. Credits – director: António Antunes da Mata; producer: AGC, H. da Costa. Approved for viewing by Inspecção-Geral dos Espectáculos AD160.
11. *África em Lisboa. Os Indígenas da Guiné na Grande Exposição Industrial Portuguesa,* 1932. Type: documentary. Sound: no. Dura-

---

1. This list is not exhaustive; I have selected only the titles most relevant to my topic.
2. From the colonial series *Angola Vista por António da Mata.*

tion: 9 min 32 s. Credits – directors: Salazar Diniz and Raul Reis; producer: Ulyssea Filme; cinematography: Salazar Diniz; intertitles: Óscar Viegas. Approved for viewing by Inspecção-Geral dos Espectáculos P380.

12. *De Lisboa a Luanda – Angola vista por António da Mata*, António Antunes da Mata, 1932.

13. *O Deserto de Angola*, António Antunes da Mata, 1932.

14. *Fazenda Açucareira «Tentativa»*, 1932.

15. *Pesca à baleia em Angola*, António Antunes da Mata, 1932.

16. *I Companhia de Infantaria Indígena de Angola em Lisboa*, 1933. Type: documentary. Sound: no. Duration: 8 min 33 s. Credits – director unknown; producer: AGC. Approved for viewing by Inspecção-Geral dos Espectáculos AO3.

17. *De Lisboa a São Tomé*, 1933.

18. *Do Lobito a Lisboa com o «Lancia» S-16570 10 Maio-20 Agosto 1933*, Gonçalo Cabral, 1933.

19. *Dragões de Moçambique*, Aníbal Contreiras, 1934.

20. *Moçambique, Ritmos Guerreiros em Cantos e Danças*, 1934. Type: documentary. Sound: no. Duration: 36 min. Credits – director: Aníbal Contreiras; producer: unknown; laboratory: Lisboa Filme; sound recording: F. Quintela. Approved for viewing by Inspecção-Geral dos Espectáculos AO.

21. *No País das Laurentinas – Colonos*, 1934. Type: documentary. Sound: no. Duration: 23 min 25 s. Credits – director: Ismael Costa; producer: AGC; intertitles: Ismael Costa (intertitles created at the graphics bench of *Notícias*); cinematography: Fernandes Tomaz.

22. *I Exposição Colonial Portuguesa – Porto 1934*, 1935. Type: documentary. Sound: no. Duration: 5 min 38 s (73 m). Credits – director, producer, cinematography, captions: Aníbal Contreiras; cinematography: J. César de Sá (Matos-Cruz and Antunes 1997: no. 6, p. 46).

23. *São Tomé, Jóia do Império*,[3] René Ginet, 1935.

24. *I Cruzeiro de Férias às Colónias do Ocidente*, 1936. Type: documentary/reportage. Duration: 65 min. Credits – director: San Payo; producer: AGC.

25. *Exposição Histórica da Ocupação*,[4] 1937. Type: documentary. Sound: yes. Duration: 8 min 9 s[5] (44 m) (Matos-Cruz 1983: 78). Credits

---

3. A film on work on the *roças* or plantations of São Tomé e Príncipe.

4. This film is incomplete; at least the first reel is missing.

5. This was the effective running time of the print I viewed in ANIM, i.e. what now remains of the film. The print, recovered from the original nitrate stock (image and sound), exhibits scratches and lacunae.

– director and narrator: António Lopes Ribeiro; producer: AGC/MCCA; studios: Tobis Portuguesa; assistant director: Carlos Filipe Ribeiro; writer: Manuel Múrias; cinematography: Manuel Luís Vieira and Isy Goldberger; distributor: SPAC; sound: Luís Sousa Santos and Paulo de Brito Aranha. Premiere: 11 May 1938, São Luís Theatre, Lisbon.

26. *A Revolução de Maio,* António Lopes Ribeiro, 1937.

27. *A Segunda Viagem Triunfal,* 1939. Type: feature-length documentary. Sound: yes. Duration: 70 min (74 min) (Matos-Cruz and Antunes 1997: no. 8, p. 60; Matos-Cruz 1981: 17). Credits – director, sound recording: Paulo de Brito Aranha; producer: SPAC; editing: Vieira de Sousa; music: Jaime Silva Jr; equipment: Tobis Portuguesa (Tobis Klangfilm system); laboratory: Lisboa Filme (image), Kodak film; distribution: SPAC; cinematography: Octávio Bobone and Artur Costa de Macedo. Approved for viewing by Inspecção-Geral dos Espectáculos BF15.

28. *Viagem do Chefe do Estado às Colónias de Angola e São Tomé e Príncipe,* 1939. Type: documentary. Sound: yes. Duration: 70 min approx. (81 min 30 s) (Matos-Cruz 1983: 78). Credits – director and editor: António Lopes Ribeiro; producer: AGC/MCCA; assistant director: Carlos Filipe Ribeiro; musical director: Pedro de Freitas Branco; music: Wenceslau Pinto; writer: Manuel Múrias; distributor: SPAC; cinematography: Isy Goldberger and Manuel Luís Vieira; narrator: Manuel Ribeiro; sound: Luís Sousa Santos and Paulo de Brito Aranha; laboratory: Lisboa Filme (image); animation: Carlos Ribeiro; sound recording by Klangfilm/Tobis Portuguesa. Premiere: 22 May 1939, Tivoli Theatre, Lisbon. Approved for viewing by Inspecção-Geral dos Espectáculos BF10.

29. *O Cortejo do Mundo Português,* 1940, Type: documentary. Colour. Sound: ? Duration: 6 min. Credits – director and producer: F. Carneiro Mendes.[6]

30. *A Exposição do Mundo Português,* 1940. Type: documentary. Colour. Sound: ? Duration: 8 min. Credits – director and producer: F. Carneiro Mendes.

31. *O Feitiço do Império,* 1940. Type: feature-length drama.[7] Sound: yes, but the copy I viewed has lost its soundtrack. Duration: 150

---

6. As this film was made by an amateur (F. Carneiro Mendes), there are no records of its having passed through the censors.

7. This copy was restored from a nitrate negative; the soundtrack has been lost. Total footage is 3,544 metres, with running time of 129 minutes. The opening credits and first part are missing; the film now opens with the departure of Luís Morais for Portugal (Matos-Cruz 1983: 409).

min (146 min) (Matos-Cruz 1981: 19, 1983: 78). Credits – director, editor, dialogues: António Lopes Ribeiro; producer: AGC/MCCA; screenplay: Joaquim Mota Júnior; distribution: SPAC; makeup: António Vilar; sound: Luís Sousa Santos and Paulo de Brito Aranha; art director: António Soares; composer: Pedro de Freitas Branco; laboratory: Lisboa Filme (image); cinematography: Manuel Luís Vieira and Isy Goldberger; music: Jaime Silva Filho and Wenceslau Pinto; studios: Tobis Portuguesa. Premiere: 23 May 1940, Eden Theatre, Lisbon. The film ran for seven weeks.

32. *As Festas do Duplo Centenário,* 1940. Type: feature-length documentary. Sound: yes. Duration: the running time of this film seems initially to have been 76 min (Matos-Cruz and Antunes 1997: no. 8, p. 63), but the print in the Cinemateca Portuguesa's ANIM archive consists of just four reels with a total running time of 36 min.[8] Credits – director and narrator: António Lopes Ribeiro; producer: SPN; cinematography: Octávio Bobone, Artur Costa de Macedo, Salazar Diniz and Manuel Luís Vieira; sound: Paulo de Brito Aranha and Luís Sousa Santos; distribution: SPAC; editor: Vieira de Sousa; laboratory: Lisboa Filme.

33. *Guiné Berço do Império,* 1940. Type: documentary. Duration: 22 min. Credits – director, writer and editor: Lopes Ribeiro; producer: AGC/MCCA; assistant director: Carlos Filipe Ribeiro; laboratory: Tobis Portuguesa; cinematography: Isy Goldberger and Manuel Luís Vieira; sound: Paulo de Brito Aranha; distribution: SPAC.

34. *Aspectos de Moçambique,* 1941. Type: documentary. Duration: 12 min. Credits – director, writer and editor: António Lopes Ribeiro; producer: AGC/MCCA; assistant director: Carlos Filipe Ribeiro; cinematography: Isy Goldberger and Manuel Luís Vieira; sound: Paulo de Brito Aranha and Luís Sousa Santos; narrator: D. João da Câmara; laboratory: Lisboa Filme; distribution: Filmes Castelo Lopes. Premiere: 1948(?).

35. *A Exposição do Mundo Português,* 1941. Type: documentary. B/W. Sound: yes. Duration: 64 min.[9] Credits – director, writer and narrator: António Lopes Ribeiro; assistant director: Carlos Filipe Ribeiro; producer and distributor: SPAC; music: Frederico de Freitas; cinematography: Octávio Bobone, Artur Costa de Macedo, Salazar

---

8. According to Matos-Cruz, the surviving footage (1,200 metres) of this film totals just 44 minutes, corresponding to the second, fourth, fifth and seventh reels. There are lacunae of image and sound on the extant print, which was recovered from the original nitrate stock (1983: 410).

9. According to Matos-Cruz, the original version of this film lasted 33 minutes, with footage of 750 m; a full positive print of this film exists (1983: 411).

Diniz and Manuel Luís Vieira; sound: J. Sá Nobre; editing: Vieira de Sousa; laboratory: Lisboa Filme, on Kodak film stock.

36. *São Tomé e Príncipe*, 1941. Type: documentary. Duration: 21 min approx. Credits – supervising director, writer and editor: António Lopes Ribeiro; assistant director: Carlos Filipe Ribeiro; cinematography: Manuel Luís Vieira; sound: Paulo de Brito Aranha and Luís Sousa Santos; laboratory: Lisboa Filme; distribution: SPAC; producer unknown. Filmed in 1938. António Lopes Ribeiro was not present during filming.

37. *Portugal na Exposição de Paris de 1937*, António Lopes Ribeiro, 1942.

38. *Viagem de Sua Eminência o Cardeal Patriarca de Lisboa*, António Lopes Ribeiro, mid-1940s (?). Type: documentary. Duration: 28 min. Credits – director: António Lopes Ribeiro; producer: SPAC; writer: Moreira das Neves; cinematography: Manuel Luís Vieira and António de Sousa.

39. *Angola Uma Nova Lusitânia*, 1944. Type: feature-length documentary. Sound: yes. Duration: 75 min. Matos-Cruz (1983: 88) gives the running time as approximately 30 minutes. Credits – director, writer, editor: António Lopes Ribeiro(?); producer: AGC/MCCA; assistant director: Carlos Filipe Ribeiro; cinematography: Manuel Luís Vieira and Isy Goldberger; distribution: SPAC; sound: Luís Sousa Santos and Paulo de Brito Aranha; camera operators: Isy Goldberger and Manuel Luiz Vieira; texts: José Osório de Oliveira; editing: Vieira de Sousa(?); narrator: Pedro Moutinho; sound operator: Américo Nobre.

40. *Gentes que Nós Civilizámos (apontamentos etnográficos de Angola)*, 1944. Type: documentary. B/W. Sound: yes. Duration: 18 min. Matos-Cruz (1988: 83) gives 18 min 30 s. Credits – director, writer: António Lopes Ribeiro; producer: AGC/MCCA; assistant director: Carlos Filipe Ribeiro; narrator: Elmano da Cunha e Costa; cinematography: Isy Goldberger and Manuel Luiz Vieira; distribution: SPAC; sound: Luís Barão; editing: Vieira de Souza;[10] laboratory: Lisboa Filme; sound: Paulo de Brito Aranha and Luís Sousa Santos. Premiere: 1944 (Matos-Cruz 1983: 11).

41. *As Ilhas Crioulas de Cabo Verde*, 1945. Type: documentary. B/W. Sound: yes. Duration: 20 min. Credits – director, narrator: António Lopes Ribeiro; producer: AGC/MCCA; assistant director: Carlos Filipe Ribeiro; distribution: SPAC; cinematography: Manuel Luiz Vieira and Isy Goldberger; sound: Luís Sousa Santos and Paulo

---

10. Matos-Cruz (1983: 88) credits António Lopes Ribeiro as the editor.

de Brito Aranha; laboratory: Lisboa Filme; writer: José Osório de Oliveira;[11] editing: Vieira de Sousa. Premiere: 7 May 1945, Trindade Theatre, Lisbon. Previewed in a 'Cape Verdean screening' in the Trindade Theatre. Filmed in 1938 (Matos-Cruz 1983: 91).

42. *Guiné Portuguesa,* 1946. Type: documentary. Duration: 27 min. Credits – director, writer and editor: António Lopes Ribeiro; producer: AGC/MCCA; assistant director: Carlos Filipe Ribeiro; cinematography: Isy Goldberger and Manuel Luís Vieira; sound: Paulo de Brito Aranha and Luís Sousa Santos; laboratory: Lisboa Filme; distribution: SPAC. Premiere: 1946. Filmed in 1938.

43. *O Cortejo Histórico com a Representação de Todas as Colónias Portuguesas em Carros Alegóricos,* 1947. Type: documentary. B/W. Sound: yes, but the print I viewed had no soundtrack. Duration: 7 min. Credits – no credits are included in the print I viewed. Cinemateca Portuguesa informed me that this film was produced by Leitão de Barros.

44. *O Cortejo Histórico de Lisboa,* 1947. Type: documentary. Colour. Duration: 25 min 30 s. Credits – director: António Lopes Ribeiro; producer: Câmara Municipal de Lisboa; cinematography: Alberto Schmidt, Álvaro Antunes, Arlindo Freixo, José Vieira, Mateus Júnior and Salvador Fernandes; narrator: Pedro Moutinho; editing: Rex Endsleigh; sound recording: British Movietone News.

45. *14 Anos de Política do Espírito. Apontamentos para uma Exposição,* António Lopes Ribeiro, 1948.

46. *O Ensino em Angola,* 1950. Type: documentary. B/W. Sound: yes. Duration: 12 min. Credits – director: Ricardo Malheiro; producer: Ministério das Colónias, Felipe de Solms and Ricardo Malheiro; assistant director: Lemos Ferreira; narrator: Pedro Moutinho; cinematography: João Silva; sound director: Luís Barão; writer: Ávila de Azevedo; laboratory: Tobis Portuguesa (image); sound recording: Lisboa Filme; editor: Carlos Marques.

47. *Epopeia da Selva,*[12] 1950. Type: drama. Duration: feature length(?). Credits – director: Raul Faria da Fonseca; cinematography: Perdigão Queiroga.

48. *Acção Missionária em Angola,* 1951. Type: documentary. B/W. Sound: yes. Duration: 10 min. Credits – directors: Lemos Pereira

---

11. Matos-Cruz (1983: 91) credits António Lopes Ribeiro as the writer.

12. An 'African adventure', shot in Angola. The film remained unfinished after its director died in a plane crash in 1950. After *O Feitiço do Império*, it was one of the most ambitious productions on a colonial theme in Portuguese cinema. *Epopeia da Selva* ('Jungle Epic') combined drama and documentary in a series of adventures and historical episodes set in Africa, such as the feats of the explorer Silva Porto.

and João Silva; producers: Ministério do Ultramar and Felipe de
Solms; writer and narrator: Pedro Moutinho; cinematography: João
Silva; sound director: Enrique Dominguez; laboratory: Tobis Portu-
guesa; editor: João Mendes; sound recording: Lisboa Filme.

49. *Chaimite,* 1953. Type: feature-length drama. B/W. Sound: yes.
Duration: 157 min (Matos-Cruz 1981: 61). Credits – director,
screenplay, editing, storyboard: Jorge Brum do Canto; producer:
Cinal – Cinematografia Nacional, Lda, with funding from Fundo
do Cinema Nacional; assistant director: Melo Pereira; distribution:
Momento Filmes; sound: Heliodoro Pires and Luís Sousa Santos;
historic and military adviser: Major Vassalo Pandayo; construc-
tion coordinator: Francisco Duarte; cinematography: J. César de
Sá and Aurélio Rodrigues; laboratory: Ulyssea Filme (image) on
Kodak and Gevaert film stock; music: Joly Braga Santos; studios:
Cinelândia; military assistants for certain African scenes: Captain
Araújo de Oliveira, Lieutenants Finsa Álvares da Costa and Almeida
Santos; art director: Mário Costa; script supervisor: Luiz Emauz;
makeup: Augusto Madureira; stills by João Martins on *Kosmos* pa-
per; dialogue translated into Ronga by Enoque Lilombo; dialogue
translated into Chengane by David Zinhôngua Manhiça; props:
Almeida e Sousa.[13] Premiere: 4 April 1953, Monumental Theatre,
Lisbon. Cast: Alfredo Pique – Mambaza; Jacinto Ramos – Mouz-
inho de Albuquerque; David Zinhôngua Manhiça – Mauéué; Car-
los Benfica – Gungunhana; Augusto Figueiredo – Caldas Xavier;
Jorge Brum do Canto – Paiva Couceiro; Emília Vilas – aunt Rosa;
Julieta Castelo – D. Maria José Mouzinho de Albuquerque; Ar-
tur Semedo – sergeant; Emílio Correia – António the interpreter;
Silva Araújo – António Enes; Carlos José Teixeira – soldier; Maria
Mayer/Lurdes Norberto – settler's daughter. Extras: César Viana,
Hanita Hallan, Amilcar Peres, Laura Ribeiro, Mário Santos, Pedro
Navarro, Carlos Bagão, Sousa Mendes, Narciso Moutinho, Roberto
Santos Castanheira.

50. *Portugal na Exposição de Bruxelas,* António Lopes Ribeiro, 1958.
51. *Nossos Irmãos, os Africanos,* Ed Keffel, 1963.
52. *Catembe,* M. G. Faria de Almeida, 1965.
53. *Portugal de Hoje,* J. N. Pascal-Angot, 1967.
54. *Portugal do meu amor,* Jean Manzon, 1967.
55. *Uma vontade maior,* Carlos Tudela, 1967.

---

13. Other crew members were: Aurélio Rodrigues, Emílio Correia, Artur Semedo, Amilcar
Peres, Jacinto Ramos, Victor Costa, Edite Sobral, Carlos Deus, António Alcazar, Augusto Quirino, José de Castro and Madalena Penedo.

56. *Portugueses no Brasil*, António Lopes Ribeiro, Miguel Spiguel, 1968.
57. *O romance do Luachimo*, Baptista Rosa, 1969.
58. *Angola na Guerra e no Progresso*, Quirino Simões, 1971.
59. *Deixem-me ao menos subir às palmeiras*, Joaquim Lopes Barbosa, 1974.
60. *Índia*, António Faria, 1975.
61. *Moçambique (Documento Vivo)*, Viriato Barreto, 1977.
62. *Esplendor Selvagem*, António de Sousa, 1978.
63. *Acto dos Feitos da Guiné*, Ideia, Fernando Matos Silva, 1981.

Films on Portugal dos Pequenitos

1. *Rumo à Vida: A Obra de Assistência Social na Beira Litoral*, 1950. Duration: 25 min. Format: CD (ISBN 972-8318-75-8. Copyright 145 318/99). Credits – director: João Mendes; writer: Henrique Galvão; cinematography: Perdigão Queiroga; producers: Felipe de Solms and Ricardo Malheiro; narrator: Pedro Moutinho.
2. *Portugal dos Pequenitos*, 1968(?). Colour. Sound: yes. Duration: 10 min. Credits – director: João Mendes; producer: Felipe de Solms; cinematography: Mário Moura; writer: Luiz Forjaz Trigueiros; music: Shegundo Galarza. A copy of this film can be viewed at Casa-Museu Bissaya-Barreto.

Texts from the *padrões* of Portugal dos Pequenitos

Modified texts of the inscriptions on the *padrões* in the streets of Overseas Portugal

At the entrance

'Of all the Europeans, the Portuguese were the pioneers of the geographical Discoveries and the opening of the world, unblocking communication between the civilizations of the earth and enabling contact between cultures on the five continents. From this great adventure the modern world was born. Following these overseas encounters and dialogue between civilizations, after five centuries of history "divided in pieces around the world" the various Portuguese-speaking countries were created, with the Luso-African-Brazilian community now one of the most important on the planet.'

Beside the Mission Chapel

'The discoveries and the overseas encounters of the Portuguese contributed to the construction of a new image of the world and the idea of dialogue among the human species. The history of planet earth was unified and men underwent a long period of learning about humanity, like big children learning to live together. This period of learning has produced much that is positive: men and cultures came together in their differences and this allowed them to understand their unity. In this way the feeling of the acceptance of difference was born – universalism, the foundation of fraternity and tolerance.'

Beside the map showing the routes sailed by the first navigators

'It was from the Atlantic that what would become the Western, modern world was created, after the great discoveries of the 15th and 16th centuries, due to the long efforts of the Portuguese and, later, of other peoples. The quest for geographic and scientific knowledge comes from the dawn of history and continues today in the age of space exploration. But the unparalleled nature of the great contribution of the voyages of the Portuguese discoveries will forever go down in history.'

Inscriptions on the *padrões* of the pavilions in Overseas Portugal

Original versions[1]

Angola

'In 1482, Diogo Cam took our caravels to Kongo. Two years later he returned there to erect the *padrão* of Portugal, and went up the river Zaire as far as the falls of Yelala, where he engraved his name and the names of his companions in the rock. He met and negotiated with the Black king of Kongo, and brought the latter's son to Portugal, where King João II had him baptized and educated. Thus began, peacefully, the civilizing action of the Portuguese in Angola – our biggest overseas province.'

Mozambique

'When Vasco da Gama went in search of India, after rounding the Cape of Good Hope he anchored at several points along the East African coast and rested on the small island of Mozambique, which offered good shelter. After this, the Portuguese ships on the India route made Mozambique and the ports on that coast their usual anchoring places, where they met the Indigenous populations and showed them the way to civilization.'

Guinea

'In the time of Henry the Navigator, Guinea was the name given to the whole of the African coast which was gradually discovered beyond Cape Bojador. A country of *Azenegues* and Blacks, some of the earliest navigatiors died here, struck down by poisoned spears. The current province of Portuguese Guinea is still home to many Black races and is

---

1. The pavilions of Timor and Macao have no original *padrão* in their interior.

like a *padrão* which attests to the excellence of our discoverers and the valour of their efforts.'

São Tomé e Príncipe
'In the reign of Dom Afonso V, his son (later Dom João II) gave new impetus to the Discoveries, which had almost stopped since 1446. The African coast was discovered in giant steps – 100 leagues a year – and in 1471 the Portuguese arrived in the Gulf of Guinea, Benin and Mina, from where much gold came to Portugal. Along this coast four islands were found, one of which received the name of the Island of the Prince and another the name of Island of Lizards (today São Tomé); the other two we later ceded to Spain. Dom João II resolved to colonize these islands, in the middle of a torrid zone which the ancients said was uninhabitable. The Portuguese colonized them in such a way that they now produce excellent coffee and the finest cocoa in the world.'

Cape Verde
'Off the cape which was named "Verde" on account of the trees which covered it, our navigators discovered the island of this archipelago one by one. The first to be sighted was the island of Santiago, by the caravels of Diogo Gomes and Antonio da Nola. Henry the Navigator made the latter captain of these islands, which were colonized by Whites and Blacks, and where the creole which is now spoken differs somewhat from Portuguese.'

India
'The discovery of the maritime route to India (by seas never before sailed) gave Dom Manuel I supremacy in Indian Ocean navigation and trade. In 1498 Vasco da Gama attempted to make peace with the peoples of India, from whom we were to buy the greatly valued spices. But the intrigues of the Moorish traders obliged us to maintain our dominion over the seas by force. The Portuguese ships defeated the Turks, the Egyptians and the Indians, and our Indian Empire established itself with the numerous fortresses which we built there, and of which those of Goa, Damão and Diu remain.'

Revised versions (altered in the early 1990s)

People's Republic of Angola
'The Portuguese first encountered Angola in 1482, when the navigator Diogo Cão established friendly relations with the African civilizations south of the Equator. This navigator sailed up the mouth of the river

Zaire, formed an alliance with the king of Kongo and conducted geographic surveys of the Angolan coast. The Portuguese presence in Angola lasted for five centuries and Portuguese sovereignty lasted until 11 November 1975, when the new country became independent.'

People's Republic of Mozambique

'The illustrious Vasco da Gama was the first Portuguese navigator to arrive in Mozambique, during his fantastic adventure in search of India. After rounding the Cape of Good Hope he stopped in various ports on the east African coast, and found in the lovely island of Mozambique the supplies he needed. In the subsequent centuries Mozambique continued to be a base for ships plying the India line and a port where the Portuguese established a lasting presence. The new country rose to independence on 25 June 1975.'

People's Republic of Guiné-Bissau

'The Portuguese navigators of the 15th century were the first to conduct geographic surveys of the coasts of West Africa and Guinea, where they made contact with the inhabitants. The presence of the Portuguese in the region of Guiné-Bissau dates from 1456, and Portuguese sovereignty lasted for over 500 years. On 24 September 1973 the new country gained its independence and became one more member of the Luso-African-Brazilian community.'

Demoractic Republic of São Tomé e Príncipe

'In their exploration of the gulf of Guinea in the time of Prince João, the Portuguese navigators found various uninhabited islands. On two of these islands, later called São Tomé and Príncipe, settlements were promoted and townships of African and European inhabitants established – the first European settlements in the equatorial zone. Portuguese sovereignty lasted until the 20th century. On 12 July 1975 the new country rose to independence.'

Republic of Cape Verde

'When the Cape Verde islands were discovered by the Portuguese in the 15th century they were still uninhabited. They were settled by inhabitants of African and European origin, setting the example for a remarkable cultural process of miscegenation. Having formerly served as an important base for navigations, the Cape Verde archipelago was later to become a meeting point of the Atlantic and African worlds as an independent country since 5 July 1975.'

Portuguese India
'With the voyage of Vasco da Gama in 1498 the Portuguese accomplished the objective which the Europeans had longed for and which Christopher Columbus had tried without success to achieve: the discovery of a maritime route to India. After this, every year regular convoys set off from Lisbon on the "India line" and the Portuguese began to establish their presence in the Orient. Of the old Portuguese Asian empire Goa, Damão and Diu remained until the 20th century, when the Indian Union took control of them on 17 December 1961.'

Timor
'The main objective of the geographic explorations conducted by the Portuguese navigators in the seas of the Malay Archipelago in the 16th century was to get to the Moluccan Islands. But other distant islands in this region so remote from Europe were also encountered for the first time by Europeans, including Timor, over which the Portuguese maintained sovereignty until the 20th century. The territory was occupied by Indonesia on 7 December 1975.'

Macao
'The Portuguese presence in the Far East dates from the early 16th century, and on the Chinese coast the principal entrepot was the city of Macao from the middle of the 16th century. Portuguese trade and government were established in the territory of Macao and were accepted peacefully by the Chinese, who originally offered the city to the Portuguese and saw it as a gateway to the world. Portuguese presence lasted until 31 December 1999, when its administration of the territory came to an end.'

Federal Republic of Brazil[2]
'After the voyage of Pedro Álvares Cabral, the Portuguese founded the great tropical nation of Brazil—well beyond the limits of the Treaty of Tordesillas—as a "continent-country", a giant which occupied almost half the territory of South America. On 7 September 1822 Brazil became a new and independent state, and the heir to the Portuguese crown was the first sovereign of the new country: Portugal's first "sister nation".'

---

2. The Brazil pavilion is closed and therefore I was unable to ascertain whether a *padrão* with an earlier version of the inscription is to be found inside.

Bibliography

Primary sources

Archives

Arquivo de História Social do Instituto de Ciências Sociais da Universidade de Lisboa – bequest of Pinto Quartim (*General Norton de Matos, Candidato à Presidência da República apresentou a sua candidatura no Supremo Tribunal de Justiça, em 9 de Julho de 1948, nos termos do Art. 27 da Lei Eleitoral em vigor*, n.o 46, doc. 212).

Arquivo Histórico Ultramarino – room 6, no. 538, maço 5, processos nos. 4/64, 4/69, 4/76, 4/82, room 1, bundle 200, process no. 118/46.

Cunha, Guilherme Abranches Ferreira da. 1940. *Relatório da Actuação do Encarregado da Representação Indígena de Moçambique à Exposição Histórica do Mundo Português*, 21 August 1940.

Arquivo Nacional das Imagens em Movimento[1]

Printed sources

A cidade da Beira na 1a Exposição Colonial do Porto. 1934. Presented by the Comissão de Administração Urbana.

Agência Geral das Colónias. 1947. *Colectânea de Legislação Colonial*. Lisbon: AGC.

Agenda Missionária. 1941. Sociedade Portuguesa das Missões Católicas Ultramarinas. Cucujães, Portugal.

Álbum-Catálogo Oficial, O Império Português na Primeira Exposição Colonial Portuguesa realizada no Palácio de Cristal do Porto de Junho a Setembro de ano de 1934. 1934. Porto: Tipografia Leitão.

Álbum dos finalistas da ESC. 1941–45. Class of 1941–1945. Lisbon.

Álbum fotográfico da 1a Exposição Colonial Portuguesa. 101 clichés fotográficos de Alvão. 1934. Porto: Litografia Nacional.

Almeida, António de. [1937] 1940a. Relatório sôbre a Organização, na Regência da 4a Cadeira do C. S. C., do Curso de Anthropologia Colonial, apresentado à Direcção da ESC, pelo Prof. Dr. António de Almeida. In *Annuário da ESC*, years XIX and XX, 1938 and 1939, 65–76. Lisbon: ESC.

---

1. See list of films in Appendix I.

————. 1940b. Das mutilações étnicas dos indígenas da Guiné portuguesa. In *Congressos do Mundo Português. Congresso Colonial.* Volume XIV, Book 1, Section 1, Lisbon: Comissão Executiva dos Centenários: 235–305.

————. [1942– 43] 1944. As investigações antropológicas e etnográficas em Angola. In *Anuário da ESC,* years 23 and 24, 1942 and 1943, 141–48. Lisbon: ESC.

————. [1943–44] 1945. Subsídio para o Estudo Antropológico da população dos Dembos (Angola) sôbre a capacidade vital dos Mahungos e dos Luangos, adultos do sexo masculino. In *Anuário da ESC,* year XXV, 1943 and 1944, 183–93. Lisbon: ESC.

Almeida, Viana de. 1935. O conhecimento da alma negra. *Vida Colonial. Jornal de Propaganda e Informação Colonial* 1, no. 3: 4.

Amorim, Guedes de. 1940. Um herói de África. Mouzinho de Albuquerque. *O Século. Suplemento dedicado ao Império Colonial Português e às comemorações, nas Províncias Ultramarinas, dos Centenários da Fundação e da Restauração de Portugal:* 71.

Andrade, Freire de. 1925. Trabalho indígena e as colónias portuguesas. *Boletim Geral das Colónias,* no. 3: 3–15.

Anonymous. 1935a. A semana das Colónias. *Vida Colonial. Jornal de Propaganda e Informação Colonial* 1, no. 2: 4.

————. 1935b. Le Congrès d'Anthropologie coloniale de Porto. In *L'Anthropologie,* t. 45. Paris: Masson et Cie.

————. 1935–38a. A antropologia na Exposição Colonial Portuguesa. In *Trabalhos da SPAE,* vol. 7. Porto: Imprensa Portuguesa.

Anonymous. 1935–1938b. I Congresso Nacional de Antropologia Colonial. *Trabalhos da SPAE,* vol. 7, nos. 7 and 8: 61. Porto: Imprensa Portuguesa.

————. 1936. Vida Ultramarina. *Boletim Geral das Colónias,* no. 127: 188–94.

————. 1938. Ilha de S. Tomé. In *Terra Lusa. Livro de Leitura para o 1º ciclo liceal (anos 1º, 2º e 3º),* ed. Rodrigo Fernandes Fontinha, 250–52. Porto: Tip. da Emprêsa Industrial Gráfica.

————. 1941. Ser português. In *Livro de Leitura para a 4ª Classe. Ensino Primário Elementar,* ed. António Figueirinhas, 3–5. Porto: Editôra Educação Nacional.

————. 1953. De Aquém e de Além-mar. In *Portugal em África. Revista de Cultura Missionária,* 2nd series, vol. 10, no. 55. Lisbon: Editorial LIAM.

Anuário da Universidade de Coimbra. 1887–88. Coimbra.

Anuário da Escola Superior Colonial. Lisboa: ISCSP. 1919–20 (vol. 1) to 1923–24 (vol. 5). 1924–27 (vols. 6–8) to 1953–54 (vol. 35).

Athayde, Alfredo de. 1953. Contribuição para o estudo psicológico dos indígenas do ultramar português. In *Estudos de Antropologia. Anais da Junta das Missões Geográficas e de Investigação do Ultramar,* vol. 8, t. III. Lisbon: JIU.

Azevedo, Aires de. 1940. A pureza bioquímica do Povo Português. In *Congressos do Mundo Português. Congresso Nacional de Ciências da População.* Volume XVII, Book 1, Section 2, Lisbon: Comissão Executiva dos Centenários: 551–64.

Azevedo, R. de. 1953. A Fuga dos Ganguelas. In *Livro de Leitura. Língua e História Pátria,* ed. J. Pereira Tavares, part II (2nd year), 214–19. Lisbon.

Barreto, Artur D., and Manuel Simões Alberto. 1953. Contribuição para o estudo dos grupos sanguíneos como característica etnológica de raças humanas. *Boletim da Sociedade de Estudos de Moçambique,* no. 80: 23–41.

Belchior, Manuel Dias. 1951. *Compreendamos os Negros!* 2nd ed. Lisbon: AGU.

Bermudes, A. 1895. *Plano económico da Exposição Universal Internacional e Colonial de Lisboa em 1897,* 4º centenário da descoberta da Índia. Lisbon.

Bíblia Sagrada, 19th ed. Lisbon: Difusora Bíblica.

Bissaya-Barreto, Fernando. 1940. Festas comemorativas dos Centenários e da Rainha Santa. A *Saúde. Mais vale prevenir do que remediar. Jornal popular, bi-mensal de Higiene e Profilaxia Sociais* 10, nos. 229 and 230: 4–7.

———. 1970. *Uma Obra Social Realizada em Coimbra.* 4 vols. Coimbra: Coimbra Editora.

Boas, Franz. [1887] 1974. The occurrence of similar inventions in areas widely apart. In *The Shaping of American Anthropology, 1883–1911: A Franz Boas Reader,* ed. G. W. Stocking Jr.: 61–63. New York: Basic Books.

———. 1907. Some principles of museum administration. *Science* 25; 921–33.

———. [1940] 1982. *Race, Language and Culture.* Chicago: University of Chicago Press.

Boléo, José de Oliveira. 1938. O Império Colonial Português. In *A escola técnica. Livro de Leitura,* José Monteiro e José de Oliveira Boléo, vol. 1, years 1 and 2, 115. Braga: Livraria Cruz.

Botelho, Teixeira. 1940. Discurso inaugural do Congresso Colonial. In *Congressos do Mundo Português. Programas, Discursos e Mensagens.* Vol. 19. Lisbon, Comissão Executivo dos Centenários: 199–212.

Braga, Teófilo. 1884. *Os centenários como synthese affectiva nas sociedades modernas.* Porto: Typ. de A. J. da Silva Teixeira.

Broca, Paul. (1861). Sur le volume et la forme du cerveau suivant les individus et suivant les races. *Bulletin Société d'Anthropologie Paris.* 2. P. 139-207, 301–321, 441–446.

Broca, Paul. 1864. *On the Phenomena of Hybridity in the Genus Homo.* London: C. Carter Blake.

———. 1879. *Instructions générales pour les recherches anthropologiques à faire sur le vivant.* Paris: Masson.

Cabral, Augusto. 1940. O problema do trabalho indígena em Moçambique. In *Congressos do Mundo Português. Congresso Colonial.* Volume XVI, Book 3, Section 3, Lisbon, Excecutive Committee for the Centenaries: 291–96.

Camacho, Brito. 1946. A preguiça indígena. In *Antologia Colonial Portuguesa,* vol. 1, *Política e Administração,* 189–94. Lisbon: AGC.

Cameroto, P. Alessandro Orsini di. 1936. A nova política colonial portuguesa. *Boletim Geral das Colónias,* no. 129: 97–104.

Camões, Luís Vaz de and Emanuel Paulo Ramos, 1956. In Ramos, Emanuel Paulo (org.), *Os Lusíadas,* Porto: Porto Editora, 3rd ed.

Capelo, H., and R. Ivens. 1930. O Feiticeiro da Nossa África. In *A Nossa Terra.*
    Livro de Leitura, ed. Xavier F. A. Rodrigues. Vol. 1, for the first and second
    years of secondary school, 6th ed., 103–4. Lisbon: Centro Tip. Colonial.
————. 1938a. O N'ganga. In *Terra Lusa. Livro de Leitura para o 1º ciclo liceal*
    (anos 1º, 2º e 3º), ed. Rodrigo Fernandes Fontinha, 455–56. Porto: Tip. da
    Emprêsa Industrial Gráfica.
————. 1938b. Procedimento dos pretos para com os mortos. In *Terra Lusa.*
    Livro de Leitura para o 1º ciclo liceal (anos 1º, 2º e 3º), ed. Rodrigo Fernan-
    des Fontinha, 456–58. Porto: Tip. da Emprêsa Industrial Gráfica.
————. 1953. Enterro de pretos. In *Livro de Leitura. Língua e História Pátria,*
    ed. J. Pereira Tavares, part II (2nd year), 259–61. Lisbon.
Carmona, António Óscar de Fragoso and António de Oliveira Salazar and Fran-
    cisco José Vieira Machado. 1936. Exposição Histórica da Ocupação. De-
    creto. *Boletim Geral das Colónias,* no. 140: 93–97.
Castro, Armando Augusto Gonçalves de Moraes. 1925. *Memória da Provín-*
    cia da Guiné destinada à Exposição Colonial Inter-Aliada de Paris. Bolama,
    Guinea-Bissau: Imprensa Nacional.
Castro, Augusto de. 1940. *A Exposição do Mundo Português e a Sua Finalidade*
    Nacional. Lisbon: Empresa Nacional de Publicidade.
Castro, Ferreira de. 1953. Macau. In *Livro de Leitura.. Língua e História Pátria,*
    ed. J. Pereira Tavares, part II (2nd year): 267–71. Lisbon.
Catálogo da Exposição Histórica da Ocupação. 1937. Vols. 1 and 2. Lisbon: AGC.
Catálogo da Exposição Insular e Colonial Portugueza em 1894 no Palacio de Crys-
    tal Portuense. 1895. Lisbon: Imprensa Nacional.
Catorze Anos de Política do Espírito. Apontamentos para uma Exposição apresenta-
    dos no S N. I. (Palácio Foz) em Janeiro de 1948. 1948. Lisbon: SNI.
Cayolla, Júlio. 1937? *Pavilhão da Colonização na Exposição do Mundo Português.*
    Lisboa: Bertrand.
Chagas, Pinheiro. 1938. 'Chegada à Índia' (adaptado de *História de Portugal).*
    In Fontinha, Rodrigo Fernandes. 1938. *Terra Lusa. Livro de Leitura para o*
    1.º ciclo liceal (anos 1.º, 2.º e 3.º). Porto: Tip. da Emprêsa Industrial Grá-
    fica. Pg. 358-60.
Comemorações centenárias. Exposição do Mundo Português. Roteiro dos Pavilhões
    (Descrição pormenorizada do seu conteúdo). Ano CCC da Restauração. 1940.
    Free distribution of 10,000 copies, series B.
Comemorações centenárias. Programa oficial. 1940. Lisbon: Oficina Gráfica.
Comissão executiva das festas centenárias de Portugal em Pernambuco. 1940. Cir-
    cular, Recife, 24 July.
Congresso do Ensino Colonial na Metrópole. Organização, Programa e Regulamento
    das Sessões. 1934. Lisbon: Casa Portuguesa.
Congressos do Mundo Português. 1940. Vols. 1–19. Lisbon: Comissão Executiva
    dos Centenários.
Corrêa, Francisco A. 1935. Sistemas de Política Colonial. In *Livro de Leitura.*
    Ensino Técnico Profissional, ed. Samuel de Matos Agostinho de Oliveira,
    Fernando Vieira Gonçalves da Silva and Manuel da Silva, vol. 1 (1st and

2nd years, Escolas Comerciais): 146–48. Lisbon: Emprêsa Nacional de Publicidade.

Correia, Alberto Carlos Germano da Silva. 1934a. Os maratas na Índia Portuguesa. In *Trabalhos do I Congresso Nacional de Antropologia Colonial,* 1st ed., vol. 1, 271–73. Porto: Exposição Colonial Portuguesa.

Correia, A. da Silva. 1934b. Os Eurafricanos de Angola. In *Trabalhos do I Congresso Nacional de Antropologia Colonial,* 1st ed. Vol. 1. 300–330. Porto: Exposição Colonial Portuguesa.

———. 1940a. Antropologia na Índia portuguesa. In *Congresso da História da Actividade Científica Portuguesa,* VIII Congresso, Book 1, section II, part I: 663–78. Lisbon: Comissão Executiva dos Centenários.

Correia, A. da Silva. 1940b. "Os grupos antropo-sanguíneos na Índia Portuguesa (contribuição ao estudo de antropo-hematologia no Hindustão)". In *Congressos do Mundo Português. Congresso Colonial.* Volume XIV. Book 1. Section 1. Lisbon: Comissão Executiva dos Centenários: 153–73.

Correia, J. Alves. 1940. A mentalidade do negro africano e a antiga evangelização portuguesa. In *Congresso da História da Actividade Científica Portuguesa.* Lisbon: Comissão Executiva dos Centenários, Book 2, Section III: 493–506.

Correia, Mendes. 1915. *Antropologia. Resumo das lições feitas pelo assistente.* Porto: Imprensa Portuguesa.

———. 1918. Antropologia angolense II. Bi-N'Bundo, Andulos e Ambuelas-Mambundas. Notas antropológicas sobre observações de Fonseca Cardoso. *Sep. de Archivo de Anatomia e Antropologia* 4, nos. 2–3.

———. 1919a. As Condições Físicas na Formação das Raças, *Annaes da Academia Polytechnica do Porto.* Coimbra: Imprensa da Universidade, Book 13: 1–30.

———. 1919b. *Raça e Nacionalidade.* Porto: Renascença.

———. 1931. *Sur quelques schémas de l'hérédité des groupes sanguins.* Paris: Librairie E. Nourry.

Correia, Mendes. 1932. "A fisionomia humana e os animais". Separata dos n.ºs 1 e 2 do vol. V (Março e Junho de 1932) do *Archivo de Medicina Legal.* Lisboa: Imprensa Nacional. P. 1-11.

———. 1934a. Os mestiços nas colónias portuguesas. In *Trabalhos do I Congresso Nacional de Antropologia Colonial,* vol. 1, 331–49. Porto: I Exposição Colonial Portuguesa.

———. 1934b. *Da biologia à história.* Porto: Instituto de Antropologia.

———. 1934c. Valor psico-social comparado das raças coloniais. In *Trabalhos do I Congresso Nacional de Antropologia Colonial,* vol. 2, 385–93. Porto: I Exposição Colonial Portuguesa.

———. 1934d. Discurso inaugural no I Congresso Nacional de Antropologia Colonial. In *Trabalhos do I Congresso Nacional de Antropologia Colonial,* vol. 1, 21–29. Porto: I Exposição Colonial Portuguesa.

———. 1934e. *O Instituto de Antropologia da Universidade do Porto e a investigação científica colonial.* Presented to the First National Colonial Anthropology Congress, Porto, 22–26 September 1934, I Exposição Colonial Portuguesa, Imprensa Portuguesa, Porto.

―――. 1935. *A etnogenia brasílica,* from Book 19 of *Anais da Faculdade de Ciências do Porto.* Porto: Imprensa Portuguesa.

―――. 1936. A propósito do 'Homo Taganus'. Africanos em Portugal. *Boletim da Junta Geral do Distrito de Santarém,* no. 43: 1–23.

―――. 1940a. Discurso na sessão inaugural do Congresso Nacional de Ciências da População. In Sep. de *Congressos do Mundo Português.* Porto: Imprensa Portuguesa: 1–20.

―――. 1940b. O mestiçamento nas colónias portuguesas. In *Congressos do Mundo Português. Congresso Colonial.* Volume XIV, Book 1, Section 1, Lisbon: Comissão Executiva dos Centenários: 113–33.

―――. 1940c. Factores degenerativos na população portuguesa e seu combate. Lisbon: Comissão Executiva dos Centenários, In *Congressos do Mundo Português. Congresso Nacional de Ciências da População.* Volume XVII, Book 1, Section II, Lisbon: Comissão Executiva dos Centenários: 577–89.

―――. 1940d. O elemento português na demografia do Brasil. In *Congressos do Mundo Português. Congresso Luso-Brasileiro de História. O Império e a República.* Volume IX, Book 3, Section II, Part II. Lisbon: Comissão Executiva dos Centenários: 243–58.

―――. 1943. *Raças do Império.* Porto: Portucalense Editora.

―――. 1945. Missões antropológicas às colónias. *Jornal do Médico* 7, no. 149: 11–12.

―――. 1952. Aumento da população, emigração, colonização. In *Extracto do Anuário da ESC,* year 32, 1951–52. Speech given to the national assembly on 12 March 1952, Lisbon.

―――. 1962. Da antropobiologia ultramarina. In *Estudos, Ensaios e Documentos,* no. 95: 145–238. A series of introductory talks on anthropobiological research in overseas Portugal.

Correia, M., and Alfredo Athayde. 1930. *Contribution à la craniologie d'Angola.* Paper presented at XV Congrès International d'Anthropologie et d'Archéologie Préhistorique, Paris, 21–30 September 1930.

―――. 1931. *Contribution à l'anthropologie de la Guinée portugaise.* Paris: Librairie E. Nourry, Paris.

Cortejo do Mundo Português. 1940. Lisbon: Oficina Gráfica dos Artistas.

Cortesão, Jaime. 1930. *L'expansion des portugais dans l'histoire de la civilization. Exposition Internationale d'Anvers.* Lisbon: AGC.

Costa, A. Celestino da. 1940. A investigação científica colonial. In *Congressos do Mundo Português. Congresso Colonial.* Volume XIV, Book 1, Section I, Lisbon: Comissão Executiva dos Centenários: 81–98.

Costa, Maria Irene Leite da. 1934. Contribuição para a avaliação do nível mental nos indígenas de Angola. In *Trabalhos do I Congresso Nacional de Antropologia Colonial,* vol. 1, 394–406. Porto: I Exposição Colonial Portuguesa.

Cunha, Francisco Carmo e. 1933. *Regulamentação das Exposições Internacionais.* Lisbon: Imprensa Nacional.

Cunha, Silva. [1949] 1955. *O Trabalho Indígena. Estudo de Direito Colonial.* 2nd ed. Lisbon: AGU.

Darwin, Charles. [1859] 1968. *A Origem das Espécies.* São Paulo: Hemus.

Delgado, Ralph. 1934. A Riqueza Indígena de Angola. *A Província de Angola. Diário da manhã, Número especial dedicado à Exposição Colonial Portuguesa e em honra da Restauração de Angola em 15 de Agosto de 1648.* 1934. Luanda: Empresa Gráfica de Angola.

Dias, Jorge. [1950] 1971. Estudos do Carácter Nacional Português. *Estudos de Antropologia Cultural,* no. 7: 7–49.

———. 1961. A expansão ultramarina à luz da moderna antropologia. *Ensaios Etnológicos. Revista de Estudos de Ciências Políticas e Sociais,* no. 52: 145–58.

Duarte, Teófilo. 1936. O problema económico de Timor. *Boletim Geral das Colónias,* no. 138: 33–58.

Estatuto dos Indígenas Portugueses nas Províncias da Guiné, Angola e Moçambique. Decreto-Lei no. 39 666 of 20 May 1954, Lourenço Marques:[2] Imprensa Nacional de Moçambique.

Estermann, Fr Carlos. 1940. As concepções religiosas entre os Bântus das colónias portuguesas. In *Congressos do Mundo Português. Congresso Colonial.* Volume XIV, Book 1, Section I, Lisbon: Comissão Executiva dos Centenários: 209–33.

Estermann, Fr Carlos and Elmano Cunha Costa. 1941. *Negros.* Lisbon: Bertrand.

Estudos Coloniais: Revista da Escola Superior Colonial. Lisboa: ESC. Various volumes.

Exposição da Colónia da Guiné. 1932, Catálogo. 1932. Lisbon: Museu Colonial, SGL.

Exposição Histórica da Ocupação no Século XIX, Principais Factos da Ocupação Ultramarina (Séculos XIX e XX, até à Grande Guerra). 1937. Lisbon: AGC.

Exposição Portuguesa em Sevilha. Catálogo Oficial. 1929. Lisbon: Comissariado-Geral da Exposição.

Exposition coloniale internationale de 1931 à Paris. Bibliographie. 1939. Lisbon: Commissariat Général du Portugal à L'Exposition Coloniale Internationale à Paris.

Exposition coloniale internationale de Paris (section portugaise). Catalogue officiel. 1931. Lisbon: Commissariat Général du Portugal à l'Exposition Internationale de Paris.

Exposition internationale coloniale, maritime et d'art flamand – Anvers, 1930. Catalogue officiel de la section portugaise. 1930. Lisbon: Commissariat de l'Exposition Portugaise à Anvers.

Ferreira, A. Liz. 1940. Observações sôbre o tipo morfológico constitucional dos indígenas de Angónia (Distrito de Tete). In *Congressos do Mundo Português. Congresso Colonial.* Volume XIV, Book 1, Section I, Lisbon: Comissão Executiva dos Centenários: 135–52.

---

2. · Lourenço Marques is the former name of Maputo.

Ferreira, Cláudio. 1932. Diferenciação das raças pelo sangue. In *Memória apresentada ao XV Congresso Internacional de Antropologia e de Arqueologia Pré-Histórica, IV Sessão do Instituto Internacional de Antropologia*, 3–12. Lisbon: Imprensa Nacional.

Ferro, António. 1931. *Hollywood, capital das imagens*. Lisbon: Portugal-Brasil Soc. Editora.

————. 1950. *Teatro e Cinema. 1936–1949*. Lisbon: SNI.

Festas comemorativas dos Centenários e da Rainha Santa. *A Saúde. Mais vale prevenir do que remediar. Jornal popular, bi-mensal de Higiene e Profilaxia Sociais* 10, nos. 229 and 230: 4–7.

Figueira, Luiz. 1940. Portugal ultramarino 1940. O que valem, o que representam e como estão apetrechadas para o futuro as províncias portuguesas do Ultramar. *O Século, Suplemento dedicado ao Império Colonial Português e às comemorações, nas Províncias Ultramarinas, dos Centenários da Fundação e da Restauração de Portugal*: 53–60.

Figueirinhas, António, ed. 1941. *Livro de Leitura para a 4ª classe. Ensino Primário Elementar*. Porto: Editôra Educação Nacional.

Fontes, Vítor. 1934. Instruções antropológicas para uso nas colónias. In *Trabalhos do I Congresso Nacional de Antropologia Colonial*, vol. 1, 188–97. Porto: I Exposição Colonial Portuguesa.

Fontinha, Rodrigo Fernandes. 1938. *Terra Lusa. Livro de Leitura para o 1º ciclo liceal (anos 1º, 2º e 3º)*. Porto: Tip. da Emprêsa Industrial Gráfica.

Fontoura, Álvaro da. 1940. O trabalho dos indígenas de Timor (Sua importância, estado actual e evolução desejável). In *Congressos do Mundo Português. Congresso Colonial*. Volume XVI, Book 3, Section III, Lisbon: Comissão Executiva dos Centenários: 297–378.

Freire, Júlio. 1940. O trabalho indígena nas colónias de S. Tomé e Príncipe e Angola (Estado actual e evolução desejável). In *Congressos do Mundo Português. Congresso Colonial*. Volume XVI, Book 3, Section III, Lisbon: Comissão Executiva dos Centenários: 257–90.

Freyre, Gilberto. [1933] 1957. *Casa Grande e Senzala. Formação da Família Brasileira sob o Regime de Economia Patriarcal*. Lisbon: Livros do Brasil.

————. 1954a. *Aventura e Rotina. Sugestões de uma viagem à procura das constantes portuguesas de carácter e de acção*. Lisbon: Livros do Brasil.

————. 1954b. *Um brasileiro em terras portuguesas. Introdução a uma possível Luso-tropicologia, acompanhada de conferências e discursos proferidos em Portugal e em terras lusitanas e ex-lusitanas da Ásia, África e do Atlântico*. Lisbon: Livros do Brasil.

Frias, César de. 1933. O pretinho de Angola na Escola. In *Caminho Florido. Livro de Leitura para a quarta classe*, ed. Estefânia Carreira and Oliveira Cabral, 122. Porto: Livraria Simões Lopes.

Galton, Francis. [1869] 1979. *Hereditary genius*. London: Lulyan Friedman.

Galvão, Henrique. 1934a. *Álbum Comemorativo da Primeira Exposição Colonial Portuguesa – 1934 – Porto*. Porto: Litografia Nacional.

————. 1934b. A Bem do Império: A I Exposição Colonial Portuguesa. *Portugal Colonial. Revista de Propaganda e Expansão Colonial* 4, nos. 38–39: 28–32.

————. 1935. *Primeira Exposição Colonial Portuguesa. Relatório e Contas.* Lisbon: AGC.

————. 1940. *Exposição do Mundo Português. Secção Colonial.* Lisbon: Neogravura.

Garrett, Tomaz de Almeida. 1937. Um batuque. In *Portugal é Grande, como se prova neste Livro de Leitura,* ed. Francisco Júlio Martins Sequeira and Manuel António de Morais Neves, 238–39. Lisbon: Livraria Popular de Francisco Franco.

Gobineau, Arthur de. [1853] 1983. *Essai sur l'inegalité des races humaines.* Paris: Gallimard/Pléiade.

Grave, João. 1929. *Livro de Leitura. IV Classe.* Porto: Livraria Chardron de Lêlo e Irmão.

Grilo, Francisco Monteiro. 1932. *Moçambique na Exposição Colonial Internacional de Paris. Relatório do Delegado da Colónia. 1930–1931.* Lourenço Marques, Mozambique: Imprensa Nacional.

Guia da Exposição do Portugal dos Pequenitos. 197?.

Guia da Exposição – Feira de Angola, Luanda, Agosto de 1938. 1938. Luanda: Agência Técnica de Publicidade.

Guia oficial da Exposição Portuguesa em Sevilha. 1929. Lisbon: Comissariado-Geral da Exposição Portuguesa em Sevilha.

Guia Oficial do Visitante da Exposição Colonial Portuguesa, Porto. 1934. Lisbon: Tipografia Leitão.

H. V. V. 1935. Le Congrès d'Anthropologie coloniale de Porto. *L'Anthropologie,* Book 45. Paris: Masson et Cie.

Jorge, Ricardo, and Manuel Barbosa Sueiro. 1942. Registo Somatológico e Somatométrico adoptado pelo Museu Bocage no estudo dos indígenas do Ultramar (Exposição do Mundo Português – Lisboa, 1940). *Arquivos do Museu Bocage.* Vol. 13. P. 73-86.

Júnior, António Campos. 193?. O combate de Magul. In *Livro de Leitura para a Quarta Classe,* ed. Ulysses Machado, 220–22. Lisbon: Tipografia Silvas.

Júnior, Joaquim Pereira Mota. 1940. *O Feitiço do Império.* Lisbon: AGC.

Júnior, Joaquim Rodrigues dos Santos. 1937a. Missão antropológica a Moçambique. In *Trabalhos da SPAE,* vol. 8, no. 2. Porto: Imprensa Portuguesa.

————. 1937b. Grupos sangüíneos nos indígenas de Tete, Zambézia. In *Trabalhos da SPAE,* vol. 8, no. 2: 213–17. Porto: Imprensa Portuguesa.

————. 1938a. Missão antropológica de Moçambique (2ª campanha). In *Trabalhos da SPAE,* vol. 8, no. 3. Porto: Imprensa Portuguesa.

————. 1938b. Relatório da missão antropológica à África do Sul e a Moçambique. In Sep. *Trabalhos da SPAE.* Vol. 8, no. 3: 1–52. Porto: Imprensa Portuguesa.

————. 1944a. Missão antropológica de Moçambique. Las Ciencias. Vol. 9, no. 3. Madrid: 1–10.

————. 1944b. *Contribuição para o estudo da Antropologia de Moçambique. Algumas tribos do distrito de Tete.* Lisbon: JIU.

————. 1956. *Antropologia de Moçambique.* Porto: Imprensa Portuguesa.

Kant, Immanuel. [1764] 1953. Osservazioni sul sentimento del Bello e del Sublime. In *Scritti precritici*: 303–63. Bari.

———. 1935. *Antropología en sentido pragmático*. Madrid: Revista de Occidente.

Le Bon, Gustav .1879. 'Recherches anatomiques et mathématiques sur les lois de variations de volume du cerveau et sur leurs relations avec l'intelligence'. *Revue d'Anthropologie*, series no. 2, vol 2. P. 27-104.

Le Bon, G. [1894] 1910. *Les lois psychologiques de l' evolution des peuples*. Paris: Felix Alcan.

Leiro, Fernando. 1935. A África vista através do cinema. *Vida Colonial. Jornal de Propaganda e Informação Colonial* 1, no. 1: 1, 7.

Leme, Carlos Câmara. 1999. "Testemunhas do Século Português - 45. Igrejas Caeiro, 82 anos, o companheiro da alegria". *Público*, 21 November 1999. N.º 3536. P. 26.

Lemos, Maximiano de. 1933. Campanhas de África. In *Caminho Florido. Livro de Leitura para a quarta classe*, ed. Estefânia Carreira and Oliveira Cabral, 181–82. Porto: Livraria Simões Lopes.

Lencastre, Júlio Garcês de. 1934. *Agência Geral das Colónias. A sua acção no período de 1933–34*. Lisbon: Impr. Libânio da Silva.

Lima, Américo Pires de, and Leopoldina F. Paulo. 1940. São os portugueses dolicocéfalos? – Um novo índice cefálico. In *Congressos do Mundo Português. Congresso Nacional de Ciências da População*. Volume XVII, Book 1, Section II, Lisbon: Comissão Executiva dos Centenários: 396–403.

Lima, Augusto César Pires de. 1932. *Portugal (Livro de Leitura), classes I and II*. Porto: privately published.

Lima, Augusto César Pires de. 1937. *Livro de Leitura para o Ensino Comercial*. Porto: privately published.

Lima, Joaquim Alberto Pires de. 1934. Estudos de Antropologia Colonial. O que temos feito e o que precisamos fazer. In *Trabalhos do I Congresso Nacional de Antropologia Colonial*, vol. 1, 105–33. Porto: I Exposição Colonial Portuguesa.

Lima, Joaquim Alberto Pires. 1940. Influência de Mouros, Judeus e Negros na Etnografia portuguesa. In *Congressos do Mundo Português. Congresso Nacional de Ciências da População*. Volume XVIII, Book 2, Section III. Lisbon: Comissão Executiva dos Centenários: 63–102.

Lima, Joaquim Alberto Pires de, and Constâncio Mascarenhas. 1930. *Contribuição para o estudo antropológico da Guiné Portuguesa*. XV Congrès International d'Anthropologie et d'Archéologie Préhistorique, Porto and Coimbra, 21–30 September 1930.

Livro de Honra do Portugal dos Pequenitos, Volume 1 (February 1950 to August 1984) and Volume 2 (January 1951 to 1982).

Livro de Leitura para a Terceira Classe. Ensino Primário Elementar. 1931. Porto: Educação Nacional.

Lobato, Alexandre. 1952. A histórica Ilha de Moçambique. *Panorama. Revista Portuguesa de Arte e Turismo*, nos. 5 and 6: 73–77.

Lopes, David. 1935. Os mouros na civilização portuguesa. In *Livro de Leitura. Ensino Técnico Profissional,* ed. Samuel de Matos Agostinho de Oliveira, Fernando Vieira Gonçalves da Silva and Manuel da Silva, vol. 1 (1st and 2nd years, business schools): 89–90. Lisbon: Emprêsa Nacional de Publicidade.

Machado, Bernardino. 1930. *O Acto Colonial da Ditadura.* Biarritz, France.

Machado, Francisco José Vieira. 1937. Do Ministro das Colónias. In *Catálogo da Exposição Histórica da Ocupação,* vols. 1 and 2. Lisbon: AGC.

Machado, Ulysses. 1930s?. *Livro de Leitura para a Quarta Classe.* Lisbon: Tipografia Silvas.

Magalhãis, A. Leite de. 1937. A Guiné. *Livro de Leitura. Língua Portuguesa, 1º ciclo (1º, 2º and 3º anos),* ed. In J. Pereira Tavares, 209–10. Lisbon: Livraria Sá da Costa.

Maia, Francisco Assis F. da. 1953. A colonização do Brasil. In *Livro de Leitura. Língua e História Pátria, parte II (2º ano),* ed. J. Pereira Tavares, 151–52. Lisbon.

Mano, Marques. 1936. A questão africana e o sentido da colonização portuguesa. *Boletim Geral das Colónias,* no. 133: 52.

Martins, E. A. Azambuja. 1940. Investigações à mentalidade do soldado indígena de Moçambique. In *Congressos do Mundo Português. Congresso da História da Actividade Científica Portuguesa.* Volume XII, Book 1, Section I, Lisbon: Comissão Executiva dos Centenários: 443–62.

Martins, J. P. Oliveira. [1880] 1888. *O Brazil e as Colónias Portuguezas.* 3rd ed. Lisbon: António Maria Pereira.

Marx, K., and F. Engels. [1848] 1959. The Communist Manifesto. In *Basic Writings on Politics and Philosophy,* ed. L. Feuer, 1–14. New York: Anchor.

Matos, Norton de. 1944. *Memórias e trabalhos da minha vida. Factos, acontecimentos e episódios que a minha memória guardou. Conferências, discursos e artigos e suas raízes no passado,* vols. 1–4. Lisbon: Editora Marítimo Colonial.

M. C. 1937. Costumes de Moçambique. In *Livro de Leitura. Língua Portuguesa, 1º ciclo (1º, 2º e 3º anos),* ed. J. Pereira Tavares, 223–24. Lisbon: Livraria Sá da Costa.

———. 1953. Costumes de Moçambique. In *Livro de Leitura. Língua e História Pátria, parte II (2º ano),* ed. J. Pereira Tavares, 206–8. Lisbon.

M., V. de. 1935. Vocação missionária de Portugal. *Boletim Geral das Colónias,* no. 126: 153–54.

Mello, Lopo Vaz de Sampaio e. 1932. Esquisso Ethnographico da População de Cabo Verde. In *Annuário da ESC,* years 12 and 13, 1931–32, 73–91. Lisbon: ESC.

———. 1936a. Da influência da eugenia no fenómeno da colonização e na política do império. *Boletim Geral das Colónias,* no. 131: 37–69.

———. 1936b. Alguns aspectos do 'Eterno Feminino' nas Colónias (Esquisso Ethnographico) (Excerto duma conferência). *O Mundo Português. Revista de Cultura e Propaganda, Arte e Literatura Coloniais* 3, no. 26: 59–63.

————. 1937. Política Indígena de Associação. *Boletim Geral das Colónias,* no. 144: 5–38.

Melo, António Brandão de, and Frédéric-Léon Zysset. 1931. *Angola. Monographie Historique, Géografique et Economique de la Colonie destinée a l'Exposition Coloniale Internationale de Paris de 1931.* Luanda: Imprimerie Nationale.

Mendes, Joaquim M. 1955. O ensino em Angola. *Portugal em África. Revista de Cultura Missionária* 12, no. 71: 432–36.

Missões Antropológicas e Etnológicas às Colónias. [1945] 1951. Decreto-Lei no. 34 478. In *Anuário da ESC,* year 32, 1950–51, 146–49. Lisbon: ESC.

Molar, Serafim. 1947. *O meu primeiro livro de leitura.* 5th ed. Bailundo, Angola: Tipografia da Missão Católica.

Monteiro, Armindo. 1934. Anotações à margem da Exposição Colonial do Pôrto. *O Mundo Português. Revista de Cultura e Propaganda, Arte e Literatura Coloniais* 1, no. 11, volume 1: 353–61.

Montenegro, Álvaro. 1928. *A Raça Negra perante a Civilização. Em redor do problema colonial.* Lisbon: Imprensa Beleza.

Mundo Português: imagens de uma exposição histórica. 1957. Lisbon: SNI.

Murinello, Francisco Ferro. [1940–41] 1942. Subsidios para um plano de pesquizas relativo ao estudo dos processos de educação e instrução indígenas do nosso império colonial. In *Annuário da ESC,* years 21 and 22, 145–66. Lisbon: ESC.

Nogueira, Rodrigo de Sá. 1940. Da necessidade de se estudar a nossa dialectologia colonial. In *Congressos do Mundo Português. Congresso Colonial.* Volume XIV, Book 1, Section I, Lisbon: Comissão Executiva dos Centenários: 545–55.

Noronha, Eduardo. 1937. A rendição do Gungunhana (adapted from *Mouzinho de Albuquerque – Século XX*). In *Livro de Leitura. Língua Portuguesa, 1º ciclo (1º, 2º and 3º anos),* ed. J. Pereira Tavares, 389–93. Lisbon: Livraria Sá da Costa.

O Cortejo Colonial no Porto, em 30 de Setembro de 1934, dia do Encerramento da «I Exposição Colonial Portuguesa». Descrição e Roteiro. 1934. Porto.

Oliveira, Fernando Correia de. 1997. No vale encantado de Charles Boxer. Uma visita ao mais importante historiador estrangeiro da época dos Descobrimentos. *Revista Pública,* no. 2637: 26–34.

Oliveira, José Osório de. 1940. Os portugueses no Brasil. *O Século. Suplemento dedicado ao Império Colonial Português e às comemorações, nas Províncias Ultramarinas, dos Centenários da Fundação e da Restauração de Portugal,* 73–74.

Osório, João de Castro, and João F. Rodrigues. 1940. Integração dos actuais régulos na obra administrativa nas colónias de Angola e Moçambique. In *Congressos do Mundo Português. Congresso Colonial.* Volume XV, Book 2, Section II, Lisbon: Comissão Executiva dos Centenários: 543–61.

Pavilhão do Brasil na Exposição Histórica do Mundo Português, 1940. 1941. Lisbon: Comissão Brasileira dos Centenários de Portugal, Neogravura.

Pereira, Gonçalves. 1935. *A ocupação científica do Ultramar.* Lisbon: ISCEF.

Pina, Luiz de. 1931. *Les angles de la base du crâne chez les indigènes des colonies portugaises africaines.* Paris: XV Congrès Intern d'Anthrop et d'Archéologie Préhistorique.

———. 1940. A medicina indígena da África Portuguesa. In *Congressos do Mundo Português. Congresso Colonial.* Volume XIV, Book 1, Section I, Lisbon: Comissão Executiva dos Centenários: 175–207.

Pinto, F. A. 1938. O minério em Angola. In *Terra Lusa. Livro de Leitura para o 1º ciclo liceal (anos 1º, 2º e 3º),* ed. Rodrigo Fernandes Fontinha, 450–52. Porto: Tip. da Emprêsa Industrial Gráfica.

Pio, Matoso. [1944–45] 1945. Bases economico-sociais de uma política de contacto de raças. In *Anuário da ESC,* year 26, 1944–45, 183–222. Lisbon: ESC.

Portugal dos Pequenitos. 1966. Coimbra: Fundação Bissaya-Barreto.

Portugal dos Pequenitos, Coimbra-Portugal. 2000. *Notícias* 3, no. 14: 4–5.

Portugal através do tempo e da história. Neste livro se acrescentam e explicam os mapas que figuram no pavilhão de «O Século» na Exposição Colonial do Porto – 1934. 1934. Lisbon: Sociedade Nacional de Tipografia.

Primeira Conferência Económica do Império Colonial Português – Parecer, Projectos de Decretos e Votos. 1936. Vol. 2. Lisbon: Ministério das Colónias.

Quintinha, Julião. 1937a. Lourenço Marques. In *Portugal é Grande, como se prova neste Livro de Leitura,* ed. Francisco Júlio Martins Sequeira and Manuel António de Morais Neves, 380–81. Lisbon: Livraria Popular de Francisco Franco.

———. 1937b. O rei do Congo. In *Portugal é Grande, como se prova neste Livro de Leitura,* ed. Francisco Júlio Martins Sequeira and Manuel António de Morais Neves, 366–68. Lisbon: Livraria Popular de Francisco Franco.

———. 1938. Os portugueses no Congo. In *Terra Lusa. Livro de Leitura para o 1º ciclo liceal (anos 1º, 2º e 3º), ed.* Rodrigo Fernandes Fontinha, 254–56. Porto: Tip. da Emprêsa Industrial Gráfica.

Regulamento da Exposição Portuguesa em Sevilha. 1929. Lisbon: Comissariado-Geral.

Renan, E. [1872] 1961. *Oeuvres completes.* Paris: Calmann Lévy.

———. [1882] 1992. *Qu'est-ce qu'une nation? et autres essais politiques.* Paris: Presses Pocket.

República Portuguesa. 1936. *Código do Trabalho dos Indígenas nas Colónias Portuguesas de África, Aprovado por Decreto no.16 199 de 6 de Dezembro de 1928. Anotado pela Direcção dos Serviços da Administração Civil.* Luanda: Imprensa Nacional de Angola.

Ribeiro, António Lopes. 1933. Filmes de propaganda. *Animatógrafo* 1, no. 4: 3–5.

Ribeiro, Tomaz. 1931. Costumes indianos. In *Livro de Leitura. A Família, A Pátria. Pequena selecta de trechos em prosa e verso para os alunos da I e II classes dos liceus, organizada de harmonia com os programas oficiais,* ed. Nicolau Rijo Micalef Pace, 2nd ed., 292–94. Coimbra: Coimbra Editora.

Rodrigues, F. A. Xavier (ed.). 1930. *A Nossa Terra. Livro de Leitura.* Vol. 1, for 1st and 2nd years of secondary school, 6th ed., 103–4. Lisbon: Centro Tip. Colonial.

Rodrigues, J. F. 1940. "Plano de um organismo e orientação da investigação científica nas Colónias". In *Congressos do Mundo Português. Congresso Colonial.* Volume XIV. Book 1. Section 1: 61–80.

Romero, Sílvio. 1888. *História da Literatura Brasileira.* Vol. 2. Rio de Janeiro: Garnier.

Ruah, Judah Bento. 1932. Mestiços (Mulatos de Moçambique). In *Annuário da ESC,* years 12 and 13, 1931–32, 399–411.

Saccadura, Fernando. 1928. *Usos e costumes de Quitéve – Terrritório de Manica e Sofala.* Sep. *Boletim da Sociedade de Geografia de Lisboa.* Nos. 3–4: 53–74; nos. 5–6: 148–62; nos. 9–10: 363–85 and nos. 11–12: 401–35.

Santa-Rita, José Gonçalo. 1936. O sentido do Acto Colonial. *Revista da Faculdade de Letras da Universidade de Lisboa* series 1, volume 3, nos. 1–2: 224–40.

———. 1940a. A investigação científica portuguesa nos últimos 100 anos. In *Congressos do Mundo Português. Congresso Colonial.* Volume XIV, Book 1, Section I, Lisbon: Comissão Executiva dos Centenários: 11–30.

———. 1940b. O contacto das raças nas colónias portuguesas. Seus efeitos políticos e sociais. Legislação portuguesa. In *Congressos do Mundo Português. Congresso Colonial.* Volume XV, Book 2, Section II. Lisbon: Comissão Executiva dos Centenários: 13–70.

———. [1944] 1945. Selvagens e civilizados. In *Anuário da ESC,* year 25, 1943–44, 163–70. Lisbon: ESC.

———. 1955. Sá da Bandeira e a política ultramarina. In *Estudos Ultramarinos.* Volume 5: 135–168.

Santos, F. Bahia. 1955. *Política Ultramarina de Portugal.* Lisbon: SGL.

Santos, João A. Correia dos, Guimarães, João Carlos. 1939. *Primeiro Livro de Leitura (Complemento da Cartilha para adultos). Guia para a Instrução e Educação do Soldado.* Lisbon: Imprensa Beleza.

Santos, Fr Faustino dos. 1925. Missões religiosas portuguesas do enclave de Cabinda. *Missões de Angola e Congo* 5, no. 12: 214–15.

Secretariado Nacional de Informação. 1955. *Portugal: propaganda.* Lisbon: SNI.

Serra, José Antunes. 1940. Novos métodos de estudo da pigmentação e sua importância racial. In *Congressos do Mundo Português. Congresso Nacional de Ciências da População.* Volume XVII, Book 1, Section II, Lisbon: Comissão Executiva dos Centenários: 453–71.

Silva, Mário Moreira da. 1952. Timor, exemplo da colonização portuguesa. *Portugal em África. Revista de Cultura Missionária,* no. 52: 219–34.

Tamagnini, Eusébio. 1902. *Dissertação para a Cadeira de Antropologia e Arqueologia Pré-Histórica.* Coimbra: IUAC.

———. 1933. Sociedade Portuguesa de Estudos Eugénicos. *Arquivo de Anatomia e Antropologia* 16: 111–34.

————. 1934. *Os problemas da mestiçagem.* Plenary conference of the I National Colonial Anthropology Congress, Exposição Colonial Portuguesa, 39–63. Porto: Imprensa Portuguesa.

————. 1934–35. Lição inaugural do ano lectivo de 1934-1935. *Revista da Faculdade de Ciências* 5, no. 1: 28.

————. 1939. Les dimensions du nez, l'indice nasal et le prétendu fort métissage négroide des portugais. Congrès International des Sciences Anthropologiques et Ethnologiques. 1: 175–76.

Tavares, J. 1953. *Livro de Leitura. Língua e História Pátria, parte II (2º ano).* Lisbon.

Tavares, Silva. 1937. *Pela fé e pelo império. Poema comemorativo da primeira exposição histórica da ocupação.* Lisbon: AGC.

Teixeira, Campos. 1931. Terra de Portugal. In *Livro de Leitura para a terceira classe. Ensino Primário Elementar,* 125–26. Porto: Livraria Educação Nacional.

Trabalhos do I Congresso Nacional de Antropologia Colonial. 1934. Vols. 1 and 2. Porto: I Exposição Colonial Portuguesa.

Trindade, Leopoldo. 1937. Esbôço ethnographico, ethnologico e anthropologico da Colonia de Moçambique. In *Annuário da ESC,* year 18: 117–37. Lisbon: ESC.

Vasconcelos, Ernesto de. 1929. As colónias. In *Portugal. Exposição Portuguesa em Sevilha,* vol. 1: 1–45. Lisbon: Livraria Sá da Costa.

————, ed. 1906. *Catálogo da Exposição colonial de algodão, borracha, cacau e café.* Lisbon: SGL.

Vasconcelos, João Teixeira de. 1937. Costumes indígenas de Angola. In *Portugal é Grande, como se prova neste Livro de Leitura,* ed. Francisco Júlio Martins Sequeira and Manuel António de Morais Neves, 375–76. Lisbon: Livraria Popular de Francisco Franco.

Vidal, João Evangelista de Lima. 1937. As nossas missões. In *Livro de Leitura. Língua Portuguesa, 1º ciclo (1º, 2º and 3º anos),* ed. J. Pereira Tavares, 408A–408D. Lisbon: Livraria Sá da Costa.

Voltaire. [1756] 1963. *Essai sur les moeurs.* Paris: Garnier.

ZZ. 1935. A Alemanha não deve possuir colónias. *Vida Colonial. Jornal de Propaganda e Informação Colonial* 1, no. 3: 12, 15.

Newspaper/periodical sources

Animatógrafo. 1933. Nos. 4 and 8. Lisbon.

A Província de Angola. Diário da manhã, Número especial dedicado à Exposição Colonial Portuguesa e em honra da Restauração de Angola em 15 de Agosto de 1648. 1934. Luanda: Empresa Gráfica de Angola.

Boletim Geral das Colónias (BGC). 1930–50. In several volumes. Lisbon: AGC.

Boletim Oficial de Angola. 1935. Vol. 1, no. 30.

Diário de Notícias. 1933–40. In several volumes. Lisbon.

Indústria Portuguesa (IP). 1932. Nos. 51–58. Lisbon: Associação Industrial Portuguesa.

O Planalto. Órgão de Defêsa da Colonização Nacional em Angola. 1931–32. Nos.
43, 82, 84 and 93. Nova Lisboa, Angola.
*O Século. Le journal de plus grand tirage au Portugal. Foire Internationale de
Bruxelles MCMXXIV, Numéro spécial pour la propagande à l'étranger,* 1 April
1924.
*O Século. Le journal de plus fort tirage au Portugal, Supplement dedié à L'Exposi-
tion Coloniale de Paris,* 1931.
*O Século, Le journal de plus grand tirage au Portugal, Supplement consacré à L'Ex-
position Internationale de Paris,* 1937.
*O Século, Número Extraordinário Comemorativo do Duplo Centenário da Funda-
ção e Restauração de Portugal,* June 1940a, Neogravura, Lisbon.
*O Século, Suplemento dedicado ao Império Colonial Português e às comemorações,
nas Províncias Ultramarinas, dos Centenários da Fundação e da Restauração
de Portugal,* June 1940b, O Século, Lisbon.
O Século, Número Especial Dedicado ao Império, 16 October 1948, Lisbon.

Secondary sources

Abu-Lughod, Lila. 1986. *Veiled Sentiments. Honor and Poetry in a Bedouin Soci-
ety.* Berkeley: University of California Press.
————. 1990. *The Romance of Resistance: Tracing Transformations of Power
through Bedouin Women. American Ethnologist* 17: 41–55.
Acciaiuoli, Margarida. 1998. *Exposições do Estado Novo, 1934, 1940.* Lisbon:
Livros Horizonte.
Alexandre, Manuel Valentim Franco. 1993. *Os Sentidos do Império. Questão
Nacional e Questão Colonial na Crise do Antigo Regime Português.* Porto:
Afrontamento.
Amorim, António, Miguel Vale de Almeida, Paulo Gama Mota, Luís Souta, Eu-
génia Cunha and João Filipe Marques. 1997. *O Que É a Raça? Um Debate
entre a Antropologia e a Biologia.* Lisbon: Oikos.
Anderson, Benedict. [1983] 1991. *Imagined Communities: Reflections on the
Origin and Spread of Nationalism.* London: Verso.
Andrews, George Reid. 1991. *Blacks and Whites in São Paulo, Brazil, 1888–
1988.* Madison: University of Wisconsin Press.
António, L. 1978. *Cinema e Censura em Portugal. 1926–1974.* Lisbon: Arcádia.
Appadurai, Arjun. 1988. Introduction: Place and Voice in Anthropological
Theory. *Cultural Anthropology* 3, no. 1: 16–20.
Appiah, Kwame Anthony. 1992. *In My Father's House: Africa in the Philosophy
of Culture.* New York: Oxford University Press.
Areia, M. R. de, and M. A. da Rocha. 1985. O ensino da antropologia em
Coimbra. In *Cem Anos de Antropologia em Coimbra, 1885–1985,* 13–60.
Coimbra: MLAUC.
Augstein, Hannah Franziska. 1996. *Race: The Origins of an Idea, 1760–1850.*
Bristol: Thoemmes Press.

Balandier, Georges. 1955. *Sociologie actuelle de l'Afrique noire. Dynamique des changements sociaux en Afrique centrale.* Paris: Presses Universitaires de France.
————. 1988. *Modernidad y Poder. El Desvio Antropologico.* Madrid: Ediciones Júcar.
Bandeirinha, J. A. Oliveira. 1996. *Quinas Vivas. Memória Descritiva de Alguns Episódios Significativos do Conflito entre Fazer Moderno e Fazer Nacional na Arquitectura Portuguesa dos Anos 40.* Porto: FAUP.
Banks, Marcus, and Howard Morphy. (1997), Introduction: Rethinking Visual Anthropology. In *Rethinking Visual Anthropology,* ed. Marcus Banks and Howard Morphy, 1–35. New Haven, CT: Yale University Press.
Banton, Michael. [1987] 1998. *Racial Theories.* Cambridge: Cambridge University Press.
Baroja, Julio Caro. [1987] (1995). *La cara, espejo del alma: historia de la fisiognómica.* Barcelona: Galaxia Gutenberg, Círculo de Lectores.
Baudet, Sabine, Marie-Christine Péan and Françoise Gauquelin. 1977. *O Corpo. Olhando as Suas Formas, Descobre-se Um Temperamento, Um Carácter, Uma Psicologia.* Lisbon: Círculo de Leitores.
Benedict, Burton. 1983. *The Anthropology of World's Fairs: San Francisco's Panama Pacific International Exposition of 1915.* London: Scholar Press.
————. 1991. International Exhibitions and National Identity. *Anthropology Today* 7, no. 3: 5–9.
Bennett, Tony. 1988. The Exhibitionary Complex. *New Formations* 4 (spring edition): 74–102.
Berman, Marshall. 1992. "Why modernism still matters" in Scott Lash & Jonathan Friedman eds. *Modernity and Identity.* Oxford & Cambridge: Blackwell. P. 33-58.
Blanchard, Pascal and Stéphane Blanchoin, Nicolas Bancel, Gilles Boëtsch and Hubert Gerbeau, (eds.). 1995. *L'Autre et Nous. «Scènes et Types».* Paris: Achac et Syros.
Blanchard, Pascal, and Stéphane Blanchoin. 1995. Les 'races' dans l'imaginaire colonial français de la Grande Guerre à Vichy. In Blanchard, Pascal and Stéphane Blanchoin, Nicolas Bancel, Gilles Boëtsch and Hubert Gerbeau (eds.). 1995, *L'Autre et Nous*: 227–33.
Boxer, Charles. 1967. *Relações Raciais no Império Colonial Português, 1415–1825.* Rio de Janeiro: Tempo Brasileiro.
————. 1969. *O Império Colonial Português.* Textos de Cultura Portuguesa. Lisbon: Edições 70.
Carreira, António. 1979. *O tráfico português de escravos na costa oriental africana nos começos do século XIX (estudo de um caso).* Lisbon: JIU / Centro de Estudos de Antropologia Cultural. From the *Estudos de Antropologia Cultural* series.
Cashmore, Ellis. [1984] 1996. *Dictionary of Race and Ethnic Relations.* London: Routledge.
Castelo, Cláudia. 1998. *O Modo Português de Estar no Mundo. O Luso-Tropicalismo e a Ideologia Colonial Portuguesa (1933–1961).* Porto: Afrontamento.

Catroga, F. 1996. Ritualizações da história. In *História da História em Portugal,
    Séculos XIX–XX,* ed. Luís Reis Torgal, José Amado Mendes and Fernando
    Catroga: 547–671. Lisbon: Círculo de Leitores.

Centlivres, Pierre. 1982. Des 'instructions' aux collections: la prodution eth-
    nographique de l'image de l'Orient. In *Collections Passion,* ed. Jaques
    Hainard and Roland Kaehr: 33–61. Neuchâtel, Switzerland: Musée
    d'Ethnographie.

Clifford, James. 1988. On Collecting Art and Culture. In *The Predicament of
    Culture. Twentieth Century Ethnography, Literature and Art,* 215–51. Cam-
    bridge, MA: Harvard University Press.

Coombes, Annie. 1991. Ethnography and the Formation of National and Cul-
    tural Identities. In *The Myth of Primitivism: Perspectives on Art,* ed. Susan
    Hiller, 189–214. London: Routledge.

Coon, C. S. 1962. *The Origin of Races.* New York: Alfred A. Knopf.

Corbey, Raymond. 1993. Ethnographic Showcases, 1870–1930. *Cultural An-
    thropology* 8, no. 3: 338–69.

Correia, M. 1982. *As Ilusões da Liberdade: A Escola Nina Rodrigues e a Antro-
    pologia no Brasil.* Doctoral thesis, Universidade de São Paulo, São Paulo,
    Brazil.

Costa, João Bénard da. 1982. Os anos 40 no cinema. In *Os Anos 40 na Arte
    Portuguesa,* vol. 1, 183–89. Lisbon: Fundação Calouste Gulbenkian.

Costa, Viana. 1934. Cinema. A sua função como agente de propaganda colo-
    nial. *A Província de Angola. Diário da manhã, Número especial dedicado à
    Exposição Colonial Portuguesa e em honra da Restauração de Angola em 15 de
    Agosto de 1648.* Luanda: Empresa Gráfica de Angola.

Coutancier, Benoît, Barthe, Christine (1995), 'Au Jardin d'Acclimatation: Re-
    présentations de l'autre (1877–1890)'. In Blanchard, Pascal and Stéphane
    Blanchoin, Nicolas Bancel, Gilles Boëtsch and Hubert Gerbeau (general
    editors), *L'Autre et Nous. «Scènes et Types».* 1995: 145–50. Paris: Achac et
    Syros.

Dias, N. 1996. O corpo e a visibilidade da diferença. In *Corpo Presente. Treze
    Reflexões Antropológicas sobre o Corpo,* ed. Miguel Vale de Almeida: 23–44.
    Oeiras, Portugal: Celta.

Dirks, Nicholas B. 1992. *Colonialism and Culture.* Ann Arbor: University of
    Michigan Press.

Edwards, Elizabeth. 1990. The Image as Anthropological Document. The Pho-
    tographic 'Types': The Pursuit of Method. *Visual Anthropology* 3: 235–58.

Escobar, Arturo. 1994. Welcome to Cyberia: Notes on the Anthropology of
    Cyberculture. *Current Anthropology* 35, no. 3: 211–31.

Fabian, Johannes. 1983. *Time and the Other: How Anthropology Makes its Ob-
    ject.* New York: Columbia University Press.

Ferro, Marc. 1986. *Comment on raconte l'histoire aux enfants à travers le monde
    entier.* Paris: Payot.

Ferro, Marc. 1987. O filme: uma contra-análise da sociedade. In *Fazer Histó-
    ria,* ed. Jacques Le Goff and Pierre Nora , vol. 3: 255–76. Venda Nova:
    Bertrand.

Fortuna, Carlos, and Claudino Ferreira. 1993. Estradas e santuários. *Revista Crítica de Ciências Sociais* 36: 55–81.

Foucault, Michel. 1966. *As Palavras e as Coisas. Uma Arqueologia das Ciências Humanas.* Lisbon: Portugália Editora.

———. [1975–76] 1992. *Genealogia del Racismo.* Madrid: Ediciones de la Piqueta.

———. 1977. *Discipline and Punish: The Birth of the Prison.* Trans. Alan Sheridan. New York: Vintage Books.

———. 1978. *The History of Sexuality,* vol. 1, *An Introduction.* New York: Random House

França, José-Augusto. 1974. *A Arte em Portugal no Século XX.* Lisbon: Bertrand.

———. 1980. *O Modernismo na Arte Portuguesa.* Lisbon: Biblioteca Breve.

Gallo, Donato. 1988. *O Saber Português. Antropologia e Colonialismo.* Lisbon: Heptágono.

Geada, E. 1977. *O Imperialismo e o Fascismo no Cinema.* Lisbon: Moraes Editores.

Giddens, Anthony. 1989. Ethnicity and Race. In *Sociology,* 242–73. Cambridge: Polity Press.

———. [1990] 1998. *As Consequências da Modernidade.* Oeiras, Portugal: Celta.

Goldberg, David Theo. 2002. Modernity, Race and Morality. In *Race Critical Theories: Text and Context,* ed. Philomena Essed and D. Theo Goldberg, 283–306. Oxford: Blackwell Publishers.

Goody, Jack. 1995. *The Expansive Moment: The Rise of Social Anthropology in Britain and Africa, 1918–1970.* Cambridge: Cambridge University Press.

Gould, Stephen Jay. 1983. *La mal-mesure de l'homme.* Paris: Editions Ramsay.

———. 1986. *O Polegar do Panda.* Lisbon: Gradiva.

Guimarães, Ângela. 1984. *Uma Corrente do Colonialismo Português. A Sociedade de Geografia de Lisboa – 1875–1895.* Lisbon: Livros Horizonte.

Haeckel, Ernest. (1900). *The Riddle of the Universe at the Close of the Nineteenth Century.* New York Harper.

Harris, Marvin. [1968] 1981. *El Desarrollo de la Teoria Antropológica. Una Historia de las Teorías de la Cultura.* Madrid: Siglo Veintiuno de España Editores.

Henriques, Isabel Castro. 1997. *Percursos da Modernidade em Angola. Dinâmicas Comerciais e Transformações Sociais em Angola.* Lisbon: IICT/ICP.

Hessen, Johannes. [1926] 1980. *Teoria do Conhecimento.* Coimbra: A. Amado.

Hinsley, Curtis M. 1991. The World as Marketplace: Commodification of the Exotic at the World's Columbian Exposition. In *Exhibiting Cultures: The Politics and Poetics of Museum Display,* ed. Ivan Karp and Steven D. Lavine, 344–65. Washington, DC: Smithsonian Institution Press.

Hobsbawm, Eric, and Terence Ranger. [1983] 1985. *The Invention of Tradition.* Cambridge: Cambridge University Press.

Jacknis, Ira. 1985. Franz Boas and Exhibits: On the Limitations of the Museum Method of Anthropology. In *Objects and Others: Essays on Museums and*

Material Culture, ed. George W. Stocking, 75–111. Madison: University of Wisconsin Press.

Jahoda, Gustav. 1999. *Images of Savages: Ancient Roots of Modern Prejudice in Western Culture.* London: Routledge.

Karp, Ivan, and Steven Lavine, eds. 1991. *Exhibiting Cultures: The Politics and Poetics of Museum Display.* Washington, DC: Smithsonian Institution Press.

Kirschenblatt-Gimblett, Barbara. 1991. Objects of Ethnography. In Karp and Lavine, *Exhibiting Cultures,* 386–443.

Kuper, Adam. 1988. *The Invention of Primitive Society: Transformations of an Illusion.* London: Routledge.

Lash, Scott, and Jonathan Friedman. 1992. *Modernity and Identity.* Oxford: Blackwell.

Latour, Bruno. [1991] 1997. *Jamais Fomos Modernos. Ensaio de Antropologia Simétrica.* Rio de Janiero: Editora 34.

Leal, João. 2000. *Etnografias Portuguesas (1870–1970). Cultura Popular e Identidade Nacional.* Lisbon: Publicações Dom Quixote.

Lévi-Strauss, Claude. [1971] 1981. *The Naked Man.* London: Cape.

Marques, João Pedro. 1999. *Os Sons do Silêncio: o Portugal de Oitocentos e a Abolição do Tráfico de Escravos.* Lisbon: ICS.

Matos, Sérgio Campos. 1998. *Historiografia e Memória Nacional no Portugal do Século XIX (1846–1898).* Lisbon: Colibri.

Matos-Cruz, J. de. 1981. *O Cais do Olhar. Fonocinema Português.* Lisbon: IPC.

———. 1983. *António Lopes Ribeiro.* Lisbon: Cinemateca Portuguesa.

Matos-Cruz, J. de, and João Antunes. 1997. *O Cinema Português. 1896–1998.* From the *Clássicos Portugueses* series. Lisbon: Lusomundo.

Mayr, E. 1963. *Animal Species and Evolution.* Cambridge, MA: Harvard University Press.

———. 1982. *The Growth of Biological Thought: Diversity, Evolution, and Inheritance.* Cambridge, MA: Harvard University Press.

Mazzoleni, Gilberto. 1992 (1990). *O Planeta Cultural. Para uma antropologia histórica.* São Paulo: Edusp - Editora da Universidade de São Paulo.

McGary, Howard. 2002. Reflections on 'a Genealogy of Modern Racism'. In Essed and Goldberg, *Race Critical Theories,* 433–36.

Mills, Charles W. 1997. *The Racial Contract.* Ithaca, NY: Cornell University Press.

Mónica, Maria Filomena. 1977. 'Deve-se ensinar o povo a ler?': a questão do analfabetismo (1926–1939) *Análise Social* 13, no. 50: 321–53.

———. 1979. *Educação e Sociedade no Portugal de Salazar.* Lisbon: Editorial Presença.

Montagu, A. 1974. The Origin of the Concept of Race. In *Man's Most Dangerous Myth: The Fallacy of Race,* 5th ed. Oxford: Oxford University Press.

Mosse, George L. [1978] 1992. *Il razzismo in Europa. Dalle origini all'olocausto.* Milan: Mondadori.

Moutinho, Mário Canova. 1982. A etnologia colonial portuguesa e o Estado Novo. In *O Fascismo em Portugal. Actas do Colóquio Realizado na Faculdade de Letras de Lisboa em Março de 1980,* 415–42. Lisbon: A Regra do Jogo.

Neto, Maria J. Baptista. 1995. *A DGEMN e a Intervenção no Património Arquitectónico em Portugal (1929–1960)*. Privately published.

Neves, Helena. 2000. *Bissaya-Barreto, Cassiano Branco e o Portugal dos Pequenitos*. In Inês Morais Viegas and Isabel Horta e Vale (coord.), *Jardim Portugal dos Pequenitos*, Lisbon: Câmara Municipal de Lisboa, Arquivo Municipal de Lisboa and Fundação Bissaya-Barreto: 10–12.

Ó, J. Ramos do. 1999. *Os Anos de Ferro. O Dispositivo Cultural durante a «Política do Espírito» 1933–1939. Ideologias, Instituições, Agentes e Práticas* Lisbon: Estampa.

Orsenna, Erik. [1988] 1989. *A Exposição Colonial*. Lisbon: Dom Quixote.

Outlaw, Lucius. 1996. *On Race and Philosophy*. London: Routledge.

Paulo, Heloísa. 1994. *Estado Novo e Propaganda em Portugal e no Brasil. O SPN/ SNI e o DIP.* Coimbra: Minerva.

Paulo, João Carlos Duarte. 1992. '*A Honra da Bandeira'. A Educação Colonial no Sistema de Ensino Português (1926–1946)*. Lisbon, privately published.

Pélissier, René. 1986. *História das Campanhas de Angola: Resistência e Revoltas (1845–1941)*. Lisbon: Estampa.

Pereira, Ana Leonor. 1997. *Darwin em Portugal (1865–1914): Filosofia, História e Engenharia Social*. Coimbra, privately published.

Pereira, Ana Leonor, and João Rui Pita. 1993. Ciências. In Mattoso, José (dir.). 1993. *História de Portugal. Quinto Volume. O Liberalismo (1807-1890)*. Lisboa: Círculo de Leitores. P. 652-667.

Pereira, Rui. 1986. Antropologia aplicada na política colonial portuguesa do Estado Novo. *Revista Internacional de Estudos Africanos*, nos. 4–5: 191–235.

———. 1989. A questão colonial na etnologia ultramarina. *Antropologia Portuguesa* 7: 61–78.

Pina, Luís de. 1977. *Documentarismo Português*. Lisbon: IPC.

Pina-Cabral, João de. 1991. *Os Contextos da Antropologia*. Lisbon: Difel.

———. 2001. Galvão Among the Cannibals: The Emotional Constitution of Colonial Power. *Identities* 8, no. 4: 483–515.

Pires, Daniel. 2000. *Dicionário da Imprensa Periódica Literária Portuguesa do Século XX (1941–1974)*, vol. 2, book 1. Lisbon: Grifo.

Poliakov, Léon. [1971] 1974. *O Mito Ariano*. São Paulo: Perspectiva.

Pomian, K. 1984. Colecção. In *Enciclopédia Einaudi* (various authors): 51–86. Lisbon: INCM.

Portela, Artur. 1982. *Salazarismo e Artes Plásticas*. London: Biblioteca Breve, Lisbon.

Porto, Nuno. 1994. *Uma Introdução à Antropologia. Aula Teórica-Prática no âmbito das Provas de Aptidão Pedagógica e Capacidade Científica*. Universidade Coimbra, Departamento de Antropologia da Faculdade de Ciências e Tecnologia. Privately published.

Rex, John. [1986] 1988. *Raça e Etnia*. Lisbon: Estampa.

Ribeiro, Félix. 1973. *Subsídios para a História do Documentarismo em Portugal: no Presente a Imagem do Passado*. Lisbon: Direcção-Geral da Educação Permanente.

Ribeiro, Orlando. 1981. *A Colonização de Angola e o Seu Fracasso.* Lisbon: INCM.

Rodrigues, A. M., ed. 1999. *Os Negros em Portugal – Séculos XV a XIX.* Lisbon: CNCDP.

Roque, Ricardo. 2001. *Antropologia e Império: Fonseca Cardoso e a expedição à Índia em 1895.* Lisbon: Imprensa de Ciências Sociais.

Ruffié, Jacques. 1983. *De la biologie à la culture.* Vol. 2. Paris: Flammarion.

Rydell, Robert W. 1992. *The Books of the Fairs.* Chicago: American Library Association.

Said, Edward W. 1995. *Orientalism.* London: Penguin Books.

Santos, Boaventura de Sousa. 1993. Modernidade, Identidade e a Cultura de Fronteira. *Revista Crítica de Ciências Sociais.* N.º 38. Dez. 1933. Coimbra: Centro de Estudos Sociais. Pg. 11-39.

Santos, Gonçalo Duro dos. 1996. *Topografias Imaginárias: as Estórias de Eusébio Tamagnini no Instituto de Antropologia de Coimbra.* Coimbra, privately published.

Santos, Ricardo Ventura. [1996] 1998. Da morfologia às moléculas, de raça a população: trajectórias conceituais em antropologia física no século XX. In *Raça, Ciência e Sociedade,* 125–39. Rio de Janeiro: Editora Fiocruz.

Santos, Rui Afonso. 1994. *O Design e a Decoração em Portugal: Exposições e Feiras.* Privately published.

Schwarcz, Lilia Moritz. 1995. *O Espectáculo das raças. cientistas, instituições e questão racial no Brasil. 1870–1930.* São Paulo: Companhia das Letras.

Seabra, J. 2000. Imagens do império. O caso de Chaimite de Jorge Brum do Canto. In *O Cinema sob o Olhar de Salazar,* ed. L. R. Torgal, 235–73. Lisbon: Círculo de Leitores.

Silva, Ana da. 2000. *Portugal nas Exposições Internacionais Coloniais e Universais (1929–1939): a Retórica Científica e Tecnológica.* Lisbon, privately published.

Silva, D. F. da, and M. Lima. 1992. Raça, género e mercado de trabalho. *Estudos Afro-Asiáticos* 23: 97–111.

Silva, Rui Ferreira da. 1990. As colónias: da visão imperial à política integracionista. In *Portugal Contemporâneo,* vol. 4, *Ascensão e Consolidação do Estado Novo,* ed. António Reis, 99–122. Lisbon: Publicações Alfa.

———. 1992. Sob o signo do império. In *Nova História de Portugal,* ed. Joel Serrão and A. H. de Oliveira Marques, vol. 12, *Portugal e o Estado Novo (1930–1960),* ed. Fernando Rosas: 355–87. Lisbon: Editorial Presença.

Skidmore, Thomas E. [1974] 1989. *Preto no Branco: Raça e Nacionalidade no Pensamento Brasileiro.* Rio de Janeiro: Paz e Terra.

Smedley, Audrey. 1993. *Race in North America: Origin and Evolution of a World View.* Oxford: Westview.

Sobral, José Manuel. 1999. Da casa à nação: passado, memória, identidade. *Etnográfica. Revista do Centro de Estudos de Antropologia Social,* no. 1: 71–86.

Sousa, J. Pais de. 1999. *Bissaya Barreto, Ordem e Progresso.* Coimbra: Minerva.

Stepan, Nancy Leys. 1982. *The Idea of Race in Science: Great Britain 1800–1960*. London: Macmillan.

———. 1991. *The Hour of Eugenics: Race, Gender and Nation in Latin America*. Ithaca, NY: Cornell University Press.

Stocking Jr., George W. 1968. *Race, Culture and Evolution: Essays in the History of Anthropology*. Chicago: University of Chicago Press.

Stocking, G. W., Jr. (ed.). 1974. *The Shaping of American Anthropology, 1883-1911: A Franz Boas Reader*. New York: Basic Books.

———. 1988. *Bones, Bodies, Behavior: Essays on Biological Anthropology*. Vol. 5. Madison: University of Wisconsin Press.

Stoler, Ann Laura, and Frederick Cooper. 1997. *Tensions of Empire. Colonial Cultures in a Bourgeois World*. Berkeley: University of California Press.

Thomaz, Omar Ribeiro. [1996] 1998. Do saber colonial ao luso-tropicalismo: 'raça' e 'nação' nas primeiras décadas do salazarismo. In *Raça, Ciência e Sociedade*, 85–106. Rio de Janeiro: Fiocruz.

———. 1997. *Ecos do Atlântico Sul: Representações sobre o Terceiro Império Português*. São Paulo, privately published.

Tinhorão, J. R. 1988. *Os Negros em Portugal. Uma Presença Silenciosa*. Lisbon: Caminho.

Torgal, Luís Reis. 1996. História, divulgação e ficção. In *História da História de Portugal, Séculos XIX–XX*, ed. Luís Reis Torgal, José Amado Mendes and Fernando Catroga, 491–545. Lisbon: Círculo de Leitores.

Turner, Victor, and Edith Turner. 1978. *Image and Pilgrimage in Christian Culture: Anthropological Perspectives*. New York: Columbia University Press.

UNESCO. 1979. *O Tráfico de Escravos Negros Séculos XV–XIX*. Trans. António Luz Correia. Lisbon: Edições 70.

Vala, Jorge, Rodrigo Brito and Diniz Lopes. 1999. *Expressões dos Racismos em Portugal*. Lisbon: Instituto de Ciências Sociais.

Vale de Almeida, Miguel. 1991. Leitura de um livro de leitura: a sociedade contada às crianças e lembrada ao povo. In *Lugares de Aqui: Actas do Seminário «Terrenos Portugueses»*, ed. B. J. O'Neill and J. Pais de Brito, 245–61. Lisbon: Dom Quixote.

———. 2000. *Um Mar da Cor da Terra. Raça, Cultura e Política da Identidade*. Oeiras, Portugal: Celta.

Valverde, P. 1997. O corpo e a busca de lugares da perfeição: escritas missionárias da África colonial portuguesa, 1930–60. *Etnográfica* 1, no. 1: 73–96.

Reixach, Juan Frigolé (ed.). 1988. *As Raças Humanas*. Lisbon: Resomnia Editores.

Viegas, Inês Morais and Isabel Horta e Vale (coord.), 2000, *Jardim Portugal dos Pequenitos*, Lisbon: Câmara Municipal de Lisboa, Arquivo Municipal de Lisboa and Fundação Bissaya-Barreto.

Wade, Peter. 1997. The Meaning of 'Race' and 'Ethnicity'. In *Race and Ethnicity in Latin America*. London: Pluto Press.

West, Cornel. 2002. A Genealogy of Modern Racism. In Essed and Goldberg, *Race Critical Theories*, 90–112.

Wieviorka, Michel. 1996. Racisme et exclusion. In *L'Exclusion. L'État des savoirs,* 344–53. Paris: Éditions La Découverte.

Wolf, Eric. 1982. The Slave Trade. In *Europe and the People without History,* 195–231. Berkeley: University of California Press.

Worth, Sol. 1981. *Studying Visual Communication.* Philadelphia: University of Pennsylvania Press.

Young, Robert J. C. 1995. *Colonial Desire: Hybridity in Theory, Culture and Race.* London: Routledge.

Index